Praise for *Oscar Wilde* by Frank
"No one can doubt that this
human and literary history th
epoch. . . . Frank Harris has
that group and moment in reached his
consummation and met his doom.

"Harris has written perhaps the best biography ever done
by an American."

"This life of Wilde is the most satisfying we possess, not
merely containing much personal data, but also vivified
and made articulate by the dramatic genius of the author."

"The best life of Wilde, . . . Wilde's life will have to
stand or fall by it."

OSCAR WILDE
FRANK HARRIS

Including
My Memories of Oscar Wilde
by George Bernard Shaw

And an introductory note by Lyle Blair

Carroll & Graf Publishers, Inc.
New York

First Carroll & Graf edition 1992

Carroll & Graf Publishers, Inc.
260 Fifth Avenue
New York, NY 10001

ISBN: 0-88184-759-3

Manufactured in the United States of America

CONTENTS

CONTENTS

Introductory Note

For some extraordinary reason this book has lain out of print in the
United States for the best part of the last thirty years, and for
some considerable length of time in the United Kingdom. It would
be easy to write that the reason for this was the animosity gen-
erated by Harris through his life; but this could not be wholly
true.

Since his death biographies and biographical studies have been
issued and whenever the literary history of his lifetime is discussed, on either side of the Atlantic, his name continues to crop
up. But this is not the place to write of his life or of his fights and
the wounds left; this has been done by the many and their works
are easily consulted. However, on reading these works one cannot
help but feel how times have changed. Harris left only bitter
memories. Others, in more recent times, whose actions may have
been little better or little worse than his, have been adored, praised
and forgiven.

Harris was undoubtedly a charlatan, unscrupulous, flamboyant,
and superbly talented. He antagonized nearly all those who knew
him, but although I find myself in my thoughts closer to Edin-
burgh and Geneva than to Canterbury and Rome, I always find
myself deeply impressed by the fact that on the artistic side he
never lost the support of Shaw, and at one time or another influenced and interested men of the calibre of Wells, Middleton,
Murray, Wilde, George Moore, and Arnold Bennett—to name

but a few. On the human side he kept the friendship and help of his lawyer and literary executor, Arthur Leonard Ross, and his wife remained with him to the end.

After several long talks with Ross I became convinced that the whole picture of Harris has never been fully understood by those of us of the generations that can get their picture of the man only through other people's books, and excellent though one or two of those books have been, the full portrait of Harris still remains to be painted. This may be, in part, rectified by the publication in 1960 of an expurgated edition of *My Life and Loves* with an introduction by Ralph G. Ross, Professor of General Studies in the University of Minnesota, and the son of Arthur Leonard Ross. Professor Ross has had at his command all the relevant materials in the possession of his father, materials which are exciting to the literary scholar and invaluable to the literary historian, and proper public acknowledgment to Mr. Ross's generosity to scholars and universities in making these materials available is long overdue.

This book was first published in the United States in 1916 under the title *Oscar Wilde: His Life and Confessions*; it was re-issued in 1918 and, as it were, republished, by Covicci-Friede in 1930. Each of these editions contained numerous and, at most times, irrelevant appendices, although, in each of these editions, as in this edition, the appendix, "My Memories of Oscar Wilde by George Bernard Shaw," was included. The Covicci-Friede edition had an extraordinary introductory section entitled, *"Including the Hitherto Unpublished Full and Final Confession by Lord Alfred Douglas."* There seems no point in including it in this edition since everybody is familiar with the story, and it was really more a continuation of one of Harris' public quarrels than a literary document relevant to the biography. As for the appendices, all of these have been dropped except for Robert Ross's (for those unfamiliar with the period it should be noted that he was no relation to Arthur Leonard Ross) letter of December 14th, 1900, which is referred to in the body of the text; this is why it has been included. There is no reason to think that the Ross letter had much veracity, and, indeed, Reggie Turner denied the whole story, or at least that part of it dealing with Wilde's actual death. Turner later stated that Wilde died quite peacefully.

INTRODUCTORY NOTE

In preparing the British edition for publication in 1938 Shaw rewrote his contribution as a preface to the book and deleted the appendices and made "a few minor emendations," to say nothing of using the preface to tilt at one or two of his own windmills. It is worth noting that this was done some years after the death of Harris, Shaw arranging for its English publication in order to help Harris' widow financially. In the preface he praised the book as much as he did when Harris was alive. Indeed, about Harris' writing Shaw said, "Harris was also an artist with a personal style as imposing in its way as the style of Wilde, and much more trenchant. Both of them transformed crude statements of fact into polished works of art": And that is as good a judgment of Harris as a writer as needs to be made.

Lyle Blair

Sydney,
New South Wales

I

Oscar's Father and Mother on Trial

ON THE 12TH OF DECEMBER, 1864, Dublin society was abuzz with excitement. A tidbit of scandal which had long been rolled on the tongue in semi-privacy was to be discussed in open court, and all women and a good many men were agog with curiosity and expectation.

The story itself was highly spiced and all the actors in it well known.

A famous doctor and oculist, recently knighted for his achievements, was the real defendant. He was married to a woman with a great literary reputation as a poet and writer who was idolised by the populace for her passionate advocacy of Ireland's claim to self-government; "Speranza" was regarded by the Irish people as a sort of Irish Muse.

The young lady bringing the action was the daughter of the professor of medical jurisprudence at Trinity College, who was also the chief at Marsh's library.

It was said that this Miss Travers, a pretty girl just out of her teens, had been seduced by Dr. Sir William Wilde while under his care as a patient. Some went so far as to say that chloroform had been used, and that the girl had been violated.

The doctor was represented as a sort of Minotaur. Lustful stories were invented and repeated with breathless delight; on

1

all faces, the joy of malicious curiosity and envious denigration. The interest taken in the case was extraordinary; the excitement beyond comparison; the first talents of the Bar were engaged on both sides; Sergeant Armstrong led for the plaintiff, helped by the famous Mr. Butt, Q.C., and Mr. Heron, Q.C., who were in turn backed by Mr. Hamill and Mr. Quinn; while Sergeant Sullivan was for the defendant, supported by Mr. Sidney, Q.C., and Mr. Morris, Q.C., and aided by Mr. John Curran and Mr. Purcell. The Court of Common Pleas was the stage, Chief Justice Monahan presiding with a special jury. The trial was expected to last a week, and not only the Court but the approaches to it were crowded.

To judge by the scandalous reports, the case should have been a criminal case, should have been conducted by the Attorney-General against Sir William Wilde; but that was not the way it presented itself. The action was not even brought directly by Miss Travers or by her father, Dr. Travers, against Sir William Wilde for rape or criminal assault, or seduction. It was a civil action brought by Miss Travers, who claimed £2,000 damages for a libel written by Lady Wilde to her father, Dr. Travers. The letter complained of ran as follows:—

TOWER, BRAY, May 6th

Sir, you may not be aware of the disreputable conduct of your daughter at Bray where she consorts with all the low newspaper boys in the place, employing them to disseminate offensive placards in which my name is given, and also tracts in which she makes it appear that she has had an intrigue with Sir William Wilde. If she chooses to disgrace herself, it is not my affair, but as her object in insulting me is in the hope of extorting money for which she has several times applied to Sir William Wilde with threats of more annoyance if not given, I think it right to inform you, as no threat of additional insult shall ever extort money from our hands. The wages of disgrace she has so basely treated for and demanded shall never be given her.

JANE F. WILDE.

2

To Dr. Travers.

The summons and plaint charged that this letter written to the father of the plaintiff by Lady Wilde was a libel reflecting on the character and chastity of Miss Travers, and as Lady Wilde was a married woman, her husband Sir William Wilde was joined in the action as a co-defendant for conformity.

The defences set up were:—

First, a plea of "No libel"; secondly, that the letter did not bear the defamatory sense imputed by the plaint: thirdly, a denial of the publication, and, fourthly, a plea of privilege. This last was evidently the real defence and was grounded upon facts which afforded some justification of Lady Wilde's bitter letter.

It was admitted that for a year or more Miss Travers had done her uttermost to annoy both Sir William Wilde and his wife in every possible way. The trouble began, the defence stated, by Miss Travers fancying that she was slighted by Lady Wilde. She thereupon published a scandalous pamphlet under the title of "Florence Boyle Price, a Warning; by Speranza," with the evident intention of causing the public to believe that the booklet was the composition of Lady Wilde under the assumed name of Florence Boyle Price. In this pamphlet Miss Travers asserted that a person she called Dr. Quilp had made an attempt on her virtue. She put the charge mildly. "It is sad," she wrote, "to think that in the nineteenth century a lady must not venture into a physician's study without being accompanied by a bodyguard to protect her."

Miss Travers admitted that Dr. Quilp was intended for Sir William Wilde; indeed she identified Dr. Quilp with the newly made knight in a dozen different ways. She went so far as to describe his appearance. She declared that he had "an animal, sinister expression about his mouth which was coarse and vulgar in the extreme. The large protruding under lip was most unpleasant. Nor did the upper part of his face redeem the lower part. His eyes were small and round, mean and prying in expression. There was no candour in the doctor's countenance, where one looked for candour." Dr. Quilp's quarrel with his victim, it appeared, was that she was "unnaturally passionless."

The publication of such a pamphlet was calculated to injure

both Sir William and Lady Wilde in public esteem, and Miss Travers was not content to let the matter rest there. She drew attention to the pamphlet by letters to the papers, and on one occasion, when Sir William Wilde was giving a lecture to the Young Men's Christian Association at the Metropolitan Hall, she caused large placards to be exhibited in the neighbourhood having upon them in large letters the words "Sir William Wilde and Speranza." She employed one of the persons bearing a placard to go about ringing a large hand bell which she, herself, had given to him for the purpose. She even published doggerel verses in the *Dublin Weekly Advertiser*, and signed them "Speranza," which annoyed Lady Wilde intensely. One read thus:—

> Your progeny is quite a pest
> To those who hate such "critters";
> Some sport I'll have, or I'm blest
> I'll fry the Wilde breed in the West
> Then you can call them Fritters.

She wrote letters to *Saunders Newsletter*, and even reviewed a book of Lady Wilde's entitled "The First Temptation," and called it a "blasphemous production." Moreover, when Lady Wilde was staying at Bray, Miss Travers sent boys to offer the pamphlet for sale to the servants in her house. In fine Miss Travers showed a keen feminine ingenuity and pertinacity in persecution worthy of a nobler motive.

But the defence did not rely on such annoyance as sufficient provocation for Lady Wilde's libellous letter. The plea went on to state that Miss Travers had applied to Sir William Wilde for money again and again, and accompanied these applications with threats of worse pen-pricks if the requests were not acceded to. It was under these circumstances, according to Lady Wilde, that she wrote the letter complained of to Dr. Travers and enclosed it in a sealed envelope. She wished to get Dr. Travers to use his parental influence to stop Miss Travers from further disgracing herself and insulting and annoying Sir William and Lady Wilde.

The defence carried the war into the enemy's camp by thus suggesting that Miss Travers was blackmailing Sir William and Lady Wilde.

The attack in the hands of Sergeant Armstrong was still more deadly and convincing. He rose early on the Monday afternoon and declared at the beginning that the case was so painful that he would have preferred not to have been engaged in it—a hypocritical statement which deceived no one, and was just as conventional-false as his wig. But with this exception the story he told was extraordinarily clear and gripping.

Some ten years before, Miss Travers, then a young girl of nineteen, was suffering from partial deafness, and was recommended by her own doctor to go to Dr. Wilde, who was the chief oculist and aurist in Dublin. Miss Travers went to Dr. Wilde, who treated her successfully. Dr. Wilde would accept no fees from her, stating at the outset that as she was the daughter of a brother-physician, he thought it an honour to be of use to her. Sergeant Armstrong assured his hearers that in spite of Miss Travers' beauty he believed that at first Dr. Wilde took nothing but a benevolent interest in the girl. Even when his professional services ceased to be necessary, Dr. Wilde continued his friendship. He wrote Miss Travers innumerable letters. He advised her as to her reading and sent her books and tickets for places of amusement. He even insisted that she should be better dressed, and pressed money upon her to buy bonnets and clothes and frequently invited her to his house for dinners and parties. The friendship went on in this sentimental kindly way for some five or six years till 1860.

The wily Sergeant knew enough about human nature to feel that it was necessary to discover some dramatic incident to change benevolent sympathy into passion, and he certainly found what he wanted.

Miss Travers, it appeared, had been burnt low down on her neck when a child. The cicatrice could still be seen, though it was gradually disappearing. When her ears were being examined by Dr. Wilde, it was customary for her to kneel on a hassock before him, and he thus discovered this burn on her neck. After her hearing improved he still continued to examine the cicatrice from time to time, pretending to note the speed with which it was disappearing. Some time in '60 or '61 Miss Travers had a corn on the sole of her foot which gave her some pain. Dr. Wilde did her the honour of paring the corn with his own hands and painting it with iodine. The cunning Sergeant could not help saying with some confusion, natural or assumed, "that it would have been just as well—at least there are men of such temperament that it would be dangerous to have such a manipulation going on." The spectators in the court smiled, feeling that in "manipulation" the Sergeant had found the most neatly suggestive word.

Naturally at this point Sergeant Sullivan interfered in order to stem the rising tide of interest and to blunt the point of the accusation. Sir William Wilde, he said, was not the man to shrink from any investigation; but he was only in the case formally, and he could not meet the allegations, which therefore were "one-sided and unfair" and so forth and so on.

After the necessary pause, Sergeant Armstrong plucked his wig straight and proceeded to read letters of Dr. Wilde to Miss Travers at this time, in which he tells her not to put too much iodine on her foot, but to rest it for a few days in a slipper and keep it in a horizontal position while reading a pleasant book. If she would send in, he would try and send her one.

"I have now," concluded the Sergeant, like an actor carefully preparing his effect, "traced this friendly intimacy down to a point where it begins to be dangerous. I do not wish to aggravate the gravity of the charge in the slightest by any rhetoric or by an unconscious over-statement; you shall therefore, gentlemen of the jury, hear from Miss Travers herself what took place between her and Dr. Wilde and what she complains of."

Miss Travers then went into the witness-box. Though thin and past her first youth, she was still pretty in a conventional way, with regular features and dark eyes. She was examined by Mr. Butt, Q.C. After confirming point by point what Sergeant Armstrong had said, she went on to tell the jury that in the summer of '62 she had thought of going to Australia, where her two brothers lived, who wanted her to come out to them. Dr. Wilde lent her £40 to go, but told her she must say it was £20 or her father might think the sum too large. She missed the ship in London and came back. She was anxious to impress on the jury the fact that she had repaid Dr. Wilde, that she had always repaid whatever he had lent her.

She went on to relate how one day Dr. Wilde had got her in a kneeling position at his feet, when he took her in his arms, declaring that he would not let her go until she called him William. Miss Travers refused to do this, and took umbrage at the embracing and ceased to visit at his house; but Dr. Wilde protested extravagantly that he had meant nothing wrong, and begged her to forgive him and gradually brought about a reconciliation which was consummated by pressing invitations to parties and by a loan of two or three pounds for a dress, which loan, like the others, had been carefully repaid.

The excitement in the court was becoming breathless. It was felt that the details were cumulative; the doctor was besieging the fortress in proper form. The story of embracings, reconciliations, and loans all prepared the public for the great scene.

The girl went on, now answering questions, now telling bits of the story in her own way, Mr. Butt, the great advocate, taking care that it should all be consecutive and clear with a due crescendo of interest. In October, 1862, it appeared Lady Wilde was not in the house at Merrion Square, but was away at Bray, as one of the children had not been well, and she thought the sea air would benefit him. Dr. Wilde was alone in the house. Miss Travers called and was admitted into Dr. Wilde's study. He put her on her knees before him and bared her neck, pretending to examine the burn; he fondled her too much and pressed her to him. She took offence and tried to draw away. Somehow or other his hand got entangled in a chain at her neck. She called out to him, "You are suffocating me," and tried to rise: but he cried out like a madman "I will, I want to," and pressed what seemed to be a handkerchief over her face. She declared that she lost consciousness.

When she came to herself she found Dr. Wilde frantically imploring her to come to her senses, while dabbing water on her face, and offering her wine to drink.

"If you don't drink," he cried, "I'll pour it over you."

For some time, she said, she scarcely realised where she was or what had occurred, though she heard him talking. But gradually consciousness came back to her, and though she would not open her eyes she understood what he was saying. He talked frantically:

"Do be reasonable, and all will be right . . . I am in your power . . . spare me, oh, spare me . . . strike me if you like. I wish to

7

God I could hate you, but I can't. I swore I would never touch your hand again. Attend to me and do what I tell you. Have faith and confidence in me and you may remedy the past and go to Australia. Think of the talk this may give rise to. Keep up appearances for your own sake. . . ."

He then took her up-stairs to a bedroom and made her drink some wine and lie down for some time. She afterwards left the house; she hardly knew how. He accompanied her to the door, she thought; but could not be certain; she was half dazed.

The judge here interposed with the crucial question:

"Did you know that you had been violated?"

The audience waited breathlessly; after a short pause Miss Travers replied:

"Yes."

Then it was true, the worst was true. The audience, excited to the highest pitch, caught breath with malevolent delight. But the thrills were not exhausted. Miss Travers next told how in Dr. Wilde's study one evening she had been vexed at some slight, and at once took four pennyworth of laudanum which she had bought. Dr. Wilde hurried her round to the house of Dr. Walsh, a physician in the neighbourhood, who gave her an antidote. Dr. Wilde was dreadfully frightened lest something should get out. . . .

She admitted at once that she had sometimes asked Dr. Wilde for money. She thought nothing of it as she had again and again repaid him the monies which he had lent her.

Miss Travers' examination in chief had been intensely interesting. The fashionable ladies had heard all they had hoped to hear, and it was noticed that they were not so eager to get seats in the court from this time on, though the room was still crowded.

The cross-examination of Miss Travers was at least as interesting to the student of human nature as the examination in chief had been, for in her story of what took place on that 14th of October, weaknesses and discrepancies of memory were discovered and at length improbabilities and contradictions in the narrative itself.

First of all it was elicited that she could not be certain of the day; it might have been the 15th or the 16th: it was Friday the 14th, she thought. . . . It was a great event to her; the most awful event in her whole life; yet she could not remember the day for certain.

"Did you tell anyone of what had taken place?"

"No."

"Not even your father?"

"No."

"Why not?"

"I did not wish to give him pain."

"But you went back to Dr. Wilde's study after the awful assault?"

"Yes."

"You went again and again, did you not?"

"Yes."

"Did he ever attempt to repeat the offence?"

"Yes."

The audience was thunderstruck; the plot was deepening. Miss Travers went on to say that the doctor was rude to her again; she did not know his intention; he took hold of her and tried to fondle her; but she would not have it.

"After the second offence you went back?"

"Yes."

"Did he ever repeat it again?"

"Yes."

Miss Travers said that once again Dr. Wilde had been rude to her.

"Yet you returned again?"

"Yes."

"And you took money from this man who had violated you against your will?"

"Yes."

"You asked him for money?"

"Yes."

"This is the first time you have told about this second and third assault, is it not?"

"Yes," the witness admitted.

So far all that Miss Travers had said hung together and seemed eminently credible; but when she was questioned about the chloroform and the handkerchief she became confused. At the outset she admitted that the handkerchief might have been a rag. She was not certain it was a rag. It was something she saw the doctor throw into the fire when she came to her senses.

"Had he kept it in his hands, then, all the time you were unconscious?"

"I don't know."

"Just to show it to you?"

The witness was silent.

When she was examined as to her knowledge of chloroform, she broke down hopelessly. She did not know the smell of it; could not describe it; did not know whether it burnt or not; could not in fact swear that it was chloroform Dr. Wilde had used; would not swear that it was anything; believed that it was chloroform or something like it because she lost consciousness. That was her only reason for saying that chloroform had been given to her.

Again the judge interposed with the probing question:

"Did you say anything about chloroform in your pamphlet?"

"No," the witness murmured.

It was manifest that the strong current of feeling in favour of Miss Travers had begun to ebb. The story was a toothsome morsel still; but it was regretfully admitted that the charge of rape had not been pushed home. It was felt to be disappointing, too, that the chief prosecuting witness should have damaged her own case.

It was now the turn of the defence, and some thought the pendulum might swing back again.

Lady Wilde was called and received an enthusiastic reception. The ordinary Irishman was willing to show at any time that he believed in his Muse, and was prepared to do more than cheer for one who had fought with her pen for "Oireland" in the *Nation*, side by side with Tom Davis.

Lady Wilde gave her evidence emphatically, but was too bitter to be a persuasive witness. It was tried to prove from her letter that she believed that Miss Travers had had an intrigue with Sir William Wilde, but she would not have it. She did not for a moment believe in her husband's guilt. Miss Travers wished to make it appear, she said, that she had an intrigue with Sir William Wilde, but in her opinion it was utterly untrue. Sir William Wilde was above suspicion. There was not a particle of truth in the accusation; *her* husband would never so demean himself.

Lady Wilde's disdainful speeches seemed to persuade the populace, but had small effect on the jury, and still less on the judge.

When she was asked if she hated Miss Travers, she replied that she did not hate anyone, but she had to admit that she disliked Miss Travers' methods of action.

"Why did you not answer Miss Travers when she wrote telling you of your husband's attempt on her virtue?"

"I took no interest in the matter," was the astounding reply.

The defence made an even worse mistake than this. When the time came, Sir William Wilde was not called.

In his speech for Miss Travers, Mr. Butt made the most of this omission. He declared that the refusal of Sir William Wilde to go into the witness box was an admission of guilt; an admission that Miss Travers' story of her betrayal was true and could not be contradicted. But the refusal of Sir William Wilde to go into the box was not, he insisted, the worst point in the defence. He reminded the jury that he had asked Lady Wilde why she had not answered Miss Travers when she wrote to her. He recalled Lady Wilde's reply:

"I took no interest in the matter."

Every woman would be interested in such a thing, he declared, even a stranger; but Lady Wilde hated her husband's victim and took no interest in her seduction beyond writing a bitter, vindictive, and libellous letter to the girl's father. . . .

The speech was regarded as a masterpiece and enhanced the already great reputation of the man who was afterwards to become the Home Rule Leader.

It only remained for the judge to sum up, for everyone was getting impatient to hear the verdict. Chief Justice Monahan made a short, impartial speech, throwing the dry, white light of truth upon the conflicting and passionate statements. First of all, he said, it was difficult to believe in the story of rape whether with or without chloroform. If the girl had been violated she would be expected to cry out at the time, or at least to complain to her father as soon as she reached home. Had it been a criminal trial, he pointed out, no one would have believed this part of Miss Travers' story. When you find a girl does not cry out at the time and does not complain afterwards, and returns to the house

11

to meet further rudeness, it must be presumed that she consented to the seduction.

But was there a seduction? The girl asserted that there was guilty intimacy, and Sir William Wilde had not contradicted her. It was said that he was only formally a defendant; but he was the real defendant and he could have gone into the box if he had liked and given his version of what took place and contradicted Miss Travers in whole or in part.

"It is for you, gentlemen of the jury, to draw your own conclusions from his omission to do what one would have thought would be an honourable man's first impulse and duty."

Finally, it was for the jury to consider whether the letter was a libel and if so what the amount of damages should be.

His Lordship recalled the jury at Mr. Butt's request to say that in assessing damages they might also take into consideration the fact that the defence was practically a justification of the libel. The fair-mindedness of the judge was conspicuous from first to last, and was worthy of the high traditions of the Irish Bench.

After deliberating for a couple of hours the jury brought in a verdict which had a certain humour in it. They awarded to Miss Travers a farthing damages and intimated that the farthing should carry costs. In other words they rated Miss Travers' virtue at the very lowest coin of the realm, while insisting that Sir William Wilde should pay a couple of thousands of pounds in costs for having seduced her.

It was generally felt that the verdict did substantial justice; though the jury, led away by patriotic sympathy with Lady Wilde, the true "Speranza," had been a little hard on Miss Travers. No one doubted that Sir William Wilde had seduced his patient. He had, it appeared, an unholy reputation, and the girl's admission that he had accused her of being "unnaturally passionless" was accepted as the true key of the enigma. This was why he had drawn away from the girl, after seducing her. And it was not unnatural under the circumstances that she should become vindictive and revengeful.

Such inferences as these, I drew from the comments of the Irish papers at the time; but naturally I wished if possible to hear some trustworthy contemporary on the matter. Fortunately such testimony was forthcoming.

A Fellow of Trinity, who was then a young man, embodied the best opinion of the time in an excellent pithy letter. He wrote to me that the trial simply established, what every one believed, that "Sir William Wilde was a pithecoid person of extraordinary sensuality and cowardice (funking the witness box left him without a defender!) and that his wife was a highfalutin' pretentious creature whose pride was as extravagant as her reputation founded on second-rate verse-making. . . . Even when a young woman she used to keep her rooms in Merrion Square in semi-darkness; she laid the paint on too thick for any ordinary light, and she gave herself besides all manner of airs."

This incisive judgment of an able and fairly impartial contemporary observer[1] corroborates, I think, the inferences which one would naturally draw from the newspaper accounts of the trial. It seems to me that both combine to give a realistic photograph, so to speak, of Sir William and Lady Wilde. An artist, however, would lean to a more kindly picture. Trying to see the personages as they saw themselves he would balance the doctor's excessive sensuality and lack of self-control by dwelling on the fact that his energy and perseverance and intimate adaptation to his surroundings had brought him in middle age to the chief place in his profession, and if Lady Wilde was abnormally vain, a verse-maker and not a poet, she was still a talented woman of considerable reading and manifold artistic sympathies.

Such were the father and mother of Oscar Wilde.

[1] As he has died since this was written, there is no longer any reason for concealing his name: R. Y. Tyrell, for many years before his death Regius Professor of Greek in Trinity College, Dublin.

Oscar Wilde as a Schoolboy

THE WILDES had three chidren, two sons and a daughter. The first son was born in 1852, a year after the marriage, and was christened after his father William Charles Kingsbury Wills. The second son was born two years later, in 1854 and the names given to him seem to reveal the Nationalist sympathies and pride of his mother. He was christened Oscar Fingal O'Flahertie Wills Wilde; but he appears to have suffered from the pompous string only in extreme youth. At school he concealed the "Fingal," as a young man he found it advisable to omit the "O'Flahertie."

In childhood and early boyhood Oscar was not considered as quick or engaging or handsome as his brother, Willie. Both boys had the benefit of the best schooling of the time. They were sent as boarders to the Portora School at Enniskillen, one of the four Royal schools of Ireland. Oscar went to Portora in 1864 at the age of nine, a couple of years after his brother. He remained at the school for seven years and left it on winning an Exhibition for Trinity College, Dublin, when he was just seventeen.

The facts hitherto collected and published about Oscar as a schoolboy are sadly meagre and insignificant. Fortunately for my readers I have received from Sir Edward Sullivan, who was a contemporary of Oscar both at school and college, an exceedingly vivid and interesting pen-picture of the lad, one of those astounding masterpieces of portraiture only to be produced by the plastic sympathies of boyhood and the intimate intercourse of years lived in common. It is love alone which in later life can achieve such a miracle of representment. I am very glad to be allowed to publish this realistic miniature, in the very words of the author.

"I first met Oscar Wilde in the early part of 1868 at Portora Royal School. He was thirteen or fourteen years of age. His long straight fair hair was a striking feature of his appearance. He was then, as he remained for some years after, extremely boyish in nature, very mobile, almost restless when out of the school-room. Yet he took no part in the school games at any time. Now and then he would be seen in one of the school boats on Loch Erne; yet he was a poor hand at an oar.

"Even as a schoolboy he was an excellent talker. His descriptive power being far above the average, and his humorous exaggerations of school occurrences always highly amusing.

"A favourite place for the boys to sit and gossip in the late afternoon in winter time was round a stove which stood in 'The Stone Hall.' Here Oscar was at his best; although his brother Willie was perhaps in those days even better than he was at telling a story.

"Oscar would frequently vary the entertainment by giving us extremely quaint illustrations of holy people in stained-glass attitudes; his power of twisting his limbs into weird contortions being very great. (I am told that Sir William Wilde, his father, possessed the same power.) It must not be thought, however, that there was any suggestion of irreverence in the exhibition.

"At one of these gatherings, about the year 1870, I remember a discussion taking place about an ecclesiastical prosecution that made a considerable stir at the time. Oscar was present and, full of the mysterious nature of the Court of Arches, he told us there was nothing he would like better in after life than to be the hero of such a *cause célèbre* and to go down to posterity as the defendant in such a case as 'Regina versus Wilde!'

"At school he was almost always called 'Oscar'—but he had a nick-name, 'Grey-crow,' which the boys would call him when they wished to annoy him, and which he resented greatly. It was derived in some mysterious way from the name of an island in the Upper Loch Erne, within easy reach of the school by boat.

"It was some little time before he left Portora that the boys got to know of his full name, Oscar Fingal O'Flahertie Wills Wilde. Just at the close of his school career he won the 'Carpenter' Greek Testament Prize,—and on presentation day was called up to the dais by Dr. Steele, by all his names—much to Oscar's annoyance, for a great deal of schoolboy chaff followed.

"He was always generous, kindly, good-tempered. I remember he and myself were on one occasion mounted as opposing jockeys on the backs of two bigger boys in what we called a 'tournament,' held in one of the class-rooms. Oscar and his horse were thrown, and the result was a broken arm for Wilde. Knowing that it was an accident, he did not let it make any difference in our friendship.

"He had, I think, no very special chums while at school. I was perhaps as friendly with him all through as anybody, though his junior in class by a year. . . .

"Willie Wilde was never very familiar with him, treating him always, in those days, as a younger brother. . . .

"When in the head class together, we with two other boys were in the town of Enniskillen one afternoon and formed part of an audience who were listening to a street orator. One of us, for the fun of the thing, got near the speaker and with a stick knocked his hat off and then ran for home followed by the other three. Several of the listeners, resenting the impertinence, gave chase, and Oscar in his hurry collided with an aged cripple and threw him down—a fact which was duly reported to the boys when we got safely back. Oscar was afterwards heard telling how he found his way barred by an angry giant with whom he fought through many rounds and whom he eventually left for dead in the road after accomplishing prodigies of valour on his redoubtable opponent. Romantic imagination was strong in him even in those schoolboy days; but there was always something in his telling of such a tale to suggest that he felt his hearers were not really being taken in; it was merely the romancing indulged in so humorously by the two principal male characters in 'The Importance of Being Earnest.' . . .

"He never took any interest in mathematics either at school or college. He laughed at science and never had a good word for a mathematical or science master, but there was nothing spiteful or malignant in anything he said against them, or indeed against anybody.

"The romances that impressed him most when at school were Disraeli's novels. He spoke slightingly of Dickens as a novelist. . . .

"The classics absorbed almost his whole attention in his later school days, and the flowing beauty of his oral translations in class, whether of Thucydides, Plato, or Virgil, was a thing not easily to be forgotten."

This photograph, so to speak, of Oscar as a schoolboy is astonishingly clear and lifelike; but I have another portrait of him from another contemporary, who has since made for himself a high name as a scholar at Trinity, which, while confirming the general traits sketched by Sir Edward Sullivan, takes somewhat more notice of certain mental qualities which came later to the fruiting.

This observer, who does not wish his name given, writes:

"Oscar had a pungent wit, and nearly all the nicknames in the school were given by him. He was very good on the literary side of scholarship, with a special leaning to poetry. . . .

"We noticed that he always liked to have editions of the classics that were of stately size with large print. . . . He was more careful in his dress than any other boy.

"He was a wide reader and read very fast indeed; how much he assimilated I never could make out. He was poor at music.

"We thought him a fair scholar but nothing extraordinary. However, he startled everyone the last year at school in the classical medal examination, by walking easily away from us all in the *viva voce* of the Greek play ('The Agamemnon')."

I may now try and accentuate a trait or two of these photographs, so to speak, and then realise the whole portrait by adding an account given to me by Oscar himself. The joy in humorous romancing and the sweetness of temper recorded by Sir Edward Sullivan were marked traits in Oscar's character all through his life. His care in dressing too, and his delight in stately editions; his love of literature "with a special leaning to poetry" were all qualities which distinguished him to the end.

"Until the last year of my school life at Portora," he said to me once, "I had nothing like the reputation of my brother Willie. I read too many English novels, too much poetry, dreamed away too much time to master the school tasks.

"Knowledge came to me through pleasure, as it always comes, I imagine. . . .

"I was nearly sixteen when the wonder and beauty of the old Greek life began to dawn upon me. Suddenly I seemed to see the white figures throwing purple shadows on the sun-baked palæstra; 'bands of nude youths and maidens'—you remember Gautier's words—'moving across a background of deep blue as on the frieze of the Parthenon.' I began to read Greek eagerly for love of it all, and the more I read the more I was enthralled:

> Oh what golden hours were for us
> As we sat together there,
> While the white vests of the chorus
> Seemed to wave up a light air;
> While the cothurns trod majestic
> Down the deep iambic lines
> And the rolling anapæstics
> Curled like vapour over shrines.

"The head master was always holding my brother Willie up to me as an example; but even he admitted that in my last year at Portora I had made astounding progress. I laid the foundation there of whatever classical scholarship I possess."

It occurred to me once to ask Oscar in later years whether the boarding school life of a great, public school was not responsible for a good deal of sensual viciousness.

"Englishmen all say so," he replied, "but it did not enter into my experience. I was very childish, Frank; a mere boy till I was over sixteen. Of course I was sensual and curious, as boys are, and had the usual boy imaginings; but I did not indulge in them excessively.

"At Portora nine out of ten boys only thought of football or cricket or rowing. Nearly every one went in for athletics— running and jumping and so forth; no one appeared to care for sex. We were healthy young barbarians and that was all.

"Did you go in for games?" I asked.

"No," Oscar replied smiling, "I never liked to kick or be kicked."

"Surely you went about with some younger boy, did you not, to whom you told your dreams and hopes, and whom you grew to care for?"

The question led to an intimate personal confession, which may take its place here.

"It is strange you should have mentioned it," he said. "There was one boy, and," he added slowly, "one peculiar incident. It occurred in my last year at Portora. The boy was a couple of years younger than I—we were great friends; we used to take long walks together and I talked to him interminably. I told him what I should have done had I been Alexander, or how I'd have played king in Athens, had I been Alcibiades. As early as I can remember I used to identify myself with every distinguished character I read about, but when I was fifteen or sixteen I noticed with some wonder that I could think of myself as Alcibiades or Sophocles more easily than as Alexander or Cæsar. The life of books had begun to interest me more than real life. . . .

"My friend had a wonderful gift for listening. I was so occupied with talking and telling about myself that I knew very little about him, curiously little when I come to think of it. But the last incident of my school life makes me think he was a sort of mute poet, and had much more in him than I imagined. It was just before I first heard that I had won an Exhibition and was to go to Trinity. Dr. Steele had called me into his study to tell me the great news; he was very glad, he said, and insisted that it was all due to my last year's hard work. The 'hard' work had been very interesting to me, or I would not have done much of it. The doctor wound up, I remember, by assuring me that if I went on studying as I had been studying during the last year I might yet do as well as my brother Willie, and be as great an honour to the school and everybody connected with it as he had been.

"This made me smile, for though I liked Willie, and knew he was a fairly good scholar, I never for a moment regarded him as my equal in any intellectual field. He knew all about football and cricket and studied the schoolbooks assiduously, whereas I read everything that pleased me, and in my own opinion always went about 'crowned.' " Here he laughed charmingly with amused deprecation of the conceit.

"It was only about the quality of the crown, Frank, that I was in any doubt. If I had been offered the Triple Tiara, it would have appeared to me only the meet reward of my extraordinary merit. . . .

"When I came out from the doctor's I hurried to my friend to tell him all the wonderful news. To my surprise he was cold and said, a little bitterly, I thought:

"You seem glad to go?"

" 'Glad to go,' I cried; I should think I was. Fancy going to Trinity College, Dublin, from this place; why, I shall meet men and not boys. Of course I am glad, wild with delight; the first step to Oxford and fame.'

" 'I mean,' my chum went on, still in the same cold way, 'you seem glad to leave me.'

"His tone startled me.

" 'You silly fellow,' I exclaimed, 'of course not; I'm always glad to be with you: but perhaps you will be coming up to Trinity too; won't you?'

" 'I'm afraid not,' he said, 'but I shall come to Dublin frequently.'

" 'Then we shall meet,' I remarked; 'you must come and see me in my rooms. My father will give me a room to myself in our house, and you know Merrion Square is the best part of Dublin. You must come and see me.'

"He looked up at me with yearning, sad, regretful eyes. But the future was beckoning to me, and I could not help talking about it, for the golden key of wonderland was in my hand, and I was wild with desires and hopes.

"My friend was very silent, I remember, and only interrupted me to ask:

" 'When do you go, Oscar?'

" 'Early,' I replied thoughtlessly, or rather full of my own thoughts, 'early to-morrow morning, I believe; the usual train.'

"In the morning just as I was starting for the station, having said 'goodbye' to everyone, he came up to me very pale and strangely quiet.

" 'I'm coming with you to the station, Oscar,' he said: 'the doctor gave me permission, when I told him what friends we had been.'

" 'I'm glad,' I cried, my conscience pricking me that I had not thought of asking for his company. 'I'm very glad. My last hours at school will always be associated with you.'

"He just glanced up at me, and the glance surprised me; it was like a dog looks at one. But my own hopes soon took possession of me again, and I can only remember being vaguely surprised by the appeal in his regard.

"When I was settled in my seat in the train, he did not say 'goodbye' and go, and leave me to my dreams; but brought me papers and things and hung about.

"The guard came and said:

" 'Now, sir, if you are going.'

"I liked the 'Sir.' To my surprise my friend jumped into the carriage and said:

" 'All right, guard, I'm going, but I shall slip out as soon as you whistle.'

"The guard touched his cap and went. I said something, I don't know what; I was a little embarrassed.

" 'You will write to me, Oscar, won't you, and tell me about everything?'

" 'Oh, yes,' I replied, 'as soon as I get settled down, you know. There will be such a lot to do at first, and I am wild to see everything. I wonder how the professors will treat me. I do hope they will not be fools or prigs; what a pity it is that all professors are not poets. . . .' And so I went on merrily, when suddenly the whistle sounded and a moment afterwards the train began to move.

" 'You must go now,' I said to him.

" 'Yes,' he replied, in a queer muffled voice, while standing with his hand on the door of the carriage. Suddenly he turned to me and cried:

" 'Oh, Oscar,' and before I knew what he was doing he had caught my face in his hot hands, and kissed me on the lips. The next moment he had slipped out of the door and was gone. . . .

"I sat there all shaken. Suddenly I became aware of cold, sticky drops trickling down my face—his tears. They affected me strangely. As I wiped them off I said to myself in amazement:

" 'This is love: this is what he meant—love.' . .

"I was trembling all over. For a long while I sat, unable to think, all shaken with wonder and remorse."

3

Trinity, Dublin: Magdalen, Oxford

OSCAR WILDE did well at school, but he did still better at college, where the competition was more severe. He entered Trinity on October 19th, 1871, just three days after his seventeenth birthday. Sir Edward Sullivan writes me that when Oscar matriculated at Trinity he was already "a thoroughly good classical scholar of a brilliant type," and he goes on to give an invaluable snap-shot of him at this time; a likeness, in fact, the chief features of which grew more and more characteristic as the years went on.

"He had rooms in College at the north side of one of the older squares, known as Botany Bay. These rooms were exceedingly grimy and ill-kept. He never entertained there. On the rare occasions when visitors were admitted, an unfinished landscape in oils was always on the easel, in a prominent place in his sitting room. He would invariably refer to it, telling one in his humorously unconvincing way that 'he had just put in the butterfly.' Those of us who had seen his work in the drawing class presided over by 'Bully' Wakeman at Portora were not likely to be deceived in the matter. . . .

"His college life was mainly one of study; in addition to working for his classical examinations, he devoured with voracity all the best English writers.

"He was an intense admirer of Swinburne and constantly

reading his poems; John Addington Symond's works too, on the Greek authors, were perpetually in his hands. He never entertained any pronounced views on social, religious or political questions while in College; he seemed to be altogether devoted to literary matters.

"He mixed freely at the same time in Dublin society functions of all kinds and was always a very vivacious and welcome guest at any house he cared to visit. All through his Dublin University days he was one of the purest minded men that could be met with.

"He was not a card player, but would on occasions join in a game of limited loo at some man's rooms. He was also an extremely moderate drinker. He became a member of the junior debating society, the Philosophical, but hardly ever took any part in their discussions.

"He read for the Berkeley medal (which he afterwards gained) with an excellent, but at the same time broken-down, classical scholar, John Townsend Mills, and, besides instruction, he contrived to get a good deal of amusement out of his readings with his quaint teacher. He told me for instance that on one occasion he expressed his sympathy for Mills on seeing him come into his rooms wearing a tall hat completely covered in crape. Mills, however, replied, with a smile, that no one was dead—it was only the evil condition of his hat that had made him assume so mournful a disguise. I have often thought that the incident was still fresh in Oscar Wilde's mind when he introduced John Worthing in 'The Importance of Being Earnest,' in mourning for his fictitious brother. . . .

"Shortly before he started on his first trip to Italy, he came into my rooms in a very striking pair of trousers. I made some chaffing remark on them, but he begged me in the most serious style of which he was so excellent a master not to jest about them.

" 'They are my Trasimenè trousers, and I mean to wear them there.' "

Already his humour was beginning to strike all his acquaintances, and what Sir Edward Sullivan here calls his "puremindedness," or what I should rather call his peculiar refinement of nature. No one ever heard Oscar Wilde tell a suggestive story; indeed he always shrank from any gross or crude expression; even his mouth was vowed always to pure beauty.

The Trinity Don whom I have already quoted about Oscar's school-days sends me a rather severe critical judgment of him as a student. There is some truth in it, however, for in part at least it was borne out and corroborated by Oscar's later achievement. It must be borne in mind that the Don was one of his competitors at Trinity, and a successful one; Oscar's mind could not limit itself to college tasks and prescribed books.

"When Oscar came to college he did excellently during the first year; he was top of his class in classics; but he did not do so well in the long examinations for a classical scholarship in his second year. He was placed fifth, which was considered very good, but he was plainly not the man for the δόλιχος (or long struggle), though first-rate for a short examination."

Oscar himself only completed these spirit-photographs by what he told me of his life at Trinity.

"It was the fascination of Greek letters, and the delight I took in Greek life and thought," he said to me once, "which made me a scholar. I got my love of the Greek ideal and my intimate knowledge of the language at Trinity from Mahaffy and Tyrrell; they were Trinity to me; Mahaffy was especially valuable to me at that time. Though not so good a scholar as Tyrrell, he had been in Greece, had lived there and saturated himself with Greek thought and Greek feeling. Besides he took deliberately the artistic standpoint towards everything, which was coming more and more to be my standpoint. He was a delightful talker, too, a really great talker in a certain way—an artist in vivid words and eloquent pauses. Tyrrell, too, was very kind to me—intensely sympathetic and crammed with knowledge. If he had known less he would have been a poet. Learning is a sad handicap, Frank, an appalling handicap," and he laughed irresistibly.

"What were the students like in Dublin?" I asked. "Did you make friends with any of them?"

"They were worse even than the boys at Portora," he replied; "they thought of nothing but cricket and football, running and jumping; and they varied these intellectual exercises with bouts of fighting and drinking. If they had any souls they diverted them with coarse *amours* among barmaids and the women of the streets; they were simply awful. Sexual vice is even coarser and more loathsome in Ireland than it is in England:—

" 'Lilies that fester smell far worse than weeds.'

"When I tried to talk they broke into my thought with stupid gibes and jokes. Their highest idea of humour was an obscene story. No, no, Tyrrell and Mahaffy represent to me whatever was good in Trinity."

In 1874 Oscar Wilde won the gold medal for Greek. The subject of the year was "The Fragments of the Greek Comic Poets, as edited by Meineke." In this year, too, he won a classical scholarship—a demyship of the annual value of £95, which was tenable for five years, which enabled him to go to Oxford without throwing an undue strain on his father's means.

He noticed with delight that his success was announced in the *Oxford University Gazette* of July 11th, 1874. He entered Magdalen College, Oxford, on October 17th, a day after his twentieth birthday.

Just as he had been more successful at Trinity than at school, so he was destined to be far more successful and win a far greater reputation at Oxford than in Dublin.

He had the advantage of going to Oxford a little later than most men, at twenty instead of eighteen, and thus was enabled to win high honours with comparative ease, while leading a life of cultured enjoyment.

He was placed in the first class in "Moderations" in 1876 and had even then managed to make himself talked about in the life of the place. The Trinity Don whom I have already quoted, after admitting that there was not a breath against his character either at school or Trinity, goes on to write that "at Trinity he did not strike us as a very exceptional person," and yet there must have been some sharp eyes at Trinity, for our Don adds with surprising divination:

"I fancy his rapid development took place after he went to Oxford, where he was able to specialize more; in fact where he could study what he most affected. It is, I feel sure, from his Oxford life more than from his life in Ireland that one would be able to trace the good and bad features by which he afterwards attracted the attention of the world."

In 1878 Oscar won a First Class in "Greats." In this same Trinity term, 1878, he further distinguished himself by gaining the Newdigate prize for English verse with his poem "Ravenna," which he recited at the annual Commemoration in the Sheldonian Theatre on June 26th. His reciting of the poem was the literary event of the year in Oxford.

There had been great curiosity about him; he was said to be the best talker of the day, and one of the ripest scholars. There were those in the University who predicted an astonishing future for him, and indeed all possibilities seemed within his reach. "His verses were listened to," said *The Oxford and Cambridge Undergraduates' Journal*, "with rapt attention." It was just the sort of thing, half poetry, half rhythmic rhetoric, which was sure to reach the hearts and minds of youth. His voice, too, was of beautiful tenor quality, and exquisitely used. When he sat down people crowded to praise him and even men of great distinction in life flattered him with extravagant compliments. Strange to say he used always to declare that his appearance about the same time as Prince Rupert, at a fancy dress ball, given by Mrs. George Morrell, at Headington Hill Hall, afforded him a far more gratifying proof of the exceptional position he had won.

"Everyone came round me, Frank, and made me talk. I hardly danced at all. I went as Prince Rupert, and I talked as he charged but with more success, for I turned all my foes into friends. I had the divinest evening; Oxford meant so much to me. . . .

"I wish I could tell you all Oxford did for me.

"I was the happiest man in the world when I entered Magdalen for the first time. Oxford—the mere word to me is full of an inexpressible, an incommunicable charm. Oxford—the home of lost causes and impossible ideals; Matthew Arnold's Oxford—with its dreaming spires and grey colleges, set in velvet lawns and hidden away among the trees, and about it the beautiful fields, all starred with cowslips and fritillaries where the quiet river winds its way to London and the sea. . . . The change, Frank, to me was astounding; Trinity was as barbarian as school, with coarseness superadded. If it had not been for two or three people, I should have been worse off at Trinity than at Portora; but Oxford—Oxford was paradise to me. My very soul seemed to expand within me to peace and joy. Oxford—the enchanted valley, holding in its flowerlet cup all the idealism of the middle ages.[1] Oxford is the

---

[1] Oscar was always fond of loosely quoting or paraphrasing in conversation the purple passages from contemporary writers. He said them exqui-

capital of romance, Frank; in its own way as memorable as Athens, and to me it was even more entrancing. In Oxford, as in Athens, the realities of sordid life were kept at a distance. No one seemed to know anything about money or care anything for it. Everywhere the aristocratic feeling; one must have money, but must not bother about it. And all the appurtenances of life were perfect: the food, the wine, the cigarettes; the common needs of life became artistic symbols, our clothes even won meaning and significance. It was at Oxford I first dressed in knee breeches and silk stockings. I almost reformed fashion and made modern dress æsthetically beautiful; a second and greater reformation, Frank. What a pity it is that Luther knew nothing of dress, had no sense of the becoming. He had courage but no fineness of perception. I'm afraid his neckties would always have been quite shocking!" and he laughed charmingly.

"What about the inside of the platter, Oscar?"

"Ah, Frank, don't ask me, I don't know; there was no grossness, no coarseness; but all delicate delights!

" 'Fair passions and bountiful pities and loves without pain,' "[1]

and he laughed mischievously at the misquotation.

"Loves?" I questioned, and he nodded his head smiling; but would not be drawn.

"All romantic and ideal affections. Every successive wave of youths from the public schools brought some chosen spirits, perfectly wonderful persons, the most graceful and fascinating disciples that a poet could desire, and I preached the old-ever-new gospel of individual revolt and individual perfection. I showed them that sin with its curiosities widened the horizons of life. Prejudices and prohibitions are mere walls to imprison the soul. Indulgence may hurt the body, Frank, but nothing except suffering hurts the spirit; it is self-denial and abstinence that maim and deform the soul."

---

sitely and sometimes his own embroidery was as good as the original. This discipleship, however, always suggested to me a lack of originality. In especial Matthew Arnold had an extraordinary influence upon him, almost as great indeed as Pater.

[1] "Stain," not "pain," in the original.

"Then they knew you as a great talker even at Oxford?" I asked in some surprise.

"Frank," he cried reprovingly, laughing at the same time delightfully, "I was a great talker at school. I did nothing at Trinity but talk, my reading was done at odd hours. I was the best talker ever seen in Oxford."

"And did you find any teacher there like Mahaffy?" I asked, "any professor with a touch of the poet?"

He came to seriousness at once.

"There were two or three teachers, Frank," he replied, "greater than Mahaffy; teachers of the world as well as of Oxford. There was Ruskin for instance, who appealed to me intensely—a wonderful man and a most wonderful writer. A sort of exquisite romantic flower; like a violet filling the whole air with the ineffable perfume of belief. Ruskin has always seemed to me the Plato of England—a Prophet of the Good and True and Beautiful, who saw as Plato saw that the three are one perfect flower. But it was his prose I loved, and not his piety. His sympathy with the poor bored me; the road he wanted us to build was tiresome. I could see nothing in poverty that appealed to me, nothing; I shrank away from it as from a degradation of the spirit; but his prose was lyrical and rose on broad wings into the blue. He was a great poet and teacher, Frank, and therefore of course a most preposterous professor; he bored you to death when he taught, but was an inspiration when he sang.

"Then there was Pater, Pater the classic, Pater the scholar, who had already written the greatest English prose; I think a page or two of the greatest prose in all literature. Pater meant everything to me. He taught me the highest form of art: the austerity of beauty. I came to my full growth with Pater. He was a sort of silent, sympathetic elder brother. Fortunately for me he could not talk at all; but he was an admirable listener, and I talked to him by the hour. I learned the instrument of speech with him, for I could see by his face when I had said anything extraordinary. He did not praise me but quickened me astonishingly, forced me always to do better than my best—an intense vivifying influence, the influence of Greek art at its supremest."

"He was the Gamaliel then," I questioned, "at whose feet you sat?"

"Oh, no, Frank," he chided, "everyone sat at my feet even then. But Pater was a very great man. Dear Pater! I remember once talking to him when we were seated together on a bench under some trees in Oxford. I had been watching the students bathing in the river; the beautiful white figures all grace and ease and virile strength. I had been pointing out how Christianity had flowered into romance, and how the crude Hebraic materialism and all the later formalities of an established creed had fallen away from the tree of life and left us the exquisite ideals of the new paganism. . . .

"The pale Christ had been outlived; his renunciations and his sympathies were mere weaknesses; we were moving to a synthesis of art where the enchanting perfume of romance should be wedded to the severe beauty of classic form. I really talked as if inspired, and when I paused, Pater—the stiff, quiet, silent Pater— suddenly slipped from his seat and knelt down by me and kissed my hand. I cried:

" 'You must not, you really must not. What would people think if they saw you?'

"He got up with a white strained face.

" 'I had to,' he muttered, glancing about him fearfully, 'I had to—once. . . . ' "

I must warn my readers that this whole incident is ripened and set in a higher key of thought by the fact that Oscar told it more than ten years after it happened.

4

Formative Influences: Oscar's Poems

THE MOST IMPORTANT event in Oscar's early life happened while he was still an undergraduate at Oxford. His father, Sir William Wilde, died in 1876, leaving to his wife, Lady Wilde, nearly all he possessed, some £7,000, the interest of which was barely enough to keep her in genteel poverty. The sum is so small that one is constrained to believe the report that Sir William Wilde in his later years kept practically open house—"lashins of whisky and a good larder"— and was besides notorious for his gallantries. Oscar's small portion, a little money and a small house with some land, came to him in the nick of time. He used the cash partly to pay some debts at Oxford, partly to defray the expenses of a trip to Greece. It was natural that Oscar Wilde, with his eager sponge-like receptivity, should receive the best academic education of his time and should better that by travel. We all get something like the education we desire, and Oscar Wilde, it always seemed to me, was over-educated, had learned, that is, too much from books and not enough from life and had thought too little for himself; but my readers will be able to judge of this for themselves.

In 1877 he accompanied Professor Mahaffy on a long tour through Greece. The pleasure and profit Oscar got from the trip were so great that he failed to return to Oxford on the date fixed. The Dons fined him forty-five pounds for the breach of discipline;

but they returned the money to him in the following year when he won First Honours in "Greats" and the Newdigate prize.

This visit to Greece when he was twenty-three confirmed the view of life which he had already formed and I have indicated sufficiently perhaps in that talk with Pater already recorded. But no one will understand Oscar Wilde who for a moment loses sight of the fact that he was a pagan born: as Gautier says, "One for whom the visible world alone exists," endowed with all the Greek sensuousness and love of plastic beauty; a pagan, like Nietzsche and Gautier, wholly out of sympathy with Christianity, one of "the Confraternity of the faithless who *cannot* believe,"[1] to whom a sense of sin and repentance are symptoms of weakness and disease.

Oscar used often to say that the chief pleasure he had in visiting Rome was to find the Greek gods and the heroes and heroines of Greek story throned in the Vatican. He preferred Niobe to the Mater Dolorosa and Helen to both; the worship of sorrow must give place, he declared, to the worship of the beautiful.

Another dominant characteristic of the young man may here find its place.

While still at Oxford his tastes—the bent of his mind and his temperament—were beginning to outline his future. He spent his vacations in Dublin and always called upon his old school friend Edward Sullivan in his rooms at Trinity. Sullivan relates that when they met, Oscar used to be full of his occasional visits to London and could talk of nothing but the impression made upon him by plays and players. From youth on the theatre drew him irresistibly; he had not only all the vanity of the actor, but what might be called the born dramatist's love for the varied life of the stage—its paintings, costumings, rhetoric—and above all the touch of emphasis natural to it which gives such opportunity for humorous exaggeration.

"I remember him telling me," Sullivan writes, "about Irving's 'Macbeth,' which made a great impression on him; he was fascinated by it. He feared, however, that the public might be similarly affected—a thing which, he declared, would destroy his enjoyment of an extraordinary performance." He admired Miss Ellen

[1] His own words in "De Profundis."

Terry, too, extravagantly, as he admired Marion Terry, Mrs. Langtry, and Mary Anderson later.

The death of Sir William Wilde put an end to the family life in Dublin and set the survivors free. Lady Wilde had lost her husband and her only daughter in Merrion Square. The house was full of sad memories to her; she was eager to leave it all and settle in London.

The *Requiescat* in Oscar's first book of poems was written in memory of this sister who died in her teens, whom he likened to "a ray of sunshine dancing about the house." He took his vocation seriously even in youth; he felt that he should sing his sorrow, give record of whatever happened to him in life. But he found no new word for his bereavement.

Willie Wilde came over to London and got employment as a journalist and was soon given almost a free hand by the editor of the society paper, *The World*. With rare unselfishness, or, if you will, with Celtic clannishness, he did a good deal to make Oscar's name known. Every clever thing that Oscar said or that could be attributed to him, Willie reported in *The World*. This puffing and Oscar's own uncommon power as a talker; but chiefly perhaps a whispered reputation for strange sins, had thus early begun to form a sort of myth around him. He was already on the way to becoming a personage; there was a certain curiosity about him, a flutter of interest in whatever he did. He had published poems in the Trinity College magazine, *Kottabos*, and elsewhere. People were beginning to take him at his own valuation as a poet and a wit; and the more readily as that ambition did not clash in any way with their more material strivings.

The time had now come for Oscar to conquer London as he had conquered Oxford. He had finished the first class in the great World-School and was eager to try the next, where his mistakes would be his only tutors and his desires his taskmasters. His University successes flattered him with the belief that he would go from triumph to triumph and be the exception proving the rule that the victor in the academic lists seldom repeats his victories on the battlefield of life.

It is not sufficiently understood that the learning of Latin and Greek and the forming of expensive habits at others' cost are a positive disability and handicap in the rough-and-tumble tussle of the great city, where greed and unscrupulous resolution rule, and where there are few prizes for feats of memory or taste in words. When the graduate wins in life he wins as a rule in spite of his so-called education and not because of it.

It is true that the majority of English 'Varsity men give themselves an infinitely better education than that provided by the authorities. They devote themselves to athletic sports with whole-hearted enthusiasm. Fortunately for them, it is impossible to develop the body without at the same time steeling the will. The would-be athlete has to live laborious days; he may not eat to his liking, nor drink to his thirst. He learns deep lessons almost unconsciously; to conquer his desires and make light of pain and discomfort. He needs no Aristotle to teach him the value of habits; he is soon forced to use them as defences against his pet weaknesses; above all he finds that self-denial has its reward in perfect health; that the thistle, pain, too, has its flower. It is a truism that 'Varsity athletes generally succeed in life; Spartan discipline proving itself incomparably superior to Greek accidence.

Oscar Wilde knew nothing of this discipline. He had never trained his body to endurance or his will to steadfastness. He was the perfect flower of academic study and leisure. At Magdalen he had been taught luxurious living, the delight of gratifying expensive tastes; he had been brought up and enervated, so to speak, in Capua. His vanity had been full-fed with cloistered triumphs; he was at once pleasure-loving, vainly self-confident and weak; he had been encouraged for years to give way to his emotions and to pamper his sensations and, as the Cap-and-Bells of Folly, to cherish a fantastic code of honour even in mortal combat, while despising the religion which might have given him some hold on the respect of his compatriots. What chance had this cultured honour-loving Sybarite in the deadly grapple of modern life where the first quality is will power, the only knowledge needed a knowledge of the value of money. I must not be understood here as in any degree disparaging Oscar. I can surely state that a flower is weaker than a weed without exalting the weed or depreciating the flower.

The first part of life's voyage was over for Oscar Wilde. Let us try to see him as he saw himself at this time and let us also determine his true relations to the world. Fortunately he has given us his own view of himself with some care.

In Foster's *Alumni Oxonienses*, Oscar Wilde described himself on leaving Oxford as a "Professor of Æsthetics and a Critic of Art"—an announcement to me at once infinitely ludicrous and pathetic. "Ludicrous" because it betrays such complete ignorance of life all given over to men industrious with muck-rakes. "Gadarene swine," as Carlyle called them, "busily grubbing and grunting in search of pignuts." "Pathetic" for it is boldly ingenuous as youth itself with a touch of youthful conceit and exaggeration. Another eager human soul on the threshold, longing to find some suitable high work in the world, all unwitting of the fact that ideal strivings are everywhere despised and discouraged—jerry-built cottages for the million being the day's demand and not oratories or palaces of art or temples for the spirit.

Not the time for a "professor of æsthetics," one would say, and assuredly not the place. One wonders whether Zululand would not be more favourable for such a man than England. Germany, France, and Italy have many positions in universities, picture-galleries, museums, opera houses for lovers of the beautiful, and above all an educated respect for artists and writers just as they have places too for servants of Truth in chemical laboratories and polytechnics endowed by the State with excellent results even from the utilitarian point of view. But rich England has only a few dozen such places in all at command and these are usually allotted with a cynical contempt for merit; miserable anarchic England, soul-starved amid its creature comforts, proving now by way of example to helots that man cannot live by bread alone:—England and Oscar Wilde! the "Black Country" and "the professor of æsthetics"—a mad world, my masters!

It is necessary for us now to face this mournful truth that in the quarrel between these two the faults were not all on one side. Mayhap England was even further removed from the ideal than the would-be professor of æsthetics, which fact may well give us pause and food for thought. Organic progress we have been told; indeed, might have seen if we had eyes, evolution, so-called, is from the simple to the complex; our rulers therefore should have provided for the ever-growing complexity of modern life and modern men. The good gardener will even make it his ambition to produce new species; our politicians, however, will not take the trouble to give even the new species that appear a chance of living; they are too busy, it appears, in keeping their jobs.

No new profession has been organized in England since the Middle Ages. In the meantime we have invented new arts, new sciences and new letters. When will these be organized and regimented in new and living professions, so that young ingenuous souls may find suitable fields for their powers and may not be forced willy-nilly to grub for pignuts when it would be more profitable for them and for us to use their nobler faculties? Not only are the poor poorer and more numerous in England than elsewhere; but there is less provision made for the "intellectuals" too. Consequently the organism is suffering at both extremities. It is high time that both maladies were taken in hand, for by universal consent England is now about the worst organized of all modern States, the furthest from the ideal.

Something too should be done with the existing professions to make them worthy of honourable ambition. One of them, the Church, is a noble body without a soul; the soul, our nostrils tell us, died some time ago, while the medical profession has got a noble spirit with a wretched half-organized body. It says much for the inherent integrity and piety of human nature that our doctors persist in trying to cure diseases when it is clearly to their self-interest to keep their patients ailing—an anarchic world, this English one, and stupefied with self-praise. What will this professor of æsthetics make of it?

Here he is, the flower of English University training, a winner of some of the chief academic prizes without any worthy means of earning a livelihood, save perchance by journalism. And journalism in England suffers from the prevailing anarchy. In France, Italy, and Germany journalism is a career in which an eloquent and cultured youth may honourably win his spurs. In many countries this way of earning one's bread can still be turned into an art by the gifted and high-minded; but in England thanks in the main to the anonymity of the press cunningly contrived by the capitalist, the journalist or modern preacher is turned into a venal voice, a soulless Cheapjack paid to puff his master's wares. Clearly our "Professor of Æsthetics and Critic of Art" is likely to have a doleful time of it in nineteenth century London.

Oscar had already dipped into his little patrimony, as we have seen, and he could not conceal from himself that he would soon have to live on what he could earn—a few pounds a week. But then he was a poet and had boundless confidence in his own ability. To the artist nature the present is everything; just for to-day he resolved that he would live as he had always lived. So he travelled first class to London and bought all the books and papers that could distract him on the way: "Give me the luxuries," he used to say, "and anyone can have the necessaries."

In the background of his mind there were serious misgivings. Long afterwards he told me that his father's death and the smallness of his patrimony had been a heavy blow to him. He encouraged himself, however, at the moment by dwelling on his brother's comparative success and waved aside fears and doubts as unworthy.

It is to his credit that at first he tried to cut down expenses and live laborious days. He took a couple of furnished rooms in Salisbury Street off the Strand, a very Grub Street for a man of fashion, and began to work at journalism while getting together a book of poems for publication. His journalism at first was anything but successful. It was his misfortune to appeal only to the best heads and good heads are not numerous anywhere. His appeal, too, was still academic and laboured. His brother Willie with his commoner sympathies appeared to be better equipped for this work. But Oscar had from the first a certain social success.

As soon as he reached London, he stepped boldly into the limelight, going to all "first nights" and taking the floor on all occasions. He was not only an admirable talker but he was invariably smiling, eager, full of life and the joy of living and, above all, given to unmeasured praise of whatever and whoever pleased him. This gift of enthusiastic admiration was not only his most engaging characteristic, but also, perhaps, the chief proof of his extraordinary ability. It was certainly, too, the quality which served him best all through his life. He went about declaring that Mrs. Langtry was more beautiful than the "Venus of Milo," and Lady Archie Campbell more charming than Rosalind and Mr. Whistler an incomparable artist. Such enthusiasm in a young and brilliant man was unexpected and delightful and doors were thrown open to him in all sets. Those who praise passionately are generally welcome guests and if Oscar could not praise he shrugged his shoulders and kept silent; scarcely a bitter word ever fell from those smiling lips. No tactics could have been more successful in England than his native gift of radiant good-humour and enthusiasm. He got to know not only all the actors and actresses, but the chief patrons and frequenters of the theatre: Lord Lytton, Lady Shrewsbury, Lady Dorothy Nevill, Lady de Grey and Mrs. Jeune; and, on the other hand, Hardy, Meredith, Browning, Swinburne, and Matthew Arnold—all Bohemia, in fact, and all that part of Mayfair which cares for the things of the intellect.

But though he went out a great deal and met a great many distinguished people, and won a certain popularity, his social success put no money in his purse. It even forced him to spend money; for the constant applause of his hearers gave him self-confidence. He began to talk more and write less, and cabs and gloves and flowers cost money. He was soon compelled to mortgage his little property in Ireland.

At the same time it must be admitted he was still indefatigably intent on bettering his mind, and in London he found more original teachers than in Oxford; notably Morris and Whistler. Morris, though greatly overpraised during his life, had hardly any message for the men of his time. He went for his ideals to an imaginary past and what he taught and praised was often totally unsuited to modern conditions. Whistler, on the other hand, was a modern of the moderns, and a great artist to boot. He had not only assimilated all the newest thought of the day, but with the alchemy of genius had transmuted it and made it his own. Before even the de Goncourts, he had admired Chinese porcelain and Japanese prints and his own exquisite intuition strengthened by Japanese example had shown him that his impression of life was more valuable than any mere transcript of it. Modern art he felt should be an interpretation and not a representment of reality, and he taught the golden rule of the artist that the half is usually more expressive than the whole. He went about London preaching new schemes of decoration and another Renaissance of Art. Had he only been a painter he would never have exercised an extraordinary influence; but he was of a singularly interesting appearance as well and an admirable talker gifted with picturesque phrases and a most caustic wit.

Oscar sat at his feet and imbibed as much as he could of the new æsthetic gospel. He even ventured to annex some of the master's most telling stories and thus came into conflict with his teacher.

One incident may find a place here.

The art critic of *The Times*, Mr. Humphry Ward, had come to see an exhibition of Whistler's pictures. Filled with an undue sense of his own importance, he buttonholed the master and pointing to one picture said:

"That's good, first-rate, a lovely bit of colour; but that, you know," he went on, jerking his finger over his shoulder at another picture, "that's bad, drawing all wrong . . . bad!"

"My dear fellow," cried Whistler, "you must never say that this painting's good or that bad, never! Good and bad are not terms to be used by you; but say, I like this, and I dislike that, and you'll be within your right. And now come and have a whiskey for you're sure to like that."

Carried away by the witty fling, Oscar cried:

"I wish I had said that."

"You will, Oscar, you will," came Whistler's lightning thrust.

Of all the personal influences which went to the moulding of Oscar Wilde's talent, that of Whistler, in my opinion was the most important; Whistler taught him that men of genius stand apart and are laws unto themselves; showed him, too, that all qualities—singularity of appearance, wit, rudeness even, count doubly in a democracy. But neither his own talent nor the bold self-assertion learned from Whistler helped him to earn money; the conquest of London seemed further off and more improbable than ever. Where Whistler had missed the laurel how could he or indeed anyone be sure of winning?

A weaker professor of æsthetics would have been discouraged by the monetary and other difficulties of his position and would have lost heart at the outset in front of the impenetrable blank wall of English philistinism and contempt. But Oscar Wilde was conscious of great ability and was driven by an inordinate vanity. Instead of diminishing his pretensions in the face of opposition he increased them. He began to go abroad in the evening in knee breeches and silk stockings wearing strange flowers in his coat— green cornflowers and gilded lilies—while talking about Baudelaire, whose name even was unfamiliar, as a world poet, and proclaiming the strange creed that "nothing succeeds like excess." Very soon his name came into everyone's mouth; London talked of him and discussed him at a thousand tea-tables. For one invitation he had received before, a dozen now poured in; he became a celebrity.

Of course he was still sneered at by many as a mere *poseur;* it still seemed to be all Lombard Street to a china orange that he would be beaten down under the myriad trampling feet of middle-class indifference and disdain.

Some circumstances were in his favour. Though the artistic movement inaugurated years before by the Pre-Raphaelites was still laughed at and scorned by the many as a craze, a few had stood firm, and slowly the steadfast minority had begun to sway the majority as is often the case in democracies. Oscar Wilde profited by the victory of these art-loving forerunners. Here and there among the indifferent public, men were attracted by the artistic view of life and women by the emotional intensity of the new creed. Oscar Wilde became the prophet of an esoteric cult. But notoriety even did not solve the monetary question, which grew more and more insistent. A dozen times he waved it aside and went into debt rather than restrain himself. Somehow or other he would fall on his feet, he thought. Men who console themselves in this way usually fall on someone else's feet and so did Oscar Wilde. At twenty-six years of age and curiously enough at the very moment of his insolent-bold challenge of the world with fantastic dress, he stooped to ask his mother for money, money which she could ill spare, though to do her justice she never wasted a second thought on money where her affections were concerned, and she not only loved Oscar but was proud of him. Still she could not give him much; the difficulty was only postponed; what was to be done?

His vanity had grown with his growth; the dread of defeat was only a spur to the society favourite; he cast about for some means of conquering the Philistines, and could think of nothing but his book of poems. He had been trying off and on for nearly a year to get it published. The publishers told him roundly that there was no money in poetry and refused the risk. But the notoriety of his knee breeches and silken hose, and above all the continual attacks in the society papers, came to his aid and his book appeared in the early summer of 1881 with all the importance that imposing form, good paper, broad margins, and high price (10/6) could give it. The truth was, he paid for the printing and production of the book himself, and David Bogue, the publisher, put his name on for a commission.

Oscar had built high fantastic hopes on this book. To the very end of his life he believed himself a poet and in the creative sense of the word he was assuredly justified, but he meant it in the singing sense as well, and there his claim can only be admitted with serious qualifications. But whether he was a singer or not the hopes founded on this book were extravagant; he expected to make not only reputation by it, but a large amount of money, and money is not often made in England by poetry.

The book had an extraordinary success, greater, it may safely be said, than any first book of real poetry has ever had in England or indeed is ever likely to have: four editions were sold in a few weeks. Two of the Sonnets in the book were addressed to Ellen Terry, one as "Portia," the other as "Henrietta Maria"; and these partly account for the book's popularity, for Miss Terry was delighted with them and praised the book and its author to the skies.[1] I reproduce the "Henrietta Maria" sonnet here as a fair specimen of the work:

QUEEN HENRIETTA MARIA

In the lone tent, waiting for victory,
    She stands with eyes marred by the mists of pain,
    Like some wan lily overdrenched with rain:
The clamorous clang of arms, the ensanguined sky,
War's ruin, and the wreck of chivalry,
    To her proud soul no common fear can bring:
    Bravely she tarrieth for her Lord the King,
Her soul aflame with passionate ecstasy.
O Hair of Gold! O Crimson Lips! O Face!
    Made for the luring and the love of man!
    With thee I do forget the toil and stress,
The loveless road that knows no resting-place,
    Time's straitened pulse, the soul's dread weariness,
My freedom and my life republican.

Lyric poetry is by its excellence the chief art of England, as music is the art of Germany. A book of poetry is almost sure of fair appreciation in the English press which does not trouble to

---

[1] In her "Recollections" Miss Terry says that she was more impressed by the genius of Oscar Wilde and of Whistler than by that of any other men.

notice a "Sartor Resartus" or the first essays of an Emerson. The excessive consideration given to Oscar's book by the critics showed that already his personality and social success had affected the reporters.

The Athenæum gave the book the place of honour in its number for the 23rd of July. The review was severe; but not unjust. "Mr. Wilde's volume of poems," it says, "may be regarded as the evangel of a new creed. From other gospels it differs in coming after, instead of before, the cult it seeks to establish. . . . We fail to see, however, that the apostle of the new worship has any distinct message."

The critic then took pains to prove that "nearly all the book is imitative" . . . and concluded: "Work of this nature has no element of endurance."

The Saturday Review dismissed the book at the end of an article on "Recent Poetry" as "neither good nor bad." The reviewer objected in the English fashion to the sensual tone of the poems; but summed up fairly enough: "This book is not without traces of cleverness, but it is marred everywhere by imitation, insincerity, and bad taste."

At the same time the notices in *Punch* were extravagantly bitter, while of course the notices in *The World*, mainly written by Oscar's brother, were extravagantly eulogistic. *Punch* declared:

"Mr. Wilde may be æsthetic, but he is not original . . . a volume of echoes. . . . Swinburne and water."

Now what did *The Athenæum* mean by taking a new book of imitative verse so seriously and talking of it as the "evangel of a new creed," besides suggesting that "it comes after the cult," and so forth?

It seems probable that *The Athenæum* mistook Oscar Wilde for a continuator of the Pre-Raphaelite movement with the sub-conscious and peculiarly English suggestion that whatever is "æsthetic" or "artistic" is necessarily weak and worthless, if not worse.

Soon after Oscar left Oxford *Punch* began to caricature him and ridicule the cult of what it christened "The Too Utterly Utter." Nine Englishmen out of ten took delight in the savage contempt poured upon what was known euphemistically as "the æsthetic craze" by the pet organ of the English middle class.

This was the sort of thing *Punch* published under the title of "A Poet's Day":

"Oscar at Breakfast! Oscar at Luncheon!!
Oscar at Dinner!!! Oscar at Supper!!!!"

" 'You see I am, after all, mortal,' remarked the poet, with an ineffable affable smile, as he looked up from an elegant but substantial dish of ham and eggs. Passing a long willowy hand through his waving hair, he swept away a stray curl-paper, with the nonchalance of a D'Orsay.

"After this effort Mr. Wilde expressed himself as feeling somewhat faint; and with a half apologetic smile ordered another portion of Ham and Eggs."

Punch's verses on the subject were of the same sort, showing spite rather than humour. Under the heading of "Sage Green" (by a fading-out Æsthete) it published such stuff as this:

> My love is as fair as a lily flower.
> (*The Peacock blue has a sacred sheen!*)
> Oh, bright are the blooms in her maiden bower.
> (*Sing Hey! Sing Ho! for the sweet Sage Green!*)

. . . .

> And woe is me that I never may win;
> (*The Peacock blue has a sacred sheen!*)
> For the Bard's hard up, and she's got no tin
> (*Sing Hey! Sing Ho! for the sweet Sage Green!*)

Taking the criticism as a whole it would be useless to deny that there is an underlying assumption of vicious sensuality in the poet which is believed to be reflected in the poetry. This is the only way to explain the condemnation which is much more bitter than the verse deserves.

The poems gave Oscar pocket money for a season; increased too his notoriety; but did him little or no good with the judicious: there was not a memorable word or a new cadence, or a sincere cry in the book. Still, first volumes of poetry are as a rule imitative and the attempt, if inferior to "Venus and Adonis," was not without interest.

Oscar was naturally disappointed with the criticism, but the sales and the stir the book made encouraged him, and he was as determined as ever to succeed. What was to be done next?

5

Oscar's Quarrel with Whistler: Marriage

THE FIRST ROUND in the battle with Fate was inconclusive. Oscar Wilde had managed to get known and talked about and had kept his head above water for a couple of years while learning something about life and more about himself. On the other hand, he had spent almost all his patrimony, had run into some debt besides; yet seemed as far as ever from earning a decent living. The outlook was disquieting.

Even as a young man Oscar had a very considerable understanding of life. He could not make his way as a journalist, the English did not care for his poetry; but there was still the lecture-platform. In his heart he knew that he could talk better than he wrote.

He got his brother to announce boldly in *The World* that owing to the "astonishing success of his 'Poems' Mr. Oscar Wilde had been invited to lecture in America."

The invitation was imaginary; but Oscar had resolved to break into this new field; there was money in it, he felt sure.

Besides he had another string to his bow. When the first rumblings of the social storm in Russia reached England, our aristocratic republican seized occasion by the forelock and wrote a play on the Nihilist Conspiracy called *Vera*. This drama was impregnated with popular English liberal sentiment. With the interest of actuality about it *Vera* was published in September, 1880; but fell flat.

The assassination of the Tsar Alexander, however, in March, 1881; the way Oscar's poems published in June of that year were taken up by Miss Terry and puffed in the press, induced Mrs. Bernard Beere, an actress of some merit, to accept *Vera* for the stage. It was suddenly announced that *Vera* would be put on by Mrs. Bernard Beere at The Adelphi in December, '81; but the author had to be content with this advertisement. December came and went and *Vera* was not staged. It seemed probable to Oscar that it might be accepted in America; at any rate, there could be no harm in trying: he sailed for New York.

It was on the cards that he might succeed in his new adventure. The taste of America in letters and art is still strongly influenced, if not formed, by English taste, and, if Oscar Wilde had been properly accredited, it is probable that his extraordinary gift of speech would have won him success in America as a lecturer.

His phrase to the Revenue officers on landing: "I have nothing to declare except my genius," turned the limelight full upon him and excited comment and discussion all over the country. But the fuglemen of his caste whose praise had brought him to the front in England were almost unrepresented in the States, and never bold enough to be partisans. Oscar faced the American Philistine public without his accustomed *claque*, and under these circumstances a half-success was evidence of considerable power. His subjects were "The English Renaissance" and "House Decoration."

His first lecture at Chickering Hall on January 9, 1882, was so much talked about that the famous impresario, Major Pond, engaged him for a tour which, however, had to be cut short in the middle as a monetary failure. *The Nation* gave a very fair account of his first lecture: "Mr. Wilde is essentially a foreign product and can hardly succeed in this country. What he has to say is not new, and his extravagance is not extravagant enough to amuse the average American audience. His knee breeches and long hair are good as far as they go; but Bunthorne has really spoiled the public for Wilde."

The Nation underrated American curiosity. Oscar lectured some ninety times from January till July, when he returned to

New York. The gross receipts amounted to some £4,000: he received about £1,200, which left him with a few hundreds above his expenses. His optimism regarded this as a triumph.

One is fain to confess today that these lectures make very poor reading. There is not a new thought in them; not even a memorable expression; they are nothing but student work, the best passages in them being mere paraphrases of Pater and Arnold, though the titles were borrowed from Whistler. Dr. Ernest Bendz in his monograph on *The Influence of Pater and Matthew Arnold in the Prose-Writings of Oscar Wilde* has established this fact with curious erudition and completeness.

Still, the lecturer was a fine figure of a man; his knee breeches and silk stockings set all the women talking, and he spoke with suave authority. Even the dullest had to admit that his elocution was excellent, and the manner of speech is keenly appreciated in America. In some of the Eastern towns, in New York especially, he had a certain success, the success of sensation and of novelty, such success as every large capital gives to the strange and eccentric.

In Boston he scored a triumph of character. Fifty or sixty Harvard students came to his lecture dressed to caricature him in "swallow tail coats, knee breeches, flowing wigs and green ties. They all wore large lilies in their button-holes and each man carried a huge sunflower as he limped along." That evening Oscar appeared in ordinary dress and went on with his lecture as if he had not noticed the rudeness. The chief Boston paper gave him due credit:

> "Everyone who witnessed the scene on Tuesday evening must feel about it very much as we do, and those who came to scoff, if they did not exactly remain to pray, at least left the Music Hall with feelings of cordial liking, and, perhaps to their own surprise, of respect for Oscar Wilde."[1]

As he travelled west to Louisville and Omaha his popularity dwindled and dwindled. Still he persevered and after leaving the States visited Canada, reaching Halifax in the autumn.

[1] By way of heaping coals of fire on the students' heads Oscar presented a cast of the Hermes (then recently unearthed) to the University of Harvard.

One incident must find a place here. On September 6, he sent £80 to Lady Wilde. I have been told that this was merely a return of money she had advanced; but there can be no doubt that Oscar, unlike his brother Willie, helped his mother again and again most generously, though Willie was always her favourite.

Oscar returned to England in April, 1883, and lectured to the Art Students at their club in Golden Square. This at once brought about a break with Whistler who accused him of plagiarism:— "Picking from our platters the plums for the puddings he peddles in the provinces."

If one compares this lecture with Oscar's on "The English Renaissance of Art," delivered in New York only a year before, and with Whistler's well-known opinions, it is impossible not to admit that the charge was justified. Such phrases as "artists are not to copy beauty but to create it . . . a picture is a purely decorative thing," proclaim their author.

The long newspaper wrangle between the two was brought to a head in 1885, when Whistler gave his famous *Ten o'clock* discourse on Art. This lecture was infinitely better than any of Oscar Wilde's. Twenty odd years older than Wilde, Whistler was a master of all his resources; he was not only witty, but he had new views on art and original ideas. As a great artist he knew that "there never was an artistic period. There never was an Art-loving nation." Again and again he reached pure beauty of expression. The masterly persiflage, too, filled me with admiration and I declared that the lecture ranked with the best ever heard in London with Coleridge's on Shakespeare and Carlyle's on Heroes. To my astonishment Oscar would not admit the superlative quality of Whistler's talk; he thought the message paradoxical and the ridicule of the professors too bitter. "Whistler's like a wasp," he cried, "and carries about with him a poisoned sting." Oscar's kindly sweet nature revolted against the disdainful aggressiveness of Whistler's attitude. Besides, in essence, Whistler's lecture was an attack on the academic theory taught in the universities, and defended naturally by a young scholar like Oscar Wilde. Whistler's view that the artist was sporadic, a happy chance, a "sport," in fact, was a new view, and Oscar had not yet reached this level; he reviewed the master in the *Pall Mall Gazette*, a review remarkable for one of the earliest gleams of that genial humour which later became his most characteristic gift: "Whistler," he said, "is indeed one of the very greatest masters of painting in my opinion. And I may add that in this opinion Mr. Whistler himself entirely concurs."

Whistler retorted in *The World* and Oscar replied, but Whistler had the best of the argument. . . . "Oscar—the amiable, irresponsible, esurient Oscar—with no more sense of a picture than of the fit of a coat, has the courage of the opinions . . . of others!"

It should be noted here that one of the bitterest of tongues could not help doing homage to Oscar Wilde's "amiability." Whistler even prefered to call him "amiable and irresponsible" rather than give his plagiarism a harsher attribute.

Oscar Wilde learned almost all he knew of art and of controversy from Whistler, but he was never more than a pupil in either field; for controversy in especial he was poorly equipped. He had neither the courage, nor the contempt, nor the joy in conflict of his great exemplar.

Unperturbed by Whistler's attacks, Oscar went on lecturing about the country on "Personal Impressions of America," and in August crossed again to New York to see his play "Vera" produced by Marie Prescott at the Union Square Theatre. It was a complete failure, as might have been expected; the serious part of it was such as any talented young man might have written. Nevertheless I find in this play for the first time, a characteristic gleam of humour, an unexpected flirt of wing, so to speak, which, in view of the future, is full of promise. At the time it passed unappreciated.

September, 1883, saw Oscar again in England. The platform gave him better results than the theatre, but not enough for freedom or ease. It is the more to his credit that as soon as he got a couple of hundred pounds ahead, he resolved to spend it in bettering his mind.

His longing for wider culture and, perhaps in part, the example of Whistler, drove him to Paris. He put up at the little provincial Hotel Voltaire on the Quai Voltaire and quickly made acquaintance with everyone of note in the world of letters, from Victor Hugo to Paul Bourget. He admired Verlaine's genius to the full, but the grotesque physical ugliness of the man himself (Verlaine was like a masque of Socrates) and his sordid and unclean way of living prevented Oscar from really getting to know him. During this stay in Paris, Oscar read enormously and his French, which had been school-boyish, became quite good. He always said that Balzac, and especially his poet, Lucien de Rubempré, had been his teachers.

While in Paris he completed his blank-verse play, "The Duchess of Padua," and sent it to Miss Mary Anderson in America, who refused it, although she had commissioned him, he always said, to write it. It seems to me inferior even to "Vera" in interest, more academic and further from life, and when produced in New York in 1891 it was a complete frost.

In a few months Oscar Wilde had spent his money and had skimmed the cream from Paris, as he thought; accordingly he returned to London and took rooms again, this time in Charles Street, Mayfair. He had learned some rude lessons in the years since leaving Oxford, and the first and most impressive lesson was the fear of poverty. Yet his taking rooms in the fashionable part of town showed that he was more determined than ever to rise and not to sink.

It was Lady Wilde who urged him to take rooms near her; she never doubted his ultimate triumph. She knew all his poems by heart, took the strass for diamonds and welcomed the chance of introducing her brilliant son to the Irish Nationalist Members and other pinchbeck celebrities who flocked about her.

It was about this time that I first saw Lady Wilde. I was introduced to her by Willie, Oscar's elder brother, whom I had met in Fleet Street. Willie was then a tall, well-made fellow of thirty or thereabouts with an expressive, taking face, lit up with a pair of deep blue laughing eyes. He had any amount of physical vivacity, and told a good story with immense verve, without for a moment getting above the commonplace: to him the Corinthian journalism of *The Daily Telegraph* was literature. Still he had the surface good nature and good humour of healthy youth and was generally liked. He took me to his mother's house one afternoon; but first he had a drink here and a chat there so that we did not reach the West End till after six o'clock.

The room and its occupants made an indelible, grotesque impression on me. It seemed smaller than it was because overcrowded with a score of women and half a dozen men. It was very dark and there were empty tea-cups and cigarette ends everywhere. Lady Wilde sat enthroned behind the tea-table looking like a sort of female Buddha swathed in wraps—a large woman with a heavy face and prominent nose; very like Oscar indeed, with the same sallow skin which always looked dirty; her eyes too were her redeeming feature—vivacious and quick-glancing as a girl's. She "made up" like an actress and naturally preferred shadowed gloom to sunlight. Her idealism came to show as soon as she spoke. It was a necessity of her nature to be enthusiastic; unfriendly critics said hysterical, but I should prefer to say high-falutin' about everything she enjoyed or admired. She was at her best in misfortune; her great vanity gave her a certain proud stoicism which was admirable.

The Land League was under discussion as we entered, and Parnell's attitude to it. Lady Wilde regarded him as the pre-destined saviour of her country. "Parnell," she said with a strong accent on the first syllable, "is the man of destiny; he will strike off the feters and free Ireland, and throne her as Queen among the nations."

A murmur of applause came from a thin bird-like woman standing opposite, who floated towards us clad in a sage-green gown, which sheathed her like an umbrella case; had she had any figure the dress would have been indecent.

"How like 'Speranza'!" she cooed, "dear Lady Wilde!" I noticed that her glance went towards Willie, who was standing on the other side of his mother, talking to a tall, handsome girl. Willie's friend seemed amused at the lyrical outburst of the green spinster, for smiling a little she questioned him:

" 'Speranza' is Lady Wilde?" she asked with a slight American accent.

Lady Wilde informed the company with all the impressiveness she had at command that she did not expect Oscar that afternoon; "he is so busy with his new poems, you know; they say there has been no such sensation since Byron." She added; "already everyone is talking of them."

"Indeed, yes," sighed the green lily, "do you remember, dear Speranza, what he said about 'The Sphinx,' that he read to us. He told us the written verse was quite different from what the printed poem would be just as the sculptor's clay model differs from the marble. Subtle, wasn't it?"

"Perfectly true, too!" cried a man, with a falsetto voice, moving into the circle; "Leonardo himself might have said that."

The whole scene seemed to me affected and middle-class, untidy, too, with an un-English note about it of shiftlessness; the æsthetic dresses were extravagant, the enthusiasms pumped up and exaggerated. I was glad to leave quietly.

It was on this visit to Lady Wilde, or a later one, that I first heard of that other poem by Oscar, "The Harlot's House," which was also said to have been written in Paris. Though published in an obscure sheet and in itself commonplace enough it made an astonishing stir. Time and advertisement had been working for him. Academic lectures and imitative poetry alike had made him widely known; and, thanks to the small body of enthusiastic admirers whom I have already spoken of, his reputation, instead of waning, had grown like the Jinn when released from the bottle.

The fuglemen were determined to find something wonderful in everything he did, and the title of "The Harlot's House," shocking Philistinism, gave them a certain opportunity which they used to the uttermost. On all sides one was asked: "Have you seen Oscar's latest?" And then the last verse would be quoted:—"Divine, don't ye think?"

> "And down the long and silent street,
>   The dawn, with silver-sandalled feet,
> Crept like a frightened girl."

In spite of all this extravagant eulogy, Oscar Wilde's early plays and poems, like his lectures, were unimportant. The small remnant of people in England who really love the things of the spirit were disappointed in them, failed to find in them the genius so loudly and so arrogantly vaunted.

But, if Oscar Wilde's early writings were failures, his talk was more successful than ever. He still tried to show off on all occasions and sometimes fell flat in consequence; but his failures in this field were few and merely comparative; constant practice was ripening his extraordinary natural gift. About this time, too, he began to develop that humorous vein in conversation, which later lent a singular distinction to his casual utterances.

His talk brought him numerous invitations to dinner and lunch and introduced him to some of the best houses in London, but it produced no money. He was earning very little and he needed money, comparatively large sums of money, from week to week. Oscar Wilde was extravagant in almost every possible way. He wished to be well-fed, well-dressed, well-wined, and prodigal of "tips." He wanted first editions of the poets; had a liking for old furniture and old silver, for fine pictures, Eastern carpets and Renaissance bronzes; in fine, he had all the artist's desires as well as those of the poet and *viveur*. He was constantly in dire need of cash and did not hesitate to borrow fifty pounds from anyone who would lend it to him. He was beginning to experience the truth of the old verse:

> 'Tis a very good world to live in,
>   To lend or to spend or to give in,
> But to beg or to borrow or to get a man's own,
>   'Tis the very worst world that ever was known.

The difficulties of life were constantly increasing upon him. He despised bread and butter and talked only of champagne and caviare; but without bread, hunger is imminent. Victory no longer seemed indubitable. It was possible; it began even to be probable that the fair ship of his fame might come to wreck on the shoals of poverty.

It was painfully clear that he must do something without further delay, must either conquer want or overleap it. Would he bridle his desires, live savingly, and write assiduously till such repute came as would enable him to launch out and indulge his tastes? He was wise enough to see the advantages of such a course. Every day his reputation as a talker was growing. Had he had a little more self-control, had he waited a little longer till his position in society was secured, he could easily have married someone with money and position who would have placed him above sordid care and fear for ever. But he could not wait; he was colossally vain; he would wear the peacock's feathers at all times and all costs. He was intensely pleasure-loving, too; his mouth watered for every fruit. Besides, he couldn't write with creditors at the door. Like Bossuet he was unable to work when bothered about small economies:—*s'il était à l'étroit dans son domestique.*

What was to be done? Suddenly he cut the knot and married the daughter of a Q.C., a Miss Constance Lloyd, a young lady without any particular qualities or beauty, whom he had met in Dublin on a lecture tour. Miss Lloyd had a few hundreds a year of her own, just enough to keep the wolf from the door. The couple went to live in Tite Street, Chelsea, in a modest little house. The drawing-room, however, was decorated by Godwin and quickly gained a certain notoriety. It was indeed a charming room with an artistic distinction and appeal of its own.

As soon as the dreadful load of poverty was removed, Oscar began to go about a great deal, and his wife would certainly have been invited with him if he had refused invitations addressed to himself alone; but from the beginning he accepted them and consequently after the first few months of marriage his wife went out but little, and later children came and kept her at home. Having earned a respite from care by his marriage, Oscar did little for the next three years but talk. Critical observers began to make up their minds that he was a talker and not a writer. "He was a power in the art," as de Quincey said of Coleridge; "and he carried a new art into the power." Every year this gift grew with him. Every year he talked more and more brilliantly, and he was allowed now, and indeed expected, to hold the table.

In London there is no such thing as conversation. Now and then one hears a caustic or witty phrase, but nothing more. The tone of good society everywhere is to be pleasant without being prominent. In every other European country, however, able men are encouraged to talk; in England alone they are discouraged. People in society use a debased jargon or slang, snobbish shibboleths for the most part, and the majority resent any one man monopolising attention. But Oscar Wilde was allowed this privileged position, was encouraged to hold forth to amuse people, as singers are brought in to sing after dinner.

Though his fame as a witty and delightful talker grew from week to week, even his marriage did not stifle the undertone of dislike and disgust. Now indignantly, now with contempt, men spoke of him as abandoned, a creature of unnatural viciousness. There were certain houses in the best set of London society which were closed to him.

6

Oscar Wilde's Faith and Practice

FROM 1884 ON I met Oscar Wilde continually, now at the theatre, now in some society drawing room; most often, I think, at Mrs. Jeune's (afterwards Lady St. Helier). His appearance was not in his favour; there was something oily and fat about him that repelled me. Naturally being British-born and young I tried to give my repugnance a moral foundation; fleshly indulgence and laziness, I said to myself, were written all over him. The snatches of his monologues which I caught from time to time seemed to me to consist chiefly of epigrams almost mechanically constructed of proverbs and familiar sayings turned upside down. Two of Balzac's characters, it will be remembered, practised this form of humour. The desire to astonish and dazzle, the love of the uncommon for its own sake, was so evident that I shrugged my shoulders and avoided him. One evening, however, at Mrs. Jeune's, I got to know him better. At the very door Mrs. Jeune came up to me:

"Have you ever met Mr. Oscar Wilde? You ought to know him: he is so delightfully clever, so brilliant!"

I went with her and was formally introduced to him. He shook hands in a limp way I disliked; his hands were flabby, greasy; his skin looked bilious and dirty. He wore a great green scarab ring on one finger. He was over-dressed rather than well-dressed; his clothes fitted him too tightly; he was too stout. He had a trick which I noticed even then, which grew on him later, of pulling his jowl with his right hand as he spoke, and his jowl was already fat and pouchy. His appearance filled me with distaste. I lay stress on this physical repulsion, because I think most people felt it, and in itself, it is a tribute to the fascination of the man that he should have overcome the first impression so completely and so quickly. I don't remember what we talked about, but I noticed almost immediately that his grey eyes were finely expressive; in turn vivacious, laughing, sympathetic; always beautiful. The carven mouth, too, with its heavy, chiselled, purple-tinged lips, had a certain attraction and significance in spite of a black front tooth which shocked one when he laughed. He was over six feet in height and both broad and thick-set; he looked like a Roman Emperor of the decadence.

We had a certain interest in each other, an interest of curiosity, for I remember that he led the way almost at once into the inner drawing room in order to be free to talk in some seclusion. After half an hour or so I asked him to lunch next day at *The Cafe Royal*, then the best restaurant in London.

At this time he was a superb talker, more brilliant than any I have ever heard in England, but nothing like what he became later. His talk soon made me forget his repellant physical peculiarities; indeed I soon lost sight of them so completely that I have wondered since how I could have been so disagreeably affected by them at first sight. There was an extraordinary physical vivacity and geniality in the man, an extraordinary charm in his gaiety, and lightning-quick intelligence. His enthusiasms, too, were infectious. Every mental question interested him, especially if it had anything to do with art or literature. His whole face lit up as he spoke and one saw nothing but his soulful eyes, heard nothing but his musical tenor voice; he was indeed what the French call a *charmeur*.

In ten minutes I confessed to myself that I liked him, and his talk was intensely quickening. He had something unexpected to say on almost every subject. His mind was agile and powerful and he took a delight in using it. He was well-read too, in several languages, especially in French, and his excellent memory stood him in good stead. Even when he merely reproduced what the great writers had said perfectly, he added a new colouring. And already his characteristic humour was beginning to illumine every topic with lambent flashes.

It was at our first lunch, I think, that he told me he had been asked by Harper's to write a book of one hundred thousand words and offered a large sum for it—I think some five thousand dollars —in advance. He wrote to them gravely that there were not one hundred thousand words in English, so he could not undertake the work, and laughed merrily like a child at the cheeky reproof.

"I have sent their letters and my reply to the press," he added, and laughed again, while probing me with inquisitive eyes: how far did I understand the need of self-advertisement?

About this time an impromptu of his moved the town to laughter. At some dinner party it appeared the ladies sat a little too long; Oscar wanted to smoke. Suddenly the hostess drew his attention to a lamp, the shade of which was smouldering.

"Please put it out, Mr. Wilde," she said, "it's smoking."

Oscar turned to do as he was told with the remark:

"Happy lamp!"

The delightful impertinence had an extraordinary success.

Early in our friendship I was fain to see that the love of the uncommon, his paradoxes and epigrams were natural to him, sprang immediately from his taste and temperament. Perhaps it would be well to define once for all his attitude towards life with more scope and particularity than I have hitherto done.

It is often assumed that he had no clear and coherent view of life, no belief, no faith to guide his vagrant footsteps; but such an opinion does him injustice. He had his own philosophy, and held to it for long years with astonishing tenacity. His attitude towards life can best be seen if he is held up against Goethe. He took the artist's view of life which Goethe was the first to state and indeed, in youth, had overstated with an astonishing persuasiveness: "the beautiful is more than the good," said Goethe; "for it includes the good."

It seemed to Oscar, as it had seemed to young Goethe, that "the extraordinary alone survives"; the extraordinary whether good or bad; he therefore sought after the extraordinary and, naturally enough, often fell into the extravagant. But how stimulating it was in London, where sordid platitudes drip and drizzle all day long, to hear someone talking brilliant paradoxes.

Goethe did not linger long in the halfway house of unbelief; the murderer may win notoriety as easily as the martyr, but his memory will not remain, *"The fashion of this world passeth away,"* said Goethe. "I would fain occupy myself with that which endures." Midway in life Goethe accepted Kant's moral imperative and restated his creed: "A man must resolve to live," he said, "for the Good, and Beautiful, and for the Common Weal."

Oscar did not push his thought so far; the transcendental was not his field.

It was a pity, I sometimes felt, that he had not studied German as thoroughly as French; Goethe might have done more for him than Baudelaire or Balzac, for in spite of all his stodgy German faults, Goethe is the best guide through the mysteries of life whom the modern world has yet produced. Oscar Wilde stopped where the religion of Goethe began; he was far more of a pagan and individualist than the great German; he lived for the beautiful and extraordinary, but not for the Good and still less for the Whole; he acknowledged no moral obligation; *in commune bonis* was an ideal which never said anything to him; he cared nothing for the common weal; he held himself above the mass of the people with an Englishman's extravagant insularity and aggressive pride. Politics, social problems, religion—everything interested him simply as a subject of art; life itself was merely material for art. He held the position Goethe had abandoned in youth.

The view was astounding in England and new everywhere in its onesidedness. Its passionate exaggeration, however, was quickening, and there is, of course, something to be said for it. The artistic view of life is often higher than the ordinary religious view; at least it does not deal in condemnations and exclusions; it is more reasonable, more catholic, more finely perceptive.

"The artist's view of life is the only possible one," Oscar used to say, "and should be applied to everything, most of all to religion and morality. Cavaliers and Puritans are interesting for their costumes and not for their convictions. . . .

"There is no general rule of health; it is all personal, individual. . . . I only demand that freedom which I willingly concede to others. No one condemns another for preferring green to gold. Why should any taste be ostracised? Liking and disliking are not under our control. I want to choose the nourishment which suits *my* body and *my* soul."

I can almost hear him say the words with his charming humorous smile and exquisite flash of deprecation, as if he were half inclined to make fun of his own statement.

It was not his views on art, however, which recommended him to the aristocratic set in London; but his contempt for social reform, or rather his utter indifference to it, and his English love of inequality. The republicanism he flaunted in his early verses was not even skin deep; his political beliefs and prejudices were the prejudices of the English governing class and were all in favour of individual freedom, or anarchy under the protection of the policeman.

"The poor are poor creatures," was his real belief, "and must always be hewers of wood and drawers of water. They are merely the virgin soil out of which men of genius and artists grow like flowers. Their function is to give birth to genius and nourish it. They have no other *raison d'être*. Were men as intelligent as bees, all gifted individuals would be supported by the community, as the bees support their queen. We should be the first charge on the state just as Socrates declared that he should be kept in the Prytaneum at the public expense.

"Don't talk to me, Frank, about the hardships of the poor. The hardships of the poor are necessities, but talk to me of the hardships of men of genius, and I could weep tears of blood. I was never so affected by any book in my life as I was by the misery of Balzac's poet, Lucien de Rubempré."

Naturally this creed of an exaggerated individualism appealed peculiarly to the best set in London. It was eminently aristocratic and might almost be defended as scientific, for to a certain extent it found corroboration in Darwinism. All progress according to Darwin comes from peculiar individuals; "sports" as men of science call them, or the "heaven-sent" as rhetoricians prefer to style them. The many are only there to produce more "sports" and ultimately to benefit by them. All this is valid enough; but it leaves the crux of the question untouched. The poor in aristocratic England are too degraded to produce "sports" of genius, or indeed any "sports" of much value to humanity. Such an extravagant inequality of condition obtains there that the noble soul is miserable, the strongest insecure. But Wilde's creed was intensely popular with the "Smart Set" because of its very onesidedness, and he was hailed as a prophet partly because he defended the cherished prejudices of the "landed" oligarchy.

It will be seen from this that Oscar Wilde was in some danger of suffering from excessive popularity and unmerited renown. Indeed if he had loved athletic sports, hunting and shooting instead of art and letters, he might have been the selected representative of aristocratic England.

In addition to his own popular qualities a strong current was sweeping him to success. He was detested by the whole of the middle or shop-keeping class which in England, according to Matthew Arnold, has "the sense of conduct—and has but little else." This class hated and feared him; feared him for his intellectual freedom and his contempt of conventionality, and hated him because of his light-hearted self-indulgence, and also because it saw in him none of its own sordid virtues. *Punch* is peculiarly the representative of this class and of all English prejudices, and *Punch* jeered at him now in prose, now in verse, week after week. Under the heading, "More Impressions" (by Oscuro Wildgoose) I find this:

"My little fancy's clogged with gush
My little lyre is false in tone,
And when I lyrically moan,
I hear the impatient critic's 'Tush!'

"But I've 'Impressions.' These are grand!
Mere dabs of words, mere blobs of tint,
Displayed on canvas or in print,
Men laud, and think they understand.

"A smudge of brown, a smear of yellow,
No tale, no subject,—there you are!
Impressions!—and the strangest far
Is—that the bard's a clever fellow."

A little later these lines appeared:

"My languid lily, my lank limp lily,
My long, lithe, lily-love, men may grin—

Say that I'm soft and supremely silly—
What care I, while you whisper still;
What care I, while you smile? Not a pin!
While you smile, while you whisper—
    'Tis sweet to decay!
I have watered with chlorodine, tears of chagrin,
The churchyard mould I have planted thee in,
    Upside down, in an intense way,
In a rough red flower-pot, *sweeter than sin,*
    That I bought for a halfpenny, yesterday!"

The italics are mine; but the suggestion was always implicit. Yet this constant wind of puritanic hatred blowing against him helped instead of hindering his progress. Strong men are made by opposition; like kites they go up against the wind.

7

Oscar's Reputation and Supporters

"Believe me, child, all the gentleman's misfortunes arose from his being educated at a public school. . . ."—FIELDING.

IN ENGLAND success is a plant of slow growth. The tone of good society, though responsive to political talent, and openly, eagerly sensitive to money-making talent, is contemptuous of genius and rates the utmost brilliancy of the talker hardly higher than the feats of an acrobat. Men are obstinate, slow, trusting a bank-balance rather than brains, and giving way reluctantly to sharp-witted superiority. The road to power or influence in England is full of pitfalls and far too arduous for those who have neither high birth nor wealth to help them. The natural inequality of men instead of being mitigated by law or custom is everywhere strengthened and increased by a thousand effete social distinctions. Even in the best class where a certain easy familiarity reigns there is circle above circle, and the summits are isolated by heredity.

The conditions of English society being what they are, it is all but impossible at first to account for the rapidity of Oscar Wilde's social success; yet if we tell over his advantages and bring one or two into the account which have not yet been reckoned, we shall find almost every element that conduces to popularity. By talent

60

and conviction he was the natural pet of the aristocracy whose selfish prejudices he defended and whose leisure he amused. The middle class, as has been noted, disliked and despised him; but its social influence is small and its papers, and especially *Punch*, made him notorious by attacking him in and out of season. The comic weekly, indeed, helped to build up his reputation by the almost inexplicable bitterness of its invective.

Another potent force was in his favour. From the beginning he set himself to play the game of the popular actor, and neglected no opportunity of turning the limelight on his own doings. As he said, his admiration of himself was "a lifelong devotion," and he proclaimed his passion on the housetops.

Our names happened to be mentioned together once in some paper, I think it was *The Pall Mall Gazette*. He asked me what I was going to reply.

"Nothing," I answered, "why should I bother? I've done nothing yet that deserves trumpeting."

"You're making a mistake," he said seriously. "If you wish for reputation and fame in this world, and success during your lifetime, you ought to seize every opportunity of advertising yourself. You remember the Latin word, 'Fame springs from one's own house.' Like other wise sayings, it's not quite true; fame comes from oneself," and he laughed delightedly; "you must go about repeating how great you are till the dull crowd comes to believe it."

"The prophet must proclaim himself, eh? and declare his own mission?"

"That's it," he replied with a smile; "that's it. Every time my name is mentioned in a paper, I write at once to admit that I am the Messiah. Why is Pears' soap successful? Not because it is better or cheaper than any other soap, but because it is more strenuously puffed. The journalist is my 'John the Baptist.' What would you give, when a book of yours comes out, to be able to write a long article drawing attention to it in *The Pall Mall Gazette*? Here you have the opportunity of making your name known just as widely; why not avail yourself of it? I miss no chance," and to do him justice he used occasion to the utmost.

Curiously enough Bacon had the same insight, and I have often wondered since whether Oscar's worldly wisdom was original or was borrowed from the great Elizabethan climber. Bacon says:

> " 'Boldly sound your own praises and some of them will stick.' . . . It will stick with the more ignorant and the populace, though men of wisdom may smile at it; and the reputation won with many will amply contervail the disdain of a few. . . . And surely no small number of those who are of solid nature, and who, from the want of this ventosity, cannot spread all sail in pursuit of their own honour, suffer some prejudice and lose dignity by their moderation."

Many of Oscar's letters to the papers in these years were amusing, some of them full of humour. For example, when he was asked to give a list of the hundred best books, as Lord Avebury and other mediocrities had done, he wrote saying that "he could not give a list of the hundred best books, as he had only written five."

Winged words of his were always passing from mouth to mouth in town. Some theatre was opened which was found horribly ugly; one spoke of it as "Early Victorian."

"No, no," replied Oscar, "nothing so distinctive. 'Early Maple,' rather."

Even his impertinences made echoes. At a great reception, a friend asked him in passing, how the hostess, Lady S——, could be recognized. Lady S—— being short and stout, Oscar replied, smiling:

"Go through this room, my dear fellow, and the next and so on till you come to someone looking like a public monument, say the effigy of Britannia or Victoria—that's Lady S——."

Though he used to pretend that all this self-advertisement was premeditated and planned, I could hardly believe him. He was eager to write about himself because of his exaggerated vanity and reflection afterwards found grounds to justify his inclination. But whatever the motive may have been, the effect was palpable. His name was continually in men's mouths, and his fame grew by repetition. As Tiberius said of Mucianus:

"*Omnium quæ dixerat feceratque, arte quadam ostentator*" (He had a knack of showing off and advertising whatever he said or did).

But no personal qualities, however eminent, no gifts, no graces of heart or head or soul could have brought a young man to Oscar Wilde's social position and popularity in a few years.

Another cause was at work lifting him steadily. From the time he left Oxford he was acclaimed and backed by a small minority of passionate admirers whom I have called his fuglemen. These admirers formed the constant factor in his progress from social height to height. For the most part they were persons usually called "sexual inverts", who looked to the brilliancy of his intellect to gild their esoteric indulgence. This class in England is almost wholly recruited from the aristocracy and the upper middle-class that apes the "smart set". It is an inevitable product of the English boarding school and University system; indeed one of the most characteristic products. I shall probably bring upon myself a host of enemies by this assertion, but it has been weighed and must stand. Fielding has already put the same view on record. He says:

"A public school, Joseph, was the cause of all the calamities which he afterwards suffered. Public schools are the nurseries of all vice and immorality. All the wicked fellows whom I remember at the University were bred at them. . . ."

If boarding-school life with its close intimacies between boys from twelve to eighteen years of age were understood by English mothers, it is safe to say that every boarding-house in every school would disappear in a single night, and Eton, Harrow, Winchester and the rest would be turned into day-schools.

Those who have learned bad habits at school or in the 'Varsity are inclined to continue the practices in later life. Naturally enough these men are usually distinguished by a certain artistic sympathy, and often by most attractive, intellectual qualities. As a rule the epicene have soft voices and ingratiating manners, and are bold enough to make a direct appeal to the heart and emotions; they are considered the very cream of London society.

These admirers and supporters praised and defended Oscar Wilde from the beginning with the persistence and courage of men who, if they don't hang together, are likely to hang separately. After his trial and condemnation *The Daily Telegraph* spoke with contempt of these "decadents" and "æsthetes" who, it asserted, "could be numbered in London society on the fingers of one hand"; but even *The Daily Telegraph* must have known that in the "smart set" alone there are hundreds of these acolytes whose intellectual and artistic culture gives them an importance out of all proportion to their number. It was the passionate support of these men in the first place which made Oscar Wilde notorious and successful.

This fact may well give pause to the thoughtful reader. In the middle ages, when birth and position had a disproportionate power in life, the Catholic Church supplied a certain democratic corrective to the inequality of social conditions. It was a sort of "Jacob's Ladder" leading from the lowest strata of society to the very heavens and offering to ingenuous, youthful talent a career of infinite hope and unlimited ambition. This great power of the Roman Church in the middle-ages may well be compared to the influence exerted by those whom I have designated as Oscar Wilde's fuglemen in the England of today. The easiest way to success in London society is to be notorious in this sense. Whatever career one may have chosen, however humble one's birth, one is then certain of finding distinguished friends and impassioned advocates. If you happen to be in the army and unmarried, you are declared to be a strategist like Cæsar, or an organizer like Moltke; if you are an artist, instead of having your faults proclaimed and your failings scourged, your qualifications are eulogised and you find yourself compared to Michael Angelo or Titian! I would not willingly exaggerate here; but I could easily give dozens of instances to prove that sexual perversion is a "Jacob's Ladder" to most forms of success in our time in London.

It seems a curious effect of the great compensatory balance of things that a masculine rude people like the English, who love nothing so much as adventures and warlike achievements, should allow themselves to be steered in ordinary times by epicene æsthetes. But no one who knows the facts will deny that these men are prodigiously influential in London in all artistic and literary matters, and it was their constant passionate support which lifted Oscar Wilde so quickly to eminence.

From the beginning they fought for him. He was regarded as a leader among them when still at Oxford. Yet his early writings show no trace of such a prepossession; they are wholly void of offence, without even a suggestion of coarseness, as pure indeed as his talk. Nevertheless, as soon as his name came up among men in town, the accusation of abnormal viciousness was either made or hinted. Everyone spoke as if there were no doubt about his tastes, and this in spite of the habitual reticence of Englishmen. I could not understand how the imputation came to be so bold and universal; how so shameful a calumny, as I regarded it, was so firmly established in men's minds. Again and again I protested against the injustice, demanded proofs; but was met only by shrugs and pitying glances as if my prejudice must indeed be invincible if I needed evidence of the obvious.

I have since been assured, on what should be excellent authority, that the evil reputation which attached to Oscar Wilde in those early years in London was completely undeserved. I, too, must say that in the first period of our friendship, I never noticed anything that could give colour even to suspicion of him; but the belief in his abnormal tastes was widespread and dated from his life in Oxford.

From about 1886-7 on, however, there was a notable change in Oscar Wilde's manners and mode of life. He had been married a couple of years, two children had been born to him; yet instead of settling down he appeared suddenly to have become wilder. In 1887 he accepted the editorship of a lady's paper, *The Woman's World*, and was always mocking at the selection of himself as the "fittest" for such a post; he had grown noticeably bolder. I told myself that an assured income and position give confidence, but at bottom a doubt began to form in me. It can't be denied that from 1887-8 on incidents occurred from time to time which kept the suspicion of him alive, and indeed pointed and strengthened it. I shall have to deal now with some of the more important of these occurrences.

8

Oscar's Growth to Originality—About 1890

THE PERIOD OF GROWTH of any organism is the most interesting
and most instructive. And there is no moment of growth in the individual life which can be compared in importance with the
moment when a man begins to outtop his age, and to suggest the
future evolution of humanity by his own genius. Usually this
final stage is passed in solitude:

> *Es bildet ein Talent sich in der Stille,*
> *Sich ein Charakter in dem Strome der Welt.*

After writing a life of Schiller which almost anyone might have
written, Carlyle retired for some years to Craigenputtoch, and
then brought forth *Sartor Resartus*, which was personal and soul-
revealing to the verge of eccentricity. In the same way Wagner
was a mere continuator of Weber in Lohengrin and Tannhaeuser,
and first came to his own in the Meistersinger and Tristan, after
years of meditation in Switzerland.

This period for Oscar Wilde began with his marriage; the
freedom from sordid anxieties allowed him to lift up his head
and be himself. Kepler, I think, it is who praises poverty as the
foster-mother of genius; but Bernard Palissy was nearer the truth
when he said:—*Pauvreté empêche bons esprits de parvenir*

66

(poverty hinders fine minds from succeeding). There is no such mortal enemy of genius as poverty except riches: a touch of the spur from time to time does good; but a constant rowelling disables. As editor of *The Woman's World* Oscar had some money of his own to spend. Though his salary was only some six pounds a week, it made him independent, and his editorial work gave him an excuse for not exhausting himself by writing. For some years after marriage; in fact, till he lost his editorship, he wrote little and talked a great deal.

During this period we were often together. He lunched with me once or twice a week and I began to know his method of work. Everything came to him in the excitement of talk, epigrams, paradoxes and stories; and when people of great position or title were about him he generally managed to surpass himself. All social distinctions appealed to him intensely. I chaffed him about this one day and he admitted the snobbishness gaily.

"I love even historic names, Frank, as Shakespeare did. Surely everyone prefers Norfolk, Hamilton and Buckingham to Jones or Smith or Robinson."

As soon as he lost his editorship, he took to writing for the reviews; his articles were merely the *résumé* of his monologues. After talking for months at this and that lunch and dinner he had amassed a store of epigrams and humorous paradoxes which he could embody in a paper for *The Fortnightly Review* or *The Nineteenth Century*.

These papers made it manifest that Wilde had at length, as Heine phrased it, reached the topmost height of the culture of his time and was now able to say new and interesting things. His *Lehrjahr* or student-time may be said to have ended with his editorship. The articles which he wrote on "The Decay of Lying," "The Critic as Artist," and "Pen, Pencil and Poison"; in fact, all the papers which in 1891 were gathered together and published in book form under the title of "Intentions," had about them the stamp of originality. They achieved a noteworthy success with the best minds, and laid the foundation of his fame. Every paper contained, here and there, a happy phrase or epigram or flirt of humour, which made it memorable to the lover of letters.

They were all, however, conceived and written from the standpoint of the artist, and the artist alone, who never takes account of ethics, but uses right and wrong indifferently as colours of his palette. "The Decay of Lying" seemed to the ordinary, matter-of-fact Englishman a cynical plea in defence of mendacity. To the majority of readers, "Pen, Pencil and Poison" was hardly more than a shameful attempt to condone cold-blooded murder. The very articles which grounded his fame as a writer helped to injure his standing and repute.

In 1889 he published a paper which did him even more damage by appearing to justify the peculiar rumours about his private life. He held the opinion, which was universal at that time, that Shakespeare had been abnormally vicious. He believed with the majority of critics that Lord William Herbert was addressed in the first series of Sonnets; but his fine sensibility or, if you will, his peculiar temperament, led him to question whether Thorpe's dedication to "Mr. W. H." could have been addressed to Lord William Herbert. He preferred the old hypothesis that the dedication was addressed to a young actor named Mr. William Hughes, a supposition which is supported by a well-known sonnet. He set forth this idea with much circumstance and considerable ingenuity in an article which he sent to me for publication in *The Fortnightly Review*. The theme was scabrous; but his treatment of it was scrupulously reserved and adroit, and I saw no offence in the paper, and to tell the truth, no great ability in his handling of the subject.

He had talked over the article with me while he was writing it, and I told him that I thought the whole theory completely mistaken. Shakespeare was as sensual as one could well be; but there was no evidence of abnormal vice; indeed, all the evidence seemed to me to be against this universal belief. The assumption that the dedication was addressed to Lord William Herbert I had found it difficult to accept, at first; the wording of it is not only ambiguous but familiar. If I assumed that "Mr. W. H." was meant for Lord William Herbert, it was only because that seemed the easiest way out of the maze. In fine, I pointed out to Oscar that his theory had very little that was new in it, and more that was untrue, and advised him not to publish the paper. My conviction that Shakespeare was not abnormally vicious, and that the first series of Sonnets proved snobbishness and toadying and not corrupt passion, seemed to Oscar the very madness of partisanship.

He smiled away my arguments, and sent his paper to the *Fortnightly* office when I happened to be abroad. Much to my chagrin, my assistant rejected it rudely, whereupon Oscar sent it to Blackwoods, who published it in their magazine. It set everyone talking and arguing. To judge by the discussion it created, the wind of hatred and of praise it caused, one would have thought that the paper was a masterpiece, though in truth it was nothing out of the common. Had it been written by anybody else it would have passed unnoticed. But already Oscar Wilde had a prodigious notoriety, and all his sayings and doings were eagerly canvassed from one end of society to the other.

"The Portrait of Mr. W. H." did Oscar incalculable injury. It gave his enemies for the first time the very weapon they wanted, and they used it unscrupulously and untiringly with the fierce delight of hatred. Oscar seemed to revel in the storm of conflicting opinions which the paper called forth. He understood better than most men that notoriety is often the forerunner of fame and is always commercially more valuable. He rubbed his hands with delight as the discussion grew bitter and enjoyed even the sneering of the envious. A wind that blows out a little fire, he knew, plays bellows to a big one. So long as people talked about him, he didn't much care what they said, and they certainly talked interminably about everything he wrote.

The inordinate popular success increased his self-confidence, and with time his assurance took on a touch of defiance. The first startling sign of this gradual change was the publication in *Lippincott's Magazine* of "The Picture of Dorian Gray." It was attacked immediately in *The Daily Chronicle*, a liberal paper usually distinguished for a certain leaning in favour of artists and men of letters, as a "tale spawned from the leprous literature of the French *decadents*—a poisonous book, the atmosphere of which is heavy with the mephitic odours of moral and spiritual putrefaction."

Oscar as a matter of course replied and the tone of his reply is characteristic of his growth in self-assurance. He no longer dreads the imputation of viciousness; he challenges it: "It is poisonous, if you like; but you cannot deny that it is also perfect, and perfection is what we artists aim at."

When Oscar republished "The Picture of Dorian Gray" in book form in April, 1891, he sent me a large paper copy and with the copy he wrote a little note, asking me to tell him what I thought of the book. I got the volume and note early one morning and read the book until noon. I then sent him a note by hand: "Other men," I wrote, "have given us wine; some claret, some burgundy, some Moselle; you are the first to give us pure champagne. Much of this book is wittier even than Congreve and on an equal intellectual level: at length, it seems to me, you have justified yourself."

Half an hour later I was told that Oscar Wilde had called. I went down immediately to see him. He was bubbling over with content.

"How charming of you, Frank," he cried, "to have written me such a divine letter."

"I have only read a hundred pages of the book," I said; "but they are delightful. No one now can deny you a place among the wittiest and most humorous writers in English."

"How wonderful of you, Frank; what do you like so much?"

Like all artists, he loved praise and I was enthusiastic, happy to have the opportunity of making up for some earlier doubting that now seemed unworthy:

"Whatever the envious may say, you're with Burke and Sheridan, among the very able Irishmen. . . .

"Of course I have heard most of the epigrams from you before, but you have put them even better in this book."

"Do you think so, really?" he asked, smiling with pleasure.

It is worth notice that some of the epigrams in "Dorian Gray" were bettered again before they appeared in his first play. For example, in "Dorian Gray" Lord Henry Wotton, who is peculiarly Oscar's mouthpiece, while telling how he had to bargain for a piece of old brocade in Wardour Street, adds, "nowadays people know the price of everything and the value of nothing." In "Lady Windermere's Fan" the same epigram is perfected. "The cynic is one who knows the price of everything and the value of nothing."

Nearly all the literary productions of our time suffer from haste; one must produce a good deal, especially while one's reputation is in the making, in order to live by one's pen. Yet great works take time to form, and fine creations are often disfigured by the stains of hurried parturition. Oscar Wilde contrived to minimize this disability by talking his works before writing them.

The conversation of Lord Henry Wotton with his uncle, and again at lunch when he wishes to fascinate Dorian Gray, is an excellent reproduction of Oscar's ordinary talk. The uncle wonders why Lord Dartmoor wants to marry an American and grumbles about her people; "Has she got any?"

Lord Henry shook his head. "American girls are as clever at concealing their parents as English women are at concealing their past," he said, rising to go.

"They are pork-packers, I suppose?"

"I hope so, Uncle George, for Dartmoor's sake. I am told that pork-packing is the most lucrative profession in America, after politics."

All this seems to me delightful humour.

The latter part of the book, however, tails off into insignificance. The first hundred pages held the result of months and months of Oscar's talk, the latter half was written off-hand to complete the story. "Dorian Gray" was the first piece of work which proved that Oscar Wilde had at length found his true vein.

A little study of it discovers both his strength and his weakness as a writer. The initial idea of the book is excellent, finer because deeper than the commonplace idea that is the foundation of Balzac's "Peau de Chagrin," though it would probably never have been written if Balzac had not written his book first; but Balzac's sincerity and earnestness grapple with the theme and wring a blessing out of it, whereas the subtler idea in Oscar's hands dwindles gradually away till one wonders if the book would not have been more effective as a short story. Oscar did not know life well enough or care enough for character to write a profound psychological study; he was at his best in a short story or play.

One day about this time Oscar first showed me the aphorisms he had written as an introduction to "Dorian Gray." Several of them I thought excellent; but I found that Oscar had often repeated himself. I cut these repetitions out and tried to show him how much better the dozen best were than eighteen of which six were inferior. I added that I should like to publish the best in "The Fortnightly." He thanked me and said it was very kind of me.

Next morning I got a letter from him telling me that he had

read over my corrections and thought that the aphorisms I had rejected were the best, but he hoped I'd publish them as he had written them.

Naturally I replied that the final judgment must rest with him and I published them at once.

The delight I felt in his undoubted genius and success was not shared by others. Friends took occasion to tell me that I should not go about with Oscar Wilde.

"Why not?" I asked.

"He has a bad name," was the reply. "Strange things are said about him. He came down from Oxford with a vile reputation. You have only got to look at the man."

"Whatever the disease may be," I replied, "It's not catching—unfortunately."

The pleasure men take in denigration of the gifted is one of the puzzles of life to those who are not envious.

Men of letters, even people who ought to have known better, were slow to admit his extraordinary talent; he had risen so quickly, had been puffed into such prominence that they felt inclined to deny him even the gifts which he undoubtedly possessed. I was surprised once to find a friend of mine taking this attitude. Francis Adams, the poet and writer, chaffed me one day about my liking for Oscar.

"What on earth can you see in him to admire?" he asked. "He is not a great writer; he is not even a good writer; his books have no genius in them; his poetry is tenth rate, and his prose is not much better. His talk even is fictitious and extravagant."

I could only laugh at him and advise him to read "The Picture of Dorian Gray."

This book, however, gave Oscar's puritanic enemies a better weapon against him than even "The Portrait of Mr. W. H." The subject, they declared, was the same as that of "Mr. W. H.," and the treatment was simply loathsome. More than one middle-class paper, such as *To-day* in the hands of Mr. Jerome K. Jerome, condemned the book as "corrupt", and advised its suppression. Freedom of speech in England is more feared than license of action. A speck on the outside of the platter disgusts your puritan, and the inside is never peeped at, much less discussed.

Walter Pater praised "Dorian Gray" in the *Bookman;* but

thereby only did himself damage without helping his friend. Oscar meanwhile went about boldly, meeting criticism now with smiling contempt.

One incident from this time will show how unfairly he was being judged and how imprudent he was to front defamation with defiance.

One day I met a handsome youth in his company named John Gray, and I could not wonder that Oscar found him interesting, for Gray had not only great personal distinction, but charming manners and a marked poetic gift, a much greater gift than Oscar possessed. He had besides an eager, curious mind, and of course found extraordinary stimulus in Oscar's talk. It seemed to me that intellectual sympathy and the natural admiration which a younger man feels for a brilliant senior formed the obvious bond between them. But no sooner did Oscar republish "Dorian Gray" than ill-informed and worse-minded persons went about saying that the eponymous hero of the book was John Gray, though "Dorian Gray" was written before Oscar had met or heard of John Gray. One cannot help admitting that this was partly Oscar's own fault. In talk he often alluded laughingly to John Gray as his hero, "Dorian". It is just an instance of the challenging contempt which he began to use about this time in answer to the inventions of hatred.

Late in this year, 1891, he published four stories completely void of offence, calling the collection "A House of Pomegranates". He dedicated each of the tales to a lady of distinction and the book made many friends; but it was handled contemptuously in the press and had no sale.

By this time people expected a certain sort of book from Oscar Wilde and wanted nothing else. They hadn't to wait long. Early in 1892 we heard that Oscar had written a drama in French called *Salomé*, and at once it was put about that Sarah Bernhardt was going to produce it in London. Then came dramatic surprise on surprise. While it was being rehearsed, the Lord Chamberlain refused to license it on the ground that it introduced Biblical characters. Oscar protested in a brilliant interview against the action of the Censor as "odious and ridiculous". He pointed out that all the greatest artists—painters and sculptors, musicians and writers—had taken many of their best subjects from the Bible, and wanted to know why the dramatist should be prevented from treating the great soul-tragedies most proper to his art. When informed that the interdict was to stand, he declared in a pet that he would settle in France and take out letters of naturalisation.

"I am not English. I am Irish—which is quite another thing." Of course the press made all the fun it could of his show of temper.

Mr. Robert Ross considers *Salomé* "the most powerful and perfect of all Oscar's dramas". I find it almost impossible to explain, much less justify, its astonishing popularity. When it appeared, the press, both in France and in England, was critical and contemptuous; but by this time Oscar had so captured the public that he could afford to disdain critics and calumny. The play was praised by his admirers as if it had been a masterpiece, and London discussed it the more because it was in French and not clapper-clawed by the vulgar.

The indescribable cold lewdness and cruelty of *Salomé* quickened the prejudice and strengthened the dislike of the ordinary English reader for its author. And when the drama was translated into English and published with the drawings of Aubrey Beardsley, it was disparaged and condemned by all the leaders of literary opinion. The colossal popularity of the play, which Mr. Robert Ross proves so triumphantly, came from Germany and Russia and is to be attributed in part to the contempt educated Germans and Russians feel for the hypocritical vagaries of English prudery. The illustrations of Aubrey Beardsley, too, it must be admitted, were an additional offence to the ordinary English reader, for they intensified the peculiar atmosphere of the drama.

Oscar used to say that he invented Aubrey Beardsley; but the truth is, it was Mr. Robert Ross who first introduced Aubrey to Oscar and persuaded him to commission the *Salomé* drawings which gave the English edition its singular value. Strange to say, Oscar always hated the illustrations and would not have the book in his house. His dislike even extended to the artist, and as Aubrey Beardsley was of easy and agreeable intercourse, the mutual repulsion deserves a word of explanation.

Aubrey Beardsley's genius had taken London by storm. At seventeen or eighteen this auburn-haired, blue-eyed, fragile looking youth had reached maturity with his astounding talent, a talent which would have given him position and wealth in any other

country. In perfection of line his drawings were superior to anything we possess. But the curious thing about the boy was that he
expressed the passions of pride and lust and cruelty more intensely
even than Rops, more spontaneously than anyone who ever held
pencil. Beardsley's precocity was simply marvellous. He seemed
to have an intuitive understanding not only of his own art but of
every art and craft, and it was some time before one realised that
he attained this miraculous virtuosity by an absolute disdain for
every other form of human endeavour. He knew nothing of the
great general or millionaire or man of science, and he cared as
little for them as for fishermen or 'bus-drivers. The current of his
talent ran narrow between stone banks, so to speak; it was the bold
assertion of it that interested Oscar.

One phase of Beardsley's extraordinary development may be
recorded here. When I first met him his letters, and even his talk
sometimes, were curiously youthful and immature, lacking altogether the personal note of his drawings. As soon as this was
noticed he took the bull by the horns and pretended that his style
in writing was out of date; he wished us to believe that he hesitated
to shock us with his "archaic sympathies". Of course we laughed
and challenged him to reveal himself. Shortly afterwards I got an
article from him written with curious felicity of phrase, in modish
polite eighteenth-century English. He had reached personal expression in a new medium in a month or so, and apparently without effort. It was Beardsley's writing that first won Oscar to
recognition of his talent, and for a while he seemed vaguely interested in what he called his "orchid-like personality".

They were both at lunch one day when Oscar declared that
he could drink nothing but absinthe when Beardsley was present.

"Absinthe," he said, "is to all other drinks what Aubrey's drawings are to other pictures; it stands alone; it is like nothing else;
it shimmers like southern twilight in opalescent colouring; it has
about it the seduction of strange sins. It is stronger than any other
spirit and brings out the subconscious self in man. It is just like
your drawings, Aubrey; it gets on one's nerves and is cruel.

"Baudelaire called his poems *Fleurs du Mal*, I shall call your
drawings *Fleurs du Péché*—flowers of sin.

"When I have before me one of your drawings I want to drink
absinthe, which changes colour like jade in sunlight and makes the

senses thrall, and then I can live myself back in imperial Rome, in the Rome of the later Cæsars."

"Don't forget the simple pleasures of that life, Oscar," said Aubrey. "Nero set Christians on fire, like large tallow candles; the only light Christians have ever been known to give," he added in a languid, gentle voice.

This talk gave me the key. In personal intercourse Oscar Wilde was more English than the English. He seldom expressed his opinion of person or prejudice boldly; he preferred to hint dislike and disapproval. His insistence on the naked expression of lust and cruelty in Beardsley's drawings showed me that direct frankness displeased him, for he could hardly object to the qualities which were making his own *Salomé* world-famous.

The complete history of the relations between Oscar Wilde and Beardsley, and their mutual dislike, merely proves how difficult it is for original artists to appreciate one another; like mountain peaks they stand alone. Oscar showed a touch of patronage, the superiority of the senior, in his intercourse with Beardsley, and often praised him ineptly, whereas Beardsley to the last spoke of Oscar as a showman, and hoped drily that he knew more about literature than he did about art. For a moment, they worked in concert, and it is important to remember that it was Beardsley who influenced Oscar, and not Oscar who influenced Beardsley. Beardsley's contempt of critics and the public, his artistic boldness and self-assertion, had a certain hardening influence on Oscar; as things turned out a most unfortunate influence.

In spite of Mr. Robert Ross's opinion I regard *Salomé*, as a student work, an outcome of Oscar's admiration for Flaubert and his "Herodias", on the one hand, and "Les Sept Princesses", of Maeterlinck on the other. He has borrowed the colour and Oriental cruelty with the banquet scene from the Frenchman, and from the Fleming the simplicity of language and the haunting effect produced by the repetition of significant phrases. Yet *Salomé* is original through the mingling of lust and hatred in the heroine and, by making this extraordinary virgin the chief and centre of the drama, Oscar has heightened the interest of the story and bettered Flaubert's design. I feel sure he copied Maeterlinck's simplicity of style because it served to disguise his imperfect knowledge of French and yet this very artlessness adds to the weird effect of the drama.

The lust that inspires the tragedy was characteristic, but the cruelty was foreign to Oscar; both qualities would have injured him in England, had it not been for two things. First of all, only a few of the best class of English people know French at all well, and for the most part they disdain the sex-morality of their race; while the vast mass of the English public regard French as in itself an immoral medium and is inclined to treat anything in that tongue with contemptuous indifference. One can only say that *Salomé* confirmed Oscar's growing reputation for abnormal viciousness.

It was in 1892 that some of Oscar's friends struck me for the first time as questionable, to say the best of them. I remember giving a little dinner to some men in rooms I had in Jermyn Street. I invited Oscar, and he brought a young friend with him. After dinner I noticed that the youth was angry with Oscar and would scarcely speak to him, and that Oscar was making up to him. I heard snatches of pleading from Oscar—"I beg of you . . . It is not true . . . You have no cause" . . . All the while Oscar was standing apart from the rest of us with an arm on the young man's shoulder; but his coaxing was in vain, the youth turned away with petulant, sullen ill-temper. This is a mere snap-shot which remained in my memory, and made me ask myself afterwards how I could have been so slow of understanding.

Looking back and taking everything into consideration—his social success, the glare of publicity in which he lived, the buzz of talk and discussion that arose about everything he did and said, the increasing interest and value of his work and, above all, the ever-growing boldness of his writing and the challenge of his conduct—it is not surprising that the black cloud of hate and slander which attended him persistently became more and more threatening .

9

The Summer of Success: Oscar's First Play

No SEASON, it is said, is so beautiful as the brief northern summer. Three-fourths of the year is cold and dark, and the ice-bound landscape is swept by snowstorm and blizzard. Summer comes like a goddess; in a twinkling the snow vanishes and Nature puts on her robes of tenderest green; the birds arrive in flocks; flowers spring to life on all sides, and the sun shines by night as by day. Such a summertide, so beautiful and so brief, was accorded to Oscar Wilde before the final desolation.

I want to give a picture of him at the topmost height of happy hours, which will afford some proof of his magical talent of speech besides my own appreciation of it, and, fortunately, the incident has been given to me. Mr. Ernest Beckett, now Lord Grimthorpe, a lover of all superiorities, who has known the ablest men of the time, takes pleasure in telling a story which shows Oscar Wilde's influence over men who were anything but literary in their tastes. Mr. Beckett had a party of Yorkshire squires, chiefly fox-hunters and lovers of an outdoor life, at Kirkstall Grange when he heard that Oscar Wilde was in the neighbouring town of Leeds. Immediately he asked him to lunch at the Grange, chuckling to himself beforehand at the sensational novelty of the experiment. Next day "Mr. Oscar Wilde" was announced and as he came into the room the sportsmen forthwith began hiding themselves behind newspapers or moving together in groups in order to avoid seeing or being introduced to the notorious writer. Oscar shook hands with his host as if he had noticed nothing, and began to talk.

"In five minutes," Grimthorpe declares, "all the papers were put down and everyone had gathered round him to listen and laugh."

At the end of the meal one Yorkshireman after the other begged the host to follow the lunch with a dinner and invite them to meet the wonder again. When the party broke up in the small hours they all went away delighted with Oscar, vowing that no man ever talked more brilliantly. Grimthorpe cannot remember a single word Oscar said: "It was all delightful," he declares, "a play of genial humour over every topic that came up, like sunshine dancing on waves."

The extraordinary thing about Oscar's talent was that he did not monopolise the conversation. He took the ball of talk wherever it happened to be at the moment and played with it so humorously that everyone was soon smiling delightedly. The famous talkers of the past, Coleridge, Macaulay, Carlyle and the others, were all lecturers; talk to them was a discourse on a favourite theme, and in ordinary life they were generally regarded as bores. But at his best Oscar Wilde never dropped the tone of good society. He could afford to give place to others; he was equipped at all points. No subject came amiss to him; he saw everything from a humorous angle and dazzled one now with word-wit, now with the very stuff of merriment.

Though he was the life and soul of every social gathering, and in constant demand, he still read omnivorously, and his mind naturally occupied itself with high themes.

For some years, the story of Jesus fascinated him and tinged all his thought. We were talking about Renan's "Life" one day. A wonderful book he called it, one of the three great biographies of the world, Plato's dialogues with Socrates as hero and Boswell's "Life of Johnson" being the other two. It was strange, he thought, that the greatest man had written the worst biography; Plato made of Socrates a mere phonograph, into which he talked his own theories. Renan did better work, and Boswell, the humble loving friend, the least talented of the three, did better still, though being English, he had to keep to the surface of things and leave the depths to be devined. Oscar evidently expected Plato and Renan to have surpassed comparison.

It seemed to me, however, that the illiterate Galilean fishermen had proved themselves still more consummate painters than Boswell, though they, too, left a great deal too much to the imagination. Love is the best of artists; the puddle of rain in the road can reflect a piece of sky marvellously.

The Gospel story had a personal interest for Oscar; he was always weaving little fables about himself as the Master.

In spite of my ignorance of Hebrew the story of Jesus had always had the strongest attraction for me, and so we often talked about Him, though from opposite poles.

Renan, I felt, had missed Jesus at his highest. He was far below the sincerity, the tenderness and sweet-thoughted wisdom of that divine spirit. Frenchman-like, he stumbled over the miracles and came to grief. Claus Sluter's head of Jesus in the museum of Dijon is a finer portrait, and so is the imaginative picture of Fra Angelico. It seemed to me possible to do a sketch from the Gospels themselves which should show the growth of the soul of Jesus and so impose itself as a true portrait.

Oscar's interest in the theme was different; he put himself frankly in the place of his model and appeared to enjoy the jarring antinomy which resulted. One or two of his stories were surprising in ironical suggestion; surprising too because they showed his convinced paganism. Here is one which reveals his exact position:

"When Joseph of Arimathea came down in the evening from Mount Calvary where Jesus had died he saw on a white stone a young man seated weeping. And Joseph went near him and said, 'I understand how great thy grief must be, for certainly that Man was a just Man.' But the young man made answer, 'Oh, it is not for that I am weeping. I am weeping because I too have wrought miracles. I also have given sight to the blind; I have healed the palsied and I have raised the dead; I too have caused the barren fig tree to wither away and I have turned water into wine . . . and yet they have not crucified me.' "

At the time this apologue amused me; in the light of later events it assumed a tragic significance. Oscar Wilde ought to have known that in this world every real superiority is pursued with hatred, and every worker of miracles is sure to be persecuted. But he had no inkling that the Gospel story is symbolic—the life-story of genius for all time, eternally true. He never looked outside himself, and as the fruits of success were now sweet in his mouth, a pursuing Fate seemed to him the most mythical of myths. His child-like self-confidence was pathetic. The laws that govern human affairs had little interest for the man who was always a law unto himself. Yet by some extraordinary prescience, some inexplicable presentiment, the approaching catastrophe cast its shadow over his mind and he felt vaguely that the life-journey of genius would be incomplete and farcical without the final tragedy; whoever lives for the highest must be crucified.

It seems memorable to me that in this brief summer of his life, Oscar Wilde should have concerned himself especially with the life-story of the Man of Sorrows who had sounded all the depths of suffering. Just when he himself was about to enter the Dark Valley, Jesus was often in his thoughts and he always spoke of Him with admiration. But after all how could he help it? Even Dekker saw as far as that:

> "The best of men
> That e'er wore earth about Him."

This was the deeper strain in Oscar Wilde's nature though he was always disinclined to show it. Habitually he lived in humorous talk, in the epithets and epigrams he struck out in the desire to please and astonish his hearers.

One evening I learned almost by chance that he was about to try a new experiment and break into a new field.

He took up the word "lose" at the table, I remember.

"We lose our chances," he said, laughing, "we lose our figures, we even lose our characters; but we must never lose our tempers. That is our duty to our neighbour, Frank; but sometimes we mislay it, don't we?"

"Is that going in a book, Oscar?" I asked, smiling, "Or in an article? You have written nothing lately."

"I have a play in my mind," he replied gravely. "Tomorrow I am going to shut myself up in my room, and stay there until it is written. George Alexander has been bothering me to write a play for some time and I've got an idea I rather like. I wonder can I do it in a week, or will it take three? It ought not to take long to beat the Pineros and the Joneses." It always annoyed Oscar when any other name but his came into men's mouths. His vanity was extraordinarily alert.

Naturally enough he minimised Mr. Alexander's initiative. The well-known actor had "bothered" Oscar by advancing him £100 before the scenario was even outlined. A couple of months later he told me that Alexander had accepted his comedy, and was going to produce "Lady Windermere's Fan." I thought the title excellent.

"Territorial names," Oscar explained, gravely, "have always a *cachet* of distinction; they fall on the ear full toned with secular dignity. That's how I get all the names of my personages, Frank. I take up a map of the English counties, and there they are. Our English villages have often exquisitely beautiful names. Windermere, for instance, or Hunstanton," and he rolled the syllables over his tongue with a soft sensual pleasure.

I had a box the first night and, thinking it might do Oscar some good, I took with me Arthur Walter of *The Times*. The first scene of the first act was as old as the hills, but the treatment gave charm to it if not freshness. The delightful, unexpected humour set off the commonplace incident; but it was only the convention that Arthur Walter would see. The play was poor, he thought, which brought me to wonder.

After the first act I went downstairs to the *foyer* and found the critics in much the same mind. There was an enormous gentleman called Joseph Knight, who cried out:

"The humour is mechanical, unreal." Seeing that I did not respond he challenged me:

"What do you think of it?"

"That is for you critics to answer," I replied.

"I might say," he laughed, "in Oscar's own peculiar way, 'Little promise and less performance.' Ha! ha! ha!"

"That's the exact opposite to Oscar's way," I retorted. "It is the listeners who laugh at his humour."

"Come now, really," cried Knight, "you cannot think much of the play?"

For the first time in my life I began to realise that nine critics out of ten are incapable of judging original work. They seem to live in a sort of fog, waiting for someone to give them the lead, and accordingly they love to discuss every new play right and left.

"I have not seen the whole play," I answered. "I was not at any of the rehearsals; but so far it is surely the best comedy in English, the most brilliant, isn't it?"

The big man started back and stared at me; then burst out laughing.

"That's good," he cried with a loud unmirthful guffaw. " 'Lady Windermere's Fan' better than any comedy of Shakespeare! Ha! ha! ha! 'more brilliant!' ho! ho!"

"Yes," I persisted, angered by his disdain, "wittier, and more humorous than 'As You Like It,' or 'Much Ado.' Strange to say, too, it is on a higher intellectual level. I can only compare it to the best of Congreve, and I think it's better." With a grunt of disapproval or rage the great man of the daily press turned away to exchange bleatings with one of his *confrères*.

The audience was a picked audience of the best heads in London, far superior in brains therefore to the average journalist, and their judgment was that it was a most brilliant and interesting play. Though the humour was often prepared, the construction showed a rare mastery of stage-effect. Oscar Wilde had at length come into his kingdom.

At the end the author was called for, and Oscar appeared before the curtain. The house rose at him and cheered and cheered again. He was smiling, with a cigarette between his fingers, wholly master of himself and his audience.

"I am so glad, ladies and gentlemen, that you like my play. I feel sure you estimate the merits of it almost as highly as I do myself."

The house rocked with laughter. The play and its humour were a seven days' wonder in London. People talked of nothing but "Lady Windermere's Fan." The witty words in it ran from lip to lip like a tidbit of scandal. Some clever Jewesses and, strange to say, one Scotchman were the loudest in applause. Mr. Archer, the well-known critic of *The World*, was the first and only journalist to perceive that the play was a classic by virtue of "genuine dramatic qualities". Mrs. Leverson turned the humorous sayings into current social coin in *Punch*, of all places in the world, and from a favourite, Oscar Wilde rapidly became the idol of smart London.

The play was an intellectual triumph. This time Oscar had not only won success but had won also the suffrages of the best. Nearly all the journalist-critics were against him and made themselves ridiculous by their brainless strictures; *Truth* and *The Times*, for example, were poisonously puritanic, but thinking people came over to his side in a body. The halo of fame was about him, and the incense of it in his nostrils made him more charming, more irresponsibly gay, more genial-witty than ever. He was as one set upon a pinnacle with the sunshine playing about him, lighting up his radiant eyes. All the while, however, the foul mists from the underworld were wreathing about him, climbing higher and higher.

IO

The First Meeting with Lord Alfred Douglas

Thou hast led me like an heathen sacrifice,
With music and with fatal pomp of flowers,
To my eternal ruin.—Webster's *The White Devil.*

"LADY WINDERMERE'S FAN" was a success in every sense of the word, and during its run London was at Oscar's feet. There were always a few doors closed to him; but he could afford now to treat his critics with laughter, call them fogies and old-fashioned and explain that they had not a decalogue but a millelogue of sins forbidden and persons tabooed because it was easier to condemn than to understand.

I remember a lunch once when he talked most brilliantly and finished up by telling the story now published in his works as "A Florentine Tragedy". He told it superbly, making it appear far more effective than in its written form. A well-known actor, piqued at being compelled to play listener, made himself ridiculous by half turning his back on the narrator. But after lunch Willie Grenfell (now Lord Desborough) a model English athlete gifted with peculiar intellectual fairness, came round to me:

"Oscar Wilde is most surprising, most charming, a wonderful talker."

At the same moment Mr. K. H——— came over to us. He was a man who went everywhere and knew everyone. He had quiet,

85

ingratiating manners, always spoke in a gentle smiling way and had a good word to say for everyone, especially for women; he was a bachelor, too, and wholly unattached. He surprised me by taking up Grenfell's praise and breaking into a lyric:

"The best talker who ever lived," he said; "most extraordinary. I am so infinitely obliged to you for asking me to meet him—a new delight. He brings a supernal air into life. I am in truth indebted to you"—all this in an affected purring tone. I noticed for the first time that there was a touch of rouge on his face; Grenfell turned away from us rather abruptly I thought.

At this first roseate dawn of complete success and universal applause, new qualities came to view in Oscar. Praise gave him the fillip needed in order to make him surpass himself. His talk took on a sort of autumnal richness of colour, and assumed a new width or range; he now used pathos as well as humour and generally brought in a story or apologue to lend variety to the entertainment. His little weaknesses, too, began to show themselves and they grew rankly in the sunshine. He always wanted to do himself well, as the phrase goes, but now he began to eat and drink more freely than before. His vanity became defiant. I noticed one day that he had signed himself, Oscar O'Flahertie Wilde, I think under some verses which he had contributed years before to his College magazine. I asked him jokingly what the O'Flahertie stood for. To my astonishment he answered me gravely:

"The O'Flaherties were kings in Ireland, and I have a right to the name; I am descended from them."

I could not help it; I burst out laughing.

"What are you laughing at, Frank?" he asked with a touch of annoyance.

"It seems humorous to me," I explained, "that Oscar Wilde should want to be an O'Flahertie," and as I spoke a picture of the greatest of the O'Flaherties, with bushy head and dirty rags, warming enormous hairy legs before a smoking peat-fire, flashed before me. I think something of the sort must have occurred to Oscar, too, for, in spite of his attempt to be grave, he could not help laughing.

"It's unkind of you, Frank," he said. "The Irish were civilised and Christians when the English kept themselves warm with tattooings."

He could not help telling one in familiar talk of Clumber or some other great house where he had been visiting; he was intoxicated with his own popularity, a little surprised, perhaps, to find that he had won fame so easily and on the primrose path, but one could forgive him everything, for he talked more delightfully than ever.

It is almost inexplicable, but nevertheless true that life tries all of us, tests every weak point to breaking, and sets off and exaggerates our powers. Burns saw this when he wrote:

> "Wha does the utmost that he can
> Will whyles do mair."

And the obverse is true: whoever yields to a weakness habitually, some day goes further than he ever intended, and comes to worse grief than he deserved. The old prayer: *Lead us not into temptation*, is perhaps a half-conscious recognition of this fact. But we moderns are inclined to walk heedlessly, no longer believing in pitfalls or in the danger of gratified desires. And Oscar Wilde was not only an unbeliever; but he had all the heedless confidence of the artist who has won world-wide popularity and has the halo of fame on his brow. With high heart and smiling eyes he went to his fate unsuspecting.

It was in the autumn of 1891 that he first met Lord Alfred Douglas. He was thirty-six and Lord Alfred Douglas a handsome, slim youth of twenty-one, with large blue eyes and golden-fair hair. His mother, the Dowager Lady Queensberry, preserves a photograph of him taken a few years before, when he was still at Winchester, a boy of sixteen with an expression which might well be called angelic.

When I met him, he was still girlishly pretty, with the beauty of youth, colouring and fair skin; though his features were merely ordinary. It was Lionel Johnson, the writer, a friend and intimate of Douglas at Winchester, who brought him to tea at Oscar's house in Tite Street. Their mutual attraction had countless hooks. Oscar was drawn by the lad's personal beauty, and enormously affected besides by Lord Alfred Douglas' name and position. He was a snob as only an English artist can be a snob; he loved titular distinctions, and Douglas is one of the few great names in

British history with the gilding of romance about it. No doubt
Oscar talked better than his best because he was talking to Lord
Alfred Douglas. To the last the mere name rolled on his tongue
gave him extraordinary pleasure. Besides, the boy admired him,
hung upon his lips with his soul in his eyes; showed, too, rare
intelligence in his appreciation, confessed that he himself wrote
verses and loved letters passionately. Could more be desired than
perfection perfected?

And Alfred Douglas on his side was almost as powerfully attracted; he had inherited from his mother all her literary tastes—
and more; he was already a master-poet with a singing faculty
worthy to be compared with the greatest. What wonder if he
took this magical talker, with the luminous eyes and charming
voice, and a range and play of thought beyond his imagining, for
a world's miracle, one of the Immortals. Before he had listened
long, I have been told, the youth declared his admiration passionately. They were an extraordinary pair and were complementary
in a hundred ways, not only in mind, but in character. Oscar had
reached originality of thought and possessed the culture of scholarship, while Alfred Douglas had youth and rank and beauty, besides being as articulate as a woman with an unsurpassable gift of
expression. Curiously enough, Oscar was as yielding and amiable
in character as the boy was self-willed, reckless, obstinate and
imperious.

Years later Oscar told me that from the first he dreaded Alfred
Douglas' aristocratic, insolent boldness:

"He frightened me, Frank, as much as he attracted me, and I
held away from him. But he wouldn't have it; he sought me out
again and again and I couldn't resist him. That is my only fault.
That's what ruined me. He increased my expenses so that I could
not meet them; over and over again I tried to free myself from
him; but he came back and I yielded—alas!"

Though this is Oscar's later gloss on what actually happened,
it is fairly accurate. He was never able to realise how his meeting
with Lord Alfred Douglas had changed the world to him and him
to the world. The effect on the harder fibre of the boy was chiefly
mental. To Alfred Douglas, Oscar was merely a quickening, inspiring, intellectual influence; but the boy's effect on Oscar was
of character and induced imitation. Lord Alfred Douglas' bold-

ness gave Oscar *outrecuidance*, an insolent arrogance; artist-like he tried to outdo his model in aristocratic disdain. Without knowing the cause, the change in Oscar astonished me again and again, and in the course of this narrative I shall have to notice many instances of it.

One other effect the friendship had of far-reaching influence. Oscar always enjoyed good living; but for years he had had to earn his bread. He knew the value of money; he didn't like to throw it away; he was accustomed to lunch or dine at a cheap Italian restaurant for a few shillings. But to Lord Alfred Douglas money was only a counter and the most luxurious living a necessity. As soon as Oscar Wilde began to entertain him, he was led to the dearest hotels and restaurants; his expenses became formidable and soon outran his large earnings. For the first time since I had known him he borrowed heedlessly right and left, and had, therefore, to bring forth play after play with scant time for thought.

Lord Alfred Douglas has declared recently:

"I spent much more in entertaining Oscar Wilde than he did in entertaining me"; but this is preposterous self-deception. An earlier confession of his was much nearer the truth: "It was a sweet humiliation to me to let Oscar Wilde pay for everything and to ask him for money."

There can be no doubt that Lord Alfred Douglas' habitual extravagance kept Oscar Wilde hard up and drove him to write without intermission.

There were other and worse results of the intimacy which need not be exposed here in so many words, though they must be indicated; for they derived of necessity from that increased self-assurance which has already been recorded. As Oscar devoted himself to Lord Alfred Douglas and went about with him continually, he came to know his friends and familiars, and went less into society so-called. Again and again Lord Alfred Douglas flaunted acquaintance with youths of the lowest class; but no one knew him or paid much attention to him; Oscar Wilde, on the other hand, was already a famous personage whose every movement provoked comment. From this time on the rumours about Oscar took definite form and shaped themselves in specific accusations; his enemies began triumphantly to predict his ruin and disgrace.

Everything is known in London society; like water on sand the truth spreads wider and wider as it gradually filters lower. The "smart set" in London has almost as keen a love of scandal as a cathedral town. About this time one heard of a dinner which Oscar Wilde had given at a restaurant in Soho, which was said to have degenerated into a sort of Roman orgy. I was told of a man who tried to get money by blackmailing him in his own house. I shrugged my shoulders at all these scandals and asked the talebearers what had been said about Shakespeare to make him rave as he raved again and again against "back-wounding calumny"; and when they persisted in their malicious stories I could do nothing but show disbelief. Though I saw but little of Oscar during the first year or so of his intimacy with Lord Alfred Douglas, one scene from this time filled me with suspicion and an undefined dread.

I was in a corner of the Café Royal one night downstairs, playing chess, and, while waiting for my opponent to move, I went out just to stretch my legs. When I returned I found Oscar throned in the very corner, between two youths. Even to my short-sighted eyes they appeared quite common. In fact they looked like grooms. In spite of their vulgar appearance, however, one was nice looking in a fresh boyish way; the other seemed merely depraved. Oscar greeted me as usual, though he seemed slightly embarrassed. I resumed my seat, which was almost opposite him, and pretended to be absorbed in the game. To my astonishment he was talking as well as if he had had a picked audience; talking, if you please, about the Olympic games, telling how the youths wrestled and were scraped with strigulæ and threw the discus and ran races and won the myrtle-wreath. His impassioned eloquence brought the sun-bathed palæstra before one with a magic of representment. Suddenly the younger of the boys asked:

"Did you sy they was niked?"

"Of course," Oscar replied, "nude, clothed only in sunshine and beauty."

"Oh, my," giggled the lad in his unspeakable Cockney way. I could not stand it.

"I am in an impossible position," I said to my opponent, who was the amateur chess player, Montagu Gattie. "Come along and let us have some dinner." With a nod to Oscar I left the place. On the way out Gattie said to me:

"So that's the famous Oscar Wilde."

"Yes," I replied, "that's Oscar, but I never saw him in such company before."

"Didn't you?" remarked Gattie quietly; "he was well known at Oxford. I was at the 'Varsity with him. His reputation was always rather—'*high*,' shall we call it?"

I wanted to forget the scene and blot it out of my memory, and remember my friend as I knew him at his best. But that Cockney boy would not be banned; he leered there with rosy cheeks, hair plastered down in a love-lock on his forehead, and low cunning eyes. I felt uncomfortable. I would not think of it. I recalled the fact that in all our talks I had never heard Oscar use a gross word. His mind, I said to myself, is like Spenser's, vowed away from coarseness and vulgarity; he's the most perfect intellectual companion in the world. He may have wanted to talk to the boys just to see what effect his talk would have on them. His vanity is greedy enough to desire even such applause as theirs. . . . Of course, that was the explanation—vanity. My affection for him, tormented by doubt, had found at length a satisfactory solution. It was the artist in him, I said to myself, that wanted a model.

But why not boys of his own class? The answer suggested itself; boys of his own class could teach him nothing; his own boyhood would supply him with all the necessary information about well-bred youth. But if he wanted a guttersnipe in one of his plays, he would have to find a gutter-lad and paint him from life. That was probably the truth, I concluded. So satisfied was I with my discovery that I developed it to Gattie; but he would not hear of it.

"Gattie has nothing of the artist in him," I decided, "and therefore cannot understand." And I went on arguing, if Gattie were right, why *two* boys? It seemed evident to me that my reading of the riddle was the only plausible one. Besides it left my affection unaffected and free. Still, the giggle, the plastered oily hair and the venal leering eyes came back to me again and again in spite of myself.

II

The Threatening Cloud Draws Nearer

THERE IS A SECRET apprehension in man counselling sobriety and moderation, a fear born of expediency distinct from conscience, which is ethical; though it seems to be closely connected with conscience acting, as it does, by warnings and prohibitions. The story of Polycrates and his ring is a symbol of the instinctive feeling that extraordinary good fortune is perilous and can not endure.

A year or so after the first meeting between Oscar Wilde and Lord Alfred Douglas I heard that they were being pestered on account of some amorous letters which had been stolen from them. There was talk of blackmail and hints of an interesting exposure.

Towards the end of the year it was announced that Lord Alfred Douglas had gone to Egypt; but this "flight into Egypt," as it was wittily called, was gilded by the fact that a little later he was appointed an honorary attaché to Lord Cromer. I regarded his absence as a piece of good fortune, for when he was in London, Oscar had no time to himself, and was seen in public with associates he would have done better to avoid. Time and again he had praised Lord Alfred Douglas to me as a charming person, a poet, and had grown lyrical about his violet eyes and honey-coloured hair. I knew nothing of Lord Alfred Douglas, and had no inkling of his poetic talent. I did not like several of Oscar's particular friends, and I had a special dislike for the father of Lord Alfred Douglas. I knew Queensberry rather well. I was a member of the old Pelican Club, and I used to go there frequently for a talk with Tom, Dick, or Harry, about athletics, or for a game of chess with George Edwards. Queensberry was there almost every night, and someone introduced me to him. I was eager to know him because he had surprised me. At some play,[1] I think it was "The Promise of May," by Tennyson, produced at the Globe, in which atheists were condemned, he had got up in his box and denounced the play, proclaiming himself an atheist. I wanted to know the Englishman who could be so contemptuous of convention. Had he acted out of aristocratic insolence, or was he by any possibility high-minded? To one who knew the man the mere question must seem ridiculous.

Queensberry was perhaps five feet nine or ten in height, with a plain, heavy, rather sullen face and quick, hot eyes. He was a mass of self-conceit, all bristling with suspicion, and in regard to money, prudent to meanness. He cared nothing for books, but liked outdoor sports and under a rather abrupt, but not discourteous, manner hid an irritable, violent temper. He was combative and courageous as very nervous people sometimes are, when they happen to be strong-willed—the sort of man who, just because he was afraid of a bull and had pictured the dreadful wound it could give, would therefore seize it by the horns.

The insane temper of the man got him into rows at the Pelican more than once. I remember one evening he insulted a man whom I liked immensely. Haseltine was a stockbroker, I think, a big, fair, handsome fellow who took Queensberry's insults for some time with cheerful contempt. Again and again he turned Queensberry's wrath aside with a fair word, but Queensberry went on working himself into a passion, and at last made a rush at him. Haseltine watched him coming and hit out in the nick of time; he caught Queensberry full in the face and literally knocked him heels over head. Queensberry got up in a sad mess. He had a swollen nose and black eye and his shirt was all stained with blood spread about by hasty wiping. Any other man would have continued the fight or else have left the club on the spot; Queensberry took a seat at

---

[1] "The Promise of May" was produced in November, 1882.

a table, and sat there for hours silent. I could only explain it to myself by saying that his impulse to fly at once from the scene of his disgrace was very acute, and therefore he resisted it, made up his mind not to budge, and so he sat there the butt of the derisive glances and whispered talk of everyone who came into the club in the next two or three hours. He was just the sort of person a wise man would avoid and a clever one would use—a dangerous, sharp, ill-handled tool.

Disliking his father, I did not care to meet Lord Alfred Douglas, Oscar's newest friend.

I saw Oscar less frequently after the success of his first play; he no longer needed my editorial services, and was, besides, busily engaged; but I have one good trait to record of him. Some time before I had lent him £50; so long as he was hard up I said nothing about it; but after the success of his second play, I wrote to him saying that the £50 would be useful to me if he could spare it. He sent me a cheque at once with a charming letter.

He was now continually about again with Lord Alfred Douglas who, it appeared, had had a disagreement with Lord Cromer and returned to London. Almost immediately scandalous stories came into circulation concerning them: "Have you heard the latest about Lord Alfred and Oscar? I'm told they're being watched by the police," and so forth and so on interminably. One day a story came to me with such wealth of weird detail that it was manifestly at least founded on fact. Oscar was said to have written extraordinary letters to Lord Alfred Douglas. A youth called Alfred Wood had stolen the letters from Lord Alfred Douglas' rooms in Oxford and had tried to blackmail Oscar with them. The facts were so peculiar and so precise that I asked Oscar about it. He met the accusation at once and very fairly, I thought, and told me the whole story. It puts the triumphant power and address of the man in a strong light, and so I will tell it as he told it to me.

"When I was rehearsing 'A Woman of No Importance' at the Haymarket," he began, "Beerbohm Tree showed me a letter I had written a year or so before to Alfred Douglas. He seemed to think it dangerous, but I laughed at him and read the letter with him, and of course he came to understand it properly. A little later a man called Wood told me he had found some letters which I had written to Lord Alfred Douglas in a suit of clothes which Lord

Alfred had given to him. He gave me back some of the letters and I gave him a little money. But the letter, a copy of which had been sent to Beerbohm Tree, was not amongst them.

"Some time afterwards a man named Allen called upon me one night in Tite Street, and said he had got a letter of mine which I ought to have.

"The man's manner told me that he was the real enemy. 'I suppose you mean that beautiful letter of mine to Lord Alfred Douglas,' I said. 'If you had not been so foolish as to send a copy of it to Mr. Beerbohm Tree, I should have been glad to have paid you a large sum for it, as I think it is one of the best I ever wrote.' Allen looked at me with sulky, cunning eyes and said:

" 'A curious construction could be put upon that letter.'

" 'No doubt, no doubt,' I replied lightly; 'art is not intelligible to the criminal classes.' He looked me in the face defiantly and said:

" 'A man has offered me £60 for it.'

" 'You should take the offer,' I said gravely; '£60 is a great price. I myself have never received such a large sum for any prose work of that length. But I am glad to find that there is someone in England who will pay such a large sum for a letter of mine. I don't know why you come to me,' I added, rising, 'you should sell the letter at once.'

"Of course, Frank, as I spoke my body seemed empty with fear. The letter could be misunderstood, and I have so many envious enemies; but I felt that there was nothing else for it but bluff. As I went to the door Allen rose too, and said that the man who had offered him the money was out of town. I turned to him and said:

" 'He will no doubt return, and I don't care for the letter at all.'

"At this Allen changed his manner, said he was very poor, he hadn't a penny in the world, and had spent a lot trying to find me and tell me about the letter. I told him I did not mind relieving his distress, and gave him half a sovereign, assuring him at the same time that the letter would shortly be published as a sonnet in a delightful magazine. I went to the door with him, and he walked away. I closed the door; but didn't shut it at once, for suddenly I heard a policeman's step coming softly towards my house—pad, pad! A dreadful moment, then he passed by. I went into the room again all shaken, wondering whether I had done right, whether Allen would hawk the letter about—a thousand vague apprehensions.

"Suddenly a knock at the street door. My heart was in my mouth, still I went and opened it; a man named Cliburn was there.

" 'I have come to you with a letter of Allen's.'

" 'I cannot be bothered any more,' I cried, 'about that letter; I don't care twopence about it. Let him do what he likes with it.'

"To my astonishment Cliburn said:

" 'Allen has asked me to give it back to you,' and he produced it.

" 'Why does he give it back to me?' I asked carelessly.

" 'He says you were kind to him and that it is no use trying to "rent" you; you only laugh at us.'

"I looked at the letter; it was very dirty, and I said:

" 'I think it is unpardonable that better care should not have been taken of a manuscript of mine.'

"He said he was sorry; but it had been in many hands. I took the letter up casually:

" 'Well, I will accept the letter. You can thank Mr. Allen for me.'

"I gave Cliburn half a sovereign for his trouble, and said to him:

" 'I am afraid you are leading a desperately wicked life.'

" 'There's good and bad in every one of us,' he replied. I said something about his being a philosopher, and he went away. That's the whole story, Frank."

"But the letter?" I questioned.

"The letter is nothing," Oscar replied; "a prose poem. I will give you a copy of it."

Here is the letter:

"My own Boy,—Your sonnet is quite lovely, and it is a marvel that those red rose-leaf lips of yours should be made no less for the madness of music and song than for the madness of kissing. Your slim-gilt soul walks between passion and poetry. No Hyacinthus followed Love so madly as you in Greek days. Why are you alone in London, and when do you go to Salisbury? Do go there and cool your hands in the grey twilight of Gothic things. Come here whenever you like. It is a lovely place and only lacks you. Do go to Salisbury first. Always with undying love,

Yours,

Oscar."

. . . .

This letter startled me; "slim-gilt" and the "madness of kissing" were calculated to give one pause; but after all, I thought, it may be merely an artist's letter, half pose, half passionate admiration. Another thought struck me.

"But how did such a letter," I cried, "ever get into the hands of a blackmailer?"

"I don't know," he replied, shrugging his shoulders. "Lord Alfred Douglas is very careless and inconceivably bold. You should know him, Frank; he's a delightful poet."

"But how did he come to know a creature like Wood?" I persisted.

"How can I tell, Frank," he answered a little shortly; and I let the matter drop, though it left in me a certain doubt, an uncomfortable suspicion.

The scandal grew from hour to hour, and the tide of hatred rose in surges.

One day I was lunching at the Savoy, and while talking to the head waiter, Cesari, who afterwards managed the Elysée Palace Hotel in Paris, I thought I saw Oscar and Douglas go out together. Being a little short-sighted I asked:

"Isn't that Mr. Oscar Wilde?"

"Yes," said Cesari, "and Lord Alfred Douglas. We wish they would not come here; it does us a lot of harm."

"How do you mean?" I asked sharply.

"Some people don't like them," the quick Italian answered immediately.

"Oscar Wilde," I remarked casually, "is a great friend of mine," but the super-subtle Italian was already warned.

"A clever writer, I believe," he said, smiling in bland acquiescence.

This incident gave me warning, strengthened again in me the exact apprehension and suspicion which the Douglas letter had bred. Oscar I knew was too self-centred, went about too continually with admirers to have any understanding of popular feeling. He would be the last man to realise how fiercely hate, malice and envy were raging against him. I wanted to warn him; but hardly knew how to do it effectively and without offence: I made up my mind to keep my eyes open and watch an opportunity.

A little later I gave a dinner at the Savoy and asked him to come. He was delightful, his vivacious gaiety as exhilarating as wine. But he was more like a Roman Emperor than ever. He had grown fat; he ate and drank too much; not that he was intoxicated, but he became flushed, and in spite of his gay and genial talk he affected me a little unpleasantly; he was gross and puffed up. But he gave one or two splendid snapshots of actors and their egregious vanity. It seemed to him a great pity that actors should be taught to read and write; they should learn their pieces from the lips of the poet.

"Just as work is the curse of the drinking classes of this country," he said laughing, "so education is the curse of the acting classes."

Yet even when making fun of the mummers there was a new tone in him of arrogance and disdain. He used always to be genial and kindly even to those he laughed at; now he was openly contemptuous. The truth is that his extraordinarily receptive mind went with an even more abnormal receptivity of character. Unlike most men of marked ability, he took colour from his associates. In this as in love of courtesies and dislike of coarse words he was curiously feminine. Intercourse with Beardsley, for example, had backed his humorous gentleness with a sort of challenging courage; his new intimacy with Lord Alfred Douglas, coming on the top of his triumph as a playwright, was lending him aggressive self-confidence. There was in him that ὕβρις (insolent self-assurance) which the Greek feared, the pride which goeth before destruction. I regretted the change in him and was nervously apprehensive.

After dinner we all went out by the door which gives on the Embankment, for it was after 12.30. One of the party proposed that we should walk for a minute or two—at least as far as the Strand, before driving home. Oscar objected. He hated walking; it was a form of penal servitude to the animal in man, he declared; but he consented, nevertheless, under protest, laughing.

When we were going up the steps to the Strand he again objected, and quoted Dante's famous lines:

> "Tu proverai si come sa di sale
> Lo pane altrui; e com' e duro calle
> Lo scendere e 'l salir per l'altrui scale."

The impression made by Oscar that evening was not only of self-indulgence but of over-confidence. I could not imagine what had given him this insolent self-complacence. I wanted to get by myself and think. Prosperity was certainly doing him no good.

All the while the opposition to him, I felt, was growing in force. How could I verify this impression, I asked myself, so as to warn him effectually?

I decided to give a lunch to him, and on purpose I put on the invitations: "To meet Mr. Oscar Wilde and hear a new story." Out of a dozen invitations sent out to men, seven or eight were refused, three or four telling me in all kindness that they would rather not meet Oscar Wilde. This confirmed my worst fears. When Englishmen speak out in this way the dislike must be near revolt.

I gave the lunch and saw plainly enough that my forebodings were justified. Oscar was more self-confident, more contemptuous of criticism, more gross of body than ever, but his talk did not suffer; indeed, it seemed to improve. At this lunch he told the charming fable of "Narcissus," which is certainly one of his most characteristic short stories.

"When Narcissus died the Flowers of the Field were plunged in grief, and asked the River for drops of water that they might mourn for him.

" 'Oh,' replied the River, 'if only my drops of water were tears, I should not have enough to weep for Narcissus myself—I loved him.'

" 'How could you help loving Narcissus?' said the flowers, 'so beautiful was he.'

" 'Was he beautiful?' asked the River.

" 'Who should know that better than you?' said the flowers, 'for every day, lying on your bank, he would mirror his beauty in your waters.' "

Oscar paused here, and then went on:

" 'If I loved him,' replied the River, 'it is because, when he hung over me, I saw the reflection of my own loveliness in his eyes.' "

After lunch I took him aside and tried to warn him, told him that unpleasant stories were being put about against him; but he paid no heed to me.

"All envy, Frank, and malice. What do I care? I go to Clumber this summer; besides I am doing another play which I rather like. I always knew that play-writing was my province. As a youth I tried to write plays in verse; that was my mistake. Now I know better; I'm sure of myself and of success."

Somehow or other in spite of his apparent assurance I felt he was in danger and I doubted his quality as a fighter. But after all it was not my business; wilful man must have his way.

It seems to me now that my mistrust dated from the second paper war with Whistler, wherein to the astonishment of everyone Oscar did not come off victorious. As soon as he met with opposition his power of repartee seemed to desert him and Whistler, using mere rudeness and man-of-the-world sharpness, held the field. Oscar was evidently not a born fighter.

I asked him once how it was he let Whistler off so lightly. He shrugged his shoulders and showed some irritation.

"What could I say, Frank? Why should I belabour the beaten? The man is a wasp and delights in using his sting. I have done more perhaps than anyone to make him famous. I had no wish to hurt him."

Was it magnanimity or weakness or, as I think, a constitutional, a feminine shrinking from struggle and strife? Whatever the cause, it was clear that Oscar was what Shakespeare called himself, "an unhurtful opposite".

It is quite possible that if he had been attacked face to face, Oscar would have given a better account of himself. At Mrs. Grenfell's (now Lady Desborough) he crossed swords once with the Prime Minister and came off victorious. Mr. Asquith began by bantering him, in appearance lightly, in reality seriously, for putting many of his sentences in italics.

"The man who uses italics," said the politician, "is like the man who raises his voice in conversation and talks loudly in order to make himself heard."

It was the well-known objection which Emerson had taken to Carlyle's overwrought style, pointed probably by dislike of the way Oscar monopolised conversation.

Oscar met the stereotyped attack with smiling good-humour. "How delightful of you, Mr. Asquith, to have noticed that! The brilliant phrase, like good wine, needs no bush. But just as the orator marks his good things by a dramatic pause, or by raising or lowering his voice, or by gesture, so the writer marks his epigrams with italics, setting the little gem, so to speak, like a jeweller—an excusable love of one's art, not all mere vanity, I like to think"—all this with the most pleasant smile and manner.

In measure as I distrusted Oscar's fighting power and admired his sweetness of nature I took sides with him and wanted to help him. One day I heard some talk at the Pelican Club which filled me with fear for him and quickened my resolve to put him on his guard. I was going in just as Queensberry was coming out with two or three of his special cronies.

"I'll do it," I heard him cry, "I'll teach the fellow to leave my son alone. I'll not have their names coupled together."

I caught a glimpse of the thrust-out combative face and the hot grey eyes.

"What's it all about?" I asked.

"Only Queensberry," said someone, "swearing he'll stop Oscar Wilde going about with that son of his, Alfred Douglas."

Suddenly my fears took form. As in a flash I saw Oscar, heedless and smiling, walking along with his head in the air, and that violent combative insane creature pouncing on him. I sat down at once and wrote begging Oscar to lunch with me the next day alone, as I had something important to say to him. He turned up in Park Lane, manifestly anxious, a little frightened, I think.

"What is it, Frank?"

I told him very seriously what I had heard and gave besides my impression of Queensberry's character, and his insane pugnacity.

"What can I do, Frank?" said Oscar, showing distress and apprehension. "It's all Bosie."

"Who is Bosie?" I asked.

"That is Lord Alfred Douglas' pet name. It's all Bosie's fault. He has quarrelled with his father, or rather his father has quarrelled with him. He quarrels with everyone; with Lady Queensberry, with Percy Douglas, with Bosie, everyone. He's impossible. What can I do?"

"Avoid him," I said. "Don't go about with Lord Alfred Douglas. Give Queensberry his triumph. You could make a friend of him as easily as possible, if you wished. Write him a conciliatory letter."

"But he'll want me to drop Bosie, and stop seeing Lady Queensberry, and I like them all; they are charming to me. Why should I cringe to this madman?"

"Because he is a madman."

"Oh, Frank, I can't," he cried. "Bosie wouldn't let me."

" 'Wouldn't let you'? I repeated angrily. "How absurd! That Queensberry man will go to violence, to any extremity. Don't you fight other people's quarrels; you may have enough of your own some day."

"You're not sympathetic, Frank," he chided weakly. "I know you mean it kindly, but it's impossible for me to do as you advise. I cannot give up my friend. I really cannot let Lord Queensberry choose my friends for me. It's too absurd."

"But it's wise," I replied. "There's a very bad verse in one of Hugo's plays. It always amused me—he likens poverty to a low door and declares that when we have to pass through it the man who stoops lowest is the wisest. So when you meet a madman, the wisest thing to do is to avoid him and not quarrel with him."

"It's very hard, Frank; of course I'll think over what you say. But really Queensberry ought to be in a madhouse. He's too absurd," and in that spirit he left me, outwardly self-confident. He might have remembered Chaucer's words:

> Beware also to spurne again a nall;
> Strive not as doeth a crocke with a wall;
> Deme thy selfe that demest others dede,
> And trouth thee shall deliver, it is no drede.

12

Danger Signals: the Challenge

THESE TWO YEARS 1893-4 saw Oscar Wilde at the very zenith of success. Thackeray, who always felt himself a monetary failure in comparison with Dickens, calls success "one of the greatest of a great man's qualities," and Oscar was not successful merely, he was triumphant. Not Sheridan the day after his marriage, not Byron when he awoke to find himself famous, ever reached such a pinnacle. His plays were bringing in so much that he could spend money like water; he had won every sort of popularity; the gross applause of the many, and the finer incense of the few who constitute the jury of Fame; his personal popularity too was extraordinary; thousands admired him, many liked him; he seemed to have everything that heart could desire, and perfect health to boot. Even his home life was without a cloud. Two stories which he told at this time paint him. One was about his two boys Vyvyan and Cyril.

"Children are sometimes interesting," he began. "The other night I was reading when my wife came and asked me to go upstairs and reprove the elder boy: Cyril, it appeared, would not say his prayers. He had quarrelled with Vyvyan and beaten him, and when he was shaken and told he must say his prayers, he would not kneel down, or ask God to make him a good boy. Of course I had to go upstairs and see to it. I took the chubby little fellow on my knee, and told him in a grave way that he had been very naughty; naughty to hit his younger brother, and naughty because he had given his mother pain. He must kneel down at once, and ask God to forgive him and make him a good boy.

" 'I was not naughty,' he pouted, 'it was Vyvyan; he was naughty.'

"I explained to him that his temper was naughty, and that he must do as he was told. With a little sigh he slipped off my knee, and knelt down and put his little hands together, as he had been taught, and began 'Our Father.' When he had finished the 'Lord's Prayer,' he looked up at me and said gravely, 'Now I'll pray to myself.'

"He closed his eyes and his lips moved. When he had finished I took him in my arms again and kissed him. 'That's right,' I said.

" 'You said you were sorry,' questioned his mother, leaning over him, 'and asked God to make you a good boy?'

" 'Yes, mother,' he nodded. 'I said I was sorry and asked God to make Vyvyan a good boy.'

"I had to leave the room, Frank, or he would have seen me smiling. Wasn't it delightful of him! We are all willing to ask God to make others good."

This story shows the lovable side of him. There was another side not so amiable. In April, 1893, "A Woman of No Importance" was produced by Herbert Beerbohm Tree at the Haymarket and ran till the end of the season, August 16th, surviving even the festival of St. Grouse. The astonishing success of this second play confirmed Oscar Wilde's popularity, gave him money to spend and increased his self-confidence. In the summer he took a house up the river at Goring, and went there to live with Lord Alfred Douglas. Weird stories came to us in London about their life together. Some time in September, I think it was, I asked him what was the truth underlying these reports.

"Scandals and slanders, Frank, have no relation to truth," he replied.

"I wonder if that's true," I said; "slander often has some substratum of truth; it resembles the truth like a gigantic shadow; there is a likeness at least in outline."

"That would be true," he retorted, "if the canvas, so to speak, on which the shadows fall were even and true; but it is not. Scandals and slander are related to the hatred of the people who invent them and are not, in any shadowy sense even, effigies or images of the person attacked."

"Much smoke, then," I queried, "and no fire?"

"Only little fires," he rejoined, "show much smoke. The foundation for what you heard is both small and harmless. The summer was very warm and beautiful, as you know and I was up at Goring with Bosie. Often in the middle of the day we were too hot to go on the river. One afternoon it was sultry-close, and Bosie proposed that I should turn the hose pipe on him. He went in and threw his things off and so did I. A few minutes later I was seated in a chair with a bath towel round me and Bosie was lying on the grass about ten yards away, when the vicar came to pay us a call. The servant told him that we were in the garden, and he came and found us there. Frank, you have no idea the sort of face he pulled. What could I say?

" 'I am the vicar of the parish,' he bowed pompously.

" 'I'm delighted to see you,' I said, getting up and draping myself carefully, 'you have come just in time to enjoy a perfectly Greek scene. I regret that I am scarcely fit to receive you, and Bosie there'—and I pointed to Bosie lying on the grass. The vicar turned his head and saw Bosie's white limbs; the sight was too much for him; he got very red, gave a gasp and fled from the place.

"I simply sat down in my chair and shrieked with laughter. How he may have described the scene, what explanation he gave of it, what vile gloss he may have invented, I don't know and I don't care. I have no doubt he wagged his head and pursed his lips and looked unutterable things. But really it takes a saint to suffer such fools gladly."

I could not help smiling when I thought of the vicar's face, but Oscar's tone was not pleasant.

The change in him had gone further than I had feared. He was now utterly contemptuous of criticism and would listen to no counsel. He was gross, too, the rich food and wine seemed to ooze out of him and his manner was defiant, hard. He was like some great pagan determined to live his own life to the very fullest, careless of what others might say or think or do. Even the stories which he wrote about this time show the worst side of his paganism:

"When Jesus was minded to return to Nazareth, Nazareth was so changed that He no longer recognized His own city. The Nazareth where he had lived was full of lamentations and tears; this city was filled with outbursts of laughter and song. . . .

"Christ went out of the house and, behold, in the street he saw a woman whose face and raiment were painted and whose feet were shod with pearls, and behind her walked a man who wore a cloak of two colours, and whose eyes were bright with lust. And Christ went up to the man and laid His hand on his shoulder, and said to him, 'Tell me, why art thou following this woman, and why dost thou look at her in such wise?' The man turned round, recognized Him and said, 'I was blind; Thou didst heal me; what else should I do with my sight?'"

The same note is played on in two or three more incidents, but the one I have given is the best, and should have been allowed to stand alone. It has been called blasphemous; it is not intentionally blasphemous; as I have said, Oscar always put himself quite naïvely in the place of any historical character.

The disdain of public opinion which Oscar now showed not only in his writings, but in his answers to criticism, quickly turned the public dislike into aggressive hatred. In 1894 a book appeared, "The Green Carnation," which was a sort of photograph of Oscar as a talker and a caricature of his thought. The gossipy story had a surprising success, altogether beyond its merits, which simply testified to the intense interest the suspicion of extraordinary viciousness has for common minds. Oscar's genius was not given in the book at all, but his humour was indicated and a malevolent doubt of his morality insisted upon again and again. Rumour had it that the book was true in every particular, that Mr. Hichens had taken down Oscar's talks evening after evening and simply reproduced them. I asked Oscar if this was true.

"True enough, Frank," he replied with a certain contempt which was foreign to him. "Hichens got to know Bosie Douglas in Egypt. They went up the Nile together, I believe with 'Dodo' Benson. Naturally Bosie talked a great deal about me and Hichens wanted to know me. When they returned to town, I thought him rather pleasant, and saw a good deal of him. I had no idea that he was going to play reporter; it seems to me a breach of confidence —ignoble."

"It is not a picture of you," I said, "but there is a certain likeness."

"A photograph is always like and unlike, Frank," he replied; "the sun too, when used mechanically, is merely a reporter, and traduces instead of reproducing you."

"The Green Carnation" ruined Oscar Wilde's character with the general public. On all sides the book was referred to as confirming the worst suspicions. The cloud which hung over him grew continually darker.

During the summer of 1894 he wrote the "Ideal Husband," which was the outcome of a story I had told him. I had heard it from an American I had met in Cairo, a Mr. Cope Whitehouse. He told me that Disraeli had made money by entrusting the Rothschilds with the purchase of the Suez Canal shares. It seemed to me strange that this statement, if true, had never been set forth authoritatively; but the story was peculiarly modern, and had possibilities in it. Oscar admitted afterwards that he had taken the idea and used it in "An Ideal Husband."

It was in this summer also that he wrote "The Importance of Being Earnest," his finest play. He went to the seaside and completed it, he said, in three weeks, and, when I spoke of the delight he must feel at having two plays performed in London at the same time, he said:

"Next year, Frank, I may have four or five; I could write one every two months with the greatest ease. It all depends on money. If I need money I shall write half a dozen plays next year."

His words reminded me of what Goethe had said about himself. In each of the ten years he spent on his "Theory of Light" he could have written a couple of plays as good as his best. The land of Might-have-been is peopled with these gorgeous shadow-shapes.

Oscar had already found his public, a public capable of appreciating the very best he could do. As soon as "The Importance of Being Earnest" was produced it had an extraordinary success, and success of the best sort. Even journalist critics had begun to cease exhibiting their own limitations in foolish fault-finding and now imitated their betters, parroting phrases of extravagant laudation.

Oscar took the praise as he had taken the scandal and slander, with complacent superiority. He had changed greatly and for the worse; he was growing coarser and harder every year. All his friends noticed this. Even M. André Gide, who was a great admirer and wrote, shortly after his death, the best account of him that appeared, was compelled to deplore his deterioration. He says:

"One felt that there was less tenderness in his looks, that there was something harsh in his laughter, and a wild madness in his joy. He seemed at the same time to be sure of pleasing and less ambitious to succeed therein. He had grown reckless, hardened and conceited. Strangely enough he no longer spoke in fables . . ."

His brother Willie made a similar complaint to Sir Edward Sullivan. Sir Edward writes:

"William Wilde told me, when Oscar was in prison, that the only trouble between him and his brother was caused by Oscar's inordinate vanity in the period before his conviction. 'He had surrounded himself,' William said, 'with a gang of parasites who praised him all day long, and to whom he used to give his cigarette-cases, breast pins, etc., in return for their sickening flattery. No one, not even I, his brother, dared offer any criticism on his works without offending him.'"

If proof were needed both of his reckless contempt for public opinion and the malignancy with which he was misjudged, it could be found in an incident which took place towards the end of 1894. A journal entitled *The Chameleon* was produced by some Oxford undergraduates. Oscar wrote for it a handful of sayings which he called "Phrases and Philosophies for the Use of the Young." His epigrams were harmless enough; but in the same number there appeared a story entitled "The Priest and the Acolyte" which could hardly be defended. The mere fact that his work was printed in the same journal called forth a storm of condemnation though he had never seen the story before it was published nor had he anything to do with its insertion.

Nemesis was following hard after him. Late in this year he spoke to me of his own accord about Lord Queensberry. He wanted my advice:

"Lord Queensberry is annoying me," he said; "I did my best to reconcile him and Bosie. One day at the Café Royal, while Bosie and I were lunching there, Queensberry came in and I made Bosie go over and fetch his father and bring him to lunch with us. He was half friendly with me till quite recently; though he wrote a shameful letter to Bosie about us. What am I to do?"

I asked him what Lord Queensberry objected to.

"He objects to my friendship with Bosie."

"Then why not cease to see Bosie?" I asked.

"It is impossible, Frank, and ridiculous; why should I give up my friends for Queensberry?"

"I should like to see Queensberry's letter," I said. "Is it possible?"

"I'll bring it to you, Frank, but there's nothing in it." A day or two later he showed me the letter, and after I had read it he produced a copy of the telegram which Lord Alfred Douglas had sent to his father in reply. Here they both are; they speak for themselves loudly enough:

ALFRED,—

It is extremely painful for me to have to write to you in the strain I must; but please understand that I decline to receive any answers from you in writing in return. After your recent hysterical impertinent ones I refuse to be annoyed with such, and I decline to read any more letters. If you have anything to say do come here and say it in person. Firstly, am I to understand that, having left Oxford as you did, with discredit to yourself, the reasons of which were fully explained to me by your tutor, you now intend to loaf and loll about and do nothing? All the time you were wasting at Oxford I was put off with an assurance that you were eventually to go into the Civil Service or to the Foreign Office, and then I was put off with an assurance that you were going to the Bar. It appears to me that you intend to do nothing. I utterly decline, however, to just supply you with sufficient funds to enable you to loaf about. You are preparing a wretched future for yourself, and it would be most cruel and wrong for me to encourage you in this. Secondly, I come to the more painful part of this letter—your intimacy with this man Wilde. It must either cease or I will disown you and stop all money supplies. I am not going to try and analyse this intimacy, and I make no charge; but to my mind to pose as a thing is as bad as to be it.

With my own eyes I saw you both in the most loathsome and disgusting relationship as expressed by your manner and expression. Never in my experience have I ever seen such a sight as that in your horrible features. No wonder people are talking as they are. Also I now hear on good authority, but this may be false, that his wife is petitioning to divorce him for sodomy and other crimes. Is this true, or do you not know of it? If I thought the actual thing was true, and it became public property, I should be quite justified in shooting him at sight. These Christian English cowards and men, as they call themselves, want waking up.

Your disgusted so-called father,

QUEENSBERRY.

In reply to this letter Lord Alfred Douglas telegraphed:

"What a funny little man you are! ALFRED DOUGLAS."

This telegram was excellently calculated to drive Queensberry frantic with rage. There was feminine cunning in its wound to vanity.

A little later Oscar told me that Queensberry, accompanied by a friend, had called on him.

"What happened?" I asked.

"I said to him, 'I suppose, Lord Queensberry, you have come to apologise for the libellous letter you wrote about me?'

" 'No,' he replied, 'the letter was privileged; it was written to my son.'

" 'How dared you say such a thing about your son and me?'

" 'You were both kicked out of the Savoy Hotel for disgusting conduct,' he replied.

" 'That's untrue,' I said, 'absolutely untrue.'

" 'You were blackmailed too for a disgusting letter you wrote my son,' he went on.

" 'I don't know who has been telling you all these silly stories,' I replied, 'but they are untrue and quite ridiculous.'

"He ended up by saying that if he caught me and his son together again he would thrash me.

" 'I don't know what the Queensberry rules are,' I retorted, 'but my rule is to shoot at sight in case of personal violence,' and with that I told him to leave my house."

"Of course he defied you?" I questioned.

"He was rude, Frank, and preposterous to the end."

As Oscar was telling me the story, it seemed to me as if another person were speaking through his mouth. The idea of Oscar "standing up" to Queensberry or "shooting at sight" was too absurd. Who was inspiring him? Alfred Douglas?

"What has happened since?" I enquired.

"Nothing," he replied, "perhaps he will be quiet now. Bosie has written him a terrible letter; he must see now that, if he goes on, he will only injure his own flesh and blood."

"That wouldn't stop him," I replied, "if I read him aright. But if I could see what Alfred Douglas wrote, I should be better able to judge of the effect it will have on Queensberry."

A little later I saw the letter; it shows better than words of mine the tempers of the chief actors in this squalid story:

"As you return my letters unopened, I am obliged to write on a postcard. I write to inform you that I treat your absurd threats with absolute indifference. Ever since your exhibition at O. W.'s house, I have made a point of appearing with him at many public restaurants such as The Berkeley, Willis's Rooms, the Café Royal, etc., and I shall continue to go to any of these places whenever I choose and with whom I choose. I am of age and my own master. You have disowned me at least a dozen times, and have very meanly deprived me of money. You have therefore no right over me, either legal or moral. If O. W. was to prosecute you in the Central Criminal Court for libel, you would get seven years' penal servitude for your outrageous libels. Much as I detest you, I am anxious to avoid this for the sake of the family; but if you try to assault me, I shall defend myself with a loaded revolver, which I always carry; and if I shoot you or if he shoots you, we shall be completely justified as we shall be acting in self-defence against a violent and dangerous rough, and I think if you were dead many people would not miss you.—A. D."

This letter of the son seemed to me appalling. My guess was right; it was he who was speaking through Oscar; the threat of shooting at sight came from him. I did not then understand all the circumstances; I had not met Lady Queensberry. I could not have imagined how she had suffered at the hands of her husband—a charming, cultivated woman, with exquisite taste in literature and art; a woman of the most delicate, aspen-like sensibilities and noble generosities, coupled with that violent, coarse animal with the hot eyes and combative nature. Her married life had been a martyrdom. Naturally the children had all taken her side in the quarrel, and Lord Alfred Douglas, her especial favourite, had practically identified himself with her, which explains to some extent, though nothing can justify, the unnatural animosity of his letter. The letter showed me that the quarrel was far deeper, far bitterer than I had imagined—one of those dreadful family quarrels, where the intimate knowledge each has of the other whips anger to madness. All I could do was to warn Oscar.

"It's the old, old story," I said. "You are putting your hand between the bark and the tree, and you will suffer for it." But he would not or could not see it.

"What is one to do with such a madman?" he asked pitiably.

"Avoid him," I replied, "as you would avoid a madman, who wanted to fight with you; or conciliate him; there is nothing else to do."

He would not be warned. A little later the matter came up again. At the first production of "The Importance of Being Earnest" Lord Queensberry appeared at the theatre carrying a large bouquet of turnips and carrots. What the meaning was of those vegetables only the man himself and his like could divine. I asked Oscar about the matter. He seemed annoyed but on the whole triumphant.

"Queensberry," he said, "had engaged a stall at the St. James's Theatre, no doubt to kick up a row; but as soon as I heard of it I got Alick (George Alexander) to send him back his money. On the night of the first performance Queensberry appeared carrying a large bundle of carrots. He was refused admittance at the box-office, and when he tried to enter the gallery the police would not let him in. He must be mad, Frank, don't you think? I am glad he was foiled."

"He is insanely violent," I said, "he will keep on attacking you."

"But what can I do, Frank?"

"Don't ask for advice you won't take," I replied. "There's a French proverb I've always liked: 'In love and war don't seek counsel.' But for God's sake, don't drift. Stop while you can."

But Oscar would have had to take a resolution and act in order to stop, and he was incapable of such energy. The wild horses of Fate had run away with the light chariot of his fortune, and what the end would be no one could foresee. It came with appalling suddenness.

One evening, in February, '95, I heard that the Marquis of Queensberry had left an insulting card for Oscar at the Albemarle Club. My informant added gleefully that now Oscar would have to face the music and we'd all see what was in him. There was no malice in this, just an Englishman's pleasure in a desperate fight, and curiosity as to the issue.

A little later I received a letter from Oscar, asking me if he could call on me that afternoon. I stayed in, and about four o'clock he came to see me.

At first he used the old imperious mask, which he had lately accustomed himself to wear.

"I am bringing an action against Queensberry, Frank," he began gravely, "for criminal libel. He is a mere wild beast. My solicitors tell me that I am certain to win. But they say some of the things I have written will be brought up against me in court. Now you know all I have written. Would you in your position as editor of *The Fortnightly* come and give evidence for me, testify for instance that 'Dorian Gray' is not immoral?"

"Yes," I replied at once, "I should be perfectly willing, and I could say more than that; I could say that you are one of the very few men I have ever known whose talk and whose writings were vowed away from grossness of any sort."

"Oh! Frank, would you? It would be so kind of you," he cried out. "My solicitors said I ought to ask you, but they were afraid you would not like to come. Your evidence will win the case. It is good of you." His whole face was shaken; he turned away to hide the tears.

"Anything I can do, Oscar," I said, "I shall do with pleasure, and, as you know, to the uttermost; but I want you to consider the matter carefully. An English court of law gives me no assurance of a fair trial or rather I am certain that in matters of art or morality an English court is about the worst tribunal in the civilised world."

He shook his head impatiently.

"I cannot help it, I cannot alter it," he said.

"You must listen to me," I insisted. "You remember the Whistler and Ruskin action. You know that Whistler ought to have won. You know that Ruskin was shamelessly in fault; but the British jury and the so-called British artists treated Whistler and his superb work with contempt. Take a different case altogether, the Belt case, where all the Academicians went into the witness box, and asserted honestly enough that Belt was an impostor, yet the jury gave him a verdict of £5,000, though a year later he was sent to penal servitude for the very frauds which the jury in the first trial had declared by their verdict he had not committed. An English law court is all very well for two average men, who are fighting an ordinary business dispute. That's what it's made for, but to judge a Whistler or the ability or the immorality of an artist is to ask the court to do what it is wholly unfit to do. There is not a judge on the bench whose opinion on such a matter is worth a moment's consideration, and the jury are a thousand years behind the judge."

"That may be true, Frank; but I cannot help it."

"Don't forget," I persisted, "all British prejudices will be against you. Here is a father, the fools will say, trying to protect his young son. If he has made a mistake; it is only through excess of laudable zeal. You would have to prove yourself a religious maniac in order to have any chance against him in England."

"How terrible you are, Frank. You know it is Bosie Douglas who wants me to fight, and my solicitors tell me I shall win."

"Solicitors live on quarrels. Of course they want a case that will bring hundreds if not thousands of pounds into their pockets. Besides, they like the fight. They will have all the kudos of it and the fun, and you will pay the piper. For God's sake don't be led into it; that way madness lies."

"But, Frank," he objected weakly, "how can I sit down under such an insult. I must do something."

"That's another story," I replied. "Let us by all means weigh what is to be done. But let us begin by putting the law-courts out of the question. Don't forget that you are challenged to mortal combat. Let us consider how the challenge should be met, but we won't fight under Queensberry rules because Queensberry happens to be the aggressor. Don't forget that if you lose and Queensberry goes free, everyone will hold that you have been guilty of nameless vice. Put the law courts out of your head. Whatever else you do, you must not bring an action for criminal libel against Queensberry. You are sure to lose it; you haven't a dog's chance, and the English despise the beaten— *væ victis!* Don't commit suicide."

Nothing was determined when the time came to part.

This conversation took place, I believe, on Friday or Saturday. I spent the whole of Sunday trying to find out what was known about Oscar Wilde and what would be brought up against him. I wanted to know how he was regarded in an ordinary middle-class English home.

My investigations had appalling results. Everyone assumed that Oscar Wilde was guilty of the worst that had ever been alleged against him; the very people who received him in their houses condemned him pitilessly and, as I approached the fountain-head of information, the charges became more and more definite; to my horror, in the Public Prosecutor's office, his guilt was said to be known and classified.

All "people of importance" agreed that he would lose his case against Queensberry; "no English jury would give Oscar Wilde a verdict against anyone," was the expert opinion.

"How unjust!" I cried.

A careless shrug was the only reply.

I returned home from my enquiries late on Sunday afternoon, and in a few minutes Oscar called by appointment. I told him I was more convinced than ever that he must not go on with the prosecution; he would be certain to lose. Without beating about the bush I declared that he had no earthly chance.

"There are letters," I said, "which are infinitely worse than your published writings, which will be put in evidence against you."

"What letters do you mean, Frank?" he questioned. "The Wood letters to Lord Alfred Douglas I told you about? I can explain all of them."

"You paid blackmail to Wood for letters you had written to Douglas," I replied, "and you will not be able to explain that fact to the satisfaction of a jury. I am told it is possible that witnesses will be called against you. Take it from me, Oscar, you have not a ghost of a chance."

"Tell me what you mean, Frank, for God's sake," he cried.

"I can tell you in a word," I replied; "you will lose your case. I have promised not to say more."

I tried to persuade him by his vanity.

"You must remember," I said, "that you are a sort of standard bearer for future generations. If you lose you will make it harder for all writers in England; though God knows it is hard enough already; you will put back the hands of the clock for fifty years."

I seemed almost to have persuaded him. He questioned me:

"What is the alternative, Frank, the wisest thing to do in your opinion? Tell me that."

"You ought to go abroad," I replied, "go abroad with your wife, and let Queensberry and his son fight out their own miserable quarrels; they are well-matched."

"Oh, Frank," he cried, "how can I do that?"

"Sleep on it," I replied; "I am going to, and we can talk it all over in a day or two."

"But I must know," he said wistfully, "to-morrow morning, Frank."

"Bernard Shaw is lunching with me to-morrow," I replied, "at the Café Royal."

He made an impatient movement of his head.

"He usually goes early," I went on, "and if you like to come after three o'clock we can have a talk and consider it all."

"May I bring Bosie?" he enquired.

"I would rather you did not," I replied, "but it is for you to do just as you like. I don't mind saying what I have to say, before anyone," and on that we parted.

Somehow or other next day at lunch both Shaw and I got interested in our talk, and we were both at the table when Oscar came in. I introduced them, but they had met before. Shaw stood up and proposed to go at once, but Oscar with his usual courtesy assured him that he would be glad if he stayed.

"Then, Oscar," I said, "perhaps you won't mind Shaw hearing what I advise?"

"No, Frank, I don't mind," he sighed with a pitiful air of depression.

I am not certain and my notes do not tell me whether Bosie Douglas came in with Oscar or a little later, but he heard the greater part of our talk. I put the matter simply.

"First of all," I said, "we start with the certainty that you are going to lose the case against Queensberry. You must give it up, drop it at once; but you cannot drop it and stay in England. Queensberry would probably attack you again and again. I know him well; he is half a savage and regards pity as a weakness; he has absolutely no consideration for others.

"You should go abroad, and, as ace of trumps, you should take your wife with you. Now for the excuse: I would sit down and write such a letter as you alone can write to *The Times*. You should set forth how you have been insulted by the Marquis of Queensberry, and how you went naturally to the Courts for a remedy, but you found out very soon that this was a mistake. No jury would give a verdict against a father, however mistaken he might be. The only thing for you to do therefore is to go abroad, and leave the whole ring, with its gloves and ropes, its sponges and pails, to Lord Queensberry. You are a maker of beautiful things, you should say, and not a fighter. Whereas the Marquis of Queensberry takes joy only in fighting. You refuse to fight with a father under these circumstances."

Oscar seemed to be inclined to do as I proposed. I appealed to Shaw, and Shaw said he thought I was right; the case would very likely go against Oscar, a jury would hardly give a verdict against a father trying to protect his son. Oscar seemed much moved. I think it was about this time that Bosie Douglas came in. At Oscar's request, I repeated my argument and to my astonishment Douglas got up at once, and cried with his little white, venomous, distorted face:

"Such advice shows you are no friend of Oscar's."

"What do you mean?" I asked in wonderment; but he turned and left the room on the spot. To my astonishment Oscar also got up.

"It is not friendly of you, Frank," he said weakly. "It really is not friendly."

I stared at him; he was parrotting Douglas' idiotic words.

"Don't be absurd," I said; but he repeated:

"No, Frank, it is not friendly," and went to the door and disappeared.

Like a flash I saw part at least of the truth. It was not Oscar who had ever misled Douglas, but Lord Alfred Douglas who was driving Oscar whither he would.

I turned to Shaw.

"Did I say anything in the heat of argument that could have offended Oscar or Douglas?"

"Nothing," said Shaw, "not a word; you have nothing to reproach yourself with." [1]

Left to myself I was at a loss to imagine what Lord Alfred Douglas proposed to himself by hounding Oscar on to attack his father. I was still more surprised by his white, bitter face. I could not get rid of the impression it left on me. While groping among these reflections I was suddenly struck by a sort of likeness, a similarity of expression and of temper between Lord Alfred Douglas and his unhappy father. I could not get it out of my head—that little face blanched with rage and the wild, hating eyes; the shrill voice, too, was Queensberry's.

[1] I am very glad that Bernard Shaw has lately put in print his memory of this conversation. The above account was printed, though not published, in 1911, and in 1914 Shaw published his recollection of what took place at this consultation. Readers may judge from the comparison how far my general story is worthy of credence. In the Introduction to his playlet, "The Dark Lady of the Sonnets," Shaw writes:

"Yet he (Harris) knows the taste and the value of humour. He was one of the few men of letters who really appreciated Oscar Wilde, though he did not rally fiercely to Wilde's side until the world deserted Oscar in his ruin. I myself was present at a curious meeting between the two when Harris on the eve of the Queensberry trial prophesied to Wilde with miraculous precision exactly what immediately afterwards happened to him and warned him to leave the country. It was the first time within my knowledge that such a forecast proved true. Wilde, though under no illusion as to the folly of the quite unselfish suit-at-law he had been persuaded to begin, nevertheless so miscalculated the force of the social vengeance he was unloosing on himself that he fancied it could be stayed by putting up the editor of *The Saturday Review* (as Mr. Harris then was) to declare that he considered *Dorian Gray* a highly moral book, which it certainly is. When Harris foretold him the truth, Wilde denounced him as a faint-hearted friend who was failing him in his hour of need and left the room in anger. Harris's idiosyncratic power of pity saved him from feeling or showing the smallest resentment; and events presently proved to Wilde how insanely he had been advised in taking the action, and how accurately Harris had gauged the situation."

13

Oscar Attacks Queensberry and Is Worsted

It was weakness in Oscar and not strength that allowed him to be driven to the conflict by Lord Alfred Douglas; it was his weakness again which prevented him from abandoning the prosecution, once it was begun. Such a resolution would have involved a breaking away from his associates and from his friends; a personal assertion of will of which he was incapable. Again and again he answered my urging with:

"I can't, Frank, I can't."

When I pointed out to him that the defence was growing bolder—it was announced one morning in the newspapers that Lord Queensberry, instead of pleading paternal privilege and minimising his accusation, was determined to justify the libel and declare that it was true in every particular—Oscar could only say weakly:

"I can't help it, Frank, I can't do anything; you only distress me by predicting disaster."

The fibres of resolution, never strong in him, had been destroyed by years of self-indulgence, while the influence whipping him was stronger than I guessed. He was hurried like a sheep to the slaughter.

Although everyone who cared to think knew that Queensberry would win the case, many persons believed that Oscar would make a brilliant intellectual fight, and carry off the honours, if not the verdict.

The trial took place at the Central Criminal Court on April 3rd, 1895. Mr. Justice Collins was the judge and the case was conducted at first with the outward seemliness and propriety which are so peculiarly English. An hour before the opening of the case the Court was crowded, not a seat to be had for love or money; even standing room was at a premium.

The Counsel were the best at the Bar; Sir Edward Clarke, Q.C., Mr. Charles Mathews, and Mr. Travers Humphreys for the prosecution; Mr. Carson, Q.C., Mr. G. C. Gill and Mr. A. Gill for the defence. Mr. Besley, Q.C., and Mr. Monckton watched the case, it was said, for the brothers, Lord Douglas of Hawick and Lord Alfred Douglas.

While waiting for the judge, the buzz of talk in the court grew loud; everybody agreed that the presence of Sir Edward Clarke gave Oscar an advantage. Mr. Carson was not so well known then as he has since become; he was regarded as a sharp-witted Irishman who had still his spurs to win. Some knew he had been at school with Oscar, and at Trinity College was as high in the second class as Oscar was in the first. It was said he envied Oscar his reputation for brilliance.

Suddenly the loud voice of the clerk called for silence.

As the judge appeared everyone stood up in complete stillness. Sir Edward Clarke opened for the prosecution. The bleak face, long upper lip and severe side whiskers made the little man look exactly like a nonconformist parson of the old days, but his tone and manner were modern—quiet and conversational. The charge, he said, was that the defendant had published a false and malicious libel against Mr. Oscar Wilde. The libel was in the form of a card which Lord Queensberry had left at a club to which Mr. Oscar Wilde belonged; it could not be justified unless the statements written on the card were true. It would, however, have been possible to have excused the card by a strong feeling, a mistaken feeling, on the part of a father, but the plea which the defendant had brought before the Court raised graver issues. He said that the statement was true and was made for the public benefit. There were besides a series of accusations in the plea (everyone held his breath), mentioning names of persons, and it was said with regard to these persons that Mr. Wilde had solicited them to commit a grave offence and that he had been guilty "with each and all of them of indecent practices. . . ." My heart seemed to stop. My worst forebodings were more than justified. Vaguely I heard Clarke's voice, "grave responsibility . . . serious allegations . . . credible witnesses . . . Mr. Oscar Wilde was the son of Sir William Wilde . . ." the voice droned on and I awoke to feverish clearness of brain. Queensberry had turned the defence into a prosecution. Why had he taken the risk? Who had given him the new and precise information? I felt that there was nothing before Oscar but ruin absolute. Could anything be done? Even now he could go abroad—even now. I resolved once more to try and induce him to fly.

My interest turned from these passionate imaginings to the actual. Would Sir Edward Clarke fight the case as it should be fought? He had begun to tell of the friendship between Oscar Wilde and Lord Alfred Douglas; the friendship too between Oscar Wilde and Lady Queensberry, who on her own petition had been divorced from the Marquis. Would he go on to paint the terrible ill-feeling that existed between Lord Alfred Douglas and his father, and show how Oscar had been dragged into the bitter family squabble? To the legal mind this had but little to do with the case.

We got, instead, a dry relation of the facts which have already been set forth in this history. Wright, the porter of the Albemarle Club, was called to say that Lord Queensberry had handed him the card produced. Witness had looked at the card; did not understand it; but put it in an envelope and gave it to Mr. Wilde.

Mr. Oscar Wilde was then called and went into the witness box. He looked a little grave but was composed and serious. Sir Edward Clarke took him briefly through the incidents of his life; his successes at school and the University; the attempts made to blackmail him; the insults of Lord Queensberry; and then directed his attention to the allegations in the plea impugning his conduct with different persons. Mr. Oscar Wilde declared that there was no truth in any of these statements. Hereupon Sir Edward Clarke sat down. Mr. Carson rose and the death duel began.

Mr. Carson brought out that Oscar Wilde was forty years of age and Lord Alfred Douglas twenty-four. Down to the interview in Tite Street Lord Queensberry had been friendly with Mr. Wilde.

"Had Mr. Wilde written in a publication called *The Chameleon?*"

"Yes."

"Had he written there a story called 'The Priest and the Acolyte'?"

"No."

"Was that story immoral?"

Oscar amused everyone by replying:

"Much worse than immoral, it was badly written," but feeling that this gibe was too light for the occasion he added:

"It was altogether offensive and perfect twaddle."

He admitted at once that he did not express his disapproval of it; it was beneath him "to concern himself with the effusions of an illiterate undergraduate."

"Did Mr. Wilde ever consider the effect in his writings of inciting to immorality?"

Oscar declared that he aimed neither at good nor evil, but tried to make a beautiful thing. When questioned as to the immorality in thought in the article in *The Chameleon*, he retorted "that there is no such thing as morality or immorality in thought." A hum of understanding and approval ran through the court; the intellect is profoundly amoral.

Again and again he scored in this way off Mr. Carson.

"No work of art ever puts forward views; views belong to the Philistines and not to artists." . . .

"What do you think of this view?"

"I don't think of any views except my own."

All this while Mr. Carson had been hitting at a man on his own level; but Oscar Wilde was above him and not one of his blows had taken effect. Every moment, too, Oscar grew more and more at his ease, and the combat seemed to be turning completely in his favour. Mr. Carson at length took up "Dorian Gray" and began cross-examining on passages in it.

"You talk about one man adoring another. Did you ever adore any man?"

"No," replied Oscar quietly, "I have never adored anyone but myself."

The Court roared with laughter. Oscar went on:

"There are people in the world, I regret to say, who cannot understand the deep affection that an artist can feel for a friend with a beautiful personality."

He was then questioned about his letter (already quoted here) to Lord Alfred Douglas. It was a prose-poem, he said, written in answer to a sonnet. He had not written to other people in the same strain, not even to Lord Alfred Douglas again; he did not repeat himself in style.

Mr. Carson read another letter from Oscar Wilde to Lord Alfred Douglas, which paints their relations with extraordinary exactness. Here it is:

> Savoy Hotel,
> Victoria Embankment, London.
>
> Dearest of All Boys,—
>   Your letter was delightful, red and yellow wine to me; but I am sad and out of sorts. Bosie, you must not make scenes with me. They kill me, they wreck the loveliness of life. I cannot see you, so Greek and gracious, distorted with passion. I cannot listen to your curved lips saying hideous things to me. I would sooner ('here a word is indecipherable,' Mr. Carson went on, 'but I will ask the witness')[1]—than have you bitter, unjust, hating. . . . I must see you soon. You are the divine thing I want, the thing of genius and beauty; but I don't know how to do it. Shall I come to Salisbury? My bill here is £49 for a week. I have also got a new sitting-room. . . . Why are you not here, my dear, my wonderful boy? I fear I must leave—no money, no credit, and a heart of lead.
>
> Your Own Oscar

Oscar said that it was an expression of his tender admiration for Lord Alfred Douglas.

"You have said," Mr. Carson went on, "that all the statements about persons in the plea of justification were false. Do you still hold to that assertion?"

"I do."

Mr. Carson then paused and looked at the judge. Justice Collins

---

[1] The words which Mr. Carson could not read were: "I would sooner be rented than, etc." Rent is a slang term for blackmail.

shuffled his papers together and announced that the cross-examination would be continued on the morrow. As the Judge went out, all the tongues in the court broke loose. Oscar was surrounded by friends congratulating him and rejoicing.

I was not so happy and went away to think the matter out. I tried to keep up my courage by recalling the humorous things Oscar had said during the cross-examination. I recalled too the dull commonplaces of Mr. Carson. I tried to persuade myself that it was all going on very well. But in the back of my mind I realized that Oscar's answers, characteristic and clever as many of them were, had not impressed the jury, were indeed rather calculated to alienate them. He had taken the purely artistic standpoint, had not attempted to go higher and reach a synthesis which would conciliate the Philistine jurymen as well as the thinking public, and the Judge.

Mr. Carson was in closer touch with the jury, being nearer their intellectual level, and there was a terrible menace in his last words. To-morrow, I said to myself, he will begin to examine about persons and not books. He did not win on the literary question, but he was right to bring it in. The passages he had quoted, and especially Oscar's letters to Lord Alfred Douglas, had created a strong prejudice in the minds of the jury. They ought not to have had this effect, I thought, but they had. My contempt for Courts of law deepened. Those twelve jurymen were anything but the peers of the accused. How could they judge him?

. . . .

The second day of the trial was very different from the first. There seemed to be a gloom over the Court. Oscar went into the box as if it had been the dock; he had lost all his spring. Mr. Carson settled down to the cross-examination with apparent zest. It was evident from his mere manner that he was coming to what he regarded as the strong part of his case. He began by examining Oscar as to his intimacy with a person named Taylor.

"Has Taylor been to your house and to your chambers?"
"Yes."
"Have you been to Taylor's rooms to afternoon tea parties?"
"Yes."

"Did Taylor's rooms strike you as peculiar?"

"They were pretty rooms."

"Have you ever seen them lit by anything else but candles even in the daytime?"

"I think so. I'm not sure."

"Have you ever met there a young man called Wood?"

"On one occasion."

"Have you ever met Sidney Mavor there at tea?"

"It is possible."

"What was your connection with Taylor?"

"Taylor was a friend, a young man of intelligence and education; he had been to a good English school."

"Did you know Taylor was being watched by the police?"

"No."

"Did you know that Taylor was arrested with a man named Parker in a raid made last year on a house in Fitzroy Square?"

"I read of it in the newspaper."

"Did that cause you to drop your acquaintance with Taylor?"

"No; Taylor explained to me that he had gone there to a dance and that the magistrate had dismissed the case against him."

"Did you get Taylor to arrange dinners for you to meet young men?"

"No; I have dined with Taylor at a restaurant."

"How many young men has Taylor introduced to you?"

"Five in all."

"Did you give money or presents to these five?"

"I may have done."

"Did they give you anything?"

"Nothing."

"Among the five men Taylor introduced you to, was one named Parker?"

"Yes."

"Did you get on friendly terms with him?"

"Yes."

"Did you call him 'Charlie' and allow him to call you 'Oscar'?"

"Yes."

"How old was Parker?"

"I don't keep a census of people's ages. It would be vulgar to ask people their age."

"Where did you first meet Parker?"

"I invited Taylor to Kettner's[1] on the occasion of my birthday, and told him to bring what friends he liked. He brought Parker and his brother.

"Did you know Parker was a gentleman's servant out of work, and his brother a groom?"

"No; I did not."

"But you did know that Parker was not a literary character or an artist, and that culture was not his strong point?"

"I did."

"What was there in common between you and Charlie Parker?"

"I like people who are young, bright, happy, careless and original. I do not like them sensible, and I do not like them old; I don't like social distinctions of any kind, and the mere fact of youth is so wonderful to me that I would sooner talk to a young man for half an hour than be cross-examined by an elderly Q.C."

Everyone smiled at this retort.

"Had you chambers in St. James's Place?"

"Yes, from October, '93, to April, '94."

"Did Charlie Parker go and have tea with you there?"

"Yes."

"Did you give him money?"

"I gave him three or four pounds because he said he was hard up."

"What did he give you in return?"

"Nothing."

"Did you give Charlie Parker a silver cigarette case at Christmas?"

"I did."

"Did you visit him one night at 12:30 at Park Walk, Chelsea?"

"I did not."

"Did you write him any beautiful prose-poems?"

"I don't think so."

"Did you know that Charlie Parker had enlisted in the Army?"

"I have heard so."

"When you heard that Taylor was arrested what did you do?"

"I was greatly distressed and wrote to tell him so."

"When did you first meet Fred Atkins?"

"In October or November, '92."

[1] A famous Italian restaurant in Soho; it had several "private rooms."

126

"Did he tell you that he was employed by a firm of book-makers?"

"He may have done."

"Not a literary man or an artist, was he?"

"No."

"What age was he?"

"Nineteen or twenty."

"Did you ask him to dinner at Kettner's?"

"I think I met him at a dinner at Kettner's."

"Was Taylor at the dinner?"

"He may have been."

"Did you meet him afterwards?"

"I did."

"Did you call him 'Fred' and let him call you 'Oscar'?"

"Yes."

"Did you go to Paris with him?"

"Yes."

"Did you give him money?"

"Yes."

"Was there ever any impropriety between you?"

"No."

"When did you first meet Ernest Scarfe?"

"In December, 1893."

"Who introduced him to you?"

"Taylor."

"Scarfe was out of work, was he not?"

"He may have been."

"Did Taylor bring Scarfe to you at St. James's Place?"

"Yes."

"Did you give Scarfe a cigarette case?"

"Yes. It was my custom to give cigarette cases to people I liked."

"When did you first meet Mavor?"

"In '93."

"Did you give him money or a cigarette case?"

"A cigarette case."

"Did you know Walter Grainger?" . . . and so on till the very air in the court seemed peopled with spectres.

127

On the whole Oscar bore the cross-examination very well; but he made one appalling slip.

Mr. Carson was pressing him as to his relations with the boy Grainger, who had been employed in Lord Alfred Douglas' rooms in Oxford.

"Did you ever kiss him?" he asked.

Oscar answered carelessly, "Oh, dear, no. He was a peculiarly plain boy. He was, unfortunately, extremely ugly. I pitied him for it."

"Was that the reason why you did not kiss him?"

"Oh, Mr. Carson, you are pertinently insolent."

"Did you say that in support of your statement that you never kissed him?"

"No. It is a childish question."

But Carson was not to be warded off; like a terrier he sprang again and again:

"Why, sir, did you mention that this boy was extremely ugly?"

"For this reason. If I were asked why I did not kiss a door-mat, I should say because I do not like to kiss door-mats." . . .

"Why did you mention his ugliness?"

"It is ridiculous to imagine that any such thing could have occurred under any circumstances."

"Then why did you mention his ugliness, I ask you?"

"Because you insulted me by an insulting question."

"Was that a reason why you should say the boy was ugly?"

(Here the witness began several answers almost inarticulately and finished none of them. His efforts to collect his ideas were not aided by Mr. Carson's sharp staccato repetition: "Why? why? why did you add that?") At last the witness answered:

"You sting me and insult me and at times one says things flippantly."

Then came the re-examination by Sir Edward Clarke, which brought out very clearly the hatred of Lord Alfred Douglas for his father. Letters were read and in one letter Queensberry declared that Oscar had plainly shown the white feather when he called on him. One felt that this was probably true. Queensberry's word on such a point could be accepted.

In the re-examination Sir Edward Clarke occupied himself chiefly with two youths, Shelley and Conway, who had been passed over casually by Mr. Carson. In answer to his questions Oscar stated that Shelley was a youth in the employ of Mathews and Lane, the publishers. Shelley had very good taste in literature and a great desire for culture. Shelley had read all his books and liked them. Shelley had dined with him and his wife at Tite Street. Shelley was in every way a gentleman. He had never gone with Charlie Parker to the Savoy Hotel.

A juryman wanted to know at this point whether the witness was aware of the nature of the article, "The Priest and the Acolyte," in *The Chameleon.*

"I knew nothing of it; it came as a terrible shock to me."

This answer contrasted strangely with the light tone of his reply to the same question on the previous day.

The re-examination did not improve Oscar's position. It left all the facts where they were, and at least a suspicion in every mind.

Sir Edward Clarke intimated that this concluded the evidence for the prosecution, whereupon Mr. Carson rose to make the opening speech for the defence. I was shivering with apprehension.

He began by admitting the grave responsibility resting on Lord Queensberry, who accepted it to the fullest. Lord Queensberry was justified in doing all he could do to cut short an acquaintance which must be disastrous to his son. Mr. Carson wished to draw the attention of the jury to the fact that all these men with whom Mr. Wilde went about were discharged servants and grooms, and that they were all about the same age. He asked the jury also to note that Taylor, who was the pivot of the whole case, had not yet been put in the box. Why not? He pointed out to the jury that the very same idea that was set forth in "The Priest and the Acolyte" was contained in Oscar Wilde's letters to Lord Alfred Douglas, and the same idea was to be found in Lord Alfred Douglas' poem, "The Two Loves," which was published in *The Chameleon.* He went on to say that when, in the story of "The Priest and the Acolyte," the boy was discovered in the priest's bed,[1] the priest made the same defense as Mr. Wilde had made, that the world does not understand the beauty of this love. The same idea was found again in "Dorian Gray," and he read two or

[1] Mr. Carson here made a mistake; there is no such incident in the story. The error merely shows how prejudiced his mind was.

three passages from the book in support of this statement. Mr. Wilde had described his letter to Lord Alfred Douglas as a prose sonnet. He would read it again to the court, and he read both the letters. "Mr. Wilde says they are beautiful," he went on, "I call them an abominable piece of disgusting immorality."

At this the Judge again shuffled his papers together and whispered in a quiet voice that the court would sit on the morrow, and left the room.

The honours of the day had all been with Mr. Carson. Oscar left the box in a depressed way. One or two friends came towards him, but the majority held aloof, and in almost unbroken silence everyone slipped out of the court. Strange to say in my mind there was just a ray of hope. Mr. Carson was still laying stress on the article in *The Chameleon* and scattered passages in "Dorian Gray"; on Oscar's letters to Lord Alfred Douglas and Lord Alfred Douglas' poems in *The Chameleon*. He must see, I thought, that all this was extremely weak. Sir Edward Clarke could be trusted to tear all such arguments, founded on literary work, to shreds. There was room for more than reasonable doubt about all such things.

Why had not Mr. Carson put some of the young men he spoke of in the box? Would he be able to do that? He talked of Taylor as "the pivot of the case," and gibed at the prosecution for not putting Taylor in the box. Would he put Taylor in the box? And why, if he had such witnesses at his beck and call, should he lay stress on the flimsy, weak evidence to be drawn from passages in books and poems and letters? One thing was clear; if he was able to put any of the young men in the box about whom he had examined Oscar, Oscar was ruined. Even if he rested his defence on the letters and poems he'd win and Oscar would be discredited, for already it was clear that no jury would give Oscar Wilde a verdict against a father trying to protect his son. The issue had narrowed down to terrible straits. Would it be utter ruin to Oscar or merely loss of the case and reputation? We had only sixteen hours to wait; they seemed to me to hold the last hope.

I drove to Tite Street, hoping to see Oscar. I was convinced that Carson had important witnesses at his command, and that the outcome of the case would be disastrous. Why should not Oscar even now, this very evening, cross to Calais, leaving a letter for his counsel and the court abandoning the idiotic prosecution.

The house at Tite Street seemed deserted. For some time no one answered my knocking and ringing, and then a man-servant simply told me that Mr. Wilde was not in. He did not know whether Mr. Wilde was expected back or not; did not think he was coming back. I turned and went home. I thought Oscar would probably say to me again:

"I can do nothing, Frank, nothing."

. . . .

The feeling in the court next morning was good tempered, even jaunty. The benches were filled with young barristers, all of whom had made up their minds that the testimony would be what one of them called "nifty." Everyone treated the case as practically over.

"But will Carson call witnesses?" I asked.

"Of course he will," they said, "but in any case Wilde does not stand a ghost of a chance of getting a verdict against Queensberry; he was a bally fool to bring such an action."

"The question is," said someone, "will Wilde face the music?"

My heart leapt. Perhaps he had gone, fled already to France to avoid this dreadful, useless torture. I could see the hounds with open mouths, dripping white fangs, and greedy eyes all closing in on the defenceless quarry. Would the huntsman give the word? We were not left long in doubt.

Mr. Carson continued his statement for the defence. He had sufficiently demonstrated to the jury, he thought, that, so far as Lord Queensberry was concerned, he was absolutely justified in bringing to a climax in the way he had, the connection between Mr. Oscar Wilde and his son. A dramatic pause.

A moment later the clever advocate resumed; unfortunately he had a more painful part of the case to approach. It would be his painful duty to bring before them one after the other the young men he had examined Mr. Wilde about and allow them to tell their tales. In no one of these cases were these young men on an equality in any way with Mr. Wilde. Mr. Wilde had told them that there was something beautiful and charming about youth which led him to make these acquaintances. That was a travesty of the facts. Mr. Wilde preferred to know nothing of these young men and their antecedents. He knew nothing about Wood; he knew nothing about Parker; he knew nothing about Scarfe, nothing about Conway, and not much about Taylor. The truth was Taylor was the procurer for Mr. Wilde and the jury would hear from this young man Parker, who would have to tell his unfortunate story to them, that he was poor, out of a place, had no money, and unfortunately fell a victim to Mr. Wilde. (Sir Edward Clarke here left the court.)

On the first evening they met, Mr. Wilde called Parker "Charlie" and Parker called Mr. Wilde "Oscar." It may be a very noble instinct in some people to wish to break down social barriers, but Mr. Wilde's conduct was not ordered by generous instincts. Luxurious dinners and champagne were not the way to assist a poor man. Parker would tell them that, after this first dinner, Mr. Wilde invited him to drive with him to the Savoy Hotel. Mr. Wilde had not told them why he had that suite of rooms at the Savoy Hotel. Parker would tell them what happened on arriving there. This was the scandal Lord Queensberry had referred to in his letter as far back as June or July last year. The jury would wonder not at the reports having reached Lord Queensberry's ears, but that Oscar Wilde had been tolerated in London society as long as he had been. Parker had since enlisted in the Army and bore a good character. Mr. Wilde himself had said that Parker was respectable. Parker would reluctantly present himself to tell his story to the jury.

All this time the court was hushed with awe and wonder; everyone was asking what on earth had induced Wilde to begin the prosecution; what madness had driven him and why had he listened to the insane advice to bring the action when he must have known the sort of evidence which could be brought against him.

After promising to produce Parker and the others Mr. Carson stopped speaking and began looking through his papers; when he began again, everyone held his breath; what was coming now? He proceeded in the same matter-of-fact and serious way to deal with the case of the youth, Conway. Conway, it appeared, had known Mr. Wilde and his family at Worthing. Conway was sixteen years of age. . . . At this moment Sir Edward Clarke returned with Mr. Charles Mathews and asked permission of the judge to have a word or two with Mr. Carson. At the close of a few minutes' talk between the counsel, Sir Edward Clarke rose and told the Judge that after communicating with Mr. Oscar Wilde he thought it better to withdraw the prosecution and submit to a verdict of "not guilty".

He minimised the defeat. He declared that, in respect to matters connected with literature and the letters, he could not resist the verdict of "not guilty", having regard to the fact that Lord Queensberry had not used a direct accusation, but the words "posing as", etc. Besides, he wished to spare the jury the necessity of investigating in detail matter of the most appalling character. He wished to make an end of the case—and he sat down.

Why on earth did S.. Edward Clarke not advise Oscar in this way weeks before? Why did he not tell him his case could not possibly be won?

I have heard since on excellent authority that before taking up the case Sir Edward Clarke asked Oscar Wilde whether he was guilty or not, and accepted in good faith his assurance that he was innocent. As soon as he realised, in court, the strength of the case against Oscar he advised him to abandon the prosecution. To his astonishment Oscar was eager to abandon it. Sir Edward Clarke afterwards defended his unfortunate client out of loyalty and pity, Oscar again assuring him of his innocence.

Mr. Carson rose at once and insisted, as was his right, that this verdict of "not guilty" must be understood to mean that Lord Queensberry had succeeded in his plea of justification.

Mr. Justice Collins thought that it was not part of the function of the Judge and jury to insist on wading through prurient details, which had no bearing on the matter at issue, which had already been decided by the consent of the prosecutors to a verdict of "not guilty". Such a verdict meant of course that the plea of justification was proved. The jury having consulted for a few moments, the Clerk of Arraigns asked:

"Do you find the plea of justification has been proved or not?"

Foreman: "Yes."

"You say that the defendant is 'not guilty,' and that is the verdict of you all?"

Foreman: "Yes, and we also find that it is for the public benefit."

The last kick to the dead lion. As the verdict was read out the spectators in the court burst into cheers.

Mr. Carson: "Of course the costs of the defence will follow?"
Mr. Justice Collins: "Yes."
Mr. C. F. Gill: "And Lord Queensberry may be discharged?"
Mr. Justice Collins: "Certainly."

The Marquis of Queensberry left the dock amid renewed cheering, which was taken up again and again in the street.

14

How Genius Is Persecuted in England

THE ENGLISH are very proud of their sense of justice, proud too of their Roman law and the practice of the Courts in which they have incorporated it. They boast of their fair play in all things as the French boast of their lightness and, if you question it, you lose caste with them, as one prejudiced or ignorant or both. English justice cannot be bought, they say, and if it is dear, excessively dear even, they rather like to feel they have paid a long price for a good article. Yet it may be that here, as in other things, they take outward propriety and decorum for the inward and ineffable grace. That a judge should be incorruptible is not so important as that he should be wise and humane.

English journalists and barristers were very much amused at the conduct of the Dreyfus case; yet, when Dreyfus was being tried for the second time in France, two or three instances of similar injustice in England were set forth with circumstance in one of the London newspapers, but no one paid any effective attention to them. If Dreyfus had been convicted in England, it is probable that no voice would ever have been raised in his favour; it is absolutely certain that there would never have been a second trial. A keen sense of abstract justice is only to be found in conjunction with a rich fount of imaginative sympathy. The English are too self-absorbed to take much interest in their neighbours' affairs, too busy to care for abstract questions of right or wrong.

Before the trial of Oscar Wilde I still believed that in a criminal case rough justice would be done in England. The bias of an English judge, I said to myself, is always in favour of the accused. It is an honourable tradition of English procedure that even the Treasury barristers should state rather less than they can prove against the unfortunate person who is being attacked by all the power and authority of the State. I was soon forced to see that these honourable and praiseworthy conventions were as withes of straw in the fire of English prejudice. The first thing to set me doubting was that the judge did not try to check the cheering in Court after the verdict in favour of Lord Queensberry. English judges always resent and resist such popular outbursts; why not in this case? After all, no judge could think Queensberry a hero; he was too well known for that, and yet the cheering swelled again and again, and the judge gathered up his papers without a word and went his way as if he were deaf. A dreadful apprehension crept over me. In spite of myself I began to realise that my belief in English justice might be altogether mistaken. It was to me as if the solid earth had become a quaking bog, or indeed as if a child had suddenly discovered its parent to be shameless. The subsequent trials are among the most painful experiences of my life. I shall try to set down all the incidents fairly.

One peculiarity had first struck me in the conduct of the case between Oscar Wilde and Lord Queensberry that did not seem to occur to any of the numberless journalists and writers who commented on the trial. It was apparent from his letter to his son (which I published in a previous chapter), and from the fact that he called at Oscar Wilde's house that Lord Queensberry at the beginning did not believe in the truth of his accusations; he set them forth as a violent man sets forth hearsay and suspicion, knowing that as a father he could do this with impunity and, accordingly, at first he pleaded privilege. Some time between the beginning of the prosecution and the trial, he obtained an immense amount of unexpected evidence. He then justified his libel and gave the names of the persons whom he intended to call to prove his case. Where did he get this new knowledge?

I have spoken again and again in the course of this narrative of

Oscar's enemies, asserting that the English middle-class, as puritans, detested his attitude and way of life, and if some fanatic or representative of the nonconformist conscience had hunted up evidence against Wilde and brought him to ruin there would have been nothing extraordinary in a vengeance which might have been regarded as a duty. Strange to say the effective hatred of Oscar Wilde was shown by a man of the upper class who was anything but a puritan. It was Mr. Charles Brookfield, I believe, who constituted himself private prosecutor in this case and raked Piccadilly to find witnesses against Oscar Wilde. Mr. Brookfield was afterwards appointed Censor of Plays on the strength apparently of having himself written one of the "riskiest" plays of the period. As I do not know Mr. Brookfield, I will not judge him. But his appointment always seemed to me, even before I knew that he had acted against Wilde, curiously characteristic of English life and of the casual, contemptuous way Englishmen of the governing class regard letters. In the same spirit Lord Salisbury as Prime Minister made a journalist Poet Laureate simply because he had puffed him for years in the columns of *The Standard*. Lord Salisbury probably neither knew nor cared that Alfred Austin had never written a line that could live. One thing Mr. Brookfield's witnesses established: every offence alleged against Oscar Wilde dated from 1892 or later—after his first meeting with Lord Alfred Douglas.

But at the time all such matters were lost for me in the questions: would the authorities arrest Oscar? or would they allow him to escape? Had the police asked for a warrant? Knowing English custom and the desire of Englishmen to pass in silence over all unpleasant sexual matters, I thought he would be given the hint to go abroad and allowed to escape. That is the ordinary, the usual English procedure. Everyone knows the case of a certain lord, notorious for similar practices, who was warned by the police that a warrant had been issued against him; taking the hint he has lived for many years past in leisured ease as an honoured guest in Florence. Nor is it only aristocrats who are so favoured by English justice. Everyone can remember the case of a Canon of Westminster who was similarly warned and also escaped. We can come down the social scale to the very bottom and find the same practice. A certain journalist unwittingly offended a great personage. Immediately he was warned by the police that a warrant issued against him in India seventeen years before would at once be acted upon if he did not make himself scarce. For some time he lived in peaceful retirement in Belgium. Moreover, in all these cases the warrants had been issued on the sworn complaints of the parties damnified or of their parents and guardians. No one had complained of Oscar Wilde. Naturally I thought the dislike of publicity which dictated such lenience to the lord and the canon and the journalist would be even more operative in the case of a man of genius like Oscar Wilde. In certain ways he had a greater position than even the son of a duke. The shocking details of his trial would have an appalling, a world-wide publicity.

Besides, I said to myself, the governing class in England is steeped in aristocratic prejudice, and particularly when threatened by democratic innovations. All superiorities, whether of birth or wealth, or talent, are conscious of the same *raison d'être* and have the same self-interest. The lord, the millionaire and the genius have all the same reason for standing up for each other, and this reason is usually effective. Everyone knows that in England the law is emphatically a respecter of persons. It is not there to promote equality, much less is it the defender of the helpless, the weak and the poor; it is a rampart for the aristocracy and the rich, a whip in the hands of the strong. It is always used to increase the effect of natural and inherited inequality, and it is not directed by a high feeling of justice; but, perverted by aristocratic prejudice and snobbishness, it is not higher than democratic equality, but lower and more sordid.

The case was just a case where an aristocratic society could and should have shown its superiority over a democratic society with its rough rule of equality. For equality is only half-way on the road to justice. More than once the House of Commons has recognized this fundamental truth; it condemned Clive but added that he had rendered "great and distinguished services to his country"; and no one thought of punishing him for his crimes.

Our time is even more tolerant and more corrupt. For a worse crime than extortion Cecil Rhodes was not even brought to trial, but honoured and fêted, while his creatures, who were condemned by the House of Commons Committee, were rewarded by the Government.

Had not Wilde also rendered distinguished services to his country? The wars waged against the Mashonas and Matabeles were a doubtful good; but the plays of Oscar Wilde had already given many hours of innocent pleasure to thousands of persons and were evidently destined to benefit tens of thousands in the future. Such a man is a benefactor of humanity in the best and truest sense and deserves peculiar consideration.

To the society favourite the discredit of the trial with Lord Queensberry was in itself a punishment more than sufficient. Everyone knew when Oscar Wilde left the court that he left it a ruined and disgraced man. Was it worth while to stir up all the foul mud again in order to beat the beaten? Alas! the English are pedants, as Goethe saw; they think little of literary men or of merely spiritual achievements. They love to abide by rules and pay no heed to exceptions, unless indeed the exceptions are men of title or great wealth, or "persons of importance" to the Government. The majority of the people are too ignorant to know the value of a book and they regard poetry as the thistle-down of speech. It does not occur to Englishmen that a phrase may be more valuable and more enduring in its effects than a long campaign and a dozen victories. Yet, the sentence, "Let him that is without sin among you first cast the stone," or Shakespeare's version of the same truth: "if we had our deserts which of us would escape whipping?" is likely to outlast the British Empire, and prove of more value to humanity.

The man of genius in Great Britain is feared and hated in exact proportion to his originality, and if he happens to be a writer or a musician he is despised to boot. The prejudice against Oscar Wilde showed itself virulently on all hands. Mr. Justice Collins did not attempt to restrain the cheering of the court that greeted the success of Lord Queensberry. Not one of the policemen who stood round the door tried to stop the "booing" of the crowd who pursued Oscar Wilde with hootings and vile cries when he left the court. He was judged already and condemned before being tried.

The police, too, acted against him with extraordinary vigour. It has been stated by Mr. Sherard in his "Life" that the police did not attempt to execute the warrant against Wilde, "till after the last train had left for Dover," and that it was only Oscar's obstinacy in remaining in London that necessitated his arrest. This idea is wholly imaginary.

It is worth while to know exactly what took place at this juncture. From Oscar's conduct in this crisis the reader will be able to judge whether he had been depicted faithfully or not in this book. He has been described as amiable, weak, of a charming disposition—easily led in action, though not in thought. Now we shall see how far we were justified, for he is at one of those moments which try the soul. Fortunately every incident of that day is known. Oscar himself told me generally what happened and the minutest details of the picture were filled in for me a little later by his best friend, Robert Ross.

In the morning Mr. Mathews, one of Oscar's counsel, came to him and said: "If you wish it, Clarke and I will keep the case going and give you time to get to Calais."

Oscar refused to stir. "I'll stay," was all he would say. Robert Ross urged him to accept Mathews' offer; but he would not. Why? I am sure he had no reason, for I put the question to him more than once, and even after reflecting, he had no explanation to give. He stayed because to stay was easier than to make an immediate decision and act on it energetically. He had very little will power to begin with, and his mode of life had weakened his original endowment.

After the judgment had been given in favour of Queensberry, Oscar drove off in a brougham, accompanied by Alfred Douglas, to consult with his solicitor, Humphreys. At the same time he gave Ross a cheque on his bank in St. James's Street. At that moment he intended to fly.

Ross noticed that he was followed by a detective. He drew about £200 from the bank and raced off to meet Oscar at the Cadogan Hotel, in Sloane Street, where Lord Alfred Douglas had been staying for the past four or five weeks. Ross reached the Cadogan Hotel about 1.45 and found Oscar there with Reggie Turner. Both of them advised Oscar to go at once to Dover and try to get to France; but he would only say, "the train has gone; it is too late." He had again lapsed into inaction.

He asked Ross to go to see his wife and tell her what had occurred. Ross did this and had a very painful scene: Mrs. Wilde wept and said, "I hope Oscar is going away abroad."

Ross returned to the Cadogan Hotel and told Oscar what his wife had said, but even this didn't move him to action.

He sat as if glued to his chair, and drank hock and seltzer steadily in almost unbroken silence. About four o'clock George Wyndham came to see his cousin, Alfred Douglas; not finding him, he wanted to see Oscar, but Oscar, fearing reproaches, sent Ross instead. Wyndham said it was a pity that Bosie Douglas should be with Oscar, and Ross immediately told him that Wilde's friends for years past had been trying to separate them and that if he, Wyndham, would keep his cousin away, he would be doing Oscar the very greatest kindness. At this Wyndham grew more civil, though still "frightfully agitated", and begged Ross to get Oscar to leave the country at once to avoid scandal. Ross replied that he and Turner had been trying to bring that about for hours. In the middle of the conversation Bosie, having returned, burst into the room with: "I want to see my cousin," and Ross rejoined Oscar. In a quarter of an hour Bosie followed him to say that he was going out with Wyndham to see someone of importance.

About five o'clock a reporter of the *Star* newspaper came to see Oscar, a Mr. Marlowe, who is now editor of *The Daily Mail*, but again Oscar refused to see him and sent Ross. Mr. Marlowe was sympathetic and quite understood the position; he informed Ross that a tape message had come through to the paper saying that a warrant for Oscar Wilde had already been issued. Ross immediately went into the other room and told Oscar, who said nothing, but "went very grey in the face."

A moment later Oscar asked Ross to give him the money he had got at the bank, though he had refused it several times in the course of the day. Ross gave it to him, naturally taking it for a sign that he had at length made up his mind to start, but immediately afterwards Oscar settled down in his chair and said, "I shall stay and do my sentence whatever it is"—a man evidently incapable of action.

For the next hour the trio sat waiting for the blow to fall. Once or twice Oscar asked querulously where Bosie was, but no one could tell him.

At ten past six the waiter knocked at the door and Ross answered it. There were two detectives. The elder entered and said, "We have a warrant here, Mr. Wilde, for your arrest on a charge of committing indecent acts." Wilde wanted to know whether he would be given bail; the detective replied:

"That is a question for the magistrate."

Oscar then rose and asked, "Where shall I be taken?"

"To Bow Street," was the reply.

As he picked up a copy of the Yellow Book and groped for his overcoat, they all noticed that he was "very drunk" though still perfectly conscious of what he was doing.

He asked Ross to go to Tite Street and get him a change of clothes and bring them to Bow Street. The two detectives took him away in a four-wheeler, leaving Ross and Turner on the curb.

Ross hurried to Tite Street. He found that Mrs. Oscar Wilde had gone to the house of a relative and there was only Wilde's man servant, Arthur, in the house, who afterwards went out of his mind, and is still, it is said, in an asylum. He had an intense affection for Oscar. Ross found that Mrs. Oscar Wilde had locked up Oscar's bedroom and study. He burst open the bedroom door and, with the help of Arthur, packed up a change of things. He then hurried to Bow Street, where he found a howling mob shouting indecencies. He was informed by an inspector that it was impossible to see Wilde or to leave any clothes for him.

Ross returned at once to Tite Street, forced open the library door and removed a certain number of letters and manuscripts of Wilde's; but unluckily he couldn't find the two MSS. which he knew had been returned to Tite Street two days before, namely, "A Florentine Tragedy" and the enlarged version of "The Portrait of Mr. W. H."

Ross then drove to his mother's and collapsed. Mrs. Ross insisted that he should go abroad, and in order to induce him to do it gave £500 for Oscar's defence. Ross went to the Terminus Hotel at Calais, where Bosie Douglas joined him a little later. They both stayed there while Oscar was being tried before Mr. Justice Charles and one day George Wyndham crossed the Channel to see Bosie Douglas.

There is of course some excuse to be made for the chief actor. Oscar was physically tired and morally broken. He had pulled the fair building of reputation and success down upon his own head and, with the "booing" of the mob still in his ears, he could think of nothing but the lost hours when he ought to have used his money to take him beyond the reach of his pursuers.

His enemies, on the other hand, had acted with the utmost promptitude. Lord Queensberry's solicitor, Mr. Charles Russell, had stated that it was not his client's intention to take the initiative in any criminal prosecution of Mr. Oscar Wilde, but, on the very same morning when Wilde withdrew from the prosecution, Mr. Russell sent a letter to the Hon. Hamilton Cuffe, the Director of Public Prosecutions, with a copy of "all our witnesses' statements, together with a copy of the shorthand notes of the trial."

The Treasury authorities were at least as eager. As soon as possible after leaving the court Mr. C. F. Gill, Mr. Angus Lewis, and Mr. Charles Russell waited on Sir John Bridge at Bow Street in his private room and obtained a warrant for the arrest of Oscar Wilde, which was executed, as we have seen, the same evening.

The police showed him less than no favour. About eight o'clock Lord Alfred Douglas drove to Bow Street and wanted to know if Wilde could be bailed out, but was informed that his application could not be entertained. He offered to procure comforts for the prisoner. This offer also was peremptorily refused by the police inspector just as Ross' offer of night clothes had been refused. It is a common belief that in England a man is treated as innocent until he has been proved guilty, but those who believe this pleasant fiction, have never been in the hands of the English police. As soon as a man is arrested on any charge he is at once treated as if he were a dangerous criminal; he is searched, for instance, with every circumstance of indignity. Before his conviction a man is allowed to wear his own clothes; but a change of linen or clothes is denied him, or accorded in part and grudgingly, for no earthly reason except to gratify the ill-will of the gaolers.

The warrant on which Oscar Wilde was arrested charged him with an offence alleged to have been committed under Section xi. of the Criminal Amendment Act of 1885; in other words, he was arrested and tried for an offence which was not punishable by law ten years before. This Act was brought in as a result of the shameful and sentimental stories (evidently for the most part manufactured) which Mr. Stead had published in *The Pall Mall Gazette* under the title of "Modern Babylon". In order to cover and justify their prophet some of the "unco guid" pressed forward this so-called legislative reform, by which it was made a criminal offence to take liberties with a girl under thirteen years of age— even with her own consent. Intimacy with minors under sixteen was punishable if they consented or even tempted. Mr. Labouchere, the Radical member, inflamed, it is said, with a desire to make the law ridiculous, gravely proposed that the section be extended, so as to apply to people of the same sex who indulged in familiarities or indecencies. The Puritan faction had no logical objection to the extension, and it became the law of the land. It was by virtue of this piece of legislative wisdom, which is without a model and without a copy in the law of any other civilised country, that Oscar Wilde was arrested and thrown into prison.

His arrest was the signal for an orgy of Philistine rancour such as even London had never known before. The puritan middle class, which had always regarded Wilde with dislike as an artist and intellectual scoffer, a mere parasite of the aristocracy, now gave free scope to their disgust and contempt, and everyone tried to outdo his neighbour in expressions of loathing and abhorrence. This middle class condemnation swept the lower class away in its train. To do them justice, the common people, too, felt a natural loathing for the peculiar vice attributed to Wilde; most men condemn the sins they have no mind to; but their dislike was rather contemptuous than profound, and with customary humour they soon turned the whole case into a bestial, obscene joke. "Oscar" took the place of their favourite word as a term of contempt, and they shouted it at each other on all sides; bus-drivers, cabbies and paper sellers using it in and out of season with the keenest relish. For the moment the upper classes lay mum-chance and let the storm blow over. Some of them of course agreed with the condemnation of the Puritans, and many of them felt that Oscar and his associates had been too bold and ought to be pulled up.

The English journals, which are nothing but middle-class shops, took the side of their patrons. Without a single exception they outdid themselves in condemnation of the man and all his works. You might have thought to read their bitter diatribes that they themselves lived saintly lives, and were shocked at sensual sin. One rubbed one's eyes in amazement. The Strand and Fleet Street, which practically belong to this class and have been fashioned by them, are the haunt of as vile a prostitution as can be found in Europe; the public houses which these men frequent are low drinking dens; yet they all lashed Oscar Wilde with every variety of insult as if they themselves had been above reproach. The whole of London seemed to have broken loose in a rage of contempt and loathing which was whipped up and justified each morning by the hypocritical articles of the "unco guid" in the daily this and the weekly that. In the streets one heard everywhere the loud jests of the vulgar, decked out with filthy anecdotes and punctuated by obscene laughter, as from the mouth of the Pit.

In spite of the hatred of the journalists pandering to the prejudice of their paymasters, one could hope still that the magistrate would show some regard for fair play. The expectation, reasonable or unreasonable, was doomed to disappointment. On Saturday morning, the 6th, Oscar Wilde, "described as a gentleman," the papers said in derision, was brought before Sir John Bridge. Mr. C. F. Gill, who had been employed in the Queensberry trial, was instructed by Mr. Angus Lewis of the Treasury, and conducted the prosecution; Alfred Taylor was placed in the dock charged with conspiracy with Oscar Wilde. The witnesses have already been described in connection with the Queensberry case. Charles Parker, William Parker, Alfred Wood, Sidney Mavor and Shelley all gave evidence.

After lasting all day the case was adjourned till the following Thursday.

Mr. Travers Humphreys applied for bail for Mr. Wilde, on the ground that he knew the warrant against him was being applied for on Friday afternoon, but he made no attempt to leave London. Sir John Bridge refused bail.

On Thursday, the 11th, the case was continued before Sir John Bridge, and in the end both the accused were committed for trial. Again Mr. Humphreys applied for bail, and again the magistrate refused to accept bail.

Now to refuse bail in cases of serious crime may be defended, but in the case of indecent conduct it is usually granted. To run away is regarded as a confession of guilt, and what could one wish for more than the perpetual banishment of the corrupt liver, consequently there is no reason to refuse bail. But in this case, though bail was offered to any amount, it was refused peremptorily in spite of the fact that every consideration should have been shown to an accused person who had already had a good opportunity to leave the country and had refused to budge. Moreover, Oscar Wilde had already been criticised and condemned in a hundred papers. There was widespread prejudice against him, no risk to the public in accepting bail, and considerable injury done to the accused in refusing it. His affairs were certain to be thrown into confusion; he was known not to be rich and yet he was deprived of the power to get money together and to collect evidence just when the power which freedom confers was most needed by him.

The magistrate was as prejudiced as the public; he had no more idea of standing for justice and fair play than Pilate; probably, indeed, he never gave himself the trouble to think of fairness in the matter. A large salary is paid to magistrates in London, £1,500 a year, but it is rare indeed that any of them rises above the vulgarest prejudice. Sir John Bridge not only refused bail but he was careful to give his reasons for refusing it. He had not the slightest scruple about prejudicing the case even before he had heard a word of the defence. After hearing the evidence for the prosecution he said:

"The responsibility of accepting or refusing bail rests upon me. The considerations that weigh with me are the gravity of the offenses and the strength of the evidence. I must absolutely refuse bail and send the prisoners for trial."

Now these reasons, which he proffered voluntarily, and especially the use of the word "absolutely," showed not only prejudice on the part of Sir John Bridge, but the desire to injure the unfortunate prisoner in the public mind and so continue the evil work of the journalists.

The effect of this prejudice and rancour on the part of the whole community had various consequences.

The mere news that Oscar Wilde had been arrested and taken to Holloway startled London and gave the signal for a strange exodus. Every train to Dover was crowded; every steamer to Calais thronged with members of the aristocratic and leisured classes, who seemed to prefer Paris, or even Nice out of the season, to a city like London, where the police might act with such unexpected vigour. The truth was that the cultured æsthetes whom I have already described had been thunderstruck by the facts which the Queensberry trial had laid bare. For the first time they learned that such houses as Taylor's were under police supervision, and that creatures like Wood and Parker were classified and watched. They had imagined that in "the home of liberty" such practices passed unnoticed. It came as a shock to their pre-conceived ideas that the police in London knew a great many things which they were not supposed to concern themselves with, and this unwelcome glare of light drove the vicious forth in wild haste.

Never was Paris so crowded with members of the English governing classes; here was to be seen a famous ex-Minister; there the fine face of the president of a Royal society; at one table in the Café de la Paix, a millionaire recently ennobled, and celebrated for his exquisite taste in art; opposite to him a famous general. It was even said that a celebrated English actor took a return ticket for three or four days to Paris, just to be in the fashion. The mummer returned quickly; but the majority of the migrants stayed abroad for some time. The wind of terror which had swept them across the Channel opposed their return, and they scattered over the Continent from Naples to Monte Carlo and from Palermo to Seville under all sorts of pretexts.

The gravest result of the magistrate's refusal to accept bail was purely personal. Oscar's income dried up at the source. His books were withdrawn from sale; no one went to see his plays; every shop keeper to whom he owed a penny took immediate action against him. Judgments were obtained and an execution put into his house in Tite Street. Within a month, at the very moment when he most needed money to fee counsel and procure evidence, he was beggared and sold up and, because of his confinement in prison, the sale was conducted under such conditions that, whereas in ordinary times his effects would have covered the claims against him three times over, all his belongings went for nothing, and the man who was making £4,000 or £5,000 a year by his plays was adjudicated a bankrupt for a little over £1,000. £600 of this sum were for Lord Queensberry's costs which the Queensberry family—Lord Douglas of Hawick, Lord Alfred Douglas and their mother—had promised in writing to pay, but when the time came, absolutely refused to pay. Most unfortunately many of Oscar's MSS. were stolen or lost in the disorder of the sheriff's legal proceedings. Wilde could have cried, with Shylock "You take my life when you do take away the means whereby I live." But at the time nine Englishmen out of ten applauded what was practically persecution.

A worse thing remains to be told. The right of free speech

which Englishmen pride themselves on had utterly disappeared, as it always does disappear in England when there is most need of it. It was impossible to say one word in Wilde's defence or even in extenuation of his sin in any London print. At this time I owned the greater part of the *Saturday Review* and edited it. Here at any rate one might have thought I could have set forth in a Christian country a sane and liberal view. I had no wish to minimise the offence. No one condemned unnatural vice more than I, but Oscar Wilde was a distinguished man of letters; he had written beautiful things, and his good works should have been allowed to speak in his favour. I wrote an article setting forth this view. My printers immediately informed me that they thought the article ill-advised, and when I insisted they said they would prefer not to print it. Yet there was nothing in it beyond a plea to suspend judgment and defer insult till after the trial. Messrs. Smith and Sons, the great booksellers, who somehow got wind of the matter (through my publisher, I believe), sent to say that they would not sell any paper that attempted to defend Oscar Wilde; it would be better even, they added, not to mention his name. The English tradesman-censors were determined that this man should have Jedburg justice. I should have ruined the *Saturday Review* by the mere attempt to treat the matter fairly.

In this extremity I went to the great leader of public opinion in England. Mr. Arthur Walter, the manager of *The Times*, had always been kind to me; he was a man of balanced mind, who had taken high honours at Oxford in his youth, and for twenty years had rubbed shoulders with the leading men in every rank of life. I went down to stay with him in Berkshire, and I urged upon him what I regarded as the aristocratic view. In England it was manifest that under the circumstances there was no chance of a fair trial, and it seemed to me the duty of *The Times* to say plainly that this man should not be condemned beforehand, and that if he were condemned, his merits should be taken into consideration in his punishment, as well as his demerits.

While willing to listen to me, Mr. Walter did not share my views. A man who had written a great poem or a great play did not rank in his esteem with a man who had won a skirmish against a handful of unarmed savages, or one who had stolen a piece of land from some barbarians and annexed it to the Empire. In his

heart he held the view of the English landed aristocracy, that
the ordinary successful general or admiral or statesman was infinitely more important than a Shakespeare or a Browning. He
could not be persuaded to believe that the names of Gladstone,
Disraeli, Wolseley, Roberts, and Wood would diminish and fade
from day to day till in a hundred years they would scarcely be
known, even to the educated; whereas the fame of Browning,
Swinburne, Meredith, or even Oscar Wilde, would increase and
grow brighter with time, till, in one hundred or five hundred
years, no one would dream of comparing pushful politicians like
Gladstone or Beaconsfield with men of genius like Swinburne
or Wilde. He simply would not see it and when he perceived
that the weight of argument was against him he declared that if
it were true, it was so much the worse for humanity. In his opinion anyone living a clean life was worth more than a writer of
love songs or the maker of clever comedies—Mr. John Smith
worth more than Shakespeare!

He was as deaf as only Englishmen can be deaf to the plea for
abstract justice.

"You don't even say Wilde's innocent," he threw at me more
than once.

"I believe him to be innocent," I declared truthfully, "but it
is better that a hundred guilty men go free than that one man
should not have a fair trial. And how can this man have a fair
trial now when the papers for weeks past have been filled with
violent diatribes against him and his works?"

One point, peculiarly English, he used again and again.

"So long as substantial justice is done," he said, "it is all we care
about."

"Substantial justice will never be done," I cried, "so long as
that is your ideal. Your arrow can never go quite so high as it is
aimed." But I got no further.

If Oscar Wilde had been a general or a so-called empire builder,
The Times might have affronted public opinion and called attention to his virtues, and argued that they should be taken in
extenuation of his offences; but as he was only a writer no one
seemed to owe him anything or to care what became of him.

Mr. Walter was fair-minded in comparison with most men of
his class. There was staying with him at this very time an Irish

gentleman, who listened to my pleading for Wilde with ill-concealed indignation. Excited by Arthur Walter's obstinacy to find fresh arguments, I pointed out that Wilde's offence was pathological and not criminal and would not be punished in a properly constituted state.

"You admit," I said, "that we punish crime to prevent it spreading; wipe this sin off the statute book and you would not increase the sinners by one. Then why punish them?"

"Oi'd whip such sinners to death, so I would," cried the Irishman; "hangin's too good for them."

"You only punished lepers," I went on, "in the middle ages, because you believed that leprosy was catching; this malady is not even catching."

"Faith, Oi'd punish it with extermination," cried the Irishman.

Exasperated by the fact that his idiot prejudice was hurting my friend, I said at length with a smile:

"You are very bitter. I'm not; you see, I have no sexual jealousy to inflame me."

On this Mr. Walter had to interfere between us to keep the peace, but the mischief was done. My advocacy remained without effect.

It is very curious how deep-rooted and enduring is the prejudice against writers in England. Not only is no attempt made to rate them at their true value, at the value which posterity puts upon their work; but they are continually treated as outcasts and denied the most ordinary justice. The various trials of Oscar Wilde are to the thinker an object lesson in the force of this prejudice, but some may explain the prejudice against Wilde on the score of the peculiar abhorrence with which the offence ascribed to him is regarded in England.

Let me take an example from the papers of to-day—I am writing in January, 1910. I find in my *Daily Mail* that at Bow Street police court a London magistrate, Sir Albert de Rutzen, ordered the destruction of 272 volumes of the English translation of Balzac's "Les Contes Drolatiques" on the ground that the book was obscene. "Les Contes Drolatiques" is an acknowledged masterpiece, and is not nearly so free spoken as "Lear" or "Hamlet" or "Tom Jones" or "Anthony and Cleopatra". What would be thought of a French magistrate or a German magistrate who ordered a fair translation of "Hamlet" or of "Lear" to be burnt, because of its obscenity? He would be regarded as demented. One can only understand such a judgment as an isolated fact. But in England this monstrous stupidity is the rule. Sir A. de Rutzen was not satisfied with ordering the books to be burnt and fining the bookseller; he went on to justify his condemnation and praise the police:

"It is perfectly clear to my mind that a more foul and filthy black spot has not been found in London for a long time, and the police have done uncommonly well in bringing the matter to light. I consider that the books are likely to do a great deal of harm."

Fancy the state of mind of the man who can talk such poisonous nonsense; who, with the knowledge of what Piccadilly is at night in his mind, can speak of the translation of a masterpiece as one of the "most filthy black spots" to be found in London. To say that such a man is insane is, I suppose, going too far; but to say that he does not know the value or the meaning of the words he uses, to say that he is driven by an extraordinary and brainless prejudice, is certainly the modesty of truth.

It is this sort of perversity on the part of Sir A. de Rutzen and of nine out of ten Englishmen that makes Frenchmen, Germans and Italians speak of them as ingrained hypocrites. But they are not nearly so hypocritical as they are uneducated and unintelligent, rebellious to the humanising influence of art and literature. The ordinary Englishman would much prefer to be called an athlete than a poet. The Puritan Commonwealth Parliament ordered the pictures of Charles I. to be sold, but such of them as were indecent to be burnt; accordingly half a dozen Titians were solemnly burnt and the nucleus of a great national gallery destroyed. One can see Sir A. de Rutzen solemnly assisting at this holocaust and devoutly deciding that all the masterpieces which showed temptingly a women's beautiful breasts were "foul and filthy black spots" and must be burnt as harmful. Or rather one can see that Sir A. de Rutzen has in two and a half centuries managed to get a little beyond this primitive Puritan standpoint. He might allow a pictorial masterpiece to-day to pass unburnt, but a written masterpiece is still to him anathema.

A part of this prejudice comes from the fact that the English have a special dislike for every form of sexual indulgence. It is not consistent with their ideal of manhood and, like the poor foolish magistrate, they have not yet grasped the truth, which one might have thought the example of the Japanese would have made plain by now to the dullest, that a nation may be extraordinarily brave, vigorous and self-sacrificing and at the same time intensely sensuous, and sensitive to every refinement of passion. If the great English middle class were as well educated as the German middle class, such a judgment as this of Sir A. de Rutzen would be scouted as ridiculous and absurd, or rather would be utterly unthinkable.

In Anglo-Saxon countries both the artist and the sexual passion are under a ban. The race is more easily moved martially than amorously and it regards its overpowering combative instincts as virtuous just as it is apt to despise what it likes to call "languishing love." The poet Middleton couldn't put his dream city in England —a city of fair skies and fairer streets:

> And joy was there; in all the city's length
> I saw no fingers trembling for the sword;
> Nathless they doted on their bodies' strength,
> That they might gentler be. Love was their lord.

Both America and England to-day offer terrifying examples of the despotism of an unenlightened and vulgar public opinion in all the highest concerns of man—in art, in literature and in religion. There is no despotism on earth so soul-destroying to the artist; it is baser and more degrading than anything known in Russia. The consequences of this tyranny of an uneducated middle class and a barbarian aristocracy are shown in detail in the trial of Oscar Wilde and in the savagery with which he was treated by the English officers of justice.

15

The Queen vs. Wilde: the First Trial

As soon as I heard that Oscar Wilde was arrested and bail refused, I tried to get permission to visit him in Holloway. I was told I should have to see him in a kind of barred cage and talk to him from the distance of at least a yard. It seemed to me too painful for both of us, so I went to the higher authorities and got permission to see him in a private room. The Governor met me at the entrance of the prison. To my surprise he was more than courteous; charmingly kind and sympathetic.

"We all hope," he said, "that he will soon be free; this is no place for him. Everyone likes him, everyone. It is a great pity."

He evidently felt much more than he said, and my heart went out to him. He left me in a bare room furnished with a small square deal table and two kitchen chairs. In a moment or two Oscar came in accompanied by a warder. In silence we clasped hands. He looked miserably anxious and pulled down and I felt that I had nothing to do but cheer him up.

"I am glad to see you," I cried. "I hope the warders are kind to you?"

"Yes, Frank," he replied in a hopeless way, "but everyone else is against me. It is hard."

"Don't harbour that thought," I answered; "many whom you don't know, and whom you will never know, are on your side.

Stand for them and for the myriads who are coming afterwards and make a fight of it."

"I'm afraid I'm not a fighter, Frank, as you once said," he replied sadly, "and they won't give me bail. How can I get evidence or think in this place of torture? Fancy refusing me bail," he went on, "though I stayed in London when I might have gone abroad."

"You should have gone," I cried in French, hot with indignation; "why didn't you go, the moment you came out of the court?"

"I couldn't think at first," he answered in the same tongue; "I couldn't think at all. I was numbed."

"Your friends should have thought of it," I insisted, not knowing then that they had done their best.

At this moment the warder, who had turned away towards the door, came back.

"You are not allowed, sir, to talk in a foreign language," he said quietly. "You will understand we have to obey the rules. Besides, the prisoner must not speak of this prison as a place of torture. I ought to report that; I'm sorry."

The misery of it all brought tears to my eyes. His gaolers even felt sorry for him. I thanked the warder and turned again to Oscar.

"Don't let yourself fear at all," I exclaimed. "You will have your chance again and must take it; only don't lose heart and don't be witty next time in court. The jury hate it. They regard it as intellectual superiority and impudence. Treat all things seriously and with grave dignity. Defend yourself as David would have defended his love for Jonathan. Make them all listen to you. I would undertake to get free with half your talent even if I were guilty; a resolution not to be beaten is always half the battle. . . . Make your trial memorable from your entrance into the court to the decision of the jury. Use every opportunity and give your real character a chance to fight for you."

I spoke with tears in my eyes and rage in my heart.

"I will do my best, Frank," he said despondingly, "I will do my best. If I were out of this place, I might think of something, but it is dreadful to be here. One has to go to bed by daylight and the nights are interminable."

"Haven't you a watch?" I cried.

"They don't allow you to have a watch in prison," he replied.

"But why not?" I asked in amazement. I did not know that every rule in an English prison is cunningly devised to annoy and degrade the unfortunate prisoner.

Oscar lifted his hands hopelessly:

"One may not smoke; not even a cigarette; and so I cannot sleep. All the past comes back; the golden hours; the June days in London with the sunshine dappling the grass and the silken rustling of the wind in the trees. Do you remember Wordsworth speaks 'of the wind in the trees'? How I wish I could hear it now, breathe it once again. I might get strength then to fight."

"Is the food good?" I asked.

"It's all right; I get it from outside. The food doesn't matter. It is the smoking I miss, the freedom, the companionship. My mind will not act when I'm alone. I can only think of what has been and torment myself. Already I've been punished enough for the sins of a lifetime."

"Is there nothing I can do for you, nothing you want?" I asked.

"No, Frank," he answered, "it was kind of you to come to see me, I wish I could tell you how kind."

"Don't think of it," I said; "if I'm any good send for me at any moment. A word will bring me. They allow you books, don't they?"

"Yes, Frank."

"I wish you would get the 'Apologia of Plato'," I said, "and take a big draught of that deathless smiling courage of Socrates."

"Ah, Frank, how much more humane were the Greeks. They let his friends see him and talk to him by the hour, though he was condemned to death. There were no warders there to listen, no degrading conditions."

"Quite true," I cried, suddenly realising how much better Oscar Wilde would have been treated in Athens two thousand years ago. "Our progress is mainly change; we don't shed our cruelty; even Christ has not been able to humanise us."

He nodded his head. At first he seemed greatly distressed; but I managed to encourage him a little, for at the close of the talk he questioned me:

"Do you really think I may win, Frank?"

"Of course you'll win," I replied. "You must win. You must not think of being beaten. Take it that they will not want to convict you. Say it to yourself in court; don't let yourself fear for a moment. Your enemies are merely stupid, unhappy creatures crawling about for a few miserable years between earth and sun, fated to die and leave no trace, no memory. Remember you are fighting for all of us, for every artist and thinker who is to be born into the English world. . . . It is better to win like Galileo than to be burnt like Giordano Bruno. Don't let them make another martyr. Use all your brains and eloquence and charm. Don't be afraid. They will not condemn you if they know you."

"I have been trying to think," he said, "trying to make up my mind to bear one whole year of this life. It's dreadful, Frank, I had no idea that prison was so dreadful."

The warder again drew his brows. I hastened to change the subject.

"That's why you must resolve not to have any more of it," I said; "I wish I had seen you when you came out of court, but I really thought you didn't want me; you turned away from me."

"Oh, Frank, how could I?" he cried. "I should have been so grateful to you."

"I'm very shortsighted," I rejoined, "and I thought you did. It is our foolish little vanities which prevent us acting as we should. But let me know if I can do anything for you. If you want me, I'll come at any moment."

I said this because the warder had already given me a sign; he now said:

"Time is up."

Once again we clasped hands.

"You must win," I said; "don't think of defeat. Even your enemies are human. Convert them. You can do it, believe me," and I went with dread in my heart, and pity and indignation.

> Be still, be still, my soul; it is but for a season:
> Let us endure an hour and see injustice done.

The Governor met me almost at the door.

"It is terrible," I exclaimed.

"This is no place for him," he answered. "He has nothing to do with us here. Everyone likes him and pities him; the warders, everyone. Anything I can do to make his stay tolerable shall be done."

We shook hands. I think there were tears in both our eyes as we parted. This humane Governor had taught me that Oscar's gentleness and kindness—his sweetness of nature—would win all hearts if it had time to make itself known. Yet there he was in prison. His face and figure came before me again and again; the unshaven face; the frightened, sad air; the hopeless, toneless voice. The cleanliness even of the bare hard room was ugly; the English are foolish enough to degrade those they punish. Revolt was blazing in me.

As I went away I looked up at the mediæval castellated gateway of the place, and thought how perfectly the architecture suited the spirit of the institution. The whole thing belongs to the middle ages, and not to our modern life. Fancy having both prison and hospital side by side; indeed a hospital even in the prison; torture and lovingkindness; punishment and pity under the same roof. What a blank contradiction and stupidity. Will civilisation never reach humane ideals? Will men always punish most severely the sins they do not understand and which hold for them no temptation? Did Jesus suffer in vain?

.   .   .   .

Oscar Wilde was committed on the 19th of April; a "true bill" was found against him by the grand jury on the 24th; and, as the case was put down for trial at the Old Bailey almost immediately, a postponement was asked for till the May sessions, on the ground first that the defence had not had time to prepare their case and further, that in the state of popular feeling at the moment, Mr. Wilde would not get a fair and impartial trial. Mr. Justice Charles, who was to try the case, heard the application and refused it peremptorily: "Any suggestion that the defendant would not have a fair trial was groundless," he declared; yet he knew better. In his summing up of the case on May 1st he stated that "for weeks it had been impossible to open a newspaper without reading some reference to the case," and when he asked the jury not to allow "preconceived opinions to weigh with them" he was admitting the truth that every newspaper reference was charged with dislike and contempt of Oscar Wilde. A fair trial indeed! The trial took place at the Old Bailey, three days later, April 27th, 1895, before Mr. Justice Charles. Mr. C. F. Gill and A. Gill with Mr. Horace Avory appeared for the Public Prosecutor. Mr. Wilde was again defended by Sir Edward Clarke, Mr. Charles Mathews and Mr. Travers Humphreys, while Mr. J. P. Grain and Mr. Paul Taylor were counsel for the other prisoner. The trial began on a Saturday and the whole of the day was taken up with a legal argument. I am not going to give the details of the case. I shall only note the chief features of it and the unfairness which characterised it.

Sir Edward Clarke pointed out that there was one set of charges under the Criminal Law Amendment Act and another set of charges of conspiracy. He urged that the charges of conspiracy should be dropped. Under the counts alleging conspiracy, the defendants could not be called on as witnesses, which put the defence at a disadvantage. In the end the Judge decided that there were inconveniences; but he would not accede to Sir Edward Clarke's request. Later in the trial, however, Mr. Gill himself withdrew the charges of conspiracy, and the Judge admitted explicitly in his summing up that, if he had known the evidence which was to be offered, he would not have allowed these charges of conspiracy to be made. By this confession he apparently cleared his conscience just as Pilate washed his hands. But the wrong had already been done. Not only did this charge of conspiracy embarrass the defence, but if it had never been made, as it should never have been made, then Sir Edward Clarke would have insisted and could have insisted properly that the two men should be tried separately, and Wilde would not have been discredited by being coupled with Taylor, whose character was notorious and who had already been in the hands of the police on a similar charge.

This was not the only instance of unfairness in the conduct of the prosecution. The Treasury put a youth called Atkins in the box, thus declaring him to be at least a credible witness; but Atkins was proved by Sir Edward Clarke to have perjured himself in the court in the most barefaced way. In fact the Treasury witnesses against Wilde were all blackmailers and people of the lowest character, with two exceptions. The exceptions were a boy named Mavor and a youth named Shelley. With regard to Mavor the judge admitted that no evidence had been offered that he could place before the jury; but in his summing up he was greatly affected by the evidence of Shelley. Shelley was a young man who seemed to be afflicted with a species of religious mania. Mr. Justice Charles gave great weight to his testimony. He invited the jury to say that "although there was, in his correspondence which had been read, evidence of excitability, to talk of him as a young man who did not know what he was saying was to exaggerate the effect of his letters." He went on to ask with much solemnity: "Why should this young man have invented a tale, which must have been unpleasant to him to present from the witness box?"

In the later trial before Mr. Justice Wills the Judge had to rule out the evidence of Shelley *in toto*, because it was wholly without corroboration. If the case before Mr. Justice Charles had not been confused with the charges of conspiracy, there is no doubt that he too would have ruled out the evidence of Shelley, and then his summing up must have been entirely in favour of Wilde.

The singular malevolence of the prosecution also can be estimated by their use of the so-called "literary argument." Wilde had written in a magazine called *The Chameleon*. *The Chameleon* contained an immoral story, with which Wilde had nothing to do, and which he had repudiated as offensive. Yet the prosecution tried to make him responsible in some way for the immorality of a writing which he knew nothing about.

Wilde had said two poems of Lord Alfred Douglas were "beautiful." The prosecution declared that these poems were in essence a defence of the vilest immorality, but is it not possible for the most passionate poem, even the most vicious, to be "beautiful"? Nothing was ever written more passionate than one of the poems of Sappho. Yet a fragment has been selected out and preserved by the admiration of a hundred generations of men. The prosecution was in the position all the time of one who declared that a man who praised a nude picture must necessarily be immoral. Such a contention would be inconceivable in any other civilised country. Even the Judge was on much the same intellectual level. It would not be fair, he admitted, to condemn a poet or dramatic writer by his works and he went on:

"It is unfortunately true that while some of our greatest writers have passed long years in writing nothing but the most wholesome literature—literature of the highest genius, and which anybody can read, such as the literature of Sir Walter Scott and Charles Dickens; it is also true that there were other great writers, more especially in the eighteenth century, perfectly noble-minded men themselves, who somehow or other have permitted themselves to pen volumes which it is painful for persons of ordinary modesty and decency to read."

It would have been more honest and more liberal to have brushed away the nonsensical indictment in a sentence. Would the Treasury have put Shakespeare on trial for "Hamlet" or "Lear," or would they have condemned the writer of "The Song of Solomon" for immorality, or sent St. Paul to prison for his "Epistle to the Corinthians"?

Middle-class prejudice and hypocritic canting twaddle from Judge and advocate dragged their weary length along for days and days. On Wednesday Sir Edward Clarke made his speech for the defence. He pointed out the unfairness of the charges of conspiracy which had tardily been withdrawn. He went on to say that the most remarkable characteristic of the case was the fact that it had been the occasion for conduct on the part of certain sections of the press which was disgraceful and which imperilled the administration of justice and was in the highest degree injurious to the client for whom he was pleading. Nothing, he concluded, could be more unfair than the way Mr. Wilde had been criticised in the press for weeks and weeks. But no judge interfered on his behalf.

Sir Edward Clarke evidently thought that to prove unfairness would not even influence the minds of the London jury. He was content to repudiate the attempts to judge Mr. Wilde by his books or by an article which he had condemned, or by poems which he had not written. He laid stress on the fact that Mr. Wilde had himself brought the charge against Lord Queeensberry which had provoked the whole investigation: "on March 30th, Mr. Wilde," he said, "knew the catalogue of accusations"; and he asked: did the jury believe that, if he had been guilty, he would have stayed in England and brought about the first trial? Insane would hardly be the word for such conduct, if Mr. Wilde really had been guilty. Moreover, before even hearing the specific accusations, Mr. Wilde had gone into the witness box to deny them.

Clarke's speech was a good one, but nothing out of the common; no new arguments were used in it; not one striking illustration.

Needless to say the higher advocacy of sympathy was conspicuous by its absence.

Again, the interesting part of the trial was the cross-examination of Oscar Wilde.

Mr. Gill examined him at length on the two poems which Lord Alfred Douglas had contributed to *The Chameleon*, which Mr. Wilde had called "beautiful." The first was in "Praise of Shame," the second was one called "Two Loves." Sir Edward Clarke, interposing, said:

"That's not Mr. Wilde's, Mr. Gill."

Mr. Gill: "I am not aware that I said it was."

Sir Edward Clarke: "I thought you would be glad to say it was not."

Mr. Gill insisted that Mr. Wilde should explain the poem in "Praise of Shame."

Mr. Wilde said that the first poem seemed obscure, but, when pressed as to the "love" described in the second poem, he let himself go for the first time and perhaps the only time during the trial; he said:

"The 'love' that dare not speak its name in this century is such a great affection of an older for a younger man as there was between David and Jonathan, such as Plato made the very base of his philosophy and such as you find in the sonnets of Michaelangelo and Shakespeare—a deep spiritual affection that is as pure as it is perfect and dictates great works of art like those of Shakespeare and Michaelangelo and those two letters of mine, such as they are, and which is in this century misunderstood—so misunderstood that, on account of it, I am placed where I am now. It is beautiful; it is fine; it is the noblest form of affection. It is intellectual, and it repeatedly exists between an elder and younger man, when the elder man has intellect, and the younger man has all the joy, hope and glamour of life. That it should be so the world does not understand. It mocks at it and sometimes puts one into the pillory for it."

At this stage there was loud applause in the gallery of the court, and the learned Judge at once said: "I shall have the Court cleared if there is the slightest manifestation of feeling. There must be complete silence preserved."

Mr. Justice Charles repressed the cheering in favour of Mr.

Oscar Wilde with great severity, though Mr. Justice Collins did not attempt to restrain the cheering which filled his court and accompanied the dispersing crowd into the street on the acquittal of Lord Queensberry.

In spite, however, of the unfair criticisms of the press; in spite of the unfair conduct of the prosecution, and in spite of the manifest prejudice and Philistine ignorance of the Judge, the jury disagreed.

Then followed the most dramatic incident of the whole trial. Once more Sir Edward Clarke applied for bail on behalf of Oscar Wilde. "After what has happened," he said, "I do not think the Crown will make any objection to this application." The Crown left the matter to the Judge, no doubt in all security; for the Judge immediately refused the application. Sir Edward Clarke then went on to say that, in the case of a re-trial, it ought not to take place immediately. He continued:

"The burden of those engaged in the case is very heavy, and I think it only right that the Treasury should have an opportunity between this and another session of considering the mode in which the case should be presented, if indeed it is presented at all."

Mr. Gill immediately rose to the challenge.

"The case will certainly be tried again," he declared, "whether it is to be tried again at once or in the next sessions will be a matter of convenience. Probably the most desirable course will be for the case to go the next sessions. That is the usual course."

Mr. Justice Charles: "If that is the usual course, let it be so."

The next session of the Central Criminal Court opened on the 20th of the same month.

Not three weeks' respite, still it might be enough. It was inconceivable that a Judge in Chambers would refuse to accept bail. Fortunately the law allows him no option.

. . . .

The application for bail was made in due course to a Judge in Chambers, and in spite of the bad example of the magistrate, and of Mr. Justice Charles, it was granted and Wilde was set free on his own recognizance of £2,500 with two other sureties for £1,250 each. It spoke volumes for the charm and fascination of the man that people were found to undertake this onerous responsibility. Their names deserve to be recorded; one was Lord Douglas of Hawick, the other a clergyman, the Rev. Stewart Headlam. I offered to be one bail; but I was not a householder at the time and my name was, therefore, not acceptable. I suppose the Treasury objected, which shows, I am inclined to think, some glimmering of sense on its part.

As soon as the bail was accepted I began to think of preparations for Oscar's escape. It was high time something was done to save him from the wolves. The day after his release a London morning journal was not ashamed to publish what it declared was a correct analysis of the voting of the jury on the various counts. According to this authority, ten jurors were generally for conviction and two against, in the case of Wilde; the statement was widely accepted because it added that the voting was more favourable to Taylor than to Wilde, which was so unexpected and so senseless that it carried with it a certain plausibility: *Credo quia incredible.*

I had seen enough of English justice and English judges and English journals to convince me that Oscar Wilde had no more chance of a fair trial than if he had been an Irish "Invincible". Everyone had made up his mind and would not even listen to reason. He was practically certain to be convicted, and if convicted perfectly certain to be punished with savage ferocity. The judge would probably think he was showing impartiality by punishing him for his qualities of charm and high intelligence. For the first time in my life I understood the full significance of Montaigne's confession that if he were accused of stealing the towers of Notre Dame, he would fly the kingdom rather than risk a trial, and Montaigne was a lawyer. I set to work at once to complete my preparations.

I did not think I ran any risk in helping Oscar to get away. The newspapers had seized the opportunity of the trials before the magistrate and before Mr. Justice Charles and had overwhelmed the public with such a sea of nauseous filth and impurity as could only be exposed to the public nostrils in pudibund England. Everyone, I thought, must be sick of the testimony and eager to have done with the whole thing. In this I may have been mistaken. The hatred of Wilde seemed universal and extraordinarily malignant.

I wanted a steam yacht. Curiously enough on the very day when

I was thinking of running down to Cowes to hire one, a gentleman at lunch mentioned that he had one in the Thames. I asked him could I charter it?

"Certainly," he replied, "and I will let you have it for the bare cost for the next month or two."

"One month will do for me," I said.

"Where are you going?" he asked.

I don't know why, but a thought came into my head: I would tell him the truth, and see what he would say. I took him aside and told him the bare facts. At once he declared that the yacht was at my service for such work as that without money. He would be too glad to lend it to me. It was horrible that such a man as Wilde should be treated as a common criminal.

He felt as Henry VIII felt in Shakespeare's play of that name:

> ". . . . there's some of ye, I see,
> More out of malice than integrity,
> Would try him to the utmost, ..."

It was not the generosity in my friend's offer that astonished me, but the consideration for Wilde; I thought the lenity so singular in England that I feel compelled to explain it. Though an Englishman born and bred my friend was by race a Jew—a man of the widest culture, who had no sympathy whatever with the vice attributed to Oscar. Feeling consoled because there was at least one generous, kind heart in the world, I went next day to Willie Wilde's house in Oakley Street to see Oscar. I had written to him on the previous evening that I was coming to take Oscar out to lunch.

Willie Wilde met me at the door; he was much excited apparently by the notoriety attaching to Oscar; he was volubly eager to tell me that, though we had not been friends, yet my support of Oscar was most friendly and he would therefore bury the hatchet. He had never interested me, and I was unconscious of any hatchet and careless whether he buried it or blessed it. I repeated drily that I had come to take Oscar to lunch.

"I know you have," he said, "and it's most kind of you; but he can't go."

"Why not?" I asked as I went in.

Oscar was gloomy, depressed, and evidently suffering. Willie's theatrical insincerity had annoyed me a little, and I was eager to get away. Suddenly I saw Sherard, who has since done his best for Oscar's memory. In his book there is a record of this visit of mine. He was standing silently by the wall.

"I've come to take you to lunch," I said to Oscar.

"But he cannot go out," cried Willie.

"Of course he can," I insisted, "I've come to take him."

"But where to?" asked Willie.

"Yes, Frank, where to?" repeated Oscar meekly.

"Anywhere you like," I said, "the Savoy if you life, the Café Royal for choice."

"Oh, Frank, I dare not," cried Oscar.

"No, no," cried Willie, "there would be a scandal; someone'll insult him and it would do harm; set people's backs up."

"Oh, Frank, I dare not," echoed Oscar.

"No one will insult him. There will be no scandal," I replied, "and it will do good."

"But what will people say?" cried Willie.

"No one ever knows what people will say," I retorted, "and people always speak best of those who don't care a damn what they do say."

"Oh, Frank, I could not go to a place like the Savoy where I am well known," objected Oscar.

"All right," I agreed, "you shall go where you like. All London is before us. I must have a talk with you, and it will do you good to get out into the air, and sun yourself and feel the wind in your face. Come, there's a hansom at the door."

It was not long before I had conquered his objections and Willie's absurdities and taken him with me. Scarcely had we left the house when his spirits began to lift, and he rippled into laughter.

"Really, Frank, it is strange, but I do not feel frightened and depressed any more, and the people don't boo and hiss at me. Is it not dreadful the way they insult the fallen?"

"We are not going to talk about it," I said; "we are going to talk of victories and not of defeats."

"Ah, Frank, there will be no more victories for me."

"Nonsense," I cried; "now where are we going?"

"Some quiet place where I shall not be known."

"You really would not like the Café Royal?" I asked. "Nothing will happen to you, and I think you would probably find that one or two people would wish you luck. You have had a rare bad time, and there must be some people who understand what you have gone through and know that it is sufficient punishment for any sin."

"No, Frank," he persisted, "I cannot, I really cannot."

At length we decided on a restaurant in Great Portland Street. We drove there and had a private room.

I had two purposes in me, springing from the one root, the intense desire to help him. I felt sure that if the case came up again for trial he would only be convicted through what I may call good, honest testimony. The jury with their English prejudice; or rather I should say with their healthy English instinct would not take the evidence of vile blackmailers against him; he could only be convicted through untainted evidence such as the evidence of the chambermaids at the Savoy Hotel, and their evidence was over two years old and was weak, inasmuch as the facts, if facts, were not acted upon by the management. Still their testimony was very clear and very positive, and, taken together with that of the blackmailers, sufficient to ensure conviction. After our lunch I laid this view before Oscar. He agreed with me that it was probably the chambermaids' testimony which had weighed most heavily against him. Their statement and Shelley's had brought about the injurious tone in the Judge's summing up. The Judge himself had admitted as much.

"The chambermaids' evidence is wrong," Oscar declared. "They are mistaken, Frank. It was not me they spoke about at the Savoy Hotel. It was —————. I was never bold enough. I went to see ——— in the morning in his room."

"Thank God," I said, "but why didn't Sir Edward Clarke bring that out?"

"He wanted to; but I would not let him. I told him he must not. I must be true to my friend. I could not let him."

"But he must," I said, "at any rate if he does not I will. I have three weeks and in that three weeks I am going to find the chambermaid. I am going to get a plan of your room and your friend's room, and I'm going to make her understand that she was mistaken. She probably remembered you because of your size. She mistook you for the guilty person; everybody has always taken you for the ringleader and not the follower."

"But what good is it, Frank, what good is it?" he cried. "Even if you convinced the chambermaid and she retracted; there would still be Shelley, and the Judge laid stress on Shelley's evidence as untainted."

"Shelley is an accomplice," I cried, "his testimony needs corroboration. You don't understand these legal quibbles; but there was not a particle of corroboration. Sir Edward Clarke should have had his testimony ruled out. " 'Twas that conspiracy charge," I cried, "which complicated the matter. Shelley's evidence, too, will be ruled out at the next trial, you'll see."

"Oh, Frank," he said, "you talk with passion and conviction, as if I were innocent."

"But you are innocent," I cried in amaze, "aren't you?"

"No, Frank," he said, "I thought you knew that all along."

I stared at him stupidly. "No," I said dully, "I did not know. I did not believe the accusation. I did not believe it for a moment."

I suppose the difference in my tone and manner struck him, for he said, timidly putting out his hand:

"This will make a great difference to you, Frank?"

"No," I said, pulling myself together and taking his hand; and after a pause I went on: "No; curiously enough it has made no difference to me at all. I do not know why; I suppose I have got more sympathy than morality in me. It has surprised me, dumbfounded me. The thing has always seemed fantastic and incredible to me and now you make it exist for me; but it has no effect on my friendship; none upon my resolve to help you. But I see that the battle is going to be infinitely harder than I imagined. In fact, now I don't think we have a chance of winning a verdict. I came here hoping against fear that it could be won, though I always felt that it would be better in the present state of English feeling to go abroad and avoid the risk of a trial. Now there is no question. You would be insane, as Clarke said, to stay in England. But why on earth did Alfred Douglas, knowing the truth, ever wish you to attack Queensberry?"

"He's very bold and obstinate, Frank," said Oscar weakly.

"Well, now I must play Crito," I resumed, smiling, "and take you away before the ship comes from Delos."

"Oh, Frank, that would be wonderful; but it's impossible, quite impossible. I should be arrested before I left London, and shamed again in public. They would boo at me and shout insults. . . . Oh, it is impossible; I could not risk it."

"Nonsense," I replied, "I believe the authorities would be only too glad if you went. I think Clarke's challenge to Gill was curiously ill-advised. He should have let sleeping dogs lie. Combative Gill was certain to take up the gauntlet. If Clarke had lain low there might have been no second trial. But that can't be helped now. Don't believe that it's even difficult to get away; it's easy. I don't propose to go by Folkestone or Dover."

"But, Frank, what about the people who have stood bail for me? I couldn't leave them to suffer; they would lose their thousands."

"I shan't let them lose," I replied, "I am quite willing to take half on my shoulders at once and you can pay the other thousand or so within a very short time by writing a couple of plays. American papers would be only too glad to pay you for an interview. The story of your escape would be worth a thousand pounds; they would give you almost any price for it.

"Leave everything to me, but in the meantime I want you to get out in the air as much as possible. You are not looking well; you are not yourself."

"That house is depressing, Frank. Willie makes such merit of giving me shelter; he means well, I suppose; but it is all dreadful."

My notes of this talk finish in this way, but the conversation left on me a deep impression of Oscar's extraordinary weakness or rather extraordinary softness of nature backed up and redeemed by a certain magnanimity. He would not leave the friends in the lurch who had gone bail for him; he would not give his friends away even to save himself; but neither would he exert himself greatly to win free. He was like a woman, I said to myself in wonder, and my pity for him grew keener. He seemed mentally stunned by the sudden fall, by the discovery of how violently men can hate. He had never seen the wolf in man before; the vile brute instinct that preys upon the fallen. He had not believed that such exultant savagery existed; it had never come within his ken; now it appalled him. And so he stood there waiting for what might happen without courage to do anything but suffer. My heart ached with pity for him, and yet I felt a little impatient with him as well. Why give up like that? The eternal quarrel of the combative nature with those who can't or won't fight.

Before getting into the carriage to drive back to his brother's, I ascertained that he did not need any money. He told me that he had sufficient even for the expenses of a second trial. This surprised me greatly, for he was very careless about money; but I found out from him later that a very noble and cultured woman, a friend of both of us, Miss S——, a Jewess by race tho' not by religion, had written to him asking if she could help him financially, as she had been distressed by hearing of his bankruptcy, and feared that he might be in need. If that were the case she begged him to let her be his banker, in order that he might be properly defended. He wrote in reply, saying that he was indeed in uttermost distress, that he wanted money, too, to help his mother as he had always helped her, and that he supposed the expenses of the second trial would be from £500 to £1,000. Thereupon Miss S—— sent him a cheque for £1,000, assuring him that it cost her little even in self-sacrifice and declaring that it was only inadequate recognition of the pleasure she had had through his delightful talks. Such actions are beyond praise; it is the perfume of such sweet and noble human sympathy that makes this wild beasts' cage of a world habitable for men.

Before parting we had agreed to meet a few nights afterwards at Mrs. Leverson's, where he had been invited to dinner, and where I also had been invited. By that time, I thought to myself, all my preparations would be perfected.

Looking back now I see clearly that my affection for Oscar Wilde dates from his confession to me that afternoon. I had been a friend of his for years; but what had bound us together had been purely intellectual, a community of literary tastes and ambitions. Now his trust in me and frankness had thrown down the barrier between us; and made me conscious of the extraordinary femininity and gentle weakness of his nature, and, instead of condemning him as I have always condemned that form of sexual indulgence, I felt only pity for him and a desire to protect and help him. From that day on our friendship became intimate. I began to divine him; I knew now that his words would always be more generous and noble than his actions; knew too that I must take his charm of manner and vivacity of intercourse for real virtues, and indeed they were as real as the beauty of flowers; and I was aware as by some sixth sense that, where his vanity was concerned, I might expect any injustice from him. I was sure beforehand, however, that I should always forgive him, or rather that I should always accept whatever he did and love him for the charm and sweetness and intellect in him and hold myself more than recompensed, for anything I might be able to do, by his delightful companionship.

16

Escape Rejected: the Second Trial and Sentence

In spite of the wit of the hostess and her exquisite cordiality, our dinner at Mrs. Leverson's was hardly a success. Oscar was not himself; contrary to his custom he sat silent and downcast. From time to time he sighed heavily, and his leaden dejection gradually infected all of us. I was not sorry, for I wanted to get them away early. By ten o'clock we had left the house and were in the Cromwell Road. He preferred to walk. Without his noticing it I turned up Queen's Gate towards the park. After walking for ten minutes I said to him:

"I want to speak to you seriously. Do you happen to know where Erith is?"

"No, Frank."

"It is a little landing place on the Thames," I went on, "not many miles away; it can be reached by a fast pair of horses and a brougham in a very short time. There at Erith is a steam yacht ready to start at a moment's notice; she has steam up now, one hundred pounds pressure to the square inch in her boilers; her captain's waiting, her crew ready—a greyhound in leash; she can do fifteen knots an hour without being pressed. In one hour she would be free of the Thames and on the high seas—(delightful phrase, eh?)—high seas indeed where there is freedom uncontrolled.

171

"If one started now one could breakfast in France, at Boulogne, let us say, or Dieppe; one could lunch at St. Malo or St. Enogat or any place you like on the coast of Normandy, and one could dine comfortably at the Sables d'Olonne, where there is not an Englishman to be found, and where sunshine reigns even in May from morning till night.

"What do you say, Oscar, will you come and try a homely French bourgeois dinner to-morrow evening at an inn I know almost at the water's edge? We could sit out on the little terrace and take our coffee in peace under the broad vine leaves while watching the silver pathway of the moon widen on the waters. We could smile at the miseries of London and its wolfish courts shivering in cold grey mist hundreds of miles away. Does not the prospect tempt you?"

I spoke at leisure, tasting each delight, looking for his gladness.

"Oh, Frank," he cried, "how wonderful; but how impossible!"

"Impossible! don't be absurd," I retorted. "Do you see those lights yonder?" and I showed him some lights at the Park gate on the top of the hill in front of us.

"Yes, Frank."

"That's a brougham," I said, "with a pair of fast horses. It will take us for a midnight visit to the steam yacht in double-quick time. There's a little library on board of French books and English; I've ordered supper in the cabin—lobster à l'Américaine and a bottle of Pommery. You've never seen the mouth of the Thames at night, have you? It's a scene from wonderland; houses like blobs of indigo fencing you in; ships drifting past like black ghosts in the misty air, and the purple sky above never so dark as the river, the river with its shifting lights of ruby and emerald and topaz, like an oily, opaque serpent gliding with a weird life of its own. . . . Come; you must visit the yacht."

I turned to him, but he was no longer by my side. I gasped; what had happened? The mist must have hidden him; I ran back ten yards, and there he was leaning against the railing, hung up with his head on his arm shaking.

"What's the matter, Oscar?" I cried. "What on earth's the matter?"

"Oh, Frank, I can't go," he cried. "I can't. It would be too wonderful; but it's impossible. I should be seized by the police. You don't know the police."

"Nonsense," I cried, "the police can't stop you and not a man of them will see you from start to finish. Besides, I have loose money for any I do meet, and none of them can resist a 'tip.' You will simply get out of the brougham and walk fifty yards and you will be on the yacht and free. In fact, if you like you shall not come out of the brougham until the sailors surround you as a guard of honour. On board the yacht no one will touch you. No warrant runs there. Come on, man!"

"Oh, Frank," he groaned, "it's impossible!"

"What's impossible?" I insisted. "Let's consider everything anew at breakfast to-morrow morning in France. If you want to come back, there's nothing to prevent you. The yacht will take you back in twenty-four hours. You will not have broken your bail; you'll have done nothing wrong. You can go to France, Germany or Siberia so long as you come back by the twentieth of May. Take it that I offer you a holiday in France for ten days. Surely it is better to spend a week with me than in that dismal house in Oakley Street, where the very door gives one the creeps."

"Oh, Frank, I'd love to," he groaned. "I see everything you say, but I can't. I dare not. I'm caught, Frank, in a trap; I can only wait for the end."

I began to get impatient; he was weaker than I had imagined, weaker a hundred times.

"Come for a trip, then, man," I cried, and I brought him within twenty yards of the carriage; but there he stopped as if he had made up his mind.

"No, no, I can't come. I could not go about in France feeling that the policeman's hand might fall on my shoulder at any moment. I could not live a life of fear and doubt; it would kill me in a month." His tone was decided.

"Why let your imagination run away with you?" I pleaded. "Do be reasonable for once. Fear and doubt would soon be over. If the police don't get you in France within a week after the date fixed for the trial, you need have no further fear, for they won't get you at all; they don't want you. You're making mountains out of molehills with nervous fancies."

"I should be arrested."

"Nonsense," I replied, "who would arrest you? No one has the right. You are out on bail: your bail answers for you till the 20th. Money talks, man; Englishmen always listen to money. It'll do you good with the public and the jury to come back from France to stand your trial. Do come," and I took him by the arm; but he would not move. To my astonishment he faced me and said:

"And my sureties?"

"We'll pay 'em," I replied, "both of 'em, if you break your bail. Come," but he would not.

"Frank, if I were not in Oakley Street to-night Willie would tell the police."

"Your brother?" I cried.

"Yes," he said, "Willie."

"Good God!" I exclaimed; "but let him tell. I have not mentioned Erith or the steam yacht to a soul. It's the last place in the world the police would suspect and before he talks we shall be out of reach. Besides they cannot do anything; you are doing nothing wrong. Please trust me, you do nothing questionable even till you omit to enter the Old Bailey on the 20th of May.

"You don't know Willie," he continued, "he has made my solicitors buy letters of mine; he has blackmailed me."

"Whew!" I whistled. "But in that case you'll have no compunction in leaving him without saying 'goodbye.' Let's go and get into the brougham."

"No, no," he repeated, "you don't understand; I can't go, I cannot go."

"Do you mean it really?" I asked. "Do you mean you will not come and spend a week yachting with me?"

"I cannot."

I drew him a few paces nearer the carriage: something of desolation and despair in his voice touched me. I looked at him. Tears were pouring down his face; he was the picture of misery, yet I could not move him.

"Come into the carriage," I said, hoping that the swift wind in his face would freshen him up, give him a moment's taste of the joy of living and sharpen the desire of freedom.

"Yes, Frank," he said, "if you will take me to Oakley Street."

"I would as soon take you to prison," I replied: "but as you wish."

The next moment we had got in and were swinging down Queen's Gate. The mist seemed to lend keenness to the air. At the bottom of Queen's Gate the coachman swept of himself to the left into the Cromwell Road; Oscar seemed to wake out of his stupor.

"No, Frank," he cried, "no, no," and he fumbled at the handle of the door, "I must get out; I will not go. I will not go."

"Sit still," I said in despair, "I'll tell the coachman," and I put my head out of the window and cried:

"Oakley Street, Oakley Street, Chelsea, Robert."

I do not think I spoke again till we got to Oakley Street. I was consumed with rage and contemptuous impatience. I had done the best I knew and had failed. Why? I had no idea. I have never known why he refused to come. I don't think he knew himself. Such resignation I had never dreamt of. It was utterly new to me. I used to think of resignation in a vague way as of something rather beautiful; ever since, I have thought of it with impatience. Resignation is the courage of the irresolute. Oscar's obstinacy was the obverse of his weakness. It is astonishing how inertia rules some natures. The attraction of waiting and doing nothing is intense for those who live in thought and detest action. As we turned into Oakley Street, Oscar said to me:

"You are not angry with me, Frank?" and he put out his hand.

"No, no," I said, "why should I be angry? You are the master of your fate. I can only offer advice."

"Do come and see me soon," he pleaded.

"My bolt is shot," I replied; "but I'll come in two or three days' time, as soon as I have anything of importance to say. . . . Don't forget, Oscar, the yacht is there and will be there waiting until the 20th; the yacht will always be ready and the brougham."

"Good night, Frank," he said, "good night, and thank you."

He got out and went into the house, the gloomy sordid house where the brother lived who would sell his blood for a price!

. . . .

Three or four days later we met again, but to my amaze Oscar had not changed his mind. To talk of him as cast down is the precise truth; he seemed to me as one who had fallen from a great height and lay half conscious, stunned on the ground. The moment you moved him, even to raise his head, it gave him pain and he cried out to be left alone. There he lay prone, and no one could help him. It was painful to witness his dumb misery. His mind even, his sunny bright intelligence, seemed to have deserted him.

Once again he came out with me to lunch. Afterwards we drove through Regent's Park as the quietest way to Hampstead and had a talk. The air and swift motion did him good. The beauty of the view from the heath seemed to revive him. I tried to cheer him up.

"You must know," I said, "that you can win if you want to. You cannot only bring the jury to doubt, but you can make the judge doubt as well. I was convinced of your innocence in spite of all the witnesses, and I knew more about you than they did. In the trial before Mr. Justice Charles, the thing that saved you was that you spoke of the love of David and Jonathan and the sweet affection which the common world is determined not to understand. There is another point against you which you have not touched on yet. Gill asked you what you had in common with those servingmen and stable boys. You have not explained that. You have explained that you love youth, the brightness and the gaiety of it, but you have not explained what seems inexplicable to most men, that you should go about with servants and strappers."

"Difficult to explain, Frank, isn't it, without the truth?" Evidently his mind was not working.

"No," I replied, "easy, simple. Think of Shakespeare. How did he know Dogberry and Pistol, Bardolph and Doll Tearsheet? He must have gone about with them. You don't go about with public school boys of your own class, for you know them; you have nothing to learn from them; they can teach you nothing. But the stable boy and servant you cannot sketch in your plays without knowing him, and you can't know him without getting on his level, and letting him call you 'Oscar' and calling him 'Charlie.' If you rub this in, the judge will see that he is face to face with the artist in you and will admit at least that your explanation is plausible. He will hesitate to condemn you, and once he hesitates you'll win.

"You fought badly because you did not show your own nature sufficiently; you did not use your brains in the witness box and alas—" I did not continue; the truth was I was filled with fear; for I suddenly realised that he had shown more courage and self-possession in the Queensberry trial than in the trial before Mr. Justice Charles when so much more was at stake; and I felt that in the next trial he would be more depressed still, and less inclined to take the initiative than ever. I had already learned too that I could not help him; that he would not be lifted out of that "sweet way of despair," which so attracts the artist spirit. But still I would do my best.

"Do you understand?" I asked.

"Of course, Frank, of course, but you have no conception how weary I am of the whole thing, of the shame and the struggling and the hatred. To see those people coming into the box one after the other to witness against me makes me sick. The self-satisfied grin of the barristers, the pompous foolish judge with his thin lips and cunning eyes and hard jaw. Oh, it's terrible. I feel inclined to stretch out my hands and cry to them, 'Do what you will with me, in God's name, only do it quickly; cannot you see that I am worn out? If hatred gives you pleasure, indulge it.' They worry one, Frank, with ravening jaws, as dogs worry a rabbit. Yet they call themselves men. It is appalling."

The day was dying, the western sky all draped with crimson, saffron and rosy curtains; a slight mist over London, purple on the horizon, closer, a mere wash of blue; here and there steeples pierced the thin veil like fingers pointing upward. On the left the dome of St. Paul's hung like a grey bubble over the city; on the right the twin towers of Westminster with the river and bridge which Wordsworth sang. Peace and beauty brooding everywhere and done there, lost in the mist, the "rat pit" that men call the Courts of Justice. There they judge their fellows, mistaking indifference for impartiality, as if anyone could judge his fellowman without love, and even with love how far short we all come of that perfect sympathy which is above forgiveness and takes delight in succouring the weak, comforting the broken-hearted.

. . . .

The days went swiftly by and my powerlessness to influence him filled me with self-contempt. Of course, I said to myself, if I knew him better I should be able to help him. Would vanity do anything? It was his mainspring; I could but try. He might be led by the hope of making Englishmen talk of him again, talk of him as one who had dared to escape; wonder what he would do next. I would try, and I did try. But his dejection foiled me; his dislike of the struggle seemed to grow from day to day.

He would scarcely listen to me. He was counting the days to the trial; willing to accept an adverse decision; even punishment and misery and shame seemed better than doubt and waiting. He surprised me by saying:

"A year, Frank, they may give me a year? half the possible sentence: the middle course, that English Judges always take: the sort of compromise they think safe?" and his eyes searched my face for agreement.

I felt no such confidence in English Judges; their compromises are usually bargainings; when they get hold of an artist they give rein to their intuitive fear and hate.

But I would not discourage him. I repeated:

"You can win, Oscar, if you like—" my litany to him. His wan dejected smile brought tears to my eyes.

. . . .

"Don't you want to make them all speak of you and wonder at you again? If you were in France, everyone would be asking: will he come back or disappear altogether? or will he manifest himself henceforth in some new comedies, more joyous and pagan than ever?"

I might as well have talked to the dead. He seemed numbed, hypnotised with despair. The punishment had already been greater than he could bear. I began to fear that prison, if he were condemned to it, would rob him of his reason; I sometimes feared that his mind was already giving way, so profound was his depression, so hopeless his despair.

. . . .

The trial opened before Mr. Justice Wills on the 21st of May, 1895. The Treasury had sent Sir Frank Lockwood, Q.C., M.P.,

178

to lead Mr. C. F. Gill, Mr. Horace Avory, and Mr. Sutton. Oscar was represented by the same counsel as on the previous occasion.

The whole trial to me was a nightmare, and it was characterised from the very beginning by atrocious prejudice and injustice. The High Priests of Law were weary of being balked; eager to make an end. As soon as the Judge took his seat, Sir Edward Clarke applied that the defendants should be tried separately. As they had already been acquitted on the charge of conspiracy, there was no reason why they should be tried together.

The Judge called on the Solicitor-General to answer the application.

The Solicitor-General had nothing to say, but thought it was in the interests of the defendants to be tried together; for, in case they were tried separately, it would be necessary to take the defendant Taylor first.

Sir Edward Clarke tore this pretext to pieces, and Mr. Justice Wills brought the matter to a conclusion by saying that he was in possession of all the evidence that had been taken at the previous trials, and his opinion was that the two defendants should be tried separately.

Sir Edward Clarke then applied that the case of Mr. Wilde should be taken first as his name stood first on the indictment, and as the first count was directed against him and had nothing to do with Taylor. . . . "There are reasons present, I am sure, too, in your Lordship's mind, why Wilde should not be tried immediately after the other defendant."

Mr. Justice Wills remarked, with seeming indifference, "It ought not to make the least difference, Sir Edward. I am sure I and the jury will do our best to take care that the last trial has no influence at all on the present."

Sir Edward Clarke stuck to his point. He urged respectfully that as Mr. Wilde's name stood first on the indictment his case should be taken first.

Mr. Justice Wills said he could not interfere with the discretion of the prosecution, nor vary the ordinary procedure. Justice and fair play on the one side and precedent on the other: justice was waved out of court with serene indifference. Thereupon Sir Edward Clarke pressed that the trial of Mr. Oscar Wilde

179

should stand over till the next sessions. But again Mr. Justice Wills refused. Precedent was silent now but prejudice was strong as ever.

The case against Taylor went on the whole day and was resumed next morning. Taylor went into the box and denied all the charges. The Judge summed up dead against him, and at 3.30 the jury retired to consider their verdict. In forty-five minutes they came into court again with a question which was significant. In answer to the judge, the foreman stated that "they had agreed that Taylor had introduced Parker to Wilde, but they were not satisfied with Wilde's guilt in the matter."

Mr. Justice Wills: "Were you agreed as to the charge on the other counts?"

Foreman: "Yes, my Lord."

Mr. Justice Wills: "Well, possibly it would be as well to take your verdict upon the other counts."

Through the foreman the jury accordingly intimated that they found Taylor guilty with regard to Charles and William Parker.

In answer to his Lordship, Sir F. Lockwood said he would take the verdict given by the jury of "guilty" upon the two counts.

A formal verdict having been entered, the judge ordered the prisoner to stand down, postponing sentence. Did he postpone the sentence in order not to frighten the next jury by the severity of it? Other reason I could find none.

Sir Edward Clarke then got up and said that as it was getting rather late, perhaps after the second jury had disagreed as to Mr. Wilde's guilt—

Sir F. Lockwood here interposed hotly: "I object to Sir Edward Clarke making these little speeches."

Mr. Justice Wills took the matter up as well.

"You can hardly call it a disagreement, Sir Edward," though what else he could call it, I was at a loss to imagine.

He then adjourned the case against Oscar Wilde till the next day, when a different jury would be impanelled. But whatever jury might be called they would certainly hear that their forerunners had found Taylor guilty and they would know that every London paper without exception had approved the finding. What a fair chance to give Wilde! It was like trying an Irish Secretary before a jury of Fenians.

The next morning, May 23rd, Oscar Wilde appeared in the dock. The Solicitor-General opened the case, and then called his witnesses. One of the first was Edward Shelley, who in cross-examination admitted that he had been mentally ill when he wrote Mr. Wilde those letters which had been put in evidence. He was "made nervous from over-study," he said.

Alfred Wood admitted that he had had money given him quite recently, practically blackmailing money. He was as venomous as possible. "When he went to America," he said, "he told Wilde that he wanted to get away from mixing with him (Wilde) and Douglas."

Charlie Parker next repeated his disgusting testimony with ineffable impudence and a certain exultation. Bestial ignominy could go no lower; he admitted that since the former trial he had been kept at the expense of the prosecution. After this confession the case was adjourned and we came out of court.

When I reached Fleet Street I was astonished to hear that there had been a row that same afternoon in Piccadilly between Lord Douglas of Hawick and his father, the Marquis of Queensberry. Lord Queensberry, it appears, had been writing disgusting letters about the Wilde case to Lord Douglas' wife. Meeting him in Piccadilly Percy Douglas stopped him and asked him to cease writing obscene letters to his wife. The Marquis said he would not and the father and son came to blows. Queensberry it seems was exasperated by the fact that Douglas of Hawick was one of those who had gone bail for Oscar Wilde. One of the telegrams which the Marquis of Queensberry had sent to Lady Douglas I must put in just to show the insane nature of the man who could exult in a trial which was damning the reputation of his own son. The letter was manifestly written after the result of the Taylor trial:

> Must congratulate on verdict, cannot on Percy's appearance. Looks like a dug up corpse. Fear too much madness of kissing. Taylor guilty. Wilde's turn to-morrow.
>
> QUEENSBERRY

In examination before the magistrate, Mr. Hannay, it was stated that Lord Queensberry had been sending similar letters to

181

Lady Douglas "full of the most disgusting charges against Lord Douglas, his wife, and Lord Queensberry's divorced wife and her family." But Mr. Hannay thought all this provocation was of no importance and bound over both father and son to keep the peace—an indefensible decision, a decision only to be explained by the sympathy everywhere shown to Queensberry because of his victory over Wilde, otherwise surely any honest magistrate would have condemned the father who sent obscene letters to his son's wife—a lady above reproach. These vile letters and the magistrate's bias, semed to me to add the final touch of the grotesque to the horrible vileness of the trial. It was all worthy of the seventh circle of Dante, but Dante had never imagined such a father and such judges!

. . . .

Next morning Oscar Wilde was again put in the dock. The evidence of the Queensberry trial was read and therewith the case was closed for the Crown.

Sir Edward Clarke rose and submitted that there was no case to go to the jury on the general counts. After a long legal argument for and against, Mr. Justice Wills said that he would reserve the question for the Court of Appeal. The view he took was that "the evidence was of the slenderest kind"; but he thought the responsibility must be left with the jury. To this judge "the slenderest kind" of evidence was worthful so long as it told against the accused.

Sir Edward Clarke then argued that the cases of Shelley, Parker and Wood failed on the ground of the absence of corroboration. Mr. Justice Wills admitted that Shelley showed "a peculiar exaltation" of mind; there was, too, mental derangement in his family, and worst of all there was no corroboration of his statements. Accordingly, in spite of the arguments of the Solicitor-General, Shelley's evidence was cut out. But Shelley's evidence had already been taken, had already prejudiced the jury. Indeed, it had been the evidence which had influenced Mr. Justice Charles in the previous trial to sum up dead against the defendant. Mr. Justice Charles called Shelley "the only serious witness."

Now it appeared that Shelley's evidence should never have been taken at all, that the jury ought never to have heard Shelley's testimony or the Judge's acceptance of it!

. . . .

When the court opened next morning I knew that the whole case depended on Oscar Wilde, and the showing he would make in the box, but alas! he was broken and numbed. He was not a fighter, and the length of this contest might have wearied a combative nature. The Solicitor-General began by examining him on his letters to Lord Alfred Douglas and we had the "prose poem" again and the rest of the ineffable nonsensical prejudice of the middle-class mind against passionate sentiment. It came out in evidence that Lord Alfred Douglas was now in Calais. His hatred of his father was the *causa causans* of the whole case; he had pushed Oscar into the fight and Oscar, still intent on shielding him, declared that he had asked him to go abroad.

Sir Edward Clarke again did his poor best. He pointed out that the trial rested on the evidence of mere blackmailers. He would not quarrel with that and discuss it, but it was impossible not to see that if blackmailers were to be listened to and believed, their profession might speedily become a more deadly mischief and danger to society than it had ever been.

The speech was a weak one; but the people in court cheered Sir Edward Clarke; the cheers were immediately suppressed by the Judge.

The Solicitor-General took up the rest of the day with a rancorous reply. Sir Edward Clarke even had to remind him that law officers of the Crown should try to be impartial. One instance of his prejudice may be given. Examining Oscar as to his letters to Lord Alfred Douglas, Sir Frank Lockwood wanted to know whether he thought them "decent"?

The witness replied, "Yes."

"Do you know the meaning of the word, sir?" was this gentleman's retort.

I went out of the court feeling certain that the case was lost. Oscar had not shown himself at all; he had not even spoken with the vigour he had used at the Queensbury trial. He seemed too despairing to strike a blow.

The summing up of the Judge on May 25th was perversely stupid and malevolent. He began by declaring that he was "absolutely impartial", though his view of the facts had to be corrected again and again by Sir Edward Clarke. He went on to regret that the charge of conspiracy should have been introduced, as it had to be abandoned. He then pointed out that he could not give a colourless summing up, which was "of no use to anybody". His intelligence can be judged from one crucial point: he fastened on the fact that Oscar had burnt the letters which he bought from Wood, which he said were of no importance, except that they concerned third parties. The Judge had persuaded himself that the letters were indescribably bad, forgetting apparently that Wood or his associates had selected and retained the very worst of them for purposes of blackmail and that this Judge himself, after reading it, couldn't attribute any weight to it; still he insisted that burning the letters was an act of madness; whereas it seemed to everyone of the slightest imagination the most natural thing in the world for an innocent man to do. At the time Oscar burnt the letters he had no idea that he would ever be on trial. His letters had been misunderstood and the worst of them was being used against him, and when he got the others he naturally threw them into the fire. The Judge held that it was madness, and built upon this inference a pyramid of guilt. "Nothing said by Wood should be believed, as he belongs to the vilest class of criminals; the strength of the accusation depends solely upon the character of the original introduction of Wood to Wilde as illustrated and fortified by the story with regard to the letters and their burning."

A pyramid of guilt carefully balanced on its apex! If the foolish Judge had only read his Shakespeare! What does Henry VI say:

> Proceed no straiter 'gainst our uncle Glouchester
> Than from true evidence of good esteem
> He be approved in practice culpable.

There was no "true evidence of good esteem" against Wilde, but the Judge turned a harmless action into a confession of guilt.

Then came an interruption which threw light on the English conception of justice. The foreman of the jury wanted to know, in view of the intimate relations between Lord Alfred Douglas and the defendant, whether a warrant against Lord Alfred Douglas was ever issued.

Mr. Justice Wills: "I should say not; we have never heard of it."

Foreman: "Or ever contemplated?"

Mr. Justice Wills: "That I cannot say, nor can we discuss it. The issue of such a warrant would not depend upon the testimony of the parties, but whether there was evidence of such act. Letters pointing to such relations would not be sufficient. Lord Alfred Douglas was not called, and you can give what weight you like to that."

Foreman: "If we are to deduce any guilt from these letters, it would apply equally to Lord Alfred Douglas."

Mr. Justice Wills concurred in that view, but after all he thought it had nothing to do with the present trial, which was the guilt of the accused.

The jury retired to consider their verdict at half past three. After being absent two hours they returned to know whether there was any evidence of Charles Parker having slept at St. James's Place.

His Lordship replied, "No."

The jury shortly afterwards returned again with the verdict of "Guilty" on all the counts.

It may be worth while to note again that the Judge himself admitted that the evidence on some of the counts was of "the slenderest kind"; but, when backed by his prejudiced summing up, it was more than sufficient for the jury.

Sir Edward Clarke pleaded that sentence should be postponed till the next sessions, when the legal argument would be heard.

Mr. Justice Wills would not be balked. Sentence, he thought, should be given immediately. Then, addressing the prisoners, he said, and again I give his exact words, lest I should do him wrong:

"Oscar Wilde and Alfred Taylor, the crime of which you have been convicted is so bad that one has to put stern restraint upon one's self to prevent one's self from describing in language which I would rather not use the sentiments which must rise to

185

the breast of every man of honour who has heard the details of these two terrible trials.

"That the jury have arrived at a correct verdict in this case I cannot persuade myself to entertain the shadow of a doubt; and I hope, at all events, that those who sometimes imagine that a Judge is half-hearted in the cause of decency and morality because he takes care no prejudice shall enter into the case may see that that is consistent at least with the utmost sense of indignation at the horrible charges brought home to both of you.

"It is no use for me to address you. People who can do these things must be dead to all sense of shame, and one cannot hope to produce any effect upon them. It is the worst case I have ever tried. . . . That you, Wilde, have been the centre of a circle of extensive corruption of the most hideous kind among young men it is impossible to doubt.

"I shall under such circumstances be expected to pass the severest sentence that the law allows. In my judgment it is totally inadequate for such a case as this.

"The sentence of the court is that each of you be imprisoned and kept to hard labour for two years."

The sentence hushed the court in shocked surprise.

Wilde rose and cried, "Can I say anything, my lord?"

Mr. Justice Wills waved his hand deprecatingly amid cries of "Shame" and hisses from the public gallery; some of the cries and hisses were certainly addressed to the Judge and well deserved. What did he mean by saying that Oscar was a "centre of extensive corruption of the most hideous kind"? No evidence of this had been brought forward by the prosecution. It was not even alleged that a single innocent person had been corrupted. The accusation was invented by this "absolutely impartial" Judge to justify his atrocious cruelty. The unmerited insults and appalling sentence would have disgraced the worst Judge of the Inquisition.

Mr. Justice Wills evidently suffered from the peculiar "exaltation" of mind which he had recognized in Shelley. This peculiarity is shared in a lesser degree by several other Judges on the English bench in all matters of sexual morality. What distinguished Mr. Justice Wills was that he was proud of his prejudice and eager to act on it. He evidently did not know, or did not care, that the sentence which he had given, declaring it was "totally inadequate", had been condemned by a Royal Commission as "inhuman". He would willingly have pushed "inhumanity" to savagery, out of sheer bewigged stupidity, and that he was probably well-meaning only intensified the revolt one felt at such brainless malevolence.

The bitterest words in Dante are not bitter enough to render my feeling:

"Non regioniam di lor ma guarde e passe."

The whole scene had sickened me. Hatred masquerading as justice, striking vindictively and adding insult to injury. The vile picture had its fit setting outside. We had not left the court when the cheering broke out in the streets, and when we came outside there were troops of the lowest women of the town dancing together and kicking up their legs in hideous abandonment, while the surrounding crowd of policemen and spectators guffawed with delight. As I turned away from the exhibition, as obscene and soul-defiling as anything witnessed in the madness of the French revolution, I caught a glimpse of Wood and the Parkers getting into a cab, laughing and leering.

These were the venal creatures Oscar Wilde was punished for having corrupted!

17

Prison and the Effects of Punishment

PRISON FOR OSCAR WILDE, an English prison with its insufficient bad food[1] and soul-degrading routine for that amiable, joyous, eloquent, pampered Sybarite. Here was a test indeed; an ordeal as by fire. What would he make of two years' hard labour in a lonely cell?

There are two ways of taking prison, as of taking most things, and all the myriad ways between these two extremes; would Oscar be conquered by it and allow remorse and hatred to corrupt his very heart, or would he conquer the prison and possess and use it? Hammer or anvil—which?

Victory has its virtue and is justified of itself like sunshine; defeat carries its own condemnation. Yet we have all tasted its bitter waters. Only "infinite virtue" can pass through life victorious, Shakespeare tells us, and we mortals are not of infinite virtue. The myriad vicissitudes of the struggle search out all our weaknesses, test all our powers. Every victory shows a more difficult height to scale, a steeper pinnacle of god-like hardship—that's the reward of victory. It provides the hero with ever-new battle-fields; no rest for him this side the grave.

[1] Some years ago *The Daily Chronicle* proved that though the general standard of living is lower in Germany and in France than in England; yet the prison food in France and especially in Germany is far better than in England and the treatment of the prisoners far more humane.

But what of defeat? What sweet is there in its bitter? This may be said for it; it is our great school. Punishment teaches pity, just as suffering teaches sympathy. In defeat the brave soul learns kinship with other men, takes the rub to heart, seeks out the reason for the fall in his own weakness, and ever afterwards finds it's impossible to judge, much less condemn his fellow. But after all no one can hurt us but ourselves; prison, hard labour, and the hate of men; what are these if they make you truer, wiser, kinder?

Have you come to grief through self-indulgence and good-living? Here are months in which men will take care that you shall eat badly and lie hard. Did you lack respect for others? Here are men who will show you no consideration. Were you careless of others' sufferings? Here now you shall agonize unheeded; gaolers and governors as well as black cells to teach you. Thank your stars then for every day's experience, for, when you have learned the lesson of it and turned its discipline into service, the prison shall transform itself into a hermitage, the dungeon into a home; the burnt skilly shall be sweet in your mouth; and your rest on the plankbed the dreamless slumber of a little child.

And if you are an artist, prison will be more to you than this; an astonishing vital and novel experience, accorded only to the chosen. What will you make of it? That's the question for you. It is a wonderful opportunity. Seen truly, a prison's more spacious than a palace; nay, richer, and for a loving soul, a far rarer experience. Thank then the spirit which steers men for the divine chance which has come to you; henceforth the prison shall be your domain; in future men will not think of it without thinking of you. Others may show them what the good things of life do for one; you will show them what suffering can do, cold and regretful sleepless hours and solitude, misery and distress. Others will teach the lessons of joy. The whole vast underworld of pity and pain, fear and horror and injustice is your kingdom. Men have drawn darkness about you as a curtain, shrouded you in blackest night; the light in you will shine the brighter. Always provided of course that the light is not put out altogether.

Hammer or anvil? How would Oscar Wilde take punishment?

.   .   .   .

We could not know for months. Yet he was an artist by nature —that gave one a glimmer of hope. We needed it. For outside at first there was an icy atmosphere of hatred and contempt. The mere mention of his name was met with expressions of disgust or frozen silence.

One bare incident will paint the general feeling more clearly than pages of invective or description. The day after Oscar's sentence Mr. Charles Brookfield, who, it will be remembered, had raked together the witnesses that enabled Lord Queensberry to "justify" his accusation; assisted by Mr. Charles Hawtrey, the actor, gave a dinner to Lord Queensberry to celebrate their triumph. Some forty Englishmen of good position were present at the banquet—a feast to celebrate the ruin and degradation of a man of genius.

Yet there are true souls in England, noble, generous hearts. I remember a lunch at Mrs. Jeune's, where one declared that Wilde was at length enjoying his deserts; another regretted that his punishment was so slight, a third with precise knowledge intimated delicately and with quiet complacence that two years' imprisonment with hard labour usually resulted in idiocy or death. Fifty per cent., it appeared, failed to win through. It was more to be dreaded on all accounts than five years' penal servitude. "You see it begins with starvation and solitary confinement, and that breaks up the strongest. I think it will be enough for our vainglorious talker." Miss Madeleine Stanley (now Lady Middleton) was sitting beside me, her fine, sensitive face clouded. I could not contain myself, I was being whipped on a sore.

"This must have been the way they talked in Jerusalem," I remarked, "after the world-tragedy."

"You were an intimate friend of his, were you not?" insinuated the delicate one gently.

"A friend and admirer," I replied, "and always shall be."

A glacial silence spread round the table, while the delicate one smiled with deprecating contempt and offered some grapes to her neighbour; but help came. Lady Dorothy Nevill was a little further down the table. She had not heard all that was said, but had caught the tone of the conversation and divined the rest.

"Are you talking of Oscar Wilde?" she exclaimed. "I'm glad to hear you say you are a friend. I am, too, and shall always be proud of having known him, a most brilliant, charming man."

"I think of giving a dinner to him when he comes out, Lady Dorothy," I said.

"I hope you'll ask me," she answered bravely. "I should be glad to come. I always admired and liked him. I feel dreadfully sorry for him."

The delicate one adroitly changed the conversation and coffee came in, but Miss Stanley said to me:

"I wish I had known him, there must have been great good in him to win such friendship."

"Great charm in any case," I replied, "and that's rarer among men than even goodness."

The first news that came to us from prison was not altogether bad. He had broken down and was in the infirmary, but was getting better. The brave Stewart Headlam, who had gone bail for him, had visited him, the Stewart Headlam who was an English clergyman, and yet, wonder of wonders, a Christian. A little later one heard that Sherard had seen him, and brought about a reconciliation with his wife. Mrs. Wilde had been very good and had gone to the prison and had no doubt comforted him. Much to be hoped from all this. . . .

For months and months the situation in South Africa took all my heart and mind.

In the first days of January, 1896, came the Jameson Raid, and I sailed for South Africa. I had work to do for *The Saturday Review*, absorbing work by day and night. In the summer I was back in England, but the task of defending the Boer farmers grew more and more arduous, and I only heard that Oscar was going on as well as could be expected.

Some time later, after he had been transferred to Reading Gaol, bad news leaked out, news that he was breaking up, was being punished, persecuted. His friends came to me, asking: could anything be done? As usual my only hope was in the supreme authority. Sir Evelyn Ruggles Brise was the head of the Prison Commission; after the Home Secretary, the most powerful person, the permanent official behind the Parliamentary figure-head; the man who knew and acted behind the man who talked. I sat down and wrote to him for an interview. By return came a courteous note giving me an appointment.

I told him what I had heard about Oscar, that his health was breaking down and his reason going, pointed out how monstrous it was to turn prison into a torture-chamber. To my utter astonishment he agreed with me, admitted, even, that an exceptional man ought to have exceptional treatment; showed not a trace of pedantry; good brains, good heart. He went so far as to say that Oscar Wilde should be treated with all possible consideration, that certain prison rules which pressed very hardly upon him should be interpreted as mildly as possible. He admitted that the punishment was much more severe to him than it would be to an ordinary criminal, and had nothing but admiration for his brilliant gifts.

"It was a great pity," he said, "that Wilde ever got into prison, a great pity."

I was pushing at an open door; besides the year or so which had elapsed since the condemnation had given time for reflection. Still, Sir Ruggles Brise's attitude was extraordinary, sympathetic at once and high-minded; another true Englishman at the head of affairs; infinite hope in that fact, and solace.

I had stuck to my text that something should be done at once to give Oscar courage and hope; he must not be murdered or left to despair.

Sir Ruggles Brise asked me finally if I would go to Reading and report on Oscar Wilde's condition and make any suggestion that might occur to me. He did not know if this could be arranged; but he would see the Home Secretary and would recommend it, if I were willing. Of course I was willing, more than willing. Two or three days later, I got another letter from him with another appointment, and again I went to see him. He received me with charming kindness. The Home Secretary would be glad if I would go down to Reading and report on Oscar Wilde's state.

"Everyone," said Sir Ruggles Brise, "speaks with admiration and delight of his wonderful talents. The Home Secretary thinks it would be a great loss to English literature if he were really injured by the prison discipline. Here is your order to see him alone, and a word of introduction to the Governor, and a request to give you all information."

I could not speak. I could only shake hands with him in silence.

What a country of anomalies England is! A judge of the High Court, a hard self-satisfied pernicious bigot, while the official in charge of the prisons is a man of wide culture and humane views, who has the courage of a noble humanity.

I went to Reading Gaol and sent in my letter. I was met by the Governor, who gave orders that Oscar Wilde should be conducted to a room where we could talk alone. I cannot give an account of my interviews with the Governor or the doctor; it would smack of a breach of confidence; besides all such conversations are peculiarly personal. Some people call forth the best in us, others the worst. Without wishing to, I may have stirred up the lees. I can only say here that I then learned for the first time the full, incredible meaning of "Man's inhumanity to man".

In a quarter of an hour I was led into a bare room where Oscar Wilde was already standing by a plain deal table. The warder who had come with him then left us. We shook hands and sat down opposite to each other. He had changed greatly. He appeared much older; his dark brown hair was streaked with grey, particularly in front and over the ears. He was much thinner, had lost at least thirty-five pounds, probably forty or more. On the whole, however, he looked better physically than he had looked for years before his imprisonment. His eyes were clear and bright; the outlines of the face were no longer swamped in fat; the voice even was ringing and musical; he had improved bodily, I thought; though in repose his face wore a nervous, depressed and harassed air.

"You know how glad I am to see you, heart-glad to find you looking so well," I began, "but tell me quickly, for I may be able to help you, what have you to complain of; what do you want?"

For a long time he was too hopeless, too frightened to talk. "The list of my grievances," he said, "would be without end. The worst of it is I am perpetually being punished for nothing; this governor loves to punish, and he punishes by taking my books from me. It is perfectly awful to let the mind grind itself away between the upper and nether millstones of regret and remorse without respite; with books my life would be livable—any life," he added sadly.

"The life, then, is hard. Tell me about it."

"I don't like to," he said, "it is all so dreadful—and ugly and painful, I would rather not think of it," and he turned away despairingly.

"You must tell me, or I shall not be able to help you." Bit by bit I won the confession from him.

"At first it was a fiendish nightmare; more horrible than anything I had ever dreamt of; from the first evening when they made me undress before them and get into some filthy water they called a bath and dry myself with a damp, brown rag and put on this livery of shame. The cell was appalling. I could hardly breathe in it, and the food turned my stomach; the smell and sight of it were enough. I did not eat anything for days and days, I could not even swallow the bread; and the rest of the food was uneatable; I lay on the so-called bed and shivered all night long. . . . Don't ask me to speak of it, please. Words cannot convey the cumulative effect of a myriad discomforts, brutal handling and slow starvation. Surely like Dante I have written on my face the fact that I have been in hell. Only Dante never imagined any hell like an English prison; in his lowest circle people could move about; could see each other, and hear each other groan. There was some change, some human companionship in misery. . . ."

"When did you begin to eat the food?" I asked.

"I can't tell, Frank," he replied. "After some days I got so hungry I had to eat a little, nibble at the outside of the bread, and drink some of the liquid; whether it was tea, coffee or gruel, I could not tell. As soon as I really ate anything it produced violent diarrhœa and I was ill all day and all night. From the beginning I could not sleep. I grew weak and had wild delusions. . . . You must not ask me to describe it. It is like asking a man who has gone through fever to describe one of the terrifying dreams. At Wandsworth I thought I should go mad; Wandsworth is the worst. No dungeon in hell can be worse; why is the food so bad? It even smelt bad. It was not fit for dogs."

"Was the food the worst of it?" I asked.

"The hunger made you weak, Frank; but the inhumanity was the worst of it. What devilish creatures men are! I had never known anything about them. I had never dreamt of such cruelties. A man spoke to me at exercise. You know you are not allowed to speak. He was in front of me, and he whispered, so that he could not be seen, how sorry he was for me, and how he hoped I would bear up. I stretched out my hands to him and cried, 'Oh, thank you, thank you.' The kindness of his voice brought tears into my eyes. Of course I was punished at once for speaking; a dreadful punishment. I won't think of it. I dare not. They are infinitely cunning in malice here, Frank; infinitely cunning in punishment. . . . Don't let us talk of it, it is too painful, too horrible that men should be so brutal."

"Give me an instance," I said, "of something less painful; something which may be bettered."

He smiled wanly. "All of it, Frank, all of it should be altered. There is no spirit in a prison but hate, hate masked in degrading formalism. They first break the will and rob you of hope, and then rule by fear. One day a warder came into my cell.

" 'Take off your boots,' he said.

"Of course I began to obey him; then I asked:

" 'What is it? Why must I take off my boots?'

"He would not answer me. As soon as he had my boots, he said:

" 'Come out of your cell.'

" 'Why?' I asked again. I was frightened, Frank. What had I done? I could not guess; but then I was often punished for nothing. What was it? No answer. As soon as we were in the corridor he ordered me to stand with my face to the wall, and went away. There I stood in my stocking feet waiting. The cold chilled me through; I began standing first on one foot and then on the other, racking my brains as to what they were going to do to me, wondering why I was being punished like this, and how long it would last; you know the thoughts fear-born that plague the mind. . . . After what seemed an eternity I heard him coming back. I did not dare to move or even look. He came up to me; stopped by me for a moment; my heart stopped; he threw down a pair of boots beside me, and said:

" 'Go to your cell and put those on,' and I went into my cell shaking. That's the way they give you a new pair of boots in prison, Frank; that's the way they are kind to you."

"The first period was the worst?" I asked.

"Oh, yes, infinitely the worst! One gets accustomed to everything in time, to the food and the bed and the silence. One learns the rules, and knows what to expect and what to fear. . . ."

"How did you win through the first period?" I asked.

"I died," he said quietly, "and came to life again, as a patient." I stared at him. "Quite true, Frank. What with the purgings and the semi-starvation and sleeplessness and, worst of all, the regret gnawing at my soul and the incessant torturing self-reproaches, I got weaker and weaker; my clothes hung on me; I could scarcely move. One Sunday morning after a very bad night I could not get out of bed. The warder came in and I told him I was ill."

" 'You had better get up,' he said; but I couldn't take the good advice.

" 'I can't,' I replied, 'you must do what you like with me.'

"Half an hour later the doctor came and looked in at the door. He never came near me; he simply called out:

" 'Get up; no malingering; you're all right. You'll be punished if you don't get up,' and he went away.

"I had to get up. I was very weak; I fell off my bed while dressing, and bruised myself; but I got dressed somehow or other, and then I had to go with the rest to chapel, where they sing hymns, dreadful hymns all out of tune in praise of their pitiless God.

"I could hardly stand up; everything kept disappearing and coming back faintly; and suddenly I must have fallen. . . ." He put his hand to his head. "I woke up feeling a pain in this ear. I was in the infirmary with a warder by me. My hand rested on a clean white sheet; it was like heaven. I could not help pushing my toes against the sheet to feel it, it was so smooth and cool and clean. The nurse with kind eyes said to me:

" 'Do eat something,' and gave me some thin white bread and butter. Frank, I shall never forget it. The water came into my mouth in streams; I was so desperately hungry, and it was so delicious; I was so weak I cried," and he put his hands before his eyes and gulped down his tears.

"I shall never forget it; the warder was so kind. I did not like to tell him I was famished; but when he went away I picked the crumbs off the sheet and ate them, and when I could find no more

I pulled myself to the edge of the bed and picked up the crumbs from the floor and ate those as well; the white bread was so good and I was so hungry."

"And now?" I asked, not able to stand more.

"Oh, now," he said, with an attempt to be cheerful, "of course it would be all right if they did not take my books away from me. If they would let me write. If only they would let me write as I wish, I should be quite content, but they punish me on every pretext. Why do they do it, Frank? Why do they want to make my life here one long misery?"

"Aren't you a little deaf still?" I asked, to ease the passion I felt of intolerable pity.

"Yes," he replied, "on this side, where I fell in the chapel. I fell on my ear, you know, and I must have burst the drum of it, or injured it in some way, for all through the winter it has ached and it often bleeds a little."

"But they could give you some cotton wool or something to put in it?" I said.

He smiled a poor wan smile:

"If you think one dare disturb a doctor or a warder for an earache, you don't know much about a prison. You would pay for it. Why, Frank, however ill I was now," and he lowered his voice to a whisper and glanced about him as if fearing to be overheard, "however ill I was I would not think of sending for the doctor. Not think of it," he said in an awestruck voice. "I have learned prison ways."

"I should rebel," I cried; "why do you let it break the spirit?"

"You would soon be broken, if you rebelled, here. Besides it is all incidental to the *System*. The *System!* No one outside knows what that means. It is an old story, I'm afraid, the story of man's cruelty to man."

"I think I can promise you," I said, "that the *System* will be altered a little. You shall have books and things to write with, and you shall not be harassed every moment by punishment."

"Take care," he cried in a spasm of dread, putting his hand on mine, "take care, they may punish me much worse. You don't know what they can do." I grew hot with indignation.

"Don't say anything, please, of what I have said to you. Promise

197

me, you won't say anything. Promise me. I never complained, I didn't." His excitement was a revelation.

"All right," I replied, to soothe him.

"No, but promise me, seriously," he repeated. "You must promise me. Think, you have my confidence, it is private what I have said." He was evidently frightened out of self-control.

"All right," I said, "I will not tell; but I'll get the facts from the others and not from you."

"Oh, Frank," he said, "you don't know what they do. There is a punishment here more terrible than the rack." And he whispered to me with white sidelong eyes: "They can drive you mad in a week, Frank."[1]

"Mad!" I exclaimed, thinking I must have misunderstood him; though he was white and trembling.

"What about the warders?" I asked again, to change the subject, for I began to feel that I had supped full on horrors.

"Some of them are kind," he sighed. "The one that brought me in here is so kind to me. I should like to do something for him, when I get out. He's quite human. He does not mind talking to me and explaining things; but some of them at Wandsworth were brutes. . . . I will not think of them again. I have sewn those pages up and you must never ask me to open them again. I dare not open them," he cried pitifully.

"But you ought to tell it all," I said, "that's perhaps the purpose you are here for; the ultimate reason."

"Oh, no, Frank, never. I would need a man of infinite strength to come here and give a truthful record of all that happened to him. I don't believe you could do it; I don't believe anybody would be strong enough. Starvation and purging alone would break down anyone's strength. Everybody knows that you are purged and starved to the edge of death. That's what two years' hard labour means. It's not the labour that's hard. It's the condi-

[1] He was referring, I suppose, to the solitary confinement in a dark cell, which English ingenuity has invented and according to all accounts is as terrible as any of the tortures of the past. For those tortures were all physical, whereas the modern Englishman addresses himself to the brain and nerves, and finds the fear of madness more terrifying than the fear of pain. What a pity it is that Mr. Justice Wills did not know twenty-four hours of it, just twenty-four hours to teach him what "adequate punishment" for sensual self-indulgence means, and adequate punishment, too, for inhuman cruelty.

tions of life that make it impossibly hard. They break you down body and soul. And if you resist, they drive you crazy. . . . But, please! don't say I said anything; you've promised, you know you have. You'll remember, won't you!"

I felt guilty. His insistense, his gasping fear showed me how terribly he must have suffered. He was beside himself with dread. I ought to have visited him sooner. I changed the subject.

"You shall have writing materials and your books, Oscar. Force yourself to write. You are looking better than you used to look; your eyes are brighter, your face clearer." The old smile came back into his eyes, the deathless humour.

"I've had a rest cure, Frank," he said, and smiled feebly.

"You should give record of this life as far as you can, and of all its influences on you. You have conquered, you know. Write the names of the inhuman brutes on their foreheads in vitriol, as Dante did for all time."

"No, no, I cannot. I will not. I want to live and forget. I could not; I dare not; I have not Dante's strength, nor his bitterness; I am a Greek born out of due time." He had said the true word at last.

"I will come again and see you," I replied. "Is there nothing else I can do? I hear your wife has seen you. I hope you have made it up with her?"

"She tried to be kind to me, Frank," he said in a dull voice, "she was kind, I suppose. She must have suffered; I'm sorry. . . ." One felt he had no sorrow to spare for others.

"Is there nothing I can do?" I asked.

"Nothing, Frank, only if you could get me books and writing materials, if I could be allowed to use them really! But you won't say anything I have said to you, you promise me you won't?"

"I promise," I replied, "and I shall come back in a short time to see you again. ꞱI think you will be better then. . . .

"Don't dread the coming out; you have friends who will work for you, great allies——" and I told him about Lady Dorothy Nevill at Mrs. Jeune's lunch.

"Isn't she a dear old lady?" he cried, "charming, brilliant, human creature! She might have stepped out of a page of Thackeray, only Thackeray never wrote a page quite dainty and charming enough. He came near it in his 'Esmond'. Oh, I remember you don't like the book, but it is beautifully written, Frank, in beautiful simple rhythmic English. It sings itself to the ear. Lady Dorothy" (how he loved the title!) "was always kind to me, but London is horrible. I could not live in London again. I must go away out of England. Do you remember talking to me, Frank, of France?" and he put both his hands on my shoulders, while tears ran down his face, and sighs broke from him. "Beautiful France, the one country in the world where they care for humane ideals and the humane life. Ah! if only I had gone with you to France," and the tears poured down his cheeks and our hands met convulsively.

"I'm glad to see you looking so well," I began again. "Books you shall have. For God's sake keep your heart up, and I will come back and see you, and don't forget you have good friends outside; lots of us!"

"Thank you, Frank; but take care, won't you, and remember your promise not to tell."

I nodded in assent and went to the door. The warder came in.

"The interview is over," I said; "will you take me downstairs?"

"If you will not mind sitting here, sir," he said, "for a minute. I must take him back first."

"I have been telling my friend," said Oscar to the warder, "how good you have been to me," and he turned and went, leaving with me the memory of his eyes and unforgettable smile; but I noticed as he disappeared that he was thin, and looked hunched up and bowed, in the ugly ill-fitting prison livery. I took out a bank note and put it under the blotting paper that had been placed on the table for me. In two or three minutes the warder came back, and as I left the room I thanked him for being kind to my friend, and told him how kindly Oscar had spoken of him.

"He has no business here, sir," the warder said. "He's no more like one of our reg'lars than a canary is like one of them cocky little spadgers. Prison ain't meant for such as him, and he ain't meant for prison. He's that soft, sir, you see, and affeckshunate. He's more like a woman, he is; you hurt 'em without meaning to. I don't care what they say, I likes him; and he do talk beautiful, sir, don't he?"

"Indeed he does," I said, "the best talker in the world. I want you to look in the pad on the table. I have left a note there for you."

"Not for me, sir, I could not take it; no, sir, please not," he cried in a hurried, fear-struck voice. "You've forgotten something, sir, come back and get it, sir, do, please. I daren't."

In spite of my remonstrance he took me back and I had to put the note in my pocket.

"I could not, you know, sir, I was not kind to him for that." His manner changed; he seemed hurt.

I told him I was sure of it, sure, and begged him to believe, that if I were able to do anything for him, at any time, I'd be glad, and gave him my address. He was not even listening—an honest, good man, full of the milk of human kindness. How kind deeds shine starlike in this prison of a world! That warder and Sir Ruggles Brise each in his own place; such men are the salt of the English world; better are not to be found on earth.

18

Mitigation of Punishment; But Not Release

ON MY RETURN TO LONDON I saw Sir Ruggles Brise. No one could have shown me warmer sympathy or more discriminating comprehension. I made my report to him and left the matter in his hands with perfect confidence. I took care to describe Oscar's condition to his friends while assuring them that his circumstances would soon be bettered. A little later I heard that the governor of the prison had been changed, that Oscar had got books and writing materials, and was allowed to have the gas burning in his cell to a late hour, when it was turned down but not out. In fact, from that time on he was treated with all the kindness possible, and soon we heard that he was bearing the confinement and discipline better than could have been expected. Sir Evelyn Ruggles Brise had evidently settled the difficulty in the most humane spirit.

Later still I was told that Oscar had begun to write "De Profundis" in prison, and I was very hopeful about that too. No news could have given me greater pleasure. It seemed to me certain that he would justify himself to men by turning the punishment into a stepping-stone. And in this belief when the time came I ventured to call on Sir Ruggles Brise with another petition.

"Surely," I said, "Oscar will not be imprisoned for the full term; surely four or five months for good conduct will be remitted?"

Sir Ruggles Brise listened sympathetically, but warned me at once that any remission was exceptional. However, he would let me know what could be done, if I would call again in a week. Much to my surprise, he did not seem certain even about the good conduct.

I returned at the end of the week, and had another long talk with him. He told me that good conduct meant, in prison parlance, absence of punishment, and Oscar had been punished pretty often. Of course his offenses were minor offenses; nothing serious; childish faults indeed for the most part. He was often talking, and he was often late in the morning; his cell was not kept so well as it might be, and so forth. Peccadilloes, all; yet a certificate of "good conduct" depended on such trifling observances. In face of Oscar's record Sir Ruggles Brise did not think that the sentence would be easily lessened. I was thunder-struck. But then no rules to me are sacrosanct. Indeed they are only tolerable because of the exceptions. I had such a high opinion of Ruggles Brise—his kindness and sense of fair play—that I ventured to show him my whole mind on the matter.

"Oscar Wilde," I said to him, "is just about to face life again. He is more than half reconciled to his wife; he has begun a book, is shouldering the burden. A little encouragement now and I believe he will do better things than he has ever done. I am convinced that he has far bigger things in him than we have seen yet. But he is extraordinarily sensitive and extraordinarily vain. The danger is that he may be frightened and blighted by the harshness and hatred of the world. He may shrink into himself and do nothing if the wind be not tempered a little for him. A hint of encouragement now, and the feeling that men like yourself think him worthful and deserving of special kindly treatment, and I feel certain he will do great things. I really believe it is in your hands to save a man of extraordinary talent, and get the best out of him, if you care to do it."

"Of course I care to do it," he cried. "You cannot doubt that, and I see exactly what you mean; but it will not be easy."

"Won't you see what can be done?" I persisted. "Put your mind to discover how it should be done, how the Home Secretary may be induced to remit the last few months of Wilde's sentence."

After a little while he replied:

"You must believe that the authorities are quite willing to help in any good work, more than willing, and I am sure I speak for the Home Secretary as well as for myself; but it is for you to give us some reason for acting—a reason that could be avowed and defended."

I did not at first catch his drift; so I persevered:

"You admit that the reason exists, that it would be a good thing to favour Wilde, then why not do it?"

"We live," he said, "under parliamentary rule. Suppose the question were asked in the House, and I think it very likely in the present state of public opinion that the question would be asked. What should we answer? It would not be an avowable reason that we hoped Wilde would write new plays and books, would it? That reason ought to be sufficient, I grant you; but, you see yourself, it would not be so regarded."

"You are right, I suppose," I had to admit. "But if I got you a petition from men of letters, asking you to release Wilde for his health's sake, would that do?"

Sir Ruggles Brise jumped at the suggestion.

"Certainly," he exclaimed, "if some men of letters, men of position, wrote asking that Wilde's sentence should be diminished by three or four months on account of his health, I think it would have the best effect."

"I will see Meredith at once," I said, "and some others. How many names should I get?"

"If you have Meredith," he replied, "you don't need many others. A dozen would do, or fewer if you find a dozen too many."

"I don't think I shall meet with any difficulty," I replied, "but I will let you know."

"You will find it harder than you think," he concluded, "but if you get one or two great names the rest may follow. In any case one or two good names will make it easier for you."

Naturally I thanked him for his kindness and went away absolutely content. I had never set myself a task which seemed simpler. Meredith could not be more merciless than a Royal Commisson. I returned to my office in *The Saturday Review* and got the Royal Commission report on this sentence of two years' imprisonment with hard labour. The Commission recommended that it should be wiped off the Statute Book as too severe. I drafted a little petition as colourless as possible:

"In view of the fact that the punishment of two years' imprisonment with hard labour has been condemned by a Royal Commission as too severe, and inasmuch as Mr. Wilde has been distinguished by his work in letters and is now, we hear, suffering in health, we, your petitioners, pray—and so forth and so on."

I got this printed, and then sat down to write to Meredith asking when I could see him on the matter. I wanted his signature first to be printed underneath the petition, and then issue it. To my astonishment Meredith did not answer at once, and when I pressed him and set forth the facts he wrote to me that he could not do what I wished. I wrote again, begging him to let me see him on the matter. For the first time in my life he refused to see me. He wrote to me to say that nothing I could urge would move him, and it would therefore only be painful to both of us to find ourselves in conflict.

Nothing ever surprised me more than this attitude of Meredith's. I knew his poetry pretty well, and knew how severe he was on every sensual weakness perhaps because it was his own pitfall. I knew too what a fighter he was at heart and how he loved the virile virtues; but I thought I knew the man, knew his tender kindliness of heart, the founts of pity in him, and I felt certain I could count on him for any office of human charity or generosity. But no, he was impenetrable, hard. He told me long afterwards that he had rather a low opinion of Wilde's capacities, instinctive, deep-rooted contempt, too, for the showman in him, and an absolute abhorrence of his vice.

"That vile, sensual self-indulgence puts back the hands of the clock," he said, "and should not be forgiven."

For the life of me I could never forgive Meredith; never afterwards was he of any importance to me. He had always been to me a standard bearer in the eternal conflict, a leader in the Liberation War of Humanity, and here I found him pitiless to another who had been wounded on the same side in the great struggle. It seemed to me appalling. True, Wilde had not been wounded in fighting for us; true, he had fallen out and come to grief, as a drunkard might. But after all he had been fighting on the right side, had been a quickening intellectual influence. It was dreadful to pass him on the wayside and allow him callously to bleed to death. It was revoltingly cruel! The foremost Englishman of his time unable even to understand Christ's example, much less reach his height!

This refusal of Meredith's not only hurt me, but almost destroyed my hope, though it did not alter my purpose. I wanted a figurehead for my petition, and the figurehead I had chosen I could not get. I began to wonder and doubt. I next approached a very different man, the late Professor Churton Collins, a great friend of mine, who, in spite of an almost pedantic rigour of mind and character, had in him at bottom a curious spring of sympathy—a little pool of pure love for the poets and writers whom he admired. I got him to dinner and asked him to sign the petition; he refused, but on grounds other than those taken by Meredith.

"Of course Wilde ought to get out," he said, "the sentence was a savage one and showed bitter prejudice; but I have children, and my own way to make in the world, and if I did this I should be tarred with the Wilde brush. I cannot afford to do it. If he were really a great man I hope I should do it, but I don't agree with your estimate of him. I cannot think I am called upon to bell the British cat in his defence. It has many claws and all sharp."

As soon as he saw the position was unworthy of him, he shifted to new ground.

"If you were justified in coming to me, I should do it; but I am no one; why don't you go to Meredith, Swinburne or Hardy?"

I had to give up the professor, as well as the poet. I knocked in turn at a great many doors, but all in vain. No one wished to take the odium on himself. One man, since become celebrated, said he had no position, his name was not good enough for the purpose. Others left my letters unanswered. Yet another sent a bare acknowledgement saying how sorry he was, but that public opinion was against Mr. Wilde; with one accord they all made excuses. . . .

One day Professor Tyrrell of Trinity College, Dublin, happened to be in my office, while I was setting forth the difference between men of letters in France and England as exemplified by this conduct. In France among authors there is a recognized *esprit de corps*, which constrains them to hold together. For instance when Zola was threatened with prosecution for "Nana," a dozen men like Cherbuliez, Feuillet, Dumas *fils*, who hated his work and regarded it as sensational, tawdry, immoral even, took up the cudgels for him at once; declared that the police were not judges of art, and should not interfere with a serious workman. All these Frenchmen, though they disliked Zola's work, and believed that his popularity was won by a low appeal, still admitted that he was a force in letters, and stood by him resolutely in spite of their own prepossessions and prejudices. But in England the feeling is altogether more selfish. Everyone consults his own sordid self-interest and is rather glad to see a social favourite come to grief; not a hand is stretched out to help him. Suddenly, Tyrrell broke in upon my exposition:

"I don't know whether my name is of any good to you," he said, "but I agree with all you have said, and my name might be classed with that of Churton Collins, though, of course, I've no right to speak for literature," and without more ado he signed the petition, adding, "Regius Professor of Greek at Trinity College, Dublin."

"When you next see Oscar," he continued, "please tell him that my wife and I asked after him. We both hold him in grateful memory as a most brilliant talker and writer, and a charming fellow to boot. Confusion take all their English Puritanism."

Merely living in Ireland tends to make an Englishman more humane; but one name was not enough, and Tyrrell's was the only one I could get. In despair, and knowing that George Wyndham had had a great liking for Oscar, and admiration for his high talent, I asked him to lunch at the Savoy; laid the matter before him, and begged him to give me his name. He refused, and in face of my astonishment he excused himself by saying that, as soon as the rumour had reached him of Oscar's intimacy with Bosie Douglas, he had asked Oscar whether there was any truth in the scandalous report.

"You see," he went on, "Bosie is by way of being a relation of mine, and so I had the right to ask. Oscar gave me his word of honour that there was nothing but friendship between them. He lied to me, and that I can never forgive."

A politician unable to forgive a lie—surely one can hear the mocking laughter of the gods! I could say nothing to such paltry affected nonsense. Politician-like Wyndham showed me how the wind of popular feeling blew, and I recognized that my efforts were in vain.

There is no fellow-feeling among English men of letters; in fact they hold together less than any other class and, by himself, none of them wished to help a wounded member of the flock. I had to tell Sir Ruggles Brise that I had failed.

I have been informed since that if I had begun by asking Thomas Hardy, I might have succeeded. I knew Hardy; but never cared greatly for his talent. I daresay if I had had nothing else to do I might have succeeded in some half degree. But all these two years I was extremely busy and anxious; the storm clouds in South Africa were growing steadily darker and my attitude to South African affairs was exceedingly unpopular in London. It seemed to me vitally important to prevent England from making war on the Boers. I had to abandon the attempt to get Oscar's sentence shortened, and comfort myself with Sir Ruggles Brise's assurance that he would be treated with the greatest possible consideration.

Still, my advocacy had had a good effect.

Oscar himself has told us what the kindness shown to him in the last six months of his prison life really did for him. He writes in *De Profundis* that for the first part of his sentence he could only wring his hands in impotent despair and cry, "What an ending, what an appalling ending!" But when the new spirit of kindness came to him, he could say with sincerity: "What a beginning, what a wonderful beginning!" He sums it all up in these words:

"Had I been released after eighteen months, as I hoped to be, I would have left my prison loathing it and every official in it with a bitterness of hatred that would have poisoned my life. I have had six months more of imprisonment, but humanity has been in the prison with us all the time, and now when I go out I shall always remember great kindnesses that I have received here from almost everybody, and on the day of my release I shall give many thanks to many people, and ask to be remembered by them in turn."

This is the man whom Mr. Justice Wills addressed as insensible to any high appeal.

Some time passed before I visited Oscar again. The change in him was extraordinary. He was light-hearted, gay, and looked better than I had ever seen him. Clearly the austerity of prison life suited him. He met me with a jest:

"It is you, Frank!" he cried as if astonished, "always original! You come back to prison of your own free-will!"

He declared that the new governor—Major Nelson was his name—had been as kind as possible to him. He had not had a punishment for months, and "Oh, Frank, the joy of reading when you like and writing as you please—the delight of living again!" He was so infinitely improved that his talk delighted me.

"What books have you?" I asked.

"I thought I should like the 'Œdipus Rex,'" he replied gravely; "but I could not read it. It all seemed unreal to me. Then I thought of St. Augustine, but he was worse still. The fathers of the Church were still further away from me; they all found it so easy to repent and change their lives. It does not seem to me easy. At last I got hold of Dante. Dante was what I wanted. I read the 'Purgatorio' all through, forced myself to read it in Italian to get the full savour and significance of it. Dante, too, had been in the depths and drunk the bitter lees of despair. I shall want a little library when I come out, a library of a score of books. I wonder if you will help me to get it. I want Flaubert, Stevenson, Baudelaire, Maeterlinck, Dumas *père*, Keats, Marlowe, Chatterton, Anatole France, Théophile Gautier, Dante, Goethe, Meredith's poems, and his 'Egoist,' the Song of Solomon, too, Job, and, of course, the Gospels."

"I shall be delighted to get them for you," I said, "if you will send me the list. By the by, I hear that you have been reconciled to your wife; is that true? I should be glad to know it's true."

"I hope it will be all right," he said gravely, "she is very good and kind. I suppose you have heard," he went on, "that my mother died since I came here, and that leaves a great gap in my life. . . . I always had the greatest admiration and love for my mother. She was a great woman, Frank, a perfect idealist. My father got into trouble once in Dublin, perhaps you have heard about it?"

"Oh, yes," I said. "I have read the case." (It is narrated in the first chapter of this book.)

"Well, Frank, she stood up in court and bore witness for him with perfect serenity, with perfect trust and without a shadow of common womanly jealousy. She could not believe that the man she loved could be unworthy, and her conviction was so complete that it communicated itself to the jury. Her trust was so noble that they became infected by it, and brought him in guiltless.[1] Extraordinary, was it not? She was quite sure too of the verdict. It is only noble souls who have that assurance and serenity. . . .

"When my father was dying it was the same thing. I always see her sitting there by his bedside with a sort of dark veil over her head—quite silent, quite calm. Nothing ever troubled her optimism. She believed that only good can happen to us. When death came to the man she loved, she accepted it with the same serenity and when my sister died she bore it in the same high way. My sister was a wonderful creature, so gay and high-spirited, 'embodied sunshine', I used to call her.

"When we lost her, my mother simply took it that it was best for the child. Women have infinitely more courage than men, don't you think? I have never known anyone with such perfect faith as my mother. She was one of the great figures of the world. What she must have suffered over my sentence I don't dare to think. I'm sure she endured agonies. She had great hopes of me. When she was told that she was going to die, and that she could not see me, for I was not allowed to go to her,[2] she said: 'May the prison help him,' and turned her face to the wall.

"She felt about the prison as you do, Frank, and really I think you are both right; it has helped me. There are things I see now that I never saw before. I see what pity means. I thought a work of art should be beautiful and joyous. But now I see that that ideal is insufficient, even shallow; a work of art must be founded on pity; a book or poem which has no pity in it, had better not be written. . . .

"I shall be very lonely when I come out, and I can't stand lone-

[1] I give Oscar's view of the trial just to show how his romantic imagination turned disagreeable facts into pleasant fiction. Oscar could only have heard of the trial, and perhaps his mother was his informant—which adds to the interest of the story.

[2] Permission to visit a dying mother is accorded in France, even to murderers. The English pretend to be more religious than the French; but are assuredly less humane.

liness and solitude; it is intolerable to me, hateful, I have had too much of it. . . .

"You see, Frank, I am breaking with the past altogether. I am going to write the history of it. I am going to tell how I was tempted and fell, how I was pushed by the man I loved into that dreadful quarrel of his, driven forward to the fight with his father and then left to suffer alone. . . .

"That is the story I am now going to tell. That is the book[1] of pity and of love which I am writing now—a terrible book. . . .

"I wonder would you publish it, Frank? I should like it to appear in *The Saturday*."

"I'd be delighted to publish anything of yours," I replied, "and happier still to publish something to show that you have at length chosen the better part and are beginning a new life. I'd pay you, too, whatever the work turns out to be worth to me; in any case much more than I pay Bernard Shaw or anyone else." I said this to encourage him.

"I'm sure of that," he answered. "I'll send you the book as soon as I've finished it. I think you'll like it"—and there for the moment the matter ended.

At length I felt sure that all would be well with him. How could I help feeling sure? His mind was richer and stronger than it had ever been; and he had broken with all the dark past. I was overjoyed to believe that he would yet do greater things than he had ever done, and this belief and determination were in him, too, as anyone can see on reading what he wrote at this time in prison:

"There is before me so much to do that I would regard it as a terrible tragedy if I died before I was allowed to complete at any rate a little of it. I see new developments in art and life, each one of which is a fresh mode of perfection. I long to live so that I can explore what is no less than a new world to me. Do you want to know what this new world is? I think you can guess what it is. It is the world in which I have been living. Sorrow, then, and all that it teaches one, is my new world. . . .

"I used to live entirely for pleasure. I shunned suffering and sorrow of every kind. I hated both. . . ."

[1] "De Profundis." What Oscar called "the terrible part" of the book—the indictment of Lord Alfred Douglas—has since been read out in Court.

211

Through the prison bars Oscar had begun to see how mistaken he had been, how much greater, and more salutary to the soul, suffering is than pleasure.

"Out of sorrow have the worlds been built, and at the birth of a child or a star there is pain."

19

His St. Martin's Summer: His Best Work

Shortly before he came out of prison, one of Oscar's intimates told me he was destitute, and begged me to get him some clothes. I took the name of his tailor and ordered two suits. The tailor refused to take the order; he was not going to make clothes for Oscar Wilde. I could not trust myself to talk to the man and therefore sent my assistant editor and friend, Mr. Blanchamp, to have it out with him. The tradesman soul yielded to the persuasiveness of cash in advance. I sent Oscar the clothes and a cheque, and shortly after his release got a letter thanking me.

A little later I heard on good authority a story which Oscar afterwards confirmed, that when he left Reading Gaol the correspondent of an American paper offered him £1,000 for an interview dealing with his prison life and experiences, but he felt it beneath his dignity to take his sufferings to market. He thought it better to borrow than to earn. He is partly to be excused, perhaps, when one remembers that he had still some pounds left of the large sums given him before his condemnation by Miss S——, Ross, More Adey, and others. Still his refusal of such a sum as that offered by the New York paper shows how utterly contemptuous he was of money, even at a moment when one would have thought money would have been his chief preoccupation. He always lived in the day and rather heedlessly.

As soon as he left prison he crossed with some friends to France, and went to stay at the Hotel de la Plage at Berneval, a quiet little village near Dieppe. M. André Gide, who called on him there almost as soon as he arrived, gives a fair mental picture of him at this time. He tells how delighted he was to find in him the "Oscar Wilde of old," no longer the sensualist puffed out with pride and good living, but "the sweet Wilde" of the days before 1891. "I found myself taken back, not two years," he says, "but four or five. There was the same dreamy look, the same amused smile, the same voice."

He told M. Gide that prison had completely changed him, had taught him the meaning of pity. "You know," he went on, "how fond I used to be of 'Madame Bovary,' but Flaubert would not admit pity into his work, and that is why it has a petty and re-strained character about it. It is the sense of pity by means of which a work gains in expanse, and by which it opens up a bound-less horizon. Do you know, my dear fellow, it was pity which pre-vented my killing myself? During the first six months in prison I was dreadfully unhappy, so utterly miserable that I wanted to kill myself; but what kept me from doing so was looking at the others, and seeing that they were as unhappy as I was, and feeling sorry for them. Oh dear! what a wonderful thing pity is, and I never knew it."

He was speaking in a low voice without any excitement.

"Have you ever learned how wonderful a thing pity is? For my part I thank God every night, yes, on my knees I thank God for having taught it to me. I went into prison with a heart of stone, thinking only of my own pleasure; but now my heart is utterly broken—pity has entered into my heart. I have learned now that pity is the greatest and the most beautiful thing in the world. And that is why I cannot bear ill-will towards those who caused my suffering and those who condemned me; no, nor to anyone, be-cause without them I should not have known all that. Alfred Douglas writes me terrible letters. He says he does not understand me, that he does not understand that I do not wish everyone ill, and that everyone has been horried to me. No, he does not under-stand me. He cannot understand me any more. But I keep on telling him that in every letter. We cannot follow the same road. He has his and it is beautiful—I have mine. His is that of Alci-biades; mine is now that of St. Francis of Assisi."

How much of this is sincere and how much merely imagined and stated in order to incarnate the new ideal to perfection would be hard to say. The truth is not so saintly simple as the christianised Oscar would have us believe. The unpublished portions of "De Profundis" which were read out in the Douglas—Ransome trial prove, what all his friends know, that Oscar Wilde found it impossible to forgive or forget what seemed to him personal ill-treatment. There are beautiful pages in "De Profundis," pages of sweetest Christlike resignation and charity and no doubt in a certain mood Oscar was sincere in writing them. But there was another mood in him, more vital and more enduring, if not so engaging, a mood in which he saw himself as one betrayed and sacrificed and abandoned, and then he attributed his ruin wholly to his friend and did not hesitate to speak of him as the "Judas" whose shallow selfishness and imperious ill-temper and unfulfilled promises of monetary help had driven a great man to disaster.

That unpublished portion of "De Profundis" is in essence, from beginning to end, one long curse of Lord Alfred Douglas, an indictment apparently impartial, particularly at first; but in reality a bitter and merciless accusation, showing in Oscar Wilde a curious want of sympathy even with the man he said he loved. Those who would know Oscar Wilde as he really was will read that piece of rhetoric with care enough to notice that he reiterates the charge of shallow selfishness with such venom, that he discovers his own colossal egotism and essential hardness of heart. "Love," we are told, "suffereth long and is kind . . . beareth all things, believeth all things, hopeth all things, endureth all things"—that sweet, generous, all-forgiving tenderness of love was not in the pagan, Oscar Wilde, and therefore even his deepest passion never won to complete reconciliation and ultimate redemption.

In this same talk with M. Gide, Oscar is reported to have said that he had known beforehand that a catastrophe was unavoidable; "there was but one end possible. . . . That state of things could not last; there had to be some end to it."

This view I believe is Gide's and not Oscar's. In any case I am sure that my description of him before the trials as full of insolent self-assurance is the truer truth. Of course he must have had forebodings; he was warned as I've related, again and again; but he took character-colour from his associates and he met Queensberry's first attempts at attack with utter disdain. He did not re-alise his danger at all. Gide reports him more correctly as adding:

"Prison has completely changed me. I was relying on it for that —Douglas is terrible. He cannot understand that—cannot under-stand that I am not taking up the same existence again. He accuses the others of having changed me."

I may publish here part of a letter of a prison warder which Mr. Stuart Mason reproduced in his excellent little book on Oscar Wilde. He says:

"No more beautiful life had any man lived, no more beautiful life could any man live than Oscar Wilde lived during the short period I knew him in prison. He wore upon his face an eternal smile; sunshine was on his face, sunshine of some sort must have been in his heart. People say he was not sincere. He was the very soul of sincerity when I knew him. If he did not continue that life after he left prison, then the forces of evil must have been too strong for him. But he tried, he honestly tried, and in prison he succeeded."

All this seems to me, in the main, true. Oscar's gay vivacity would have astonished any stranger. Besides, the regular hours and scant plain food of prison had improved his health and the solitude and suffering had lent him a deeper emotional life. But there was an intense bitterness in him, a profound underlying sense of injury which came continually to passionate expression. Yet as soon as the miserable petty persecution of the prison was lifted from him, all the joyous gaiety and fun of his nature bubbled up irresistibly. There was no contradiction in this complexity. A man can hold in himself a hundred conflicting passions and impulses without confusion. At this time the dominant chord in Oscar was pity for others.

To my delight the world had evidence of this changed Oscar Wilde in a very short time. On May 28th, a few days after he left prison, there appeared in *The Daily Chronicle* a letter more than two columns in length, pleading for the kindlier treatment of little children in English prisons. The letter was written because Warder Martin[1] of Reading prison had been dismissed by the

---

[1] The notes were written on scraps of paper and pushed under his cell-door; they are among the most convincing evidences of Oscar's essential humanity and kindness of heart.

Commissioners for the dreadful crime of "having given some sweet biscuits to a little hungry child."

I must quote a few paragraphs of this letter, because it shows how prison had deepened Oscar Wilde, how his own suffering had made him, as Shakespeare says, "pregnant to good pity," and also because it tells us what life was like in an English prison in our time. Oscar wrote:

"I saw the three children myself on the Monday preceding my release. They had just been convicted and were standing in a row in the central hall in their prison dress carrying their sheets under their arms, previous to their being sent to the cells allotted to them. . . . They were quite small children, the youngest—the one to whom the warder gave the biscuits—being a tiny chap, for whom they had evidently been unable to find clothes small enough to fit. I had, of course, seen many children in prison during the two years during which I was myself confined. Wandsworth prison, especially, contained always a large number of children. But the little child I saw on the afternoon of Monday, the 17th, at Reading, was tinier than any one of them. I need not say how utterly distressed I was to see these children at Reading, for I knew the treatment in store for them. The cruelty that is practised by day and night on children in English prisons is incredible except to those that have witnessed it and are aware of the brutality of the system.

"People nowadays do not understand what cruelty is. . . . Ordinary cruelty is simply stupidity.

"The prison treatment of children is terrible, primarily from people not understanding the peculiar psychology of the child's nature. A child can understand a punishment inflicted by an individual, such as a parent, or guardian, and bear it with a certain amount of acquiescence. What it cannot understand is a punishment inflicted by society. It cannot realise what society is. . . .

"The terror of a child in prison is quite limitless. I remember once in Reading, as I was going out to exercise, seeing in the dimly lit cell opposite mine a small boy. Two warders—not unkindly men—were talking to him, with some sternness apparently, or perhaps giving him some useful advice about his conduct. One was in the cell with him, the other was standing outside. The child's face was like a white wedge of sheer terror. There was in his eyes the terror of a hunted animal. The next morning I heard him at breakfast time crying, and calling to be let out. His cry was for his parents. From time to time I could hear the deep voice of the warder on duty telling him to keep quiet. Yet he was not even convicted of whatever little offence he had been charged with. He was simply on remand. That I knew by his wearing his own clothes, which seemed neat enough. He was, however, wearing prison socks and shoes. This showed that he was a very poor boy, whose own shoes, if he had any, were in a bad state. Justices and magistrates, an entirely ignorant class as a rule, often remand children for a week, and then perhaps remit whatever sentence they are entitled to pass. They call this 'not sending a child to prison'. It is of course a stupid view on their part. To a little child, whether he is in prison on remand or after conviction is not a subtlety of position he can comprehend. To him the horrible thing is to be there at all. In the eyes of humanity it should be a horrible thing for him to be there at all.

"This terror that seizes and dominates the child, as it seizes the grown man also, is of course intensified beyond power of expression by the solitary cellular system of our prisons. Every child is confined to its cell for twenty-three hours out of the twenty-four. This is the appalling thing. To shut up a child in a dimly lit cell for twenty-three hours out of the twenty-four is an example of the cruelty of stupidity. If an individual, parent or guardian, did this to a child, he would be severely punished. . . .

"The second thing from which a child suffers in prison is hunger. The food that is given to it consists of a piece of usually badly baked prison bread and a tin of water for breakfast at half past seven. At twelve o'clock it gets dinner, composed of a tin of coarse Indian meal stirabout, and at half past five it gets a piece of dry bread and a tin of water for its supper. This diet in the case of a strong man is always productive of illness of some kind, chiefly, of course, diarrhœa, with its attendant weakness. In fact, in a big prison, astringent medicines are served out regularly by the warders as a matter of course. A child is as a rule incapable of eating the food at all. Anyone who knows anything about children knows how easily a child's digestion is upset by a fit of crying or trouble and mental distress of any kind. A child who has been crying all day long and perhaps half the night, in a lonely, dimly lit cell, and is preyed upon by terror, simply cannot eat food of this coarse, horrible kind. In the case of the little child to whom Warder Martin gave the biscuits, the child was crying with hunger on Tuesday morning, and utterly unable to eat the bread and water served to it for breakfast.

"Martin went out after the breakfast had been served and bought the few sweet biscuits for the child rather than see it starving. It was a beautiful action on his part and was so recognized by the child, who, utterly unconscious of the regulation of the Prison Board, told one of the senior warders how kind this junior warder had been to him. The result was, of course, a report and a dismissal.[1]

"I know Martin extremely well, and I was under his charge for the last seven weeks of my imprisonment. . . . I was struck by the singular kindness and humanity of the way in which he spoke to me and to the other prisoners. Kind words are much in prison, and a pleasant 'good-morning' or 'good-evening' will make one as happy as one can be in prison. He was always gentle and considerate. . . .

"A great deal has been talked and written lately about the contaminating influence of prison on young children. What is said is quite true. A child is utterly contaminated by prison life. But this contaminating influence is not that of the prisoners. It is that of the whole prison system—of the governor, the chaplain, the warders, the solitary cell, the isolation, the revolting food, the rules of the Prison Commissioners, the mode of discipline, as it is termed, of the life.

"Of course no child under fourteen years of age should be sent to prison at all. It is an absurdity, and, like many absurdities, of absolutely tragical results. . . ."

This letter, I am informed, brought about some improvement in the treatment of young children in British prisons. But in regard to adults the British prison is still the torture chamber it was in Wilde's time; prisoners are still treated more brutally there than anywhere else in the civilised world; the food is the worst in Europe, insufficient indeed to maintain health; in many cases men

[1] The Home Secretary, Sir Matthew White Ridley, when questioned by Mr. Michael Davitt in the House of Commons, May 25, 1897, declared that this dismissal of a warder for feeding a little hungry child at his own expense was "fully justified" and a "proper step". This same Home Secretary appointed his utterly incompetent brother to be a judge of the High Court.

are only saved from death by starvation through being sent to the infirmary. Though these facts are well known, *Punch*, the pet organ of the British middle-class, was not ashamed a little while ago to make a mock of some suggested reform, by publishing a picture of a British convict, with the villainous face of a Bill Sykes, lying on a sofa in his cell smoking a cigar with champagne at hand. This is not altogether due to stupidity, as Oscar tried to believe, but to reasoned selfishness. *Punch* and the class for which it caters would like to believe that many convicts are unfit to live, whereas the truth is that a good many of them are superior in humanity to the people who punish and slander them.

While waiting for his wife to join him, Oscar rented a little house, the Châlet Bourgeat, about two hundred yards away from the hotel at Berneval, and furnished it. Here he spent the whole of the summer writing, bathing, and talking to the few devoted friends who visited him from time to time. Never had he been so happy; never in such perfect health. He was full of literary projects; indeed, no period of his whole life was so fruitful in good work. He was going to write some Biblical plays; one entitled "Pharaoh" first, and then one called "Ahab and Jezebel," which he pronounced Isabelle. Deeper problems, too, were much in his mind; he was already at work on "The Ballad of Reading Gaol," but before coming to that let me first show how happy the song-bird was and how divinely he sang when the dreadful cage was opened and he was allowed to use his wings in the heavenly sunshine.

Here is a letter from him shortly after his release which is one of the most delightful things he ever wrote. Fitly enough it was addressed to his friend of friends, Robert Ross, and I can only say that I am extremely obliged to Ross for allowing me to publish it:

Hotel de la Plage. Berneval, near Dieppe,
Monday night, May 31st (1897).

My dearest Robbie,
I have decided that the only way in which to get boots properly is to go to France to receive them. The *Douane*

charged 3 francs. How could you frighten me as you did? The next time you order boots please come to Dieppe to get them sent to you. It is the only way and it will be an excuse for seeing you.

I am going to-morrow on a pilgrimage. I always wanted to be a pilgrim, and I have decided to start early to-morrow to the shrine of Notre Dame de Liesse. Do you know what Liesse is? It is an old word for joy. I suppose the same as Letizia, Lætitia. I just heard to-night of the shrine or chapel, by chance, as you would say, from the sweet woman of the *auberge*, who wants me to live always at Berneval. She says Notre Dame de Liesse is wonderful, and helps everyone to the secret of joy— I do not know how long it will take me to get to the shrine, as I must walk. But, from what she tells me, it will take at least six or seven minutes to get there, and as many to come back. In fact the chapel of Notre Dame de Liesse is just fifty yards from the hotel. Isn't it extraordinary? I intend to start after I have had my coffee, and then to bathe. Need I say that this is a miracle? I wanted to go on a pilgrimage, and I find the little grey stone chapel of Our Lady of Joy is brought to me. It has probably been waiting for me all these purple years of pleasure, and now it comes to meet me with Liesse as its message. I simply don't know what to say. I wish you were not so hard to poor heretics,[1] and would admit that even for the sheep who has no shepherd there is a Stella Maris to guide it home. But you and More, especially More, treat me as a Dissenter. It is very painful and quite unjust.

Yesterday I attended Mass at 10 o'clock and afterwards bathed. So I went into the water without being a pagan. The consequence was that I was not tempted by either sirens or mermaidens, or any of the green-haired following of Glaucus. I really think that this is a remarkable thing. In my Pagan days the sea was always full of Tritons, blowing conchs, and other unpleasant things. Now it is quite different. And yet you treat me as the President of Mansfield College; and after I had canonised you too.

Dear boy, I wish you would tell me if your religion makes you happy. You conceal your religion from me in a monstrous way. You treat it like writing in the *Saturday Review* for Pollock, or dining in Wardour Street off the fascinating dish

---

[1] The correspondent to whom Wilde writes and the other friend referred to are Roman Catholics.

that is served with tomatoes and makes men mad.[1] I know it
is useless asking you, so don't tell me.

I felt an outcast in Chapel yesterday—not really, but a little
in exile. I met a dear farmer in a corn field and he gave me a
seat on his *banc* in church: so I was quite comfortable. He now
visits me twice a day, and as he has no children, and is rich, I
have made him promise to adopt *three*—two boys and a girl.
I told him that if he wanted them, he would find them. He
said he was afraid that they would turn out badly. I told him
everyone did that. He really has promised to adopt three
orphans. He is now filled with enthusiasm at the idea. He is
to go to the *Curé* and talk to him. He told me that his own
father had fallen down in a fit one day as they were talking
together, and that he had caught him in his arms, and put him
to bed, where he died, and that he himself had often thought
how dreadful it was that if he had a fit there was no one to
catch him in his arms. It is quite clear that he must adopt
orphans, is it not?

I feel that Berneval is to be my home. I really do. Notre
Dame de Liesse will be sweet to me, if I go on my knees to
her, and she will advise me. It is extraordinary being brought
here by a white horse that was a native of the place, and knew
the road, and wanted to see its parents, now of advanced years.
It is also extraordinary that I knew Berneval existed and was
arranged for me.

M. Bonnet[2] wants to build me a Châlet, 1,000 metres of
ground (I don't know how much that is—but I suppose about
100 miles) and a Châlet with a studio, a balcony, a salle-à-
manger, a huge kitchen, and three bedrooms—a view of the
sea, and trees—all for 12,000 francs—£480. If I can write a
play I am going to have it begun. Fancy one's own lovely
house and grounds in France for £480. No rent of any kind.
Pray consider this, and approve, if you think well. Of course,
not till I have done my play.

An old gentleman lives here in the hotel. He dines alone in
his room, and then sits in the sun. He came here for two days
and has stayed two years. His sole sorrow is that there is no
theatre. Monsieur Bonnet is a little heartless about this, and
says that as the old gentleman goes to bed at 8 o'clock a
theatre would be of no use to him. The old gentleman says

[1] This refers to a story which Wilde was much interested in at the time.
[2] The proprietor of the hotel.

he only goes to bed at 8 o'clock because there is no theatre. They argued the point yesterday for an hour. I sided with the old gentleman, but Logic sides with Monsieur Bonnet, I believe.

I had a sweet letter from the Sphinx.[1] She gives me a delightful account of Ernest[2] subscribing to Romeike while his divorce suit was running, and not being pleased with some of the notices. Considering the growing appreciation of Ibsen I must say that I am surprised the notices were not better, but nowadays everybody is jealous of everyone else, except, of course, husband and wife. I think I shall keep this last remark of mine for my play.

Have you got my silver spoon[3] from Reggie? You got my silver brushes out of Humphreys,[4] who is bald, so you might easily get my spoon out of Reggie, who has so many, or used to have. You know my crest is on it. It is a bit of Irish silver, and I don't want to lose it. There is an excellent substitute called Britannia metal, very much liked at the Adelphi and elsewhere. Wilson Barrett writes, "I prefer it to silver." It would suit dear Reggie admirably. Walter Besant writes, "I use none other." Mr. Beerbohm Tree also writes, "Since I have tried it I am a different actor; my friends hardly recognize me." So there is obviously a demand for it.

I am going to write a Political Economy in my heavier moments. The first law I lay down is, "Whenever there exists a demand, there is *no* supply." This is the only law that explains the extraordinary contrast between the soul of man and man's surroundings. Civilisations continue because people hate them. A modern city is the exact opposite of what everyone wants. Nineteenth-century dress is the result of our horror of the style. The tall hat will last as long as people dislike it.

Dear Robbie, I wish you would be a little more considerate and not keep me up so late talking to you. It is very flattering to me and all that, but you should remember that I need rest. Good-night. You will find some cigarettes and some flowers by your bedside. Coffee is served below at 8 o'clock. Do you mind? If it is too early for you I don't at all mind lying in bed

[1] The Sphinx is a nickname for Mrs. Leverson, author of "The Eleventh Hour," and other witty novels.

[2] Ernest was her husband.

[3] The silver spoon is a proposed line for a play given by Ross to Turner (Reggie).

[4] Wilde's solicitor in Regina v. Wilde.

an extra hour. I hope you will sleep well. You should as Lloyd is not on the Verandah.[1]

TUESDAY MORNING, 9.30.

The sea and sky are opal—no horrid drawing master's line between them—just one fishing boat, going slowly, and drawing the wind after it. I am going to bathe.

6 O'CLOCK.

Bathed and have seen a Châlet here which I wish to take for the season—quite charming—a splendid view, a large writing room, a dining room, and three lovely bedrooms—besides servants' rooms and also a huge balcony.

[In this blank space he had roughly drawn a ground plan of the imagined Châlet.]
1. Salle-à-manger.
2. Salon.
3. Balcony.

I don't know the scale of the drawing, but the rooms are larger than the plan is. All on ground floor with steps from balcony to ground.

The rent for the season or year is, what do you think?—£32.

Of course I must have it. I will take my meals here—separate and reserved table; it is within two minutes walk. Do tell me to take it. When you come again your room will be waiting for you. All I need is a *domestique*. The people here are most kind.

I made my pilgrimage—the interior of the Chapel is of course a modern horror—but there is a black image of Notre Dame de Liesse—the chapel is as tiny as an undergraduate's room at Oxford. I hope to get the Curé to celebrate Mass in it soon; as a rule the service is only held there in July and August; but I want to see a Mass quite close.

There is also another thing I must write to you about.

I adore this place. The whole country is lovely, and full of forest and deep meadow. It is simple and healthy. If I live in Paris I may be doomed to things I don't desire. I am afraid of big towns. Here I get up at 7.30. I am happy all day. I go to bed at 10. I am frightened of Paris. I want to live here.

I have seen the "terrain". It is the best here, and the only one left. I must build a house. If I could build a châlet for 12,000 francs—£500—and live in a home of my own, how happy I would be. I must raise the money somehow. It would

[1] A reference to the "Vailima Letters" of Stevenson which Wilde read when he was in prison.

give me a home, quiet, retired, healthy, and near England. If I live in Egypt I know what my life would be. If I live in the south of Italy I know I should be idle and worse. I want to live here. Do think over this and send me over the architect.[1] M. Bonnet is excellent and is ready to carry out any idea. I want a little châlet of wood and plaster walls, the wooden beams showing and the white square of plaster diapering the framework—like, I regret to say—Shakespeare's house—like old English sixteenth-century farmers' houses. So your architect has me waiting for him, as he is waiting for me.

Do you think the idea absurd?

I got the *Chronicle*, many thanks. I see the writer on Prince —A.2.11.—does not mention my name—foolish of her—it is a woman.

I, as you, the poem of my days, are away, am forced to write. I have begun something that I think will be very good.

I breakfast to-morrow with the Stannards. What a great passionate, splendid writer John Strange Winter is! How little people understand her work! *Bootle's Baby* is an "œuvre symboliste"—it is really only the style and the subject that are wrong. Pray never speak lightly of *Bootle's Baby*—Indeed pray never speak of it at all—I never do.

Yours,

OSCAR.

Please send a *Chronicle* to my wife.

    Mrs. C. M. Holland,

        Maison Benguerel,

            Bevaix,

                Pres de Neuchatel,

just marking it—and if my second letter appears, mark that.

Also cut out the letter[2] and enclose it in an envelope to:

MR. ARTHUR CRUTHENDEN,

    Poste Restante, G.P.O., Reading,

with just these lines:

Dear friend,

The enclosed will interest you. There is also another letter waiting in the post office for you from me with a little money. Ask for it if you have not got it.

Yours sincerely,

C. 3. 3.

[1] An architect who sent Wilde books on his release from prison.

[2] His letter to *The Daily Chronicle* about Warder Martin and the little children.

I have no one but you, dear Robbie, to do anything. Of course the letter to Reading must go at once, as my friends come out on Wednesday morning early.

This letter displays almost every quality of Oscar Wilde's genius in perfect efflorescence—his gaiety, joyous merriment and exquisite sensibility. Who can read of the little Chapel to Notre Dame de Liesse without emotion quickly to be changed to mirth by the sunny humour of those delicious specimens of self-advertisement: "Mr. Beerbohm Tree also writes: 'Since I have tried it, I am a different actor, my friends hardly recognize me.'"

This letter is the most characteristic thing Oscar Wilde ever wrote, a thing produced in perfect health at the topmost height of happy hours, more characteristic even than "The Importance of Being Earnest", for it has not only the humour of that delightful farce-comedy, but also more than a hint of the deeper feeling which was even then forming itself into a master-work that will form part of the inheritance of men forever.

"The Ballad of Reading Gaol" belongs to this summer of 1897. A fortunate conjuncture of circumstances—the prison discipline excluding all sense-indulgence, the kindness shown him towards the end of his imprisonment and of course the delight of freedom —gave him perfect physical health and hope and joy in work, and so Oscar was enabled for a few brief months to do better than his best. He assured me and I believe that the conception of "The Ballad" came to him in prison and was due to the alleviation of his punishment and the permission accorded to him to write and read freely—a divine fruit born directly of his pity for others and the pity others felt for him.

"The Ballad of Reading Gaol"[1] was published in January, 1898, over the signature of C. 3. 3., Oscar's number in prison. In a few weeks it ran through dozens of editions in England and America and translations appeared in almost every European

---

[1] The Ballad was finished in Naples and Alfred Douglas has since declared that he helped Oscar Wilde to write it. I have no wish to dispute this: Alfred Douglas' poetic gift was extraordinary, far greater than Oscar Wilde's. The poem was conceived in prison and a good deal of it was printed before Oscar went near Alfred Douglas and some of the best stanzas in it are to be found in this earlier portion. No part of the credit of it, in my opinion, belongs to Alfred Douglas.

language, which is proof not so much of the excellence of the poem as the great place the author held in the curiosity of men. The enthusiasm with which it was accepted in England was astounding. One reviewer compared it with the best of Sophocles; another said that "nothing like it has appeared in our time." No word of criticism was heard; the most cautious called it a "simple poignant ballad, . . . one of the greatest in the English language." This praise is assuredly not too generous. Yet even this was due to a revulsion of feeling in regard to Oscar himself rather than to any understanding of the greatness of his work. The best public felt that he had been dreadfully over-published, and made a scapegoat for worse offenders and was glad to have the opportunity of repairing its own fault by over-emphasizing Oscar's repentance and over-praising, as it imagined, the first fruits of the converted sinner.

"The Ballad of Reading Gaol" is far and away the best poem Oscar Wilde every wrote; we should try to appreciate it as the future will appreciate it. We need not be afraid to trace it to its source and note what is borrowed in it and what is original. After all necessary qualifications are made, it will stand as a great and splendid achievement.

Shortly before "The Ballad" was written, a little book of poetry called "A Shropshire Lad" was published by A. E. Housman, now I believe professor of Latin at Cambridge. There are only a hundred odd pages in the booklet; but it is full of high poetry— sincere and passionate feeling set to varied music. His friend, Reginald Turner, sent Oscar a copy of the book and one poem in particular made a deep impression on him. It is said that "his actual model for 'The Ballad of Reading Gaol' was 'The Dream of Eugene Aram' with 'The Ancient Mariner' thrown in on technical grounds"; but I believe that Wilde owed most of his inspiration to "A Shropshire Lad". .

Here are some verses from Housman's poem and some verses from "The Ballad":

> On moonlit heath and lonesome bank
>   The sheep beside me graze;
> And yon the gallows used to clank
>   Fast by the four cross ways.

A careless shepherd once would keep
    The flocks by moonlight there,[1]
And high amongst the glimmering sheep
    The dead men stood on air.

They hang us now in Shrewsbury jail:
    The whistles blow forlorn,
And trains all night groan on the rail
    To men that die at morn.

There sleeps in Shrewsbury jail to-night,
    Or wakes, as may betide,
A better lad, if things went right,
    Than most that sleep outside.

And naked to the hangman's noose
    The morning clocks will ring
A neck God made for other use
    Than strangling in a string.

And sharp the link of life will snap,
    And dead on air will stand
Heels that held up as straight a chap
    As treads upon the land.

So here I'll watch the night and wait
    To see the morning shine
When he will hear the stroke of eight
    And not the stroke of nine;

And wish my friend as sound a sleep
    As lads I did not know,
That shepherded the moonlit sheep
    A hundred years ago.

THE BALLAD OF READING GAOL

It is sweet to dance to violins
    When Love and Life are fair:
To dance to flutes, to dance to lutes,
    Is delicate and rare:
But it is not sweet with nimble feet
    To dance upon the air!

[1] Hanging in chains was called keeping sheep by moonlight.

And as one sees most fearful things
  In the crystal of a dream,
We saw the greasy hempen rope
  Hooked to the blackened beam
And heard the prayer the hangman's snare
  Strangled into a scream.

And all the woe that moved him so
  That he gave that bitter cry,
And the wild regrets, and the bloody sweats,
  None knew so well as I:
For he who lives more lives than one
  More deaths than one must die.

There are better things in "The Ballad of Reading Gaol" than those inspired by Housman. In the last of the three verses I quote there is a distinction of thought which Housman hardly reached.

"For he who lives more lives than one
  More deaths than one must die."

There are verses, too, wrung from the heart which have a diviner influence than any product of the intellect:

The Chaplain would not kneel to pray
  By his dishonoured grave:
Nor mark it with that blessed Cross
  That Christ for sinners gave,
Because the man was one of those
  Whom Christ came down to save.

. . . .

This too I know—and wise were it
  If each could know the same—
That every prison that men build
  Is built with bricks of shame,
And bound with bars lest Christ should see
  How men their brothers maim.

With bars they blur the gracious moon,
  And blind the goodly sun:

229

And they do well to hide their Hell,
    For in it things are done
That Son of God nor son of man
    Ever should look upon!

The vilest deeds like poison weeds
    Bloom well in prison-air:
It is only what is good in Man
    That wastes and withers there:
Pale Anguish keeps the heavy gate,
    And the Warder is Despair.

.   .   .   .

And he of the swollen purple throat,
    And the stark and staring eyes,
Waits for the holy hands that took
    The Thief to Paradise;
And a broken and a contrite heart
    The Lord will not despise.

"The Ballad of Reading Gaol" is beyond all comparison the greatest ballad in English; one of the noblest poems in the langauge. This is what prison did for Oscar Wilde.

When speaking to him later about this poem I remember assuming that his prison experiences must have helped him to realise the suffering of the condemned soldier and certainly lent passion to his verse. But he would not hear of it.

"Oh, no, Frank," he cried, "never; my experiences in prison were too horrible, too painful to be used. I simply blotted them out altogether and refused to recall them."

"What about the verse?" I asked:

"We sewed the sacks, we broke the stones,
    We turned the dusty drill:
We banged the tins, and bawled the hymns,
    And sweated on the mill:
And in the heart of every man
    Terror was lying still."

"Characteristic details, Frank, merely the *décor* of prison life, not its reality; that no one could paint, not even Dante, who had to turn away his eyes from lesser suffering."

It may be worth while to notice here, as an example of the hatred with which Oscar Wilde's name and work were regarded, that even after he had paid the penalty for his crime the publisher and editor, alike in England and America, put anything but a high price on his best work. They would have bought a play readily enough because they would have known that it would make them money, but a ballad from his pen nobody seemed to want. The highest price offered in America for "The Ballad of Reading Gaol" was one hundred dollars. Oscar found difficulty in getting even £20 for the English rights from the friend who published it; yet it has sold since by hundreds of thousands and is certain always to sell.

I must insert here part of another letter from Oscar Wilde which appeared in *The Daily Chronicle*, 24th March, 1898, on the cruelties of the English prison system; it was headed, "Don't read this if you want to be happy to-day," and was signed by "The Author of 'The Ballad of Reading Gaol.'" It was manifestly a direct outcome of his prison experiences. The letter was simple and affecting; but it had little or no influence on the English conscience. The Home Secretary was about to reform (!) the prison system by appointing more inspectors. Oscar Wilde pointed out that inspectors could do nothing but see that the regulations were carried out. He took up the position that it was the regulations which needed reform. His plea was irrefutable in its moderation and simplicity; but it was beyond the comprehension of an English Home Secretary apparently, for all the abuses pointed out by Oscar Wilde still flourish. I can't help giving some extracts from this memorable indictment, memorable for its reserve and sanity and complete absence of any bitterness:

". . . The prisoner who has been allowed the smallest privilege dreads the arrival of the inspectors. And on the day of any prison inspection the prison officials are more than usually brutal to the prisoners. Their object is, of course, to show the splendid discipline they maintain.

"The necessary reforms are very simple. They concern the needs of the body and the needs of the mind of each unfortunate prisoner.

"With regard to the first, there are three permanent punishments authorised by law in English prisons:

"1. Hunger.

"2. Insomnia.

"3. Disease.

"The food supplied to prisoners is entirely inadequate. Most of it is revolting in character. All of it is insufficient. Every prisoner suffers day and night from hunger. . . .

"The result of the food—which in most cases consists of weak gruel, badly baked bread, suet and water—is disease in the form of incessant diarrhœa. This malady, which ultimately with most prisoners becomes a permanent disease, is a recognized institution in every prison. At Wandsworth Prison, for instance—where I was confined for two months, till I had to be carried into hospital, where I remained for another two months—the warders go round twice or three times a day with astringent medicine, which they serve out to the prisoners as a matter of course. After about a week of such treatment it is unnecessary to say that the medicine produces no effect at all.

"The wretched prisoner is thus left a prey to the most weakening, depressing and humiliating malady that can be conceived, and if, as often happens, he fails from physical weakness to complete his required evolutions at the crank, or the mill, he is reported for idleness and punished with the greatest severity and brutality. Nor is this all.

"Nothing can be worse than the sanitary arrangements of English prisons. . . . The foul air of the prison cells, increased by a system of ventilation that is utterly ineffective, is so sickening and unwholesome that it is not uncommon for warders, when they come into the room out of the fresh air, and open and inspect each cell, to be violently sick. . . .

"With regard to the punishment of insomnia, it only exists in Chinese and English prisons. In China it is inflicted by placing the prisoner in a small bamboo cage; in England by means of the plank bed. The object of the plank bed is to produce insomnia. There is no other object in it, and it invariably succeeds. And even when one is subsequently allowed a hard mattress, as happens in the course of imprisonment, one still suffers from insomnia. It is a revolting and ignorant punishment.

"With regard to the needs of the mind, I beg that you will allow me to say something.

"The present prison system seems almost to have for its aim

the wrecking and the destruction of the mental faculties. The production of insanity is, if not its object, certainly its result. That is a well-ascertained fact. Its causes are obvious. Deprived of books, of all human intercourse, isolated from every humane and humanising influence, condemned to eternal silence, robbed of all intercourse with the external world, treated like an unintelligent animal, brutalised below the level of any of the brute-creation, the wretched man who is confined in an English prison can hardly escape becoming insane."

This letter ended by saying that if all the reforms suggested were carried out much would still remain to be done. It would still be advisable to "humanise the governors of prisons, to civilise the warders, and to Christianise the Chaplains."

This letter was the last effort of the new Oscar, the Oscar who had manfully tried to put the prison under his feet and to learn the significance of sorrow and the lesson of love which Christ brought into the world.

In the beautiful pages about Jesus which form the greater part of *De Profundis*, also written in those last hopeful months in Reading Gaol, Oscar shows, I think, that he might have done much higher work than Tolstoi or Renan had he set himself resolutely to transmute his new insight into some form of art. Now and then he divined the very secret of Jesus:

"When he says 'Forgive your enemies' it is not for the sake of the enemy, but for one's own sake that he says so, and because love is more beautiful than hate. In his own entreaty to the young man, 'Sell all that thou hast and give to the poor', it is not of the state of the poor that he is thinking but of the soul of the young man, the soul that wealth was marring."

In many of these pages Oscar Wilde really came close to the divine Master; "the image of the Man of Sorrows," he says, "has fascinated and dominated art as no Greek god succeeded in doing." . . . . And again:

"Out of the carpenter's shop at Nazareth had come a personality infinitely greater than any made by myth and legend, and one, strangely enough, destined to reveal to the world the mystical meaning of wine and the real beauties of the lilies of the field as none, either on Cithæron or Enna, has ever done. The song of Isaiah, 'He is despised and rejected of men, a man of sorrows and acquainted with grief: and we hid as it were our faces from him,' had seemed to him to prefigure himself, and in him the prophecy was fulfilled."

In this spirit Oscar made up his mind that he would write about "Christ as the precursor of the romantic movement in life" and about "The artistic life considered in its relation to conduct."

By bitter suffering he had been brought to see that the moment of repentance is the moment of absolution and self-realisation, that tears can wash out even blood. In "The Ballad of Reading Gaol" he wrote:

> And with tears of blood he cleansed the hand,
>   The hand that held the steel:
> For only blood can wipe out blood,
>   And only tears can heal:
> And the crimson stain that was of Cain
>   Became Christ's snow-white seal.

This is the highest height Oscar Wilde ever reached, and alas! he only trod the summit for a moment. But as he says himself: "One has perhaps to go to prison to understand that. And, if so, it may be worth while going to prison." He was by nature a pagan who for a few months became a Christian, but to live as a lover of Jesus was impossible to this "Greek born out of due time", and he never even dreamed of a reconciling synthesis. . . .

The arrest of his development makes him a better representative of his time. He was an artistic expression of the best English mind; a Pagan and Epicurean, his rule of conduct was a selfish Individualism:—"Am I my brother's keeper?" This attitude must entail a dreadful Nemesis, for it condemns one Briton in every four to a pauper's grave. The result will convince the most hardened that such selfishness is not a creed by which human beings can live in society.

.   .   .   .

This summer of 1897 was the harvest time in Oscar Wilde's Life; and his golden Indian summer. We owe it "De Profundis," the best pages of prose he ever wrote, and "The Ballad of Reading Gaol," his only original poem; yet one that will live as long as the language. We owe it also that sweet and charming letter to Robbie Ross which shows him in his habit as he lived. I must still say a word or two about him in this summer in order to show the ordinary working of his mind.

On his release, and, indeed, for a year or two later, he called himself Sebastian Melmoth. But one had hardly spoken a half a dozen words to him, when he used to beg to be called Oscar Wilde. I remember how he pulled up someone who had just been introduced to him, who persisted in addressing him as Mr. Melmoth.

"Call me Oscar Wilde," he pleaded, "Mr. Melmoth is unknown, you see."

"I thought you preferred it," said the stranger excusing himself.

"Oh, dear, no," interrupted Oscar smiling, "I only use the name Melmoth to spare the blushes of the postman, to preserve his modesty," and he laughed in the old delightful way.

It was always significant to me the eager delight with which he shuffled off the new name and took up the old one which he had made famous.

An anecdote from his life in the Châlet at this time showed that the old witty pagan in Oscar was not yet extinct.

An English lady who had written a great many novels and happened to be staying in Dieppe heard of him, and out of kindness or curiosity, or perhaps a mixture of both motives, wrote and invited him to luncheon. He accepted the invitation. The good lady did not know how to talk to Mr. Sebastian Melmoth, and time went heavily. At length she began to expatiate on the cheapness of things in France; did Mr. Melmoth know how wonderfully cheap and good the living was?

"Only fancy," she went on, "you would not believe what that claret you are drinking costs."

"Really?" questioned Oscar, with a polite smile.

"Of course I get it wholesale," she explained, "but it only costs me sixpence a quart."

"Oh, my dear lady, I'm afraid you have been cheated," he exclaimed, "ladies should never buy wine. I'm afraid you have been sadly overcharged."

The humour may excuse the discourtesy, but Oscar was so uniformly polite to everyone that the incident simply shows how ineffably he had been bored.

This summer of 1897 was the decisive period and final turning-point in Oscar Wilde's career. So long as the sunny weather lasted and friends came to visit him from time to time Oscar was content to live in the Châlet Bourgeat; but when the days began to draw in and the weather became unsettled, the dreariness of a life passed in solitude, indoors, and without a library became insupportable. He was being drawn in two opposite directions. I did not know it at the time; indeed he only told me about it months later when the matter had been decided irrevocably; but this was the moment when his soul was at stake between good and evil. The question was whether his wife would come to him again or whether he would yield to the solicitations of Lord Alfred Douglas and go to live with him.

Mr. Sherard has told in his book how he brought about the first reconciliation between Oscar and his wife; and how immediately afterwards he received a letter from Lord Alfred Douglas threatening to shoot him like a dog, if, by any words of his, Wilde's friendship was lost to him, Douglas.

Unluckily Mrs. Wilde's family were against her going back to her husband; they begged her not to go; talked to her of her duty to her children and herself, and the poor woman hesitated. Finally his advisers decided for her, and Mrs. Wilde wrote this decision to Oscar's solicitors shortly before his release: Oscar's probation was to last at least a year. I do not know enough about Mrs. Wilde and her relations with her family and with her husband even to discuss her inaction. I dare not criticise her; but she did not go to her husband when if she had gone boldly she might have saved him. She knew Lord Alfred Douglas' influence over him; knew that it had already brought him to grief. Gide says, and Oscar himself told me afterwards, that he had come out of prison determined not to go back to Alfred Douglas and the old life. It seems a pity that his wife did not act promptly; she allowed herself to believe that a time of probation was necessary. The delay wounded Oscar, and all the while, as he told me a little later, he was resisting an influence which had dominated his life in the past.

"I got a letter almost every day, Frank, begging me to come

to Posilippo, to the villa which Lord Alfred Douglas had rented. Every day I heard his voice calling, 'Come, come, to sunshine and to me. Come to Naples with its wonderful museum of bronzes and Pompeii and Pæstum, the city of Poseidon: I am waiting to welcome you. Come.'

"Who could resist it, Frank? love calling, calling with out-stretched arms; who could stay in bleak Berneval and watch the sheets of rain falling, falling—and the grey mist shrouding the grey sea, and think of Naples and love and sunshine; who could resist it all? I could not, Frank, I was so lonely and I hated solitude. I resisted as long as I could, but when chill October came and Bosie came to Rouen for me, I gave up the struggle and yielded."

Could Oscar Wilde have won and made for himself a new and greater life? The majority of men are content to think that such a victory was impossible to him. Everyone knows that he lost; but I at least believe that he might have won. His wife was on the point of yielding, I have since been told; on the point of complete reconciliation when she heard that he had gone to Naples and returned to his old habit of living; a few days made all the difference.

It was at the instigation of Lord Alfred Douglas that Oscar began the insane action against Lord Queensberry, in which he put to hazard his success, his position, his good name and liberty, and lost them all. Two years later at the same tempting, he committed soul-suicide.

He was not only better in health than he had ever been; but he was talking and writing better than ever before and full of literary projects which would certainly have given him money and position and a measure of happiness besides increasing his reputation. From the moment he went to Naples he was lost, and he knew it himself; he never afterwards wrote anything. As he used to say, he could never afterwards face his own soul.

He could never have won up again, the world says, and shrugs careless shoulders. It is a cheap, unworthy conclusion. Some of us still persist in believing that Oscar Wilde might easily have won and never been again caught in that dreadful wind which whips the victims of sensual desire about unceasingly, driving them hither and thither without rest in that awful place where: "Nulla speranza gli conforta mai." (No hope ever comforts!)

237

❦

20

The Results of His Second Fall: His Genius

"Non dispetto, ma doglia."—Dante.

OSCAR WILDE did not stay long in Naples, a few brief months; the forbidden fruit quickly turned to ashes in his mouth.

I give the following extracts from a letter he wrote to Robert Ross in December, 1897, shortly after leaving Naples, because it describes the second great crisis in his life and is besides the bitterest thing he ever wrote and therefore of peculiar value:

"The facts of Naples are very bald. Bosie for four months, by endless lies, offered me a home. He offered me love, affection, and care, and promised that I should never want for anything. After four months I accepted his offer, but when we met on our way to Naples, I found he had no money, no plans, and had forgotten all his promises. His one idea was that I should raise the money for us both; I did so to the extent of £120. On this Bosie lived quite happy. When it came to his having to pay his own share he became terribly unkind and penurious, except where his own pleasures were concerned, and when my allowance ceased, he left.

"With regard to the £500[1] which he said was a debt of

[1] This was the sum promised by the whole Queensberry family and by Lord Alfred Douglas in particular to Oscar to defray the costs of that first action for libel which they persuaded him to bring against Lord Queensberry. Ross has since stated in court that it was never paid. The history of the monies promised and supplied to Oscar at that time is so extraordinary

238

honour, he has written to me to say that he admits the debt of honour, but as lots of gentlemen don't pay their debts of honour, it is quite a common thing and no one thinks any the worse of them.

"I don't know what you said to Constance, but the bald fact is that I accepted the offer of the home, and found that I was expected to provide the money, and when I could no longer do so I was left to my own devices. It is the most bitter experience of a bitter life. It is a blow quite awful. It had to come, but I know it is better I should never see him again, I don't want to; it fills me with horror."

A word of explanation will explain his reference to his wife, Constance, in this letter. By a deed of separation made at the end of his imprisonment, Mrs. Wilde undertook to allow Oscar £150 a year for life, under the condition that the allowance was to be forfeited if Oscar ever lived under the same roof with Lord Alfred Douglas. Having forfeited the allowance Oscar got Robert Ross to ask his wife to continue it, and in spite of the forfeiture Mrs. Wilde continually sent Oscar money through Robert Ross, merely stipulating that her husband should not be told whence the money came. Ross, too, who had also sent him £150 a year, resumed his monthly payments as soon as he left Douglas.

My friendship with Oscar Wilde, which had been interrupted after he left prison by a silly gibe directed rather against the go-between he had sent to me than against him, was renewed in Paris early in 1898. I had never felt anything but the most cordial affection for Oscar and as soon as I went to Paris and met him I explained what had seemed to him unkind. When I asked him about his life since his release he told me simply that he had quarrelled with Bosie Douglas.

I did not attribute much importance to this; but I could not help noticing the extraordinary change that had taken place in him since he had been in Naples. His health was almost as good as ever;

---

and so characteristic of the age that it might well furnish a chapter to itself. Here it is enough just to say that those who ought to have supplied him with money evaded the obligation, while others upon whom he had no claim, helped him liberally; but even large sums of money slipped through his careless fingers like water.

in fact, the prison discipline with its two years of hard living had done him so much good that his health continued excellent almost to the end.

But his whole manner and attitude to life had again changed. He now resembled the successful Oscar of the early nineties. I caught echoes, too, in his speech of a harder, smaller nature; "that talk about reformation, Frank, is all nonsense; no one ever really reforms or changes. I am what I always was."

He was mistaken. He took up again the old pagan standpoint; but he was not the same; he was reckless now, not thoughtless, and, as soon as one probed a little beneath the surface, depressed almost to despairing. He had learnt the meaning of suffering and pity, had sensed their value; he had turned his back upon them all, it is true, but he could not return to pagan carelessness and the light-hearted enjoyment of pleasure. He did his best and almost succeeded; but the effort was there. His creed now was what it used to be about 1892: "Let us get what pleasure we may in the fleeting days; for the night cometh, and the silence that can never be broken."

The old doctrine of original sin, we now call reversion to type; the most lovely garden rose, if allowed to go without discipline and tendance, will in a few generations become again the common scentless dog-rose of our hedges. Such a reversion to type had taken place in Oscar Wilde. It must be inferred perhaps that the old pagan Greek in him was stronger than the Christian virtues which had been called into being by the discipline and suffering of prison. Little by little, as he began to live his old life again, the lessons learned in prison seemed to drop from him and be forgotten. But in reality the high thoughts he had lived with, were not lost; his lips had been touched by the divine fire; his eyes had seen the world-wonder of sympathy, pity and love and, strangely enough, this higher vision helped, as we shall soon see, to shake his individuality from its centre, and thus destroyed his power of work and completed his soul-ruin. Oscar's second fall—this time from a height—was fatal and made writing impossible to him. It is all clear enough now in retrospect though I did not understand it at the time. When he went to live with Bosie Douglas he threw off the Christian attitude, but afterwards had to recognize that "De Profundis" and "The Ballad of Reading Gaol" were deeper and better work than any of his earlier writings. He resumed the pagan position; outwardly and for the time being he was the old Oscar again, with his Greek love of beauty and hatred of disease, deformity and ugliness, and whenever he met a kindred spirit, he absolutely revelled in gay paradoxes and brilliant flashes of humour. But he was at war with himself, like Milton's Satan always conscious of his fall, always regretful of his lost estate and, by reason of this division of spirit, unable to write. Perhaps because of this he threw himself more than ever into talk.

He was beyond all comparison the most interesting companion I have ever known, the most brilliant talker, I cannot but think, that ever lived. No one surely ever gave himself more entirely in speech. Again and again he declared that he had only put his talent into his books and plays, but his genius into his life. If he had said into his talk, it would have been the exact truth.

People have differed a great deal about his mental and physical condition after he came out of prison. All who knew him really, Ross, Turner, More Adey, Lord Alfred Douglas and myself, are agreed that in spite of a slight deafness he was never better in health, never indeed so well. But some French friends were determined to make him out a martyr.

In his picture of Wilde's last years, Gide tells us that "he had suffered too grievously from his imprisonment. . . . His will had been broken . . . nothing remained in his shattered life but a mouldy ruin, painful to contemplate, of his former self. At times he seemed to wish to show that his brain was still active. Humour there was; but it was far-fetched, forced and threadbare."

These touches may be necessary in order to complete a French picture of the social outcast. They are not only untrue when applied to Oscar Wilde, but the reverse of the truth; he never talked so well, was never so charming a companion as in the last years of his life.

In the very last year his talk was more genial, more humorous, more vivid than ever, with a wider range of thought and intenser stimulus than before. He was a born *improvisatore*. At the moment he always dazzled one out of judgment. A phonograph would have discovered the truth; a great part of his charm was physical; much of his talk mere topsy-turvy paradox, the very froth of thought carried off by gleaming, dancing eyes; smiling, happy lips, and a melodious voice.

The entertainment usually started with some humorous play on words. One of the company would say something obvious or trivial, repeat a proverb or commonplace tag such as, "Genius is born, not made," and Oscar would flash in smiling, "not 'paid,' my dear fellow, not 'paid.'"

An interesting comment would follow on some doing of the day, a skit on some accepted belief or a parody of some pretentious solemnity, a winged word on a new book or a new author, and when everyone was smiling with amused enjoyment, the fine eyes would become introspective, the beautiful voice would take on a grave music and Oscar would begin a story, a story with symbolic second meaning or a glimpse of new thought, and when all were listening enthralled, of a sudden the eyes would dance, the smile break forth again like sunshine and some sparkling witticism would set everyone laughing.

The spell was broken, but only for a moment. A new clue would soon be given and at once Oscar was off again with renewed brio to finer effects.

The talking itself warmed and quickened him extraordinarily. He loved to show off and astonish his audience, and usually talked better after an hour or two than at the beginning. His verve was inexhaustible. But always a great part of the fascination lay in the quick changes from grave to gay, from pathos to mockery, from philosophy to fun.

There was but little of the actor in him. When telling a story he never mimicked his personages; his drama seldom lay in clash of character, but in thought; it was the sheer beauty of the words, the melody of the cadenced voice, the glowing eyes which fascinated you and always and above all the scintillating, coruscating humour that lifted his monologues into works of art.

Curiously enough he seldom talked of himself or of the incidents of his past life. After the prison he always regarded himself as a sort of Prometheus and his life as symbolic; but his earlier experiences never suggested themselves to him as specially significant; the happenings of his life after his fall seemed predestined and fateful to him; yet of those he spoke but seldom. Even when carried away by his own eloquence, he kept the tone of good society.

When you came afterwards to think over one of those wonderful evenings when he had talked for hours, almost without interruption, you hardly found more than an epigram, a fugitive flash of critical insight, an apologue or pretty story charmingly told. Over all this he had cast the glittering, sparkling robe of his Celtic gaiety, verbal humour, and sensual enjoyment of living. It was all like champagne; meant to be drunk quickly; if you let it stand, you soon realised that some still wines had rarer virtues. But there was always about him the magic of a rich and *puissant* personality; like some great actor he could take a poor part and fill it with the passion and vivacity of his own nature, till it became a living and memorable creation.

He gave the impression of wide intellectual range, yet in reality he was not broad; life was not his study nor the world-drama his field. His talk was all of literature and art and the vanities; the light drawing-room comedy on the edge of farce was his kingdom; there he ruled as a sovereign.

Anyone who has read Oscar Wilde's plays at all carefully, especially "The Importance of Being Earnest", must, I think, see that in kindly, happy humour he is without a peer in literature. Who can ever forget the scene between the town and country girl in that delightful farce-comedy? As soon as the London girl realises that the country girl has hardly any opportunity of making new friends or meeting new men, she exclaims:

"Ah! now I know what they mean when they talk of agricultural depression."

This sunny humour is Wilde's especial contribution to literature. He calls forth a smile whereas others try to provoke laughter. Yet he was as witty as anyone of whom we have record, and some of the best epigrams in English are his. "The cynic knows the price of everything and the value of nothing" is better than the best of La Rochefoucauld, as good as the best of Vauvenargues or Joubert. He was as wittily urbane as Congreve. But all the witty things that one man can say may be numbered on one's fingers. It was through his humour that Wilde reigned supreme. It was his humour that lent his talk its singular attraction. He was the only man I have ever met or heard of who could keep one smiling with amusement hour after hour. True, much of the humour was merely verbal, but it was always gay and genial; summer-lightning humour, I used to call it, unexpected, dazzling, full of colour yet harmless.

Let me try and catch here some of the fleeting iridescence of that radiant spirit. Some years before I had been introduced to Mlle. Marie Anne de Bovet by Sir Charles Dilke. Mlle. de Bovet was a writer of talent and knew English uncommonly well; but in spite of masses of fair hair and vivacious eyes she was certainly very plain. As soon as she heard I was in Paris, she asked me to present Oscar Wilde to her. He had no objection, and so I made a meeting between them. When he caught sight of her, he stopped short: seeing his astonishment, she cried to him in her quick, abrupt way:

"*N'est-ce pas, M. Wilde, que je suis la femme la plus laide de France?*" (Come, confess, Mr. Wilde, that I am the ugliest woman in France.)

Bowing low, Oscar replied with smiling courtesy:

"*Du monde, Madame, du monde.*" (In the world, madame, in the world.)

No one could help laughing; the retort was irresistible. He should have said: "*Au monde, Madame, au monde,*" but the meaning was clear.

Sometimes this thought-quickness and happy dexterity had to be used in self-defence. Jean Lorrain was the wittiest talker I have ever heard in France, and a most brilliant journalist. His life was as abandoned as it could well be; in fact, he made a parade of strange vices. In the days of Oscar's supremacy he always pretended to be a friend and admirer. About this time Oscar wanted me to know Stephane Mallarmé. He took me to his rooms one afternoon when there was a reception. There were a great many people present. Mallarmé was standing at the other end of the room leaning against the chimney piece. Near the door was Lorrain, and we both went towards him, Oscar with outstretched hands:

"Delighted to see you, Jean."

For some reason or other, most probably out of tawdry vanity, Lorrain folded his arms theatrically and replied:

"I regret I cannot say as much: I can no longer be one of your friends, M. Wilde."

The insult was stupid, brutal; yet everyone was on tiptoe to see how Oscar would answer it.

"How true that is," he said quietly, as quickly as if he had expected the traitor-thrust, "how true and how sad! At a certain time in life all of us who have done anything like you and me, Lorrain, must realise that we no longer have any friends in this world; but only lovers." *(Plus d'amis, seulement des amants.)*

A smile of approval lighted up every face.

"Well said, well said," was the general exclamation. His humour was almost invariably generous, kind.

One day in a Paris studio the conversation turned on the character of Marat. One Frenchman would have it that he was a fiend, another saw in him the incarnation of the revolution, a third insisted the he was merely the gamin of the Paris streets grown up. Suddenly one turned to Oscar, who was sitting silent, and asked his opinion: he took the ball at once, gravely.

"Ce malheureux! Il n'avait pas de veine—pour une fois qu'il a pris un bain . . ." (Poor devil, he was unluckly! To come to such grief for once taking a bath.)

For a little while Oscar was interested in the Dreyfus case, and especially in the Commandant Esterhazy, who played such a prominent part in it with the infamous *bordereau* which brought about the conviction of Dreyfus. Most Frenchmen now know that the *bordereau* was a forgery and without any real value.

I was curious to see Esterhazy, and Oscar brought him to lunch one day at Durand's. He was a little below middle height, extremely thin and as dark as any Italian, with an enormous hook nose and heavy jaw. He looked to me like some foul bird of prey. Greed and cunning in the restless brown eyes set close together, quick resolution in the outthrust, bony jaws and hard chin; but manifestly he had no capacity, no mind; he was meagre in all ways. For a long time he bored us by insisting that Dreyfus was a traitor, a Jew, and a German; to him a trinity of faults, whereas he, Esterhazy, was perfectly innocent and had been very badly treated. At length Oscar leant across the table and said to him in French with, strange to say, a slight Irish accent, not noticeable when he spoke English:

"The innocent," he said, "always suffer, M. le Commandant; it is their *métier*. Besides, we are all innocent till we are found out; it is a poor, common part to play and within the compass of the meanest. The interesting thing surely is to be guilty and so wear as a halo the seduction of sin."

Esterhazy appeared put out for a moment, and then he caught

the genial gaiety of the reproof and the hint contained in it. His vanity would not allow him to remain long in a secondary *rôle*, and so, to our amazement, he suddenly broke out:

"Why should I not make my confession to you? I will. It is I, Esterhazy, who alone am guilty. I wrote the *bordereau*. I put Dreyfus in prison, and all France can not liberate him. I am the maker of the plot, and the chief part in it is mine."

To his surprise we both roared with laughter. The influence of the larger nature on the smaller to such an extraordinary issue was irresistibly comic. At the time no one even suspected Esterhazy in connection with the *bordereau*.

Another example, this time of Oscar's wit, may find a place here. Sir Lewis Morris was a voluminous poetaster with a common mind. He once bored Oscar by complaining that his books were boycotted by the press; after giving several instances of unfair treatment he burst out: "There's a conspiracy against me, a conspiracy of silence; but what can one do? What should I do?"

"Join it," replied Oscar smiling.

Oscar's humour was for the most part intellectual, and something like it can be found in others, though the happy fecundity and lightsome gaiety of it belonged to the individual temperament and perished with him. I remember once trying to give an idea of the different sides of his humour, just to see how far it could be imitated.

I made believe to have met him at Paddington, after his release from Reading, though he was brought to Pentonville in private clothes by a warder on May 18th, and was released early the next morning, two years to the hour from the commencement of the Sessions at which he was convicted on May 25th. The Act says that you must be released from the prison in which you are first confined. I pretended, however, that I had met him. The train, I said, ran into Paddington Station early in the morning. I went across to him as he got out of the carriage. Grey dawn filled the vast echoing space; a few porters could be seen scattered about; it was all chill and depressing.

"Welcome, welcome, Oscar!" I cried holding out my hands. "I am sorry I'm alone. You ought to have been met by troops of boys and girls flower-crowned, but alas! you will have to content yourself with one middle-aged admirer."

"Yes, it's really terrible, Frank," he replied gravely. "If England persists in treating her criminals like this, she does not deserve to have any. . . ."

"Ah," said an old lady to him one day at lunch, "I know you people who pretend to be a great deal worse than you are, I know you. I shouldn't be afraid of you."

"Naturally we pretend to be bad, dear lady," he replied; "it is the only way to make ourselves interesting to you. Everyone believes a man who pretends to be good, he is such a bore; but no one believes a man who says he is evil. That makes him interesting."

"Oh, you are too clever for me," replied the old lady nodding her head. "You see, in my day, none of us went to Girton and Newnham. There were no schools then for the higher education of women."

"How absurd such schools are, are they not?" cried Oscar. "Were I a despot, I should immediately establish schools for the lower education of women. That's what they need. It usually takes ten years living with a man to complete a woman's education."

"Then what would you do," asked someone, "about the lower education of man?"

"That's already provided for, my dear fellow, amply provided for; we have our public schools and universities to see to that. What we want are schools for the higher education of men, and schools for the lower education of women."

Genial persiflage of this sort was his particular *forte* whether my imitation of it is good or bad.

His kindliness was ingrained. I never heard him say a gross or even a vulgar word, hardly even a sharp or unkind thing. Whether in company or with one person, his mind was all dedicated to genial, kindly, flattering thoughts. He hated rudeness or discussion or insistence as he hated ugliness or deformity.

One evening of this summer a trivial incident showed me that he was sinking deeper in the mud-honey of life.

A new play was about to be given at the Français and because he expressed a wish to see it I bought a couple of tickets. We went in and he made me change places with him in order to be able to talk to me; he was growing nearly deaf in the bad ear. After the first act we went outside to smoke a cigarette.

"It's stupid," Oscar began, "fancy us two going in there to listen to what that foolish Frenchman says about love; he knows nothing about it; either of us could write much better on the theme. Let's walk up and down here under the columns and talk."

The people began to go into the theatre and, as they were disappearing, I said:

"It seems rather a pity to waste our tickets; so many wish to see the play."

"We shall find someone to give them to," he said indifferently, stopping by one of the pillars.

At that very moment as if under his hand appeared a boy of about fifteen or sixteen, one of the gutter-snipe of Paris. To my amazement, he said:

"*Bon soir, Monsieur Wilde.*"

Oscar turned to him smiling.

"*Vous êtes Jules, n'est-ce pas?*" (you are Jules, aren't you?) he questioned.

"*Oui, M. Wilde.*"

"Here is the very boy you want," Oscar cried; "let's give him the tickets, and he'll sell them, and make something out of them," and Oscar turned and began to explain to the boy how I had given two hundred francs for the tickets, and how, even now, they should be worth a louis or two.

"*Des jaunets*" (yellow boys), cried the youth, his sharp face lighting up, and in a flash he had vanished with the tickets.

"You see he knows me, Frank," said Oscar, with the childish pleasure of gratified vanity.

"Yes," I replied drily, "not an acquaintance to be proud of, I should think."

"I don't agree with you, Frank," he said, resenting my tone, "did you notice his eyes? He is one of the most beautiful boys I have ever seen; an exact replica of Emilienne D'Alençon,[1] I call him Jules D'Alençon, and I tell her he must be her brother. I had them both dining with me once and the boy is finer than the girl, his skin far more beautiful.

"By the way," he went on, as we were walking up the Avenue de l'Opera, "why should we not see Emilienne; why should she

[1] One of the prettiest daughters of the game to be found in Paris at the time.

not sup with us, and you could compare them? She is playing at Olympai, near the Grand Hotel. Let's go and compare Aspasia and Agathon, and for once I shall be Alcibiades, and you the moralist, Socrates."

"I would rather talk to you," I replied.

"We can talk afterwards, Frank, when all the stars come out to listen; now is the time to live and enjoy."

"As you will," I said, and we went to the Music Hall and got a box, and he wrote a little note to Emilienne D'Alençon, and she came afterwards to supper with us. Though her face was pretty she was pre-eminently dull and uninteresting without two ideas in her bird's head. She was all greed and vanity, and could talk of nothing but the hope of getting an engagement in London. Could he help her, or would Monsieur, referring to me, as a journalist get her some good puffs in advance? Oscar promised everything gravely.

While we were supping inside, Oscar caught sight of the boy passing along the Boulevard. At once he tapped on the window, loud enough to attract his attention. Nothing loth, the boy came in, and the four of us had supper together—a strange quartette.

"Now, Frank," said Oscar, "compare the two faces and you will see the likeness," and indeed there was in both the same Greek beauty—the same regularity of feature, the same low brow and large eyes, the same perfect oval.

"I am telling my friend," said Oscar to Emilienne in French, "how alike you two are, true brother and sister in beauty and in the finest of arts, the art of living," and they both laughed.

"The boy is better looking," he went on to me in English. "Her mouth is coarse and hard; her hands common, while the boy is quite perfect."

"Rather dirty, don't you think?" I could not help remarking.

"Dirty, of course, but that's nothing; nothing is so immaterial as colouring; form is everything, and his form is perfect, as exquisite as the David of Donatello. That's what he's like, Frank, the David of Donatello," and he pulled his jowl, delighted to have found the painting word.

As soon as Emilienne saw that we were talking of the boy, her interest in the conversation vanished, even more quickly than her appetite. She had to go, she said suddenly; she was so sorry, and

249

the discontented curiosity of her look gave place again to the smirk of affected politeness.

"*Au revoir, n'est-ce pas? à Charing Cross, n'est-ce pas, Monsieur? Vous ne m'oublierez pas?* . . ."

As we turned to walk along the boulevard I noticed that the boy, too, had disappeared. The moonlight was playing with the leaves and boughs of the plane trees and throwing them in Japanese shadow-pictures on the pavement. I was given over to thought; evidently Oscar imagined I was offended, for he launched out into a panegyric on Paris.

"The most wonderful city in the world, the only civilised capital; the only place on earth where you find absolute toleration for all human frailties, with passionate admiration for all human virtues and capacities.

"Do you remember Verlaine, Frank? His life was nameless and terrible; he did everything to excess, was drunken, dirty and debauched, and yet there he would sit in a café on the Boul' Mich', and everybody who came in would bow to him, and call him *maître* and be proud of any sign of recognition from him because he was a great poet.

"In England they would have murdered Verlaine, and men who call themselves gentlemen would have gone out of their way to insult him in public. England is still only half-civilised; Englishmen touch life at one or two points without suspecting its complexity. They are rude and harsh."

All the while I could not help thinking of Dante and his condemnation of Florence, and its "hard, malignant people", the people who still had something in them of "the mountain and rock" of their birthplace:—"*E tiene ancor del monte e del macigno.*"

"You are not offended, Frank, are you, with me, for making you meet two caryatides of the Parisian temple of pleasure?"

"No, no," I cried, "I was thinking how Dante condemned Florence and its people, its ungrateful malignant people, and how when his teacher, Brunetto Latini, and his companions came to him in the underworld, he felt as if he, too, must throw himself into the pit with them. Nothing prevented him from carrying out his good intention (*buona voglia*) except the fear of being himself burned and baked as they were. I was just thinking that it was his great love for Latini which gave him the deathless words:

> .... "Non dispetto, ma doglia
> La vostra condizion dentro mi fisse.

"Not contempt but sorrow. . . ."

"Oh, Frank," cried Oscar, "what a beautiful incident! I remember it all. I read it this last winter in Naples. . . . Of course Dante was full of pity as are all great poets, for they know the weakness of human nature."

But even "the sorrow" of which Dante spoke seemed to carry with it some hint of condemnation; for after a pause he went on:

"You must not judge me, Frank; you don't know what I have suffered. No wonder I snatch now at enjoyment with both hands. They did terrible things to me. Did you know that when I was arrested the police let the reporters come to the cell and stare at me. Think of it—the degradation and the shame—as if I had been a monster on show. Oh! you knew! Then you know, too, how I was really condemned before I was tried; and what a farce my trial was. That terrible judge with his insults to those he was sorry he could not send to the scaffold.

"I never told you the worst thing that befell me. When they took me from Wandsworth to Reading, we had to stop at Clapham Junction. We were nearly an hour waiting for the train. There we sat on the platform. I was in the hideous prison clothes, handcuffed between two warders. You know how the trains come in every minute. Almost at once I was recognized, and there passed before me a continual stream of men and boys, and one after the other offered some foul sneer or gibe or scoff. They stood before me, Frank, calling me names and spitting on the ground—an eternity of torture."

My heart bled for him.

"I wonder if any punishment will teach humanity to such people, or understanding of their own baseness?"

After walking a few paces he turned to me:

"Don't reproach me, Frank, even in thought. You have no right to. You don't know me yet. Some day you will know more and then you will be sorry, so sorry that there will be no room for any reproach of me. If I could tell you what I suffered this winter!"

"This winter!" I cried. "In Naples?"

"Yes, in gay, happy Naples. It was last autumn that I really fell to ruin. I had come out of prison filled with good intentions, with all good resolutions. My wife had promised to come back to me. I hoped she would come very soon. If she had come at once, if she only had, it might all have been different. But she did not come. I have no doubt she was right from her point of view. She has always been right.

"But I was there alone in Berneval, and Bosie kept on calling me, calling, and as you know I went to him. At first it was all wonderful. The bruised leaves began to unfold in the light and warmth of affection; the sore feeling began to die out of me.

"But at once my allowance from my wife was stopped. Yes, Frank," he said, with a touch of the old humour, "they took it away when they should have doubled it. I did not care. When I had money I gave it to him without counting, so when I could not pay I thought Bosie would pay, and I was content. But at once I discovered that he expected me to find the money. I did what I could; but when my means were exhausted, the evil days began. He expected me to write plays and get money for us both as in the past; but I couldn't; I simply could not. When we were dunned his temper went to pieces. He has never known what it is to want really. You have no conception of the wretchedness of it all. He has a terrible, imperious, irritable temper."

"He's the son of his father," I interjected.

"Yes," said Oscar, "I am afraid that's the truth, Frank; he is the son of his father; violent, and irritable, with a tongue like a lash. As soon as the means of life were straitened, he became sullen and began reproaching me; why didn't I write? Why didn't I earn money? What was the good of me? As if I could write under such conditions. No man, Frank, has ever suffered worse shame and humiliation.

"At last there was a washing bill to be paid; Bosie was dunned for it, and when I came in, he raged and whipped me with his tongue. It was appalling; I had done everything for him, given him everything, lost everything, and now I could only stand and see love turned to hate; the strength of love's wine making the bitter more venomous. Then he left me, Frank, and now there is no hope for me. I am lost, finished, a derelict floating at the mercy of the stream, without plan or purpose. . . . And the worst of it is, I know, if men have treated me badly, I have treated myself worse; it is our sins against ourselves we can never forgive. . . . Do you wonder that I snatch at any pleasure?"

He turned and looked at me all shaken; I saw the tears pouring down his cheeks.

"I cannot talk any more, Frank," he said in a broken voice, "I must go."

I called a cab. My heart was so heavy within me, so sore, that I said nothing to stop him. He lifted his hand to me in sign of farewell, and I turned again to walk home alone, understanding, for the first time in my life, the full significance of the marvellous line in which Shakespeare summed up his impeachment of the world and his own justification: the only justification of any of us mortals:

"A man more sinn'd against than sinning."

21

His Sense of Rivalry: His Love of Life and Laziness

THE MORE I CONSIDERED THE MATTER, the more clearly I saw, or thought I saw, that the only chance of salvation for Oscar was to get him to work, to give him some purpose in life, and the reader should remember here that at this time I had not read "De Profundis" and did not know that Oscar in prison had himself recognized this necessity. After all, I said to myself, nothing is lost if he will only begin to write. A man should be able to whistle happiness and hope down the wind and take despair to his bed and heart and win courage from his harsh companion. Happiness is not essential to the artist; happiness never creates anything but memories. If Oscar would work and not brood over the past and study himself like an Indian Fakir, he might yet come to soul-health and achievement. He could win back everything; his own respect, and the respect of his fellows, if indeed that were worth winning. An artist, I knew, must have at least the self-abnegation of the hero, and heroic resolution to strive and strive, or he will never bring it far even in his art. If I could only get Oscar to work, it seemed to me everything might yet come right. I spent a week with him, lunching and dining and putting all this before him, in every way.

I noticed that he enjoyed the good eating and the good drinking as intensely as ever. He was even drinking too much I thought, was beginning to get stout and flabby again, but the good living was a necessity to him, and it certainly did not prevent him from talking charmingly. But as soon as I pressed him to write he would shake his head:

"Oh, Frank, I cannot, you know my rooms; how could I write there? A horrid bedroom like a closet, and a little sitting room without any outlook. Books everywhere; and no place to write; to tell you the truth I cannot even read in it. I can do nothing in such miserable poverty."

Again and again he came back to this. He harped upon his destitution, so that I could not but see purpose in it. He was already cunning in the art of getting money without asking for it. My heart ached for him; one goes down hill with such fatal speed and ease, and the mire at the bottom is so loathsome. I hastened to say:

"I can let you have a little money; but you ought to work, Oscar. After all why should anyone help you, if you will not help yourself? If I cannot aid you to save yourself, I am only doing you harm."

"A base sophism, Frank, mere sophistry, as you know; a good lunch is better than a bad one for any living man."

I smiled, "Don't do yourself injustice. You could easily gain thousands and live like a prince again. Why not make the effort?"

"If I had pleasant, sunny rooms I'd try. . . . It's harder than you think."

"Nonsense, it's easy for you. Your punishment has made your name known in every country in the world. A book of yours would sell like wildfire; a play of yours would draw in any capital. You might live here like a prince. Shakespeare lost love and friendship, hope and health to boot—everything, and yet forced himself to write 'The Tempest.' Why can't you?"

"I'll try, Frank, I'll try."

I may just mention here that any praise of another man, even of Shakespeare, was sure to move Oscar to emulation. He acknowledged no superior. In some articles in *The Saturday Review* I had said that no one had ever given completer record of himself than Shakespeare. "We know him better than we know any of our contemporaries," I went on, "and he is better worth knowing." At once Oscar wrote to me objecting to this phrase. "Surely,

Frank, you have forgotten me. Surely, I am better worth knowing than Shakespeare?"

The question astonished me so that I could not make up my mind at once; but when he pressed me later I had to tell him that Shakespeare had reached higher heights of thought and feeling than any modern, though I was probably wrong in saying that I knew him better than I knew a living man.

I had to go back to England and some little time elapsed before I could return to Paris; but I crossed again early in the summer, and found he had written nothing.

I often talked with him about it; but now he changed his ground a little.

"I can't write, Frank. When I take up my pen all the past comes back. I cannot bear the thoughts . . . regret and remorse, like twin dogs, wait to seize me at any idle moment. I must go out and watch life, amuse, interest myself, or I should go mad. You don't know how sore it is about my heart, as soon as I am alone. I am face to face with my own soul; the Oscar of four years ago, with his beautiful secure life, and his glorious easy triumphs, comes up before me, and I cannot stand the contrast. . . . My eyes burn with tears. If you care for me, Frank, you will not ask me to write."

"You promised to try," I said somewhat harshly, "and I want you to try. You haven't suffered more than Dante suffered in exile and poverty; yet you know if he had suffered ten times as much, he would have written it all down. Tears, indeed! the fire in his eyes would have dried the tears."

"True enough, Frank, but Dante was all of one piece whereas I am drawn in two different directions. I was born to sing the joy and pride of life, the pleasure of living, the delight in everything beautiful in this most beautiful world, and they took me and tortured me till I learned pity and sorrow. Now I cannot sing the joy, heartily, because I know the suffering, and I was never made to sing of suffering. I hate it, and I want to sing the love songs of joy and pleasure. It is joy alone which appeals to my soul; the joy of life and beauty and love—I could sing the song of Apollo the Sun-God, and they try to force me to sing the song of the tortured Marsyas."

This to me was his true and final confession. His second fall after leaving prison had put him "at war with himself". This is, I think, the very heart of truth about his soul; the song of sorrow, of pity and renunciation was not his song, and the experience of suffering prevented him from singing the delight of life and the joy he took in beauty. It never seemed to occur to him that he could reach a faith which should include both self-indulgence and renunciation in a larger acceptance of life.

In spite of his sunny nature he had a certain amount of jealousy and envy in him which was always brought to light by the popular success of those whom he had known and measured. I remember his telling me once that he wrote his first play because he was annoyed at the way Pinero was being praised—"Pinero, who can't write at all; he is a stage-carpenter and nothing else. His characters are made of dough; and never was there such a worthless style, or rather such a complete absence of style. He writes like a grocer's assistant."

I noticed now that this trait of jealousy was stronger in him than ever. One day I showed him an English illustrated paper which I had bought on my way to lunch. It contained a picture of George Curzon (I beg his pardon, Lord Curzon) as Viceroy of India. He was photographed in a carriage with his wife by his side; the gorgeous state carriage drawn by four horses, with outriders, and escorted by cavalry and cheering crowds—all the paraphernalia and pomp of imperial power.

"Do you see that?" cried Oscar angrily; "fancy George Curzon being treated like that. I know him well; a more perfect example of plodding mediocrity was never seen in the world. He had never a thought or phrase above the common."

"I know him pretty well, too," I replied. "His incurable commonness is the secret of his success. He 'voices', as he would say himself, the opinion of the average man on every subject. He might be a leader-writer on the *Mail* or *Times*. What do you know of the average man or of his opinions? But the man in the street, as he is called to-day, can only learn from the man who is just one step above himself, and so the George Curzons come to success in life. That, too, is the secret of the popularity of this or that writer. Hall Caine is an even larger George Curzon, a better endowed mediocrity."

"But why should he have fame and state and power?" Oscar cried indignantly.

"State and power, because he is George Curzon, but fame he will never have, and I suspect if the truth were known, in the moments when he too comes face to face with his own soul, as you say, he would give a good deal of his state and power for a very little of your fame."

"That is probably true, Frank," cried Oscar, "that is almost certainly the crumpled rose-leaf of his couch, but how grossly he is over-estimated and over-rewarded. . . . Do you know Wilfred Blunt?"

"I have met him," I replied, "but don't know him. We met once and he bragged preposterously about his Arab ponies. I was at that time editor of *The Evening News;* and Mr. Blunt tried hard to talk down to my level."

"He is by way of being a poet, and he has a very real love of literature."

"I know," I said; "I really know his work and a good deal about him and have nothing but praise for the way he championed the Egyptians, and for his poetry when he has anything to say."

"Well, Frank, he had a sort of club at Crabbett Park, a club for poets, to which only poets were invited, and he was a most admirable and perfect host. Lady Blunt could never make out what he was up to. He used to get us all down to Crabbett, and the poet who was received last had to make a speech about the new poet—a speech in which he was supposed to tell the truth about the new-comer. Blunt took the idea, no doubt, from the custom of the French Academy. Well, he asked me down to Crabbett Park, and George Curzon, if you please, was the poet picked to make the speech about me."

"Good God," I cried, "Curzon a poet. It's like Kitchener being taken for a great captain, or Salisbury for a statesman."

"He writes verses, Frank, but of course there is not a line of poetry in him: his verses are good enough though, well-turned, I mean, and sharp, if not witty. Well, Curzon had to make this speech about me after dinner. We had a delightful dinner, quite perfect, and then Curzon got up. He had evidently prepared his speech carefully; it was bristling with innuendoes, sneering side-hits at strange sins. Everyone looked at this fellow and thought the speech the height of bad taste.

"Mediocrity always detests ability, and loathes genius; Curzon wanted to prove to himself that at any rate in the moralities he was my superior.

"When he sat down I had to answer him. That was the programme. Of course I had not prepared a speech, had not thought about Curzon, or what he might say, but I got up, Frank, and told the kindliest truth about him, and everyone took it for the bitterest sarcasm, and cheered and cheered me, though what I said was merely the truth. I told how difficult it was for Curzon to work and study at Oxford. Everyone wanted to know him because of his position, because he was going into Parliament, and certain to make a great figure there; and everyone tried to make up to him, but he knew that he must not yield to such seduction, so he sat in his room with a wet towel about his head, and worked and worked without ceasing.

"In the earlier examinations, which demand only memory, he won first honours. But even success could not induce him to relax his efforts; he lived laborious days and took every college examination seriously; he made out dates in red ink, and hung them on his wall, and learnt pages of uninteresting events and put them in blue ink in his memory, and at last came out of the 'Final Schools' with second honours. And now, I concluded, 'this model youth is going into life, and he is certain to treat it seriously, certain to win at any rate second honours in it, and have a great and praiseworthy career.'

"Frank, they roared with laughter, and, to do Curzon justice, at the end he came up to me and apologised, and was charming. Indeed, they all made much of me and we had a great night.

"I remember we talked all the night through, or rather I talked and everyone else listened, for the great principle of the division of labour is beginning to be understood in English Society. The host gives excellent food, excellent wine, excellent cigarettes, and super-excellent coffee, that's his part, and all the men listen, that's theirs; while I talk and the stars twinkle their delight.

"Wyndham was there, too; you know George Wyndham, with his beautiful face and fine figure. He is infinitely cleverer than Curzon but he had not Curzon's push and force, or perhaps, as you say, he is not in such close touch with the average man as Curzon; he was charming to me.

"In the morning we all trooped out to see the dawn, and some of the young ones, wild with youth and high spirits, Curzon of course among the number, stripped off their clothes and rushed down to the lake and began swimming and diving about like a lot of schoolboys. There is a great deal of the schoolboy in all Englishmen, that is what makes them so lovable. When they came out they ran over the grass to dry themselves, and then began playing lawn tennis, just as they were, stark naked, the future rulers of England. I shall never forget the scene. Wilfred Blunt had gone up to his wife's apartments and had changed into some fantastic pyjamas; suddenly he opened an upper window and came out and perched himself, cross-legged, on the balcony, looking down at the mad game of lawn tennis, for all the world like a sort of pink and green Buddha, while I strolled about with someone, and ordered fresh coffee and talked till the dawn came with silent silver feet lighting up the beautiful greenery of the park. . . .

"Now George Curzon plays king in India. Wyndham is on the way to power, and I'm hiding in shame and poverty here in Paris, an exile and outcast. Do you wonder that I cannot write, Frank? The awful injustice of life maddens me. After all, what have they done in comparison with what I have done?

"Close the eyes of all of us now and fifty years hence, or a hundred years hence, no one will know anything about Curzon or Wyndham or Blunt. Whether they lived or died will be a matter of indifference to everyone; but my comedies and my stories and "The Ballad of Reading Gaol" will be known and read by millions, and even my unhappy fate will call forth world-wide sympathy."

It was all true enough, and good to keep in mind; but even when Oscar spoke of greater men than himself, he took the same attitude. His self-esteem was extraordinary. He did not compare his work with that of others, was not anxious to find his true place, as even Shakespeare was. From the beginning, from youth on, he was convinced that he was a great man and going to do great things. Many of us have the same belief and are just as persuaded, but the belief is not ever present with us as it was with Oscar, moulding all his actions. For instance, I remarked once that his handwriting was unforgettable and characteristic. "I worked at it," he said, "as a boy; I wanted a distinctive handwriting; it had to be clear and beautiful and peculiar to me. At length I got it but it took time and patience. I always wanted everything about me to be distinctive," he added, smiling.

He was proud of his physical appearance, inordinately pleased with his great height, vain of it even. "Height gives distinction," he declared, and once even went so far as to say, "One can't picture Napoleon as small; one thinks only of his magnificent head and forgets the little podgy figure; it must have been a great nuisance to him. Small men have no dignity."

All this utterly unconscious of the fact that most tall men have no ever present sense of their height as an advantage. Yet on the whole one agrees with Montaigne that height is the chief beauty of a man; it gives presence.

Oscar never learned anything from criticism; he had a good deal of personal dignity in spite of his amiability, and when one found fault with his work, he would smile vaguely or change the subject as if it didn't interest him.

Again and again I played on his self-esteem to get him to write; but always met the same answer.

"Oh, Frank, it's impossible, impossible for me to work under these disgraceful conditions."

"But you can have better conditions now and lots of money if you'll begin to work."

He shook his head despairingly. Again and again I tried, but failed to move him, even when I dangled money before him. I didn't then know that he was receiving regularly more than £300 a year. I thought he was completely destitute, dependent on such casual help as friends could give him. I have a letter from him about this time asking me for even £5 as if he were in extremest need.

On one of my visits to Paris after discussing his position, I could not help saying to him:

"The only thing that will make you write, Oscar, is absolute, blank poverty. That's the sharpest spur after all—necessity."

"You don't know me," he replied sharply. "I would kill myself. I can endure to the end; but to be absolutely destitute would show me suicide as the open door."

Suddenly his depressed manner changed and his whole face lighted up.

"Isn't it comic, Frank, the way the English talk of the 'open door,' while their doors are always locked and barred and bolted, even their church doors? Yet it is not hypocrisy in them; they simply cannot see themselves as they are; they have no imagination."

A long pause, and he went on gravely:

"Suicide, Frank, is always the temptation of the unfortunate, a great temptation."

"Suicide is the natural end of the world-weary," I replied; "but you enjoy life intensely. For you to talk of suicide is ridiculous."

"Do you know that my wife is dead, Frank?"

"I had heard it," I said.

"My way back to hope and a new life ends in her grave," he went on. "Everything I do, Frank, is irrevocable."

He spoke with a certain grave sincerity.

"The great tragedies of the world are all final and complete; Socrates would not escape death, though Crito opened the prison door for him. I could not avoid prison, though you showed me the way to safety. We are fated to suffer, don't you think? as an example to humanity—'an echo and a light unto eternity'."

"I think it would be finer, instead of taking the punishment lying down, to trample it under your feet, and make it a rung of the ladder."

"Oh, Frank, you would turn all the tragedies into triumphs, you are a fighter. My life is done."

"You love life," I cried, "as much as ever you did; more than anyone I have ever seen."

"It is true," he cried, his face lighting up quickly, "more than anyone, Frank. Life delights me. The people passing on the Boulevards, the play of the sunshine in the trees; the noise, the quick movement of the cabs, the costumes of the *cochers* and *sergents-de-ville;* workers and beggars, pimps and prostitutes—all please me to the soul, charm me, and if you would only let me talk instead of bothering me to write I should be quite happy. Why should I write any more? I have done enough for fame.

"I will tell you a story, Frank," he broke off, and he told me a slight thing about Judas. The little tale was told delightfully, with eloquent inflections of voice and still more eloquent pauses. . . .

"The end of all this is," I said before going back to London, "that you will not write?"

"No, no, Frank," he said, "that I cannot write under these conditions. If I had money enough; if I could shake off Paris, and forget those awful rooms of mine and get to the Riviera for the winter and live in some seaside village of the Latins with the blue sea at my feet and the blue sky above and God's sunlight about me and no care for money, then I would write as naturally as a bird sings, because I should be happy and could not help it. . . .

"You write stories taken from the fight of life; you are careless of surroundings, I am a poet and can only sing in the sunshine when I am happy."

"All right," I said, snatching at the half-promise. "It is just possible that I may get hold of some money during the next few months, and, if I do, you shall go and winter in the South, and live as you please without care of money. If you can only sing when the cage is beautiful and sunlight floods it, I know the very place for you."

With this sort of vague understanding we parted for some months.

❦

22

"A Great Romantic Passion!"

THERE IS NO more difficult problem for the writer, no harder task than to decide how far he should allow himself to go in picturing human weakness. We have all come from the animal and can all, without any assistance from books, imagine easily enough the effects of unrestrained self-indulgence. Yet it is instructive and pregnant with warning to remark that, as soon as the sheet anchor of high resolve is gone, the frailties of man tend to become master-vices. All our civilization is artificially built up by effort; all high humanity is the reward of constant striving against natural desires.

In the fall of this year, 1898, I sold *The Saturday Review* to Lord Hardwicke and his friends, and as soon as the purchase was completed, I think in November, I wired to Oscar that I should be in Paris in a short time and ready to take him to the South for his holiday. I sent him some money to pave the way.

A few days later I crossed and wired to him from Calais to dine with me at Durand's, and to begin dinner if I happened to be late.

While waiting for dinner, I said:

"I want to stay two or three days in Paris to see some pictures. Would you be ready to start South on Thursday next?" It was then Monday, I think.

"On Thursday?" he repeated. "Yes, Frank, I think so."

"There is some money for anything you may want to buy,"

I said and handed him a cheque I had made payable to self and signed, for he knew where he could cash it.

"How good of you, Frank, I cannot thank you enough. You start on Thursday," he added, as if considering it.

"If you would rather wait a little," I said, "say so. I'm quite willing."

"No, Frank, I think Thursday will do. We are really going to the South for the whole winter. How wonderful; how gorgeous it will be."

We had a great dinner and talked and talked. He spoke of some of the new Frenchmen, and at length of Pierre Louÿs, whom he described as a disciple:

"It was I, Frank, who induced him to write his 'Aphrodite' in prose." He spoke, too, of the Grand Guignol Theatre.

"Le Grand Guignol is the first theatre in Paris. It looks like a nonconformist chapel, a barn of a room with a gallery at the back and a little wooden stage. There you see the primitive tragedies of real life. They are as ugly and as fascinating as life itself. You must see it and we will go to Antoine's as well. You must see Antoine's new piece; he is doing great work."

We kept dinner up to an unconscionable hour. I had much to tell of London and much to hear of Paris, and we talked and drank coffee till one o'clock, and when I proposed supper Oscar accepted the idea with enthusiasm.

"I have often lunched with you from two o'clock till nine, Frank, and now I am going to dine with you from nine o'clock till breakfast to-morrow morning."

"What shall we drink?" I asked.

"The same champagne, Frank, don't you think?" he said, pulling his jowl; "there is no wine so inspiring as that dry champagne with the exquisite *bouquet*. You were the first to say my plays were the champagne of literature."

When we came out it was three o'clock and I was tired and sleepy with my journey, and Oscar had drunk perhaps more than was good for him. Knowing how he hated walking I got a *voiture de cercle* and told him to take it, and I would walk to my hotel. He thanked me and seemed to hesitate.

"What is it now?" I asked, wanting to get to bed.

"Just a word with you," he said, and drew me away from the

carriage where the *chasseur* was waiting with the rug. When he got me three or four paces away he said, hesitatingly:

"Frank, could you . . . can you let me have a few pounds? I'm very hard up."

I stared at him; I had given him a cheque at the beginning of the dinner. Had he forgotten? Or did he perchance want to keep the hundred pounds intact for some reason? Suddenly it occurred to me that he might be without even enough for the carriage. I took out a hundred franc note and gave it to him.

"Thank you, so much," he said, thrusting it into his waistcoat pocket, "It's very kind of you."

"You will turn up to-morrow at lunch at one?" I said, as I put him into the little brougham.

"Yes, of course, yes," he cried, and I turned away.

Next day at lunch he seemed to meet me with some embarrassment:

"Frank, I want to ask you something. I'm really confused about last night; we dined most wisely, if too well. This morning I found you had given me a cheque, and I found besides in my waistcoat pocket a note for a hundred francs. Did I ask you for it at the end? 'Tap' you, the French call it," he added, trying to laugh.

I nodded.

"How dreadful!" he cried. "How dreadful poverty is! I had forgotten that you had given me a cheque, and I was so hard up, so afraid you might go away without giving me anything, that I asked you for it. Isn't poverty dreadful?"

I nodded; I could not say a word. The fact told so much.

The chastened mood of self-condemnation did not last long with him or go deep; soon he was talking as merrily and gaily as ever.

Before parting I said to him:

"You won't forget that you are going on Thursday night?"

"Oh, really!" he cried, to my surprise. "Thursday is very near; I don't know whether I shall be able to come."

"What on earth do you mean?" I asked.

"The truth is, you know, I have debts to pay, and I have not enough."

"But I will give you more," I cried, "what will clear you?"

"Fifty more I think will do. How good you are!"

"I will bring it with me to-morrow morning."

"In notes please, will you? French money. I find I shall want it to pay some little things at once, and the time is short."

I thought nothing of the matter. The next day at lunch I gave him the money in French notes. That night I said to him:

"You know we are going away to-morrow evening. I hope you'll be ready? I have got the tickets for the *Train de Luxe*."

"Oh, I'm so sorry!" he cried, "I can't be ready."

"What is it now?" I asked.

"Well, it's money. Some more debts have come in."

"Why will you not be frank with me, and tell me what you owe? I will give you a cheque for it. I don't want to drag it out of you bit by bit. Tell me a sum that will make you free, and I will give it to you. I want you to have a perfect six months, and how can you if you are bothered with debts?"

"How kind you are to me! Do you really mean it?"

"Of course I do."

"Really?" he said.

"Yes," I said, "tell me what it is."

"I think, I believe . . . would another fifty be too much?"

"I will give it you to-morrow. Are you sure that will be enough?"

"Oh, yes, Frank; but let's go on Sunday. Sunday is such a good day for travelling, and it's always so dull everywhere, we might just as well spend it on the train. Besides, no one travels on Sunday in France, so we are sure to be able to take our ease in our train. Won't Sunday do, Frank?"

"Of course it will," I replied laughing; but a day or two later he was again embarrassed, and again told me it was money, and then he confessed to me that he was afraid at first I should not have paid all his debts, if I had known how much they were, and so he thought by telling me of them little by little, he would make sure at least of something. This pitiful, pitiable confession depressed me on his account. It showed practice in such petty tricks and all too little pride. Of course it did not alter my admiration of his qualities; nor weaken in any degree my resolve to give him a fair chance. If he could be saved, I was determined to save him.

We met at the Gare de Lyons on Sunday evening. I found he

had dined at the buffet. There was a surprising number of empty bottles on the table; he seemed terribly depressed.

"Someone was dining with me, Frank, a friend," he offered by way of explanation.

"Why did he not wait? I should like to have seen him."

"Oh, he was no one you would have cared about, Frank," he replied.

I sat with him and took a cup of coffee, whilst waiting for the train. He was wretchedly gloomy; scarcely spoke indeed. I could not make it out. From time to time he sighed heavily, and I noticed that his eyes were red, as if he had been crying.

"What is the matter?" I asked.

"I will tell you later, perhaps. It is very hard; parting is like dying," and his eyes filled with tears.

We were soon in the train running out into the night. I was as light-hearted as could be. At length I was free of journalism, I thought, and I was going to the South to write my Shakespeare book, and Oscar would work, too, when the conditions were pleasant. But I could not win a single smile from him; he sat downcast, sighing hopelessly from time to time.

"What on earth's the matter?" I cried. "Here you are going to the sunshine, to blue skies, and the wine-tinted Mediterranean, and you're not content. We shall stop in a hotel near a little sun-baked valley running down to the sea. You walk from the hotel over a carpet of pine needles, and when you get into the open, violets and anemones bloom about your feet, and the scent of rosemary and myrtle will be in your nostrils; yet instead of singing for joy the bird droops his feathers and hangs his head as if he had the 'pip'."

"Oh, don't," he cried, "don't," and he looked at me with tears filling his eyes; "you don't know, Frank, what a great romantic passion is."

"Is that what you are suffering from?"

"Yes, a great romantic passion."

"Good God!" I laughed; "who has inspired this new devotion?"

"Don't make fun of me, Frank, or I will not tell you; but if you will listen I will try to tell you all about it, for I think you should know, besides, I think telling it may ease my pain, so come into the cabin and listen.

"Do you remember once in the summer you wired me from Calais to meet you at Maire's restaurant, meaning to go afterwards to Antoine's Theatre, and I was very late? You remember, the evening Rostand was dining at the next table. Well, it was that evening. I drove up to Maire's in time, and I was just getting out of the victoria when a little soldier passed, and our eyes met. My heart stood still; he had great dark eyes and an exquisite olive-dark face—a Florentine bronze, Frank, by a great master. He looked like Napoleon when he was first Consul, only—less imperious, more beautiful. . . .

"I got out hypnotised, and followed him down the Boulevard as in a dream; the *cocher* came running after me, I remember, and I gave him a five franc piece, and waved him off; I had no idea what I owed him; I did not want to hear his voice; it might break the spell; mutely I followed my fate. I overtook the boy in a short time and asked him to come and have a drink, and he said to me in his quaint French way:

"*'Ce n'est pas de rufus!*' (Too good to refuse.)

"We went into a café, and I ordered something, I forget what, and we began to talk. I told him I liked his face; I had had a friend once like him; and I wanted to know all about him. I was in a hurry to meet you, but I had to make friends with him first. He began by telling me all about his mother, Frank, yes, his mother." Oscar smiled here in spite of himself.

"But at last I got from him that he was always free on Thursdays, and he would be very glad to see me then, though he did not know what I could see in him to like. I found out that the thing he desired most in the world was a bicycle; he talked of nickel-plated handle bars, and chains—and finally I told him it might be arranged. He was very grateful and so we made a rendezvous for the next Thursday, and I came on at once to dine with you."

"Goodness!" I cried laughing. "A soldier, a nickel-plated bicycle and a great romantic passion!"

"If I had said a brooch, or a necklace, some trinket which would have cost ten times as much, you would have found it quite natural."

"Yes," I admitted, "but I don't think I'd have introduced the necklace the first evening if there had been any romance in the affair, and the nickel-plated bicycle to me seems irresistibly comic."

"Frank," he cried reprovingly, "I cannot talk to you if you laugh; I am quite serious. I don't believe you know what a great romantic passion is; I am going to convince you that you don't know the meaning of it."

"Fire away," I replied, "I am here to be convinced. But I don't think you will teach me that there is any romance except where there is another sex."

"Don't talk to me of the other sex," he cried with distaste in voice and manner. "First of all in beauty there is no comparison between a boy and a girl. Think of the enormous, fat hips which every sculptor has to tone down, and make lighter, and the great udder breasts which the artist has to make small and round and firm, and then picture the exquisite slim lines of a boy's figure. No one who loves beauty can hesitate for a moment. The Greeks knew that; they had the sense of plastic beauty, and they understood that there is no comparison."

"You must not say that," I replied; "you are going too far; the Venus of Milo is as fine as any Apollo, in sheer beauty; the flowing curves appeal to me more than your weedy lines."

"Perhaps they do, Frank," he retorted, "but you must see that the boy is far more beautiful. It is your sex-instinct, your sinful sex-instinct which prevents you worshipping the higher form of beauty. Height and length of limb give distinction; slightness gives grace; women are squat! You must admit that the boy's figure is more beautiful; the appeal it makes far higher, more spiritual."

"Six of one and half-a-dozen of the other," I barked. "Your sculptor knows it is just as hard to find an ideal boy's figure as an ideal girl's; and if he has to modify the most perfect girl's figure, he has to modify the most perfect boy's figure as well. If he refines the girl's breasts and hips he has to pad the boy's ribs and tone down the great staring knee-bones and the unlovely large ankles; but please go on, I enjoy your special pleading and your romantic passion interests me; though you have not yet come to the romance, let alone the passion."

"Oh, Frank," he cried, "the story is full of romance; every meeting was an event in my life. You have no idea how intelligent he is; every evening we spent together he was different; he had grown, developed. I lent him books and he read them, and his mind opened from week to week like a flower, till in a short time, a few months, he became an exquisite companion and disciple. Frank, no girl grows like that; they have no minds, and what intelligence they have is all given to wretched vanities and personal jealousies. There is no intellectual companionship possible with them. They want to talk of dress, and not of ideas, and how persons look and not of what they are. How can you have the flower of romance without a brotherhood of soul?"

"Sisterhood of soul seems to me infinitely finer," I said, "but go on."

"I shall convince you," he declared; "I must be able to, because all reason is on my side. Let me give you one instance. Of course my boy had his bicycle; he used to come to me on it and go to and fro from the barracks on it. When you came to Paris in September, you invited me to dine one night, one Thursday night, when he was to come to me. I told him I had to go and dine with you. He didn't mind; but was glad when I said I had an English editor for a friend, glad that I should have someone to talk to about London and the people I used to know. If it had been a woman I loved, I should have been forced to tell lies; she would have been jealous of my past. I told him the truth, and when I spoke about you he grew interested and excited, and at last he put a wish before me. He wanted to know if he might come and leave his bicycle outside and look through the window of the restaurant, just to see us at dinner. I told him there might possibly be women-guests. He replied that he would be delighted to see me in dress-clothes talking to gentlemen and ladies.

"Might he come? he persisted.

"Of course I said he could come, and he came, but I never saw him.

"The next time we met he told me all about it; how he had picked you out from my description of you, and how he knew Baüer from his likeness to Dumas *père*, and he was delightful about it all.

"Now, Frank, would any girl have come to see you enjoying yourself with other people? Would any girl have stared through the window and been glad to see you inside amusing yourself with other men and women? You know there's not a girl on earth with such unselfish devotion. There is no comparison, I tell you, between the boy and the girl; I say again deliberately, you don't know what a great romantic passion is or the high unselfishness of true love."

"You have put it with extraordinary ability," I said, "as of course I knew you would. I think I can understand the charm of such companionship; but only from the young boy's point of view, not from yours. I can understand how you have opened to him a new heaven and a new earth, but what has he given you? Nothing. On the other hand any finely gifted girl would have given you something. If you had really touched her heart, you would have found in her some instinctive tenderness, some proof of unselfish, exquisite devotion that would have made your eyes prickle with a sense of inferiority.

"After all, the essence of love, the finest spirit of that companionship you speak about, of the sisterhood of soul, is that the other person should quicken you, too; open to you new horizons, discover new possibilities; and how could your soldier boy help you in any way? He brought you no new ideas, no new feelings, could reveal no new thoughts to you. I can see no romance, no growth of soul in such a connection. But the girl is different from the man in all ways. You have as much to learn from her as she has from you, and neither of you can come to ideal growth in any other way: you are both half-parts of humanity—complements, and in need of each other."

"You have put it very cunningly, Frank, as I expected you would, to return your compliment, but you must admit that with the boy, at any rate, you have no jealousy, no mean envyings, no silly inanities. There it is, Frank, some of us hate 'cats.' I can give reasons for my dislike, which to me are conclusive."

"The boy who would beg for a bicycle is not likely to be without mean envyings," I replied. "Now you have talked about romance and companionship," I went on, "but can you really feel passion?"

"Frank, what a silly question! Do you remember how Socrates says he felt when the chlamys blew aside and showed him the limbs of Charmides? Don't you remember how the blood throbbed in his veins and how he grew blind with desire, a scene more magical than the passionate love-lines of Sappho?

"There is no other passion to be compared with it. A woman's passion is degrading. She is continually tempting you. She wants your desire as a satisfaction for her vanity more than anything else, and her vanity is insatiable if her desire is weak, and so she continually tempts you to excess, and then blames you for the physical satiety and disgust which she herself has created. With a boy there is no vanity in the matter, no jealousy, and therefore none of the tempting, not a tenth part of the coarseness; and consequently desire is always fresh and keen. Oh, Frank, believe me, you don't know what a great romantic passion is."

"What you say only shows how little you know women," I replied. "If you explained all this to the girl who loves you, she would see it at once, and her tenderness would grow with her self-abnegation; we all grow by giving. If the woman cares more than the man for caresses and kindness, it is because she feels more tenderness, and is capable of intenser devotion."

"You don't know what you are talking about, Frank," he retorted. "You repeat the old accepted commonplaces. The boy came to the station with me to-night. He knew I was going away for six months. His heart was like lead, tears gathered in his eyes again and again in spite of himself, and yet he tried to be gay and bright for my sake; he wanted to show me how glad he was that I should be happy, how thankful he was for all I had done for him, and the new mental life I had created in him. He did his best to keep my courage up. I cried, but he shook his tears away. 'Six months will soon be over,' he said, 'and perhaps you will come back to me, and I shall be glad again.' Meantime he will write charming letters to me, I'm sure.

"Would any girl take a parting like that? No; she would be jealous and envious, and wonder why you were enjoying yourself in the South while she was condemned to live in the rainy, cold North. Would she ask you to tell her of all the beautiful girls you met, and whether they were charming and bright, as the boy asked me to tell him of all the interesting people I should meet, so that he, too, might take an interest in them? A girl in his place would have been ill with envy and malice and jealousy. Again I repeat, you don't know what a high romantic passion is."

"Your argument is illogical," I cried. "If the girl is jealous, it is because she has given herself more completely; her exclusiveness is the other side of her devotion and tenderness; she wants to do everything for you, to be with you and help you in every way, and in case of illness or poverty or danger, you would find how much more she had to give than your red-breeched soldier."

"That's merely a rude gibe and not an argument, Frank."

"As good an argument as your 'cats'," I replied; "your little soldier boy with his nickel-plated bicycle only makes me grin," and I grinned.

"You are unpardonable," he cried, "unpardonable, and in your soul you know that all the weight of argument is on my side. In your soul you must know it. What is the food of passion, Frank, but beauty, beauty alone, beauty always, and in beauty of form and vigour of life there is no comparison. If you loved beauty as intensely as I do, you would feel as I feel. It is beauty which gives me joy, makes me drunk as with wine, blind with insatiable desire. . . ."

23

His Judgments of Writers and of Women

He was an incomparable companion, perfectly amiable, yet vivid, and eager as a child, always interested and interesting. We awoke at Avignon and went out in pyjamas and overcoats to stretch our legs and get a bowl of coffee on the platform in the pearly grey light of early morning. After coffee and cigarettes he led the way to the other end of the platform, that we might catch a glimpse of the town wall which, though terribly restored, yet, when seen from a distance, transports one back five hundred years to the age of chivalry.

"How I should have loved to be a troubadour, or a *trouvère*, Frank; that was my true *métier*, to travel from castle to castle singing love songs and telling romantic stories to while away the tedium of the lives of the great. Fancy the reception they would have given me for bringing a new joy into their castled isolation, new ideas, new passions—a breath of gossip and scandal from the outside world to relieve the intolerable boredom of the middle ages. I should have been kept at the Court of Aix. I think they would have bound me with flower-chains, and my fame would have spread all through the sunny vineyards and grey olive-clad hills of Provence."

When we got into the train again he began:

"We stop next at Marseilles, don't we, Frank? A great historic town for nearly three thousand years. One really feels a barbarian in comparison, and yet all I know of Marseilles is that it is famous for *bouillabaisse*. Suppose we stop and get some?"

"*Bouillabaisse*," I replied, "is not peculiar to Marseilles or the *Rue Cannebière*. You can get it all along this coast. There is only one thing necessary to it and that is *rascasse*, a fish caught only among the rocks: you will get excellent *bouillabaisse* at lunch where we are going."

"Where are we going? You have not told me yet."

"It is for you to decide," I answered. "If you want perfect quiet there are two places in the Esterel mountains, Agay and La Napoule. Agay is in the middle of the Esterel. You would be absolutely alone there except for the visit of an occasional French painter. La Napoule is eight or ten miles from Cannes, so that you are within reach of a town and its amusements. There is still another place I had thought of, quieter than either, in the mountains behind Nice."

"Nice sounds wonderful, Frank, but I should meet too many English people there who would know me, and they are horribly rude. I think we will choose La Napoule."

About ten o'clock we got out at La Napoule and installed ourselves in the little hotel, taking up three of the best rooms on the second or top floor, much to the delight of the landlord. At twelve we had breakfast under a big umbrella in the open air, looking over the sea. I had put the landlord on his mettle, and he gave us a fry of little red mullet, which made us understand how tasteless whitebait are; then a plain beefsteak *aux pommes*, a morsel of cheese, and a sweet omelette. We both agreed that we had had a most excellent breakfast. The coffee left a good deal to be desired, and there was no champagne on the list fit to drink; but both these faults could be remedied by the morrow, and were remedied.

We spent the rest of the day wandering between the seashore and the pine-clad hills. The next morning I put in some work, but in the afternoon I was free to walk and explore. On one of my first tramps I discovered a monastery among the hills hundreds of feet above the sea, built and governed by an Italian monk. I got to know the Père Vergile[1] and had a great talk with him. He was both wise and strong, with ingratiating, gentle manners. Had

[1] He lived till November, 1910.

he gone as a boy from his little Italian fishing village to New York or Paris, he would have certainly come to greatness and honour. One afternoon I took Oscar to see him. The monastery was not more than three-quarters of an hour's stroll from our hotel; but Oscar grumbled at the walk as a nuisance, said it was miles and miles; the road, too, was rough, and the sun hot. The truth was, he was abnormally lazy. But he fascinated the Italian with his courteous manner and vivid speech, and as soon as we were alone the Abbé asked me who he was.

"He must be a great man," he said, "he has the stamp of a great man, and he must have lived in courts. He has the charming, grace-ful, smiling courtesy of the great."

"Yes," I nodded mysteriously, "a great man—incognito."

The Abbé kept us to dinner, made us taste of his oldest wines, and a special liqueur of his own distilling; told us how he had built the monastery with no money, and when we exclaimed with wonder, reproved us gently:

"All great things are built with faith, and not with money; why wonder that this little building stands firmly on that everlasting foundation?"

When we came out of the monastery it was already night, and the moonlight was throwing fantastic leafy shadows on the path, as we walked down through the avenue of forest to the sea shore.

"You remember those words of Vergil, Frank—*per amica si-lentia lunæ*—they always seem to me indescribably beautiful; the most magic line about the moon ever written, except Browning's in the poem in which he mentioned Keats—'him even'. I love that 'amica silentia.' What a beautiful nature the man had who could feel 'the *friendly* silences of the moon'."

When we got down the hill he declared himself tired.

"Tired after a mile?" I asked.

"Tired to death, worn out," he said, laughing at his own laziness.

"Shall we get a boat and row across the bay?"

"How splendid! of course, let's do it," and we went down to the landing stage. I had never seen the water so calm; half the bay was veiled by the mountain, and opaque like unpolished steel; a little further out, the water was a purple shield, emblazoned with shimmering silver. We called a fisherman and explained what we wanted. When we got into the boat, to my astonishment, Oscar began calling the fisher boy by his name; evidently he knew him quite well. When we landed I went up from the boat to the hotel, leaving Oscar and the boy together. . . .

A fortnight taught me a good deal about Oscar at this time; he was intensely indolent; quite content to kill time by the hour talking to the fisher lads, or he would take a little carriage and drive to Cannes and amuse himself at some wayside café.

He never cared to walk and I walked for miles daily, so that we spent only one or at most two afternoons a week together, meeting so seldom that nearly all our talks were significant. Several times contemporary names came up and I was compelled to notice for the first time that really he was contemptuous of almost everyone, and had a sharp word to say about many who were supposed to be his friends. One day we spoke of Ricketts and Shannon. I was saying that had Ricketts lived in Paris he would have had a great reputation. Many of his designs I thought extraordinary, and his intellect was peculiarly French—*mordant* even. Oscar did not like to hear praise of anyone.

"Do you know my word for them, Frank? I like it. I call them 'Temper and Temperament.'"

Was his punishment making him a little spiteful or was it the temptation of the witty phrase?

"What do you think of Arthur Symons?" I asked.

"Oh, Frank, I said of him long ago that he was a sad example of an Egoist who had no Ego."

"And what of your compatriot, George Moore? He's popular enough," I continued.

"Popular, Frank, as if that counted. George Moore has conducted his whole education in public. He had written two or three books before he found out there was such a thing as English grammar. He at once announced his discovery and so won the admiration of the illiterate. A few years later he discovered that there was something architectural in style, that sentences had to be built up into a paragraph, and paragraphs into chapters and so on. Naturally he cried this revelation, too, from the housetops, and thus won the admiration of the journalists who had been making rubble-heaps all their lives without knowing it. I'm much afraid, Frank, in spite of all his efforts, he will die before he reaches the level from which writers start. It's a pity because he has certainly a little real talent. He differs from Symons in that he has an Ego, but his Ego has five senses and no soul."

"What about Bernard Shaw?" I probed further, "after all he's going to count."

"Yes, Frank, a man of real ability but with a bleak mind. Humorous gleams as of wintry sunlight on a bare, harsh landscape. He has no passion, no feeling, and without passionate feeling how can one be an artist? He believes in nothing, loves nothing, not even Bernard Shaw, and really, on the whole, I don't wonder at his indifference," and he laughed mischievously.

"And Wells?" I asked.

"A scientific Jules Verne," he replied with a shrug.

"Did you ever care for Hardy?" I continued.

"Not greatly. He has just found out that women have legs underneath their dresses, and this discovery has almost wrecked his life. He writes poetry, I believe, in his leisure moments, and I am afraid it will be very hard reading. He knows nothing of love; passion to him is a childish illness like measles—poor unhappy spirit!"

"You might be describing Mrs. Humphry Ward," I cried.

"God forbid, Frank," he exclaimed with such mock horror I had to laugh. "After all, Hardy is a writer and a great landscape painter."

"I don't know why it is," he went on, "but I am always matchmaking when I think of English celebrities. I should so much like to have introduced Mrs. Humphry Ward blushing at eighteen or twenty to Swinburne, who would of course have bitten her neck in a furious kiss, and she would have run away and exposed him in court, or else have suffered agonies of mingled delight and shame in silence.

"And if one could only marry Thomas Hardy to Victoria Cross he might have gained some inkling of real passion with which to animate his little keepsake pictures of starched ladies. A great many writers, I think, might be saved in this way, but there would still be left the Corellis and Hall Caines that one could do nothing with except bind them back to back, which would not even tantalise them, and throw them into the river, a new *noyade*: the Thames at Barking, I think, would be about the place for them. . . . "

"Where do you go every afternoon?" I asked him once casually.

"I go to Cannes, Frank, and sit in a café and look across the sea to Capri, where Tiberius used to sit like a spider watching, and I think of myself as an exile, the victim of one of his inscrutable suspicions, or else I am in Rome looking at the people dancing naked, but with gilded lips, through the streets at the *Floralia*. I sup with the *arbiter elegantiarum* and come back to La Napoule, Frank," and he pulled his jowl, "to the simple life and the charm of restful friendship."

More and more clearly I saw that the effort, the hard work, of writing was altogether beyond him. He was now one of those men of genius, talkers merely, half artists, half dreamers, whom Balzac describes contemptuously as wasting their lives, "talking to hear themselves talk"; capable indeed of fine conceptions and of occasional fine phrases, but incapable of the punishing toil of execution; charming companions, fated in the long run to fall to misery and destitution.

Constant creation is the first condition of art as it is the first condition of life.

I asked him one day if he remembered the terrible passage about those "eunuchs of art" in "La Cousine Bette".

"Yes, Frank," he replied; "but Balzac was probably envious of the artist-talker; at any rate, we who talk should not be condemned by those to whom we dedicate our talents. It is for posterity to blame us; but after all I have written a good deal. Do you remember how Browning's Sarto defends himself?

"Some good son
Paint my two hundred pictures—let him try."

He did not see that Balzac, one of the greatest talkers that ever lived according to Théophile Gautier, was condemning the temptation to which he himself had no doubt yielded too often. To my surprise, Oscar did not even read much now. He was not eager to hear new thoughts, a little rebellious to any new mental influence. He had reached his zenith, I suppose, had begun to fossilise, as men do when they cease to grow.

One day at lunch I questioned him:

"You told me once that you always imagined yourself in the

place of every historic personage. Suppose you had been Jesus, what religion would you have preached?"

"What a wonderful question!" he cried. "What religion is mine? What belief have I?

"I believe most of all in personal liberty for every human soul. Each man ought to do what he likes, to develop as he will. England, or rather London, for I know little of England ouside London, was an ideal place to me, till they punished me because I did not share their tastes. What an absurdity it all was, Frank. How dared they punish me for what is good in my eyes? How dared they?" and he fell into moody thought. . . . The idea of a new gospel did not really interest him.

It was about this time he first told me of a new play he had in mind.

"It has a great scene, Frank," he said. "Imagine a *roué* of forty-five who is married; incorrigible, of course, Frank, a great noble who gets the person he is in love with to come and stay with him in the country. One evening his wife, who has gone upstairs to lie down with a headache, is behind a screen in a room half asleep; she is awakened by her husband's courting. She cannot move, she is bound breathless to her couch; she hears everything. Then, Frank, the husband comes to the door and finds it locked, and knowing that his wife is inside with the host, beats upon the door and will have entrance, and while the guilty ones whisper together —the woman blaming the man, the man trying to think of some excuse, some way out of the net—the wife gets up very quietly and turns on the lights while the two cowards stare at her with wild surprise. She passes to the door and opens it and the husband rushes in to find his hostess as well as the host and his wife. I think it is a great scene, Frank, a great stage picture."

"It is," I said, "a great scene; why don't you write it?"

"Perhaps I shall, Frank, one of these days, but now I am thinking of some poetry, a 'Ballad of a Fisher Boy', a sort of companion to 'The Ballad of Reading Gaol', in which I sing of liberty instead of prison, joy instead of sorrow, a kiss instead of an execution. I shall do this joy-song much better than I did the song of sorrow and despair."

"Like Davidson's 'Ballad of a Nun'," I said, for the sake of saying something.

"Naturally Davidson would write the 'Ballad of a Nun', Frank;

his talent is Scotch and severe; but I should like to write 'The Ballad of a Fisher Boy'," and he fell to dreaming.

The thought of his punishment was often with him. It seemed
to him hideously wrong and unjust. But he never questioned the
right of society to punish. He did not see that, if you once grant
that, the wrong done to him could be defended.

"I used to think myself a lord of life," he said. "How dared
those little wretches condemn me and punish me? Everyone of
them tainted with a sensuality which I loathe."

To call him out of this bitter way of regret I quoted Shakespeare's sonnet:

"For why should others' false adulterate eyes
        Give salutation to my sportive blood?
Or on my frailties why are frailer spies,
        Which in their wills count bad what I think good?"

"His complaint is exactly yours, Oscar."

"It's astonishing, Frank, how well you know him, and yet you
deny his intimacy with Pembroke. To you he is a living man; you
always talk of him as if he had just gone out of the room, and yet
you persist in believing in his innocence."

"You misapprehend me," I said, "the passion of his life was for
Mary Fitton, to give her a name; I mean the 'dark lady' of the sonnets, who was Beatrice, Cressida and Cleopatra, and you yourself
admit that a man who has a mad passion for a woman is immune,
I think the doctors call it, to other influences."

"Oh, yes, Frank, of course; but how could Shakespeare with
his beautiful nature love a woman to that mad excess?"

"Shakespeare hadn't your overwhelming love of plastic beauty,"
I replied; "he fell in love with a dominant personality, the com-
plement of his own yielding, amiable disposition."

"That's it," he broke in, "our opposites attract us irresistibly—
the charm of the unknown!"

"You often talk now," I went on, "as if you had never loved
a woman; yet you must have loved—more than one."

"My salad days, Frank," he quoted, smiling, "when I was green
in judgment, cold of blood."

"No, no," I persisted, "it is not a great while since you praised Lady So and So and the Terrys enthusiastically."

"Lady ————," he began gravely (and I could not but notice that the mere title seduced him to conventional, poetic language), "moves like a lily in water; I always think of her as a lily; just as I used to think of Lily Langtry as a tulip, with a figure like a Greek vase carved in ivory. But I always adored the Terrys. Marion is a great actress with subtle charm and enigmatic fascination. She was my 'Woman of No Importance', artificial and enthralling; she belongs to my theatre ————"

As he seemed to have lost the thread, I questioned again.

"And Ellen?"

"Oh, Ellen's a perfect wonder," he broke out, "a great character. Do you know her history?" And then, without waiting for an answer, he continued:

"She began as a model for Watts, the painter, when she was only some fifteen or sixteen years of age. In a week she read him as easily as if he had been a printed book. He treated her with condescending courtesy, *en grand seigneur*, and, naturally, she had her revenge on him.

"One day her mother came in and asked Watts what he was going to do about Ellen. Watts said he didn't understand. 'You have made Ellen in love with you,' said the mother, 'and it is impossible that could have happened unless you had been attentive to her.'

"Poor Watts protested and protested, but the mother broke down and sobbed, and said the girl's heart would be broken, and at length, in despair, Watts asked what he was to do, and the mother could only suggest marriage.

"Finally they were married."

"You don't mean that," I cried, "I never knew that Watts had married Ellen Terry."

"Oh, yes," said Oscar, "they were married all right. The mother saw to that, and to do him justice, Watts kept the whole family like a gentleman. But like an idealist, or, as a man of the world would say, a fool, he was ashamed of his wife; he showed great reserve to her, and when he gave his usual dinners or receptions, he invited only men and so, carefully, left her out.

"One evening he had a dinner; a great many well-known people were present and a bishop was on his right hand, when, suddenly, between the cheese and the pear, as the French would say, Ellen came dancing into the room in pink tights with a basket of roses around her waist with which she began pelting the guests. Watts was horrified, but everyone else delighted, the bishop in especial, it is said, declared he had never seen anything so romantically beautiful. Watts nearly had a fit, but Ellen danced out of the room with all their hearts in her basket instead of her roses.

"To me that's the true story of Ellen Terry's life. It may be true or false in reality, but I believe it to be true in fact as in symbol; it is not only an image of her life, but of her art. No one knows how she met Irving or learned to act, though, as you know, she was one of the best actresses that ever graced the English stage. A great personality. Her children even have inherited some of her talent."

It was only famous actresses such as Ellen Terry and Sarah Bernhardt and great ladies that Oscar ever praised. He was a snob by nature; indeed this was the chief link between him and English society. Besides, he had a rooted contempt for women and especially for their brains. He said once, of some one: "he is like a woman, sure to remember the trivial and forget the important."

It was this disdain of the sex which led him, later, to take up our whole dispute again.

"I have been thinking over our argument in the train," he began; "really it was preposterous of me to let you off with a drawn battle; you should have been beaten and forced to haul down your flag. We talked of love and I let you place the girl against the boy; it is all nonsense. A girl is not made for love; she is not even a good instrument of love."

"Some of us care more for the person than the pleasure," I replied, "and others —. You remember Browning:

Nearer we hold of God
Who gives, than of His tribes that take, I must believe."

"Yes, yes," he replied impatiently, "but that's not the point. I mean that a woman is not made for passion and love; but to be a mother.

"When I married, my wife was a beautiful girl, white and slim as a lily, with dancing eyes and gay rippling laughter like music. In a year or so the flower-like grace had all vanished; she became heavy, shapeless, deformed. She dragged herself about the house in uncouth misery with drawn blotched face and hideous body, sick at heart because of our love. It was dreadful. I tried to be kind to her, forced myself to touch and kiss her; but she was sick always, and—oh! I cannot recall it, it is all loathsome. . . . I used to wash my mouth and open the window to cleanse my lips in the pure air. Oh, nature is disgusting; it takes beauty and defiles it; it defaces the ivory-white body we have adored, with the vile cicatrices of maternity; it befouls the altar of the soul.

"How can you talk of such intimacy as love? How can you idealise it? Love is not possible to the artist unless it is sterile."

"All her suffering did not endear her to you?" I asked in amazement; "did not call forth that pity in you which you used to speak of as divine?"

"Pity, Frank," he exclaimed impatiently; "pity has nothing to do with love. How can one desire what is shapeless, deformed, ugly? Desire is killed by maternity; passion buried in conception," and he flung away from the table.

At length I understood his dominant motive: *trahit sua quemque voluptas*, his Greek love of form, his intolerant cult of physical beauty, could take no heed of the happiness or well-being of the beloved.

"I will not talk to you about it, Frank; I am like a Persian, who lives by warmth and worships the sun, talking to some Eskimo, who answers me with praise of blubber and night spent in ice houses and baths of foul vapour. Let's talk of something else."

24

We Argue About His "Pet Vice" and Punishment

A LITTLE LATER I was called to Monte Carlo and went for a few days, leaving Oscar, as he said, perfectly happy, with good food, excellent champagne, absinthe and coffee, and his simple fisher friends.

When I came back to La Napoule, I found everything altered and altered for the worse. There was an Englishman of a good class named M ———— staying at the hotel. He was accompanied by a youth of seventeen or eighteen whom he called his servant. Oscar wanted to know if I minded meeting him.

"He is charming, Frank, and well read, and he admires me very much. You won't mind his dining with us, will you?"

"Of course not," I replied. But when I saw M ———— I thought him an insignificant, foolish creature, who put to show a great admiration for Oscar, and drank in his words with parted lips; and well he might, for he had hardly any brains of his own. He had, however, a certain liking for the poetry and literature of passion.

To my astonishment Oscar was charming to him, chiefly I think because he was well off, and was pressing Oscar to spend the summer with him at some place he had in Switzerland. This support made Oscar recalcitrant to any influence I might have had over him. When I asked him if he had written anything whilst I was away, he replied casually:

"No, Frank, I don't think I shall be able to write any more. What is the good of it? I cannot force myself to write."

"And your 'Ballad of a Fisher Boy'?" I asked.

"I have composed three or four verses of it," he said, smiling at me, "I have got them in my head," and he recited two or three, one of which was quite good, but none of them startling.

Not having seen him for some days, I noticed that he was growing stout again. The good living and constant drinking seemed to ooze out of him; he began to look as he looked in the old days in London just before the catastrophe.

One morning I asked him to put the verses on paper which he had recited to me, but he would not; and when I pressed him, cried:

"Let me live, Frank; tasks remind me of prison. You do not know how I abhor even the memory of it. It was degrading, inhuman!"

"Prison was the making of you," I could not help retorting, irritated by what seemed to me a mere excuse. "You came out of it better in health and stronger than I have ever known you. The hard living, regular hours and compulsory chastity did you all the good in the world. That is why you wrote those superb letters to the 'Daily Chronicle' and the 'Ballad of Reading Gaol'; the State ought really to put you in prison and keep you there."

For the first time in my life I saw angry dislike in his eyes.

"You talk poisonous nonsense, Frank," he retorted. "Bad food is bad for everyone, and abstinence from tobacco is mere torture to me. Chastity is just as unnatural and devilish as hunger; I hate both. Self-denial is the shining sore on the leprous body of Christianity."

To all this M ——— giggled applause, which naturally excited the combative instincts in me—always too alert.

"All great artists," I replied, "have had to practise chastity; it is chastity alone which gives vigour and tone to mind and body, while building up a reserve of extraordinary strength. Your favourite Greeks never allowed an athlete to go into the palæstra unless he had previously lived a life of complete chastity for a whole year. Balzac, too, practised it and extolled its virtues, and goodness knows he loved all the mud-honey of Paris."

"You are hopelessly wrong, Frank. What madness will you

preach next? You are always bothering one to write, and now forsooth you recommend chastity and 'skilly', though I admit," he added laughing, "that your 'skilly' includes all the indelicacies of the season, with champagne, Mocha coffee, and absinthe to boot. But surely you are getting too puritanical. It's absurd of you; the other day you defended conventional love against my ideal passion."

He provoked me. His tone was that of rather contemptuous superiority. I kept silent. I did not wish to retort as I might have done if M ——— had not been present.

But Oscar was determined to assert his peculiar view. One or two days afterwards he came in very red and excited and more angry than I had ever seen him.

"What do you think has happened, Frank?"

"I do not know. Nothing serious, I hope."

"I was sitting by the roadside on the way to Cannes. I had taken out a Vergil with me and had begun reading it. As I sat there reading, I happened to raise my eyes, and who should I see but George Alexander—George Alexander on a bicycle. I had known him intimately in the old days, and naturally I got up delighted to see him, and went towards him. But he turned his head aside and pedalled past me deliberately. He meant to cut me. Of course I know that just before my trial in London he took my name off the bill of my comedy, though he went on playing it. But I was not angry with him for that, though he might have behaved as well as Wyndham,[1] who owed me nothing, don't you think?

"Here there was nobody to see him, yet he cut me. What brutes men are! They not only punish me as a society, but now they are trying as individuals to punish me, and after all I have not done worse than they do. What difference is there between one form of sexual indulgence and another? I hate hypocrisy and hypo-

[1] The incident is worth recording for the honour of human nature. At the moment of Oscar's trial Charles Wyndham had let his theatre, the Criterion, to Lewis Waller and H. H. Morell to produce in it "An Ideal Husband" which had been running for over 100 nights at the Haymarket. When Alexander took Oscar's name off the bill, Wyndham wrote to the young managers, saying that, if under the altered circumstances they wished to cancel their agreement, he would allow them to do so. But if they "put on" a play of Mr. Wilde's, the author's name must be on all the bills and placards as usual. He could not allow his theatre to be used to insult a man who was on trial.

crites! Think of Alexander, who made all his money out of my works, cutting me. Alexander! It is too ignoble. Wouldn't you be angry, Frank?"

"I daresay I should be," I replied coolly, hoping the incident would be a spur to him.

"I've always wondered why you gave Alexander a play? Surely you didn't think him an actor?"

"No, no!" he exclaimed, a sudden smile lighting up his face; "Alexander doesn't act on the stage; he behaves. But wasn't it mean of him?"

I couldn't help smiling, the dart was so deserved.

"Begin another play," I said, "and the Alexanders will immediately go on their knees to you again. On the other hand, if you do nothing you may expect worse than discourtesy. Men love to condemn their neighbours' pet vice. You ought to know the world by this time."

He did not even notice the hint to work, but broke out angrily:

"What you call vice, Frank, is not vice. It is as good to me as it was to Cæsar, Alexander, Michelangelo and Shakespeare. It was first of all made a sin by monasticism, and it has been made a crime in recent times, by the Goths—the Germans and English—who have done little or nothing since to refine or exalt the ideals of humanity. They all damn the sins they have no mind to, and that's their morality. A brutal race; they overeat and overdrink and condemn the lusts of the flesh, while revelling in all the vilest sins of the spirit. If they would read the 23rd chapter of St. Matthew and apply it to themselves, they would learn more than by condemning a pleasure they don't understand. Why, even Bentham refused to put what you call a 'vice' in his penal code, and you yourself admitted that it should not be punished as a crime; for it carries no temptation with it. It may be a malady; but, if so, it appears only to attack the highest natures. It is disgraceful to punish it. The wit of man can find no argument which justifies its punishment."

"Don't be too sure of that," I retorted.

"I have never heard a convincing argument which condemns it, Frank; I do not believe such a reason exists."

"Don't forget," I said, "that this practice which you defend is condemned by a hundred generations of the most civilised races of mankind."

"Mere prejudice of the unlettered, Frank."

"And what is such a prejudice?" I asked. "It is the reason of a thousand generations of men, a reason so sanctified by secular experience that it has passed into flesh and blood and become an emotion and is no longer merely an argument. I would rather have one such prejudice held by men of a dozen different races than a myriad reasons. Such a prejudice is incarnate reason approved by immemorial experience.

"What argument have you against cannibalism; what reason is there why we should not fatten babies for the spit and eat their flesh? The flesh is sweeter, African travellers tell us, than any other meat, tenderer at once and more sustaining; all reasons are in favour of it. What hinders us from indulging in this appetite but prejudice, sacred prejudice, an instinctive loathing at the bare idea?

"Humanity, it seems to me, is toiling up a long slope leading from the brute to the god. Again and again whole generations, sometimes whole races, have fallen back and disappeared in the abyss. Every slip fills the survivors with fear and horror which with ages have become instinctive, and now you appear and laugh at their fears and tell them that human flesh is excellent food, and that sterile kisses are the noblest form of passion. They shudder from you and hate and punish you, and if you persist they will kill you. Who shall say they are wrong? Who shall sneer at their instinctive repulsion hallowed by ages of successful endeavour?"

"Fine rhetoric, I concede," he replied, "but mere rhetoric. I never heard such a defence or prejudice before. I should not have expected it from you. You admit you don't share the prejudice; you don't feel the horror, the instinctive loathing you describe. Why? Because you are educated, Frank, because you know that the passion Socrates felt was not a low passion, because you know that Cæsar's weakness, let us say, or the weakness of Michelangelo or of Shakespeare, is not despicable. If the desire is not a characteristic of the highest humanity, at least it is consistent with it."

"I cannot admit that," I answered. "First of all, let us leave Shakespeare out of the question, or I should have to ask you for proofs of his guilt, and there are none. About the others there is this to be said; it is not by imitating the vices and weaknesses of great men that we shall get to their level. And suppose we are fated to climb above them, then their weaknesses are to be dreaded.

"I have not even tried to put the strongest reasons before you; I should have thought your own mind would have supplied them; but surely you see that the historical argument is against you. This vice of yours is dropping out of life, like cannibalism. It is no longer a practice of the highest races. It may have seemed natural enough to the Greeks; to us it is unnatural. Even the best Athenians condemned it; Socrates took pride in never having yielded to it; all moderns denounce it disdainfully. You must see that the whole progress of the world, the current of educated opinion, is against you, that you are now a 'sport,' a peculiarity, an abnormality, a man with six fingers: not a 'sport' that is, full of promise for the future, but a 'sport' of the dim backward and abysm of time, an arrested development."

"You are bitter, Frank, almost rude."

"Forgive me, Oscar, forgive me, please; it is because I want you at long last to open your eyes, and see things as they are."

"But I thought you were with us, Frank, I thought at least you condemned the punishment, did not believe in the barbarous penalties."

"I disbelieve in all punishment," I said; "it is by love and not by hate that men must be redeemed. I believe, too, that the time is already come when the better law might be put in force, and above all, I condemn punishment which strikes a man, an artist like you, who has done beautiful and charming things as if he had done nothing. At least the good you have accomplished should be set against the evil. It has always seemed monstrous to me that you should have been punished like a Taylor. The French were right in their treatment of Verlaine. They condemned the sin, while forgiving the sinner because of his genius. The rigour in England is mere puritanic hypocrisy, shortsightedness and racial self-esteem."

"All I can say, Frank, is, I would not limit individual desire in any way. What right has society to punish us unless it can prove we have hurt or injured someone else against his will? Besides, if you limit passion you impoverish life, you weaken the mainspring of art, and narrow the realm of beauty."

"All societies," I replied, "and most individuals, too, punish what they dislike, right or wrong. There are bad smells which do not injure anyone; yet the manufacturers of them would be indicted for committing a nuisance. Nor does your plea, that by limiting the choice of passion you impoverish life, appeal to me. On the contrary, I think I could prove that passion, the desire of the man for the woman and the woman for the man, has been enormously strengthened in modern times. Christianity has created, or at least cultivated, modesty, and modesty has sharpened desire. Christianity has helped to lift woman to an equality with man, and this modern intellectual development has again intensified passion out of all knowledge. The woman who is not a slave but an equal, who gives herself according to her own feeling, is infinitely more desirable to a man than any submissive serf who is always waiting on his will. And this movement intensifying passion is every day gaining force.

"We have a far higher love in us than the Greeks, infinitely higher and more intense than the Romans knew; our sensuality is like a river banked in with stone parapets; the current flows higher and more vehemently in the narrower bed."

"You may talk as you please, Frank, but you will never get me to believe that what I know is good to me is evil. Suppose I like a food that is poison to other people, and yet quickens me; how dare they punish me for eating of it?"

"They would say," I replied, "that they only punish you for inducing others to eat it."

He broke in: "It is all ignorant prejudice, Frank; the world is slowly growing more tolerant and one day men will be ashamed of their barbarous treatment of me, as they are now ashamed of the torturings of the Middle Ages. The current of opinion is making in our favour and not against us."

"You don't believe what you say," I cried; "if you really thought humanity was going your way, you would have been delighted to play Galileo. Instead of writing a book in prison condemning your companion who pushed you to discovery and disgrace, you would have written a book vindicating your actions. 'I am a martyr,' you would have cried, 'and not a criminal, and everyone who holds the contrary is wrong.'

"You would have said to the jury:

" 'In spite of your beliefs, and your cherished dogmas; in spite of your religion and prejudice and fanatical hatred of me, you are wrong and I am right; the world does move.'

"But you didn't say that, and you don't think it. If you did you would be glad you went into the Queensberry trial, glad you were accused, glad you were imprisoned and punished because all these things must bring your vindication more quickly; you are sorry for them all, because in your heart you know you were wrong. This old world in the main is right; it's you who are wrong."

"Of course everything can be argued, Frank; but I hold to my conviction: the best minds even now don't condemn us, and the world is becoming more tolerant. I didn't justify myself in court because I was told I should be punished lightly if I respected the common prejudices, and when I tried to speak afterwards the judge would not let me."

"And I believe," I retorted, "that you were hopelessly beaten and could never have made a fight of it, because you felt the Time-spirit was against you. How else was a silly, narrow judge able to wave you to silence? Do you think he could have silenced me? Not all the judges in Christendom. Let me give you an example. I believe with Voltaire that when modesty goes out of life it goes into the language as prudery. I am quite certain that our present habit of not discussing sexual questions in our books is bound to disappear, and that free and dignified speech will take the place of our present prurient mealy-mouthedness. I have long thought it possible, probable even, in the present state of society in England, where we are still more or less under the heel of the illiterate and prudish Philistinism of our middle class, that I might be had up to answer some charge of publishing an indecent book. The current of the time appears to be against me. In the spacious days of Elizabeth, in the modish time of the Georges, a freedom of speech was habitual which to-day is tabooed. Our cases, therefore, are somewhat alike. Do you think I should dread the issue or allow myself to be silenced by a judge? I would set forth my defence before the judge and before the jury with the assurance of victory in me! I should not minimise what I had written; I should not try to explain it away; I should seek to make it stronger. I should justify every word, and finally I'd warn both judge and jury that if they condemned and punished me they would only make my ultimate triumph more conspicuous. 'All the great men of the past are with me,' I would cry; 'all the great minds of to-day in other countries, and some of the best in England. Condemn me at your peril; you will only condemn yourselves. You are spitting against the wind and the shame will be on your own faces.'

"Do you believe I should be left to suffer? I doubt it even in England to-day. If I'm right, and I'm sure I'm right, then about me there would be an invisible cloud of witnesses. You would see a strange movement of opinion in my favour. The judge would probably lecture me and bind me over to come up for judgment; but if he sentenced me vindictively then the Home Secretary[1] would be petitioned and the movement in my favour would grow, till it swept away opposition. This is the very soul of my faith. If I did not believe with every fibre in me that this poor stupid world is honestly groping its way up the altar stairs to God, and not down, I would not live in it an hour.'

"Why do you argue against me, Frank? It is brutal of you."

"To induce you even now to turn and pull yourself out of the mud. You are forty odd years of age, and the keenest sensations of life are over for you. Turn back whilst there's time, get to work, write your ballad and your plays, and not the Alexanders alone, but all the people who really count, the best of all countries —the salt of the earth—will give you another chance. Begin to work and you'll be borne up on all hands. No one sinks to the dregs but by his own weight. If you don't bear fruit why should men care for you?"

He shrugged his shoulders and turned from me with disdainful indifference.

"I've done enough for their respect, Frank, and received nothing but hatred. Every man must dree his own weird. Thank heaven, life's not without compensations. I'm sorry I cannot please you," and he added carelessly, "M_____ has asked me to go and spend the summer with him at Gland in Switzerland. *He* does not mind whether I write or not."

"I assure you," I cried, "it is not my pleasure I am thinking about. What can it matter to me whether you write or not? It is your own good I am thinking of."

[1] This was written years before a Home Secretary, Mr. Reginald Mac-Kenna, tortured women and girls in prison in England by forcible feeding because they tried to present petitions in favour of Woman's Suffrage. He afterwards defended himself in Parliament by declaring that "'forcible feeding' was not unpleasant." The torturers of the Inquisition also befouled cruelty with hypocritical falsehood. They would burn their victims; but would not shed blood.

"Oh, bother good! One's friends like one as one is; the outside public hate one or scoff at one as they please."

"Well, I hope I shall always be your friend," I replied, "but you will yet be forced to see, Oscar, that everyone grows tired of holding up an empty sack."

"Frank, you insult me."

"I don't mean to; I'm sorry; I shall never be so brutally frank again; but you had to hear the truth for once."

"Then, Frank, you only cared for me in so far as I agreed with you?"

"Oh, that's not fair," I replied. "I have tried with all my strength to prevent you committing soul-suicide, but if you are resolved on it, I can't prevent you. I must draw away. I can do no good."

"Then you won't help me for the rest of the winter?"

"Of course I will," I replied, "I shall do all I promised and more; but there's a limit now, and till now the only limit was my power, not my will."

It was at La Napoule a few days later that an incident occurred which gave me to a certain extent a new sidelight on Oscar's nature by showing just what he thought of me. I make no scruple of setting forth his opinion here in its entirety, though the confession took place after a futile evening when he had talked to M———— of great houses in England and the great people he had met there. The talk had evidently impressed M———— as much as it had bored me. I must first say that Oscar's bedroom was separated from mine by a large sitting-room we had in common. As a rule I worked in my bedroom in the mornings and he spent a great deal of time out of doors. On this especial morning, however, I had gone into the sitting-room early to write some letters. I heard him get up and splash about in his bath. Shortly afterwards he must have gone into the next room, which was M————'s, for suddenly he began talking to him in a loud voice from one room to the other, as if he were carrying on a conversation already begun, through the open door.

"Of course it's absurd of Frank talking of social position or the great people of English society at all. He never had any social position to be compared with mine!" (The petulant tone made me smile; but what Oscar said was true; nor did I ever pretend to have such a position.)

"He had a house in Park Lane and owned *The Saturday Review* and had a certain power; but I was the centre of every party, the most honoured guest everywhere, at Clieveden and Taplow Court and Clumber. The difference was Frank was proud of meeting Balfour while Balfour was proud of meeting me: d'ye see?" (I was so interested I was unconscious of any indiscretion in listening. It made me smile to hear that I was proud of meeting Arthur Balfour. It would never have occurred to me that I should be proud of that; still no doubt Oscar was right in a general way.)

"When Frank talks of literature, he amuses me. He pretends to bring new standards into it. He does; he brings America to judge Oxford and London, much like bringing Macedon or Bœotia to judge Athens—quite ridiculous! What can Americans know about English literature? . . .

"Yet the curious thing is he has read a lot and has a sort of vision; that Shakespeare stuff of his is extraordinary; but he takes sincerity for style, and poetry as poetry has no appeal for him. You heard him admit that himself last night. . . .

"He's comic, really; curiously provincial like all Americans. Fancy a Jeremiad preached by a man in a fur coat! Frank's comic. But he's really kind and fights for his friends. He helped me in prison greatly. Sympathy is a sort of religion to him; that's why we can meet without murder and separate without suicide. . . .

"Talking literature with him is very like playing Rugby football. . . . I never did play football, you know; but talking literature with Frank must be very like playing Rugby where you end by being kicked violently through your own goal," and he laughed delightedly.

I had listened without thinking as I often listened to his talk for the mere music of the utterance. Now, at a break in the monologue, I went into the next room, feeling that to listen consciously would be unworthy. On the whole his view of me was not unkindly. He disliked to hear any opinion that differed from his own and it never came into his head that Oxford was no nearer the meridian of truth than Lawrence, Kansas, and certainly at least as far from heaven.

Some weeks later I left La Napoule and went on a visit to some friends. He wrote complaining that without me the place was dull. I wired him and went over to Nice to meet him and we lunched together at the Café de la Regence. He was terribly downcast and yet rebellious. He had come over to stay at Nice, and stopped at the Hotel Terminus, a tenth-rate hotel near the station; the proprietor called on him two or three days afterwards and informed him he must leave the hotel, as his room had been let.

"Evidently someone has told him, Frank, who I am. What am I to do?"

I soon found him a better hotel where he was well treated, but the incident coming on top of the Alexander affair seemed to have frightened him.

"There are too many English on this coast," he said to me one day, "and they are all brutal to me. I think I should like to go to Italy if you would not mind."

"The world is all before you," I replied. "I shall only be too glad for you to get a comfortable place," and I gave him the money he wanted. He lingered on at Nice for nearly a week. I saw him several times. He lunched with me at the Reserve once at Beaulieu, and was full of delight at the beauty of the bay and the quiet of it. In the middle of the meal some English people came in and showed their dislike of him rudely. He at once shrank into himself, and as soon as possible made some pretext to leave. Of course I went with him. I was more than sorry for him, but I felt as unable to help him as I should have been unable to hold him back if he had determined to throw himself down a precipice.

25

The Last Hope Lost

> "The Gods are just and of our pleasant vices
> Make instruments to plague us."

IT WAS FULL SUMMER before I met Oscar again; he had come back to Paris and taken up his old quarters in the mean little hotel in the Rue des Beaux Arts. He lunched and dined with me as usual. His talk was as humorous and charming as ever, and he was just as engaging a companion. For the first time, however, he complained of his health:

"I ate some mussels and oysters in Italy, and they must have poisoned me; for I have come out in great red blotches all over my arms and chest and back, and I don't feel well."

"Have you consulted a doctor?"

"Oh, yes, but doctors are no good. They all advise you differently; the best of it is they all listen to you with an air of intense interest when you are talking about yourself—which is an excellent tonic."

"They sometimes tell one what's the matter; give a name and significance to the unknown," I interjected.

"They bore me by forbidding me to smoke and drink. They are worse than M_____, who grudged me his wine."

"What do you mean?" I asked in wonder.

"A tragi-comic history, Frank. You were so right about M_____ and I was mistaken in him. You know he wanted me to stay with him at Gland in Switzerland, begged me to come, said he would do everything for me. When the weather got warm at Genoa I went to him. At first he seemed very glad to see me and made me welcome. The food was not very good, the drink anything but good; still I could not complain, and I put up with the discomforts. But in a week or two the wine disappeared, and beer took its place, and I suggested I must be going. He begged me so cordially not to go that I stayed on; but in a little while I noticed that the beer got less and less in quantity, and one day when I ventured to ask for a second bottle at lunch he told me that it cost a great deal and that he could not afford it. Of course I made some decent pretext and left his house as soon as possible. If one has to suffer poverty, one had best suffer alone. But to get discomforts grudgingly as a charity is the extremity of shame. I prefer to look on it from the other side; M_____ grudging me his small beer belongs to farce."

He spoke with bitterness and contempt, as he used never to speak of anyone.

I could not help sympathising with him, though visible the cloth was wearing threadbare. He asked me now at once for money, and a little later again and again. Formerly he had invented pretexts; he had not received his allowance when he expected it, or he was bothered by a bill and so forth; but now he simply begged and begged, railing the while at fortune. It was distressing. He wanted money constantly, and spent it as always like water, without a thought.

I asked him one day whether he had seen much of his soldier boy since he had returned to Paris.

"I have seen him, Frank, but not often," and he laughed gaily. "It's a farce-comedy; sentiment always begins romantically and ends in laughter—*tabulae solvuntue risu*. I taught him so much, Frank, that he was made a corporal and forthwith a nursemaid fell in love with his stripes. He's devoted to her. I suppose he likes to play teacher in his turn."

"And so the great romantic passion comes to this tame conclusion?"

"What would you, Frank? Whatever begins must also end."

"Is there anyone else?" I asked, "or have you learned reason at last?"

"Of course there's always someone else, Frank. Change is the essence of passion. The *reason* you talk of is merely another name for impotence."

"Montaigne declares," I said, "that love belongs to early youth, 'the next period after infancy', is his phrase, but that is at the best a Frenchman's view of it. Sophocles was nearer the truth when he called himself happy in that age had freed him from the whip of passion. When are you going to reach that serenity?"

"Never, Frank, never, I hope. Life without desire would not be worth living to me. As one gets older one is more difficult to please; but the sting of pleasure is even keener than in youth and far more egotistic.

"One comes to understand the Marquis de Sade and that strange, scarlet story of de Retz—the pleasure they got from inflicting pain, the curious, intense underworld of cruelty—"

"That's unlike you, Oscar," I broke in. "I thought you shrank from giving pain always; to me it's the unforgivable sin."

"To me, also," he rejoined instantly, "intellectually one may understand it; but in reality it's horrible. I want my pleasure un-embittered by any drop of pain. That reminds me: I read a ter-rible, little book the other day, Octave Mirbeau's 'Le Jardin des Supplices'; it is quite awful, a *sadique* joy in pain pulses through it; but for all that it's wonderful. His soul seems to have wandered in fearsome places. You with your contempt of fear, will face the book with courage—I————"

"I simply couldn't read it," I replied; "it was revolting to me, impossible——"

"A sort of grey adder," he summed up and I nodded in complete agreement.

I passed the next winter on the Riviera. A speculation which I had gone in for there had caused me heavy loss and much anxiety. In the spring I returned to Paris, and of course, asked him to meet me. He was much brighter than he had been for a long time. Lord Alfred Douglas, it appeared, had come in for a large legacy from his father's estate and had given him some money, and he was much more cheerful. We had a great lunch at Durand's and he was at his very best. I asked him about his health.

"I'm all right, Frank, but the rash continually comes back, a ghostly visitant, Frank. I'm afraid the doctors are in league with the devil. It generally returns after a good dinner, a sort of aftermath of champagne. The doctors say I must not drink champagne and must stop smoking, the silly people, who regard pleasure as their natural enemies; whereas it is our pleasures which provide them with a living!"

He looked fairly well, I thought; he was a little fatter, his skin a little dingier than of old, and he had grown very deaf, but in every other way he seemed at his best, though he was certainly drinking too freely—spirits between times as well as wine at meals.

I had heard on the Riviera during the winter that Smithers had tried to buy a play from him, so one day I brought up the subject.

"By the way, Smithers says that you have been working on your play; you know the one I mean, the one with the great screen scene in it."

"Oh, yes, Frank," he remarked indifferently.

"Won't you tell me what you've done?" I asked. "Have you written any of it?"

"No, Frank," he replied casually, it's the scenario Smithers talked about."

A little while afterwards he asked me for money. I told him I could not afford any at the moment, and pressed him to write his play.

"I shall never write again, Frank," he said. "I can't, I simply can't face my thoughts. Don't ask me!" Then suddenly: "Why don't you buy the scenario and write the play yourself?"

"I don't care for the stage," I replied; "it's a sort of rude encaustic work I don't like; its effects are theatrical!"

"A play pays far better than a book, you know——"

But I was not interested. That evening, thinking over what he had said, I realised all at once that a story I have in mind to write would suit "the screen scene" of Oscar's scenario; why shouldn't I write a play instead of a story? When we met next day I broached the idea to Oscar:

"I have a story in my head," I said, "which would fit into that scenario of yours, so far as you have sketched it to me. I could write it as a play and do the second, third and fourth acts very quickly, as all the personages are alive to me. Could you do the first act?"

"Of course I could, Frank."

"But," I said, "will you?"

"What would be the good, you could not sell it, Frank."

"In any case," I went on, "I could try; but I would infinitely prefer you to write the whole play if you would; then it would sell fast enough."

"Oh, Frank, don't ask me."

The idea of the collaboration was a mistake; but it seemed to me at the moment the best way to get him to do something. Suddenly he asked me to give him £50 for the scenario at once, then I could do what I liked with it.

After a good deal of talk I consented to give him the £50 if he would promise to write the first act; he promised and I gave him the money.

A little later I noticed a certain tension in his relations with Lord Alfred Douglas. One day he told me frankly that Lord Alfred Douglas had come into a fortune of £15,000 or £20,000, "and," he added, "of course he's always able to get money. He'll marry an American millionairess or some rich widow" (Oscar's ideas of life were nearly all conventional, derived from novels and plays); "and I wanted him to give me enough to make my life comfortable, to settle enough on me to make a decent life possible to me. It would only have cost him two or three thousand pounds, perhaps less. I get £150 a year and I wanted him to make it up to £300.[1] I lost that through going to him at Naples. I think he ought to give me that at the very least, don't you? Won't you speak to him, Frank?"

"I could not possibly interfere," I replied.

"I gave him everything," he went on, in a depressed way. "When I had money, he never had to ask for it; all that was mine was his. And now that he is rich, I have to beg from him, and he gives me small sums and puts me off. It is terrible of him; it is really very, very wrong of him."

I changed the subject as soon as I could; there was a note of bit-

---

[1] Oscar was already getting £300 a year from his wife and Robert Ross, to say nothing of the hundreds given to him from time to time by other friends.

terness which I did not like, which indeed I had already remarked in him.

I was destined very soon to hear the other side. A day or two later Lord Alfred Douglas told me that he had bought some race horses and was training them at Chantilly; would I come down and see them?

"I am not much of a judge of race horses," I replied, "and I don't know much about racing; but I should not mind coming down one evening. I could spend the night at an hotel and see the horses and your stable in the morning. The life of the English stable lads in France must be rather peculiar."

"It is droll," he said, "a complete English colony in France. There are practically no French jockeys or trainers worth their salt; it is all English, English slang, English ways, even English food and of course English drinks. No French boy seems to have nerve enough to make a good rider."

I made an arrangement with him and went down. I missed my train and was very late; I found that Lord Alfred Douglas had dined and gone out. I had my dinner, and about midnight went up to my room. Half an hour later there came a knocking at the door. I opened it and found Lord Alfred Douglas.

"May I come in?" he asked. "I'm glad you've not gone to bed yet."

"Of course," I said, "what is it?" He was pale and seemed extraordinarily excited.

"I have had such a row with Oscar," he jerked out, nervously moving about (I noticed the strained white face I had seen before at the Café Royal), "such a row, and I wanted to speak to you about it. Of course you know in the old days when his plays were being given in London he was rich and gave me some money, and now he says I ought to settle a large sum on him; I think it ridiculous, don't you?"

"I would rather not say anything about it," I replied; "I don't know enough about the circumstances."

He was too filled with a sense of his own injuries; too excited to catch my tone or understand any reproof in my attitude.

"Oscar is really too dreadful," he went on; "he is quite shameless now; he begs and begs and begs, and of course I have given him money, have given him hundreds, quite as much as he ever gave me, but he is insatiable and recklessly extravagant besides. Of course I want to be quite fair to him. I've already given him back all he gave me. Don't you think that is all anyone can ask of me?"

I looked at him in astonishment.

"That is for you and Oscar," I said, "to decide together. No one else can judge between you."

"Why not?" he snapped out in his irritable way, "you know us both and our relations."

"No," I replied, "I don't know all the obligations and the interwoven services. Besides, I could not judge fairly between you."

He turned on me angrily, though I had spoken with as much kindness as I could.

"He seemed to want to make you judge between us," he cried. "I don't care who's the judge. I think if you give a man back what he has given you, that is all he can ask. It's a damned lot more than most people get in this world."

After a pause he started off on a new line of thought:

"The first time I ever noticed any fault in Oscar was over that 'Salome' translation. He's appallingly conceited. You know I did the play into English. I found that his choice of words was poor, anything but good; his prose is wooden. . . .

"Of course he's not a poet," he broke off contemptuously, "even you must admit that."

"I know what you mean," I replied; "though I should have to make a vast reservation in favour of the man who wrote 'The Ballad of Reading Gaol'."

"One ballad doesn't make a man a poet," he barked. "I mean by poet one to whom verse lends powers; in that sense he's not a poet and I am." His tone was that of defiant challenge.

"You are certainly," I replied.

"Well, I did the translation of 'Salome' very carefully, as no one else could have done it," and he flushed angrily, "and all the while Oscar kept on altering it for the worse. At last I had to tell him the truth, and we had a row. He imagines he's the greatest person in the world, and the only person to be considered. His conceit is stupid. . . . I helped[1] him again and again with that 'Ballad of Reading Gaol' you're always praising. I suppose he'd deny that now.

[1] The truth about this I have already stated.

"He's got his money back; what more can he want? He disgusts me when he begs."

I could not contain myself altogether.

"He seems to blame you," I said quietly, "for egging him on to that insane action against your father which brought him to ruin."

"I've no doubt he'd find some reason to blame me," he whipped out. "How did I know how the case would go? . . . Why did he take my advice, if he didn't want to? He was surely old enough to know his own interest. . . . He's simply disgusting now; he's getting fat and bloated, and always demanding money, money, money, like a daughter of the horseleech—just as if he had a claim to it."

I could not stand it any longer; I had to try to move him to kindness.

"Sometimes one gives willingly to a man one has never had anything from. Misery and want in one we like and admire have a very strong claim."

"I do not see that there is any claim at all," he cried bitterly, as if the very word maddened him, "and I am not going to pamper him any more. He could earn all the money he wants if he would only write; but he won't do anything. He is lazy, and getting lazier, and lazier every day; and he drinks far too much. He is intolerable. I thought when he kept asking me for the money to-night, he was like an old prostitute."

"Good God!" I cried. "Good God! Has it come to that between you?"

"Yes," he repeated, not heeding what I said, "he was just like an old fat prostitute," and he gloated over the word, "and I told him so."

I looked at the man but could not speak; indeed there was nothing to be said. Surely at last, I thought, Oscar Wilde has reached the lowest depth. I could think of nothing but Oscar; this hard, small, bitter nature made Oscar's suffering plain to me.

"As I can do no good," I said, "do you mind letting me sleep? I'm simply tired to death."

"I'm sorry," he said, looking for his hat; "will you come out in the morning and see the 'gees'?"

"I don't think so," I replied, "I'm incapable of a resolution now,

I'm so tired I would rather sleep. I think I'll go up to Paris in the morning. I have something rather urgent to do."

He said "Good night" and went away.

I lay awake, my eyes prickling with sorrow and sympathy for poor Oscar, insulted in his misery and destitution, outraged and trodden on by the man he had loved, by the man who had thrust him into the Pit. . . .[1]

The Dead Poet

I dreamed of him last night, I saw his face
All radiant and unshadowed of distress,
And as of old, in music measureless,
I heard his golden voice and marked him trace
Under the common thing the hidden grace,
And conjure wonder out of emptiness,
Till mean things put on beauty like a dress
And all the world was an enchanted place.
And then methought outside a fast locked gate
I mourned the loss of unrecorded words,
Forgotten tales and mysteries half said
Wonders that might have been articulate,
And voiceless thoughts like murdered singing birds
And so I woke and knew that he was dead.

I made up my mind to go to Oscar at once and try to comfort him a little. After all, I thought, another fifty pounds or so wouldn't make a great deal of difference to me, and I dwelt on the many delightful hours I had passed with him, hours of gay talk and superb intellectual enjoyment.

I went up by the morning train to Paris, and drove across the river to Oscar's hotel.

He had two rooms, a small sitting-room and a still smaller bed-

[1] Though I have reported this conversation as faithfully as I can and have indeed softened the impression Lord Alfred Douglas made upon me at the time; still I am conscious that I may be doing him some injustice. I have never really been in sympathy with him and it may well be that in reporting him here faithfully I am showing him at his worst. I am aware that the incident does not reveal him at his best. He has proved since in his writings and notably in some superb sonnets that he had a real affection and admiration for Oscar Wilde. If I have been in any degree unfair to him I can best correct it, I think, by reproducing here the noble sonnet he wrote on Oscar after his death; in sheer beauty and sincerity of feeling it ranks with Shelley's lament for Keats:

room adjoining. He was lying half-dressed on the bed as I entered. The rooms affected me unpleasantly. They were ordinary, mean little French rooms, furnished without taste; the usual mahogany chairs, gilt clock on the mantelpiece and a preposterous bilious paper on the walls. What struck me was the disorder everywhere; books all over the round table; books on the chairs; books on the floor and higgledy-piggledy, here a pair of socks, there a hat and cane, and on the floor his overcoat. The sense of order and neatness which he used to have in his rooms at Tite Street was utterly lacking. He was not living here, intent on making the best of things; he was merely existing without plan or purpose.

I told him I wanted him to come to lunch. While he was finishing dressing it came to me that his clothes had undergone much the same change as his dwelling. In his golden days in London he had been a good deal of a dandy; he usually wore white waistcoats at night; was particular about the flowers in his buttonhole, his gloves and cane. Now he was decently dressed and that was all; as far below the average as he had been above it. Clearly, he had let go of himself and no longer took pleasure in the vanities. It seemed to me a bad sign.

I had always thought of him as very healthy, likely to live till sixty or seventy; but he had no longer any hold on himself and that depressed me; some spring of life seemed broken in him. Bosie Douglas' second betrayal had been the coup de grâce.

In the carriage he was preoccupied, out of sorts, and immediately began to apologise.

"I shall be poor company, Frank," he warned me with quivering lips.

The fragrant summer air in the Champs Elysées seemed to revive him a little, but he was evidently lost in bitter reflections and scarcely noticed where he was going. From time to time he sighed heavily as if oppressed. I talked as well as I could of this and that, tried to lure him away from the hateful subject that I knew must be in his mind; but all in vain. Towards the end of the lunch he said gravely:

"I want you to tell me something, Frank; I want you to tell me honestly if you think I am in the wrong. I wish I could think I was. . . . You know I spoke to you the other day about Bosie;

he is rich now and he is throwing his money away with both hands in racing.

"I asked him to settle £1,500 or £2,000 on me to buy me an annuity, or to do something that would give me £150 a year. You said you did not care to ask him, so I did. I told him it was really his duty to do it at once, and he turned round and lashed me savagely with his tongue. He called me dreadful names. Said dreadful things to me, Frank. I did not think it was possible to suffer more than I suffered in prison, but he has left me bleeding . . ." and the fine eyes filled with tears. Seeing that I remained silent, he cried out:

"Frank, you must tell me for our friendship's sake. Is it my fault? Was he wrong or was I wrong?"

His weakness was pathetic, or was it that his affection was still so great that he wanted to blame himself rather than his friend?

"Of course he seems to me to be wrong," I said, "utterly wrong." I could not help saying it and I went on:

"But you know his temper is insane; if he even praises himself, as he did to me lately, he gets into a rage in order to do it, and perhaps unwittingly you annoyed him by the way you asked. If you put it to his generosity and vainglory you would get it easier than from his sense of justice and right. He has not much moral sense."

"Oh, Frank," he broke in earnestly, "I put it to him as well as I could, quite quietly and gently. I talked of our old affection, of the good and evil days we had passed together. You know I could never be harsh to him, never.

"There never was," he burst out, in a sort of exaltation, "there never was in the world such a betrayal. Do you remember once telling me that the only flaw you could find in the perfect symbolism of the gospel story was that Jesus was betrayed by Judas, the foreigner from Kerioth, when he should have been betrayed by John, the beloved disciple; for it is only those we love who can betray us? Frank, how true, how tragically true that is! It is those we love who betray us with a kiss."

He was silent for some time and then went on wearily, "I wish you would speak to him, Frank, and show him how unjust and unkind he is to me."

"I cannot possibly do that, Oscar," I said, "I do not know all the relations between you and the myriad bands that unite you. I should only do harm and not good."

"Frank," he cried, "you do know, you must know that he is responsible for everything, for my downfall and my ruin. It was he who drove me to fight with his father. I begged him not to, but he whipped me to it; asked me what his father could do; pointed out to me contemptuously that he could prove nothing; said he was the most loathsome, hateful creature in the world, and that it was my duty to stop him, and that if I did not, everyone would be laughing at me, and he could never care for a coward. All his family, his brother and his mother, too, begged me to attack Queensberry, all promised me their support and afterwards—

"You know, Frank, in the Café Royal before the trial how Bosie spoke to you, when you warned me and implored me to drop the insane suit and go abroad; how angry he got. You were not a friend of mine, he said. You know he drove me to ruin in order to revenge himself on his father, and then left me to suffer.

"And that's not the worst of it, Frank. I came out of prison determined not to see him any more. I promised my poor wife I would not see him again. I had forgiven him; but I did not want to see him. I had suffered too much by him and through him, far too much. And then he wrote and wrote of his love, crying it to me every hour, begging me to come, telling me he only wanted me, in order to be happy, me in the whole world. How could I help believing him, how could I keep away from him? At last I yielded and went to him, and as soon as the difficulties began he turned on me in Naples like a wild beast, blaming me and insulting me.

"I had to fly to Paris, having lost everything through him— wife and income and self-respect, everything; but I always thought that he was at least generous as a man of his name should be. I had no idea he could be stingy and mean; but now he is comparatively rich, he prefers to squander his money on jockeys and trainers and horses, of which he knows nothing, instead of lifting me out of my misery. Surely it is not too much to ask him to give me a tenth when I gave him all? Won't you ask him?"

"I think he ought to have done what you want, without asking," I admitted, "but I am certain my speaking would not do any good. He shows me hatred already whenever I do not agree with him. Hate is nearer to him always than sympathy. He is his father's son, Oscar, and I can do nothing. I cannot even speak to him about it."

"Oh, Frank, you ought to," said Oscar.

"But suppose he retorted and said you led him astray, what could I answer?"

"Led him astray!" cried Oscar, starting up, "you cannot believe that. You know better than that. It is not true. It is he who always led, always dominated me; he is as imperious as a Cæsar. It was he who began our intimacy; he who came to me in London when I did not want to see him, or rather, Frank, I wanted to but I was afraid; at the very beginning I was afraid of what it would all lead to, and I avoided him; the desperate aristocratic pride in him, the dreadful bold, imperious temper in him terrified me. But he came to London and sent for me to come to him, said he would come to my house if I didn't. I went, thinking I could reason with him; but it was impossible. When I told him we must be very careful, for I was afraid of what might happen, he made fun of my fears, and encouraged me. He knew that they'd never dare to punish him; he's allied to half the peerage and he did not care what became of me. . . .

"He led me first to the street, introduced me to the male prostitution in London. From the beginning to the end he has driven me like the Œstrum of which the Greeks wrote, which drove the ill-fated to disaster.

"And now he says he owes me nothing; I have no *claim*, I who gave to him without counting; he says he needs all his money for himself: he wants to win races and to write poetry, Frank, the pretty verses which he thinks poetry.

"He has ruined me, soul and body, and now he puts himself in the balance against me and declares he outweighs me. Yes, Frank, he does; he told me the other day I was not a poet, not a true poet, and he was, Alfred Douglas greater than Oscar Wilde.

"I have not done much in the world," he went on hotly, "I know it better than anyone, not a quarter of what I should have done, but there are some things I have done which the world will not forget, can hardly forget. If all the tribe of Douglas from the beginning and all their achievements were added together and thrown into the balance, they would not weigh as dust in comparison. Yet he reviled me, Frank, whipped me, shamed me. . . .

He has broken me, he has broken me, the man I loved; my very heart is a cold weight in me," . . . and he got up and moved aside with the tears pouring down his cheeks.

"Don't take it so much to heart," I said in a minute or two, going after him, "the loss of affection I cannot help, but a hundred or so a year is not much; I will see that you get that every year."

"Oh, Frank, it is not the money; it is his denial, his insults, his hate that kills me; the fact that I have ruined myself for someone who cares nothing; who puts a little money before me; it is as if I were choked with mud. . . .

"Once I thought myself master of my life; lord of my fate, who could do what I pleased and would always succeed. I was as a crowned king till I met him, and now I am an exile and outcast and despised.

"I have lost my way in life; the passers-by all scorn me and the man whom I loved whips me with foul insults and contempt. There is no example in history of such a betrayal, no parallel. I am finished. It is all over with me now—all! I hope the end will come quickly," and he moved away to the window, his tears falling heavily.

26

The End

In a day or two, however, the clouds lifted and the sun shone as brilliantly as ever. Oscar's spirits could not be depressed for long. He took a child's joy in living and in every incident of life. When I left him in Paris a week or so later, in midsummer, he was full of gaiety and humour, talking as delightfully as ever with a touch of cynicism that added piquancy to his wit. Shortly after I arrived in London, he wrote saying he was ill, and that I really ought to send him some money. I had already paid him more than the amount we had agreed upon at first for his scenario, and I was hard up and anything but well. I had chronic bronchitis which prostrated me time and again that autumn. Having heard from mutual friends that Oscar's illness did not hinder him from dining out and enjoying himself, I received his plaints and requests with a certain impatience, and replied to him curtly. His illness appeared to me to be merely a pretext. When my play was accepted his demands became as insistent as they were extravagant.

Finally I went back to Paris in September to see him, persuaded that I could settle everything amicably in five minutes' talk; he must remember our agreement.

I found him well in health, but childishly annoyed that my play was going to be produced and resolved to get all the money he could from me by hook or by crook. I never met such persistence in demands. I could only settle with him decently by paying him a further sum, which I did.

In the course of this bargaining and begging I realised that contrary to my previous opinion he was not gifted as a friend, and did not attribute any importance to friendship. His affection for Bosie Douglas even had given place to hatred. Indeed his liking for him had never been founded on understanding or admiration; it was almost wholly snobbish. He loved the title, the romantic name—Lord Alfred Douglas. Robert Ross was the only friend of whom he always spoke with liking and appreciation: "One of the wittiest of men," he used to call him and would jest at his handwriting, which was peculiarly bad, but always good-naturedly; "a letter merely shows that Bobbie has something to conceal"; but he would add, "how kind he is, how good," as if Ross's devotion surprised him, as in fact it did. Ross has since told me that Oscar never cared much for him. Indeed Oscar cared so little for anyone that an unselfish affection astonished him beyond measure; he could find in himself no explanation of it. His vanity was always more active than his gratitude, as indeed it is with most of us. Now and then when Ross played mentor or took him to task, he became prickly at once and would retort: "Really, Bobbie, you ride the high horse so well, and so willingly, it seems a pity that you never tried Pegasus"—not a sneer exactly, but a rap on the knuckles to call his monitor to order. Like most men of charming manners, Oscar was selfish and self-centered, too convinced of his own importance to spend much thought on others, yet generous to the needy and kind to all.

After my return to London he kept on begging for money by almost every post. As soon as my play was advertised I found myself dunned and persecuted by a horde of people who declared that Oscar had sold them the scenario he afterwards sold to me. Several of them threatened to get injunctions to prevent me staging my play, "Mr. and Mrs. Daventry", if I did not first settle with them. Naturally, I wrote rather sharply to Oscar for having led me into this hornets' nest.

It was in the midst of all this unpleasantness that I heard from Turner, in October, I believe, that Oscar was seriously ill, and that if I owed him money, as he asserted, it would be a kindness to send it, as he was in great need. The letter found me in bed. I could not say now whether I answered it or not. It made me impatient; his friends must have known that I owed Oscar nothing; but later I received a telegram from Ross, saying that Oscar was not expected to live. I was ill and unable to move, or I should have gone at once to Paris. As it was I sent for my friend, Bell, gave him some money and a cheque, and begged him to go across and let me know if Oscar were really in danger, which I could hardly believe. As luck would have it, the next afternoon, when I hoped Bell had started, his wife came to tell me that he had had a severe asthmatic attack, but would cross as soon as he dared.

I was too hard up myself to wire money that might not be needed, and Oscar had cried "wolf" about his health too often to be a credible witness. Yet I was dissatisfied with myself and anxious for Bell to start.

Day after day passed in troubled doubts and fears; but it was not long when a period was put to all my anxiety. A telegram came telling me he was dead. I could hardly believe my eyes; it seemed incredible—the fount of joy and gaiety; the delightful source of intellectual vivacity and interest stilled forever. The world went greyer to me because of Oscar Wilde's death.

Months afterwards Robert Ross gave me the particulars of his last illness.

Ross went to Paris in October. As soon as he saw Oscar, he was shocked by the change in his appearance; he insisted on taking him to a doctor; but to his surprise the doctor saw no ground for immediate alarm. If Oscar would only stop drinking wine and *a fortiori* spirits, he might live for years. Absinthe was absolutely forbidden. But Oscar paid no heed to the warning and Ross could only take him for drives whenever the weather permitted and seek to amuse him harmlessly.

The will to live had almost left Oscar. So long as he could live pleasantly and without effort he was content; but as soon as ill-health came, or pain, or even discomfort, he grew impatient for deliverance.

But to the last he kept his joyous humour and charming gaiety. His disease brought with it a certain irritation of the skin, annoying rather than painful. Meeting Ross one morning after a day's separation he apologised for scratching himself:

"Really," he explained, "I'm more like a great ape than ever; but I hope you'll give me a lunch, Bobbie, and not a nut."

On one of the last drives with this friend he asked for champagne and when it was brought declared that he was dying as he had lived, "beyond his means"—his happy humour lighting up even his last hours.

Early in November Ross left Paris to go down to the Riviera with his mother; for Reggie Turner had undertaken to stay with Oscar. Reggie Turner describes how he grew gradually feebler and feebler, though to the end flashes of the old humour would astonish his attendants. He persisted in saying that Reggie, with his perpetual prohibitions, was qualifying for a doctor. "When you can refuse bread to the hungry, Reggie," he would say, "and drink to the thirsty, you can apply for your diploma."

Towards the end of November Reggie wired for Ross and Ross left everything and reached Paris next day.

When all was over he wrote to a friend giving him a very complete account of the last hours of Oscar Wilde; that account he generously allows me to reproduce and it will be found word for word in the Appendix; it is too long and too detailed to be used here.

Ross's letter should be read by the student; but several touches in it are too timid; certain experiences that should be put in high relief are slurred over. In conversation with me he told more and told it better.

For example, when talking of his drives with Oscar, he mentions casually that Oscar "insisted on drinking absinthe," and leaves it at that. The truth is that Oscar stopped the victoria at almost the first café, got down and had an absinthe. Two or three hundred yards further on, he stopped the carriage again to have another absinthe; at the stoppage a few minutes later Ross ventured to remonstrate:

"You'll kill yourself, Oscar," he cried, "you know the doctors said absinthe was poison to you!"

Oscar stopped on the sidewalk:

"And what have I to live for, Bobbie?" he asked gravely. And Ross looking at him and noting the wreck—the symptoms of old age and broken health—could only bow his head and walk on with him in silence. What indeed had he to live for who had abandoned all the fair uses of life?

The second scene is horrible, but is, so to speak, the inevitable resultant of the first, and has its own awful moral. Ross tells how he came one morning to Oscar's death-bed and found him practically insensible. He describes the dreadful loud death-rattle of his breath, and says: "terrible offices had to be carried out."

The truth is still more appaling. Oscar had eaten too much and drunk too much almost habitually ever since the catastrophe in Naples. The dreadful disease from which he was suffering, or from the after effects of which he was suffering, weakens all the tissues of the body, and this weakness is aggravated by drinking wine and still more by drinking spirits. Suddenly, as the two friends sat by the bedside in sorrowful anxiety, there was a loud explosion; mucus poured out of Oscar's mouth and nose, and—Even the bedding had to be burned.

If it is true that all those who draw the sword shall perish by the sword, it is no less certain that all those who live for the body shall perish by the body, and there is no death more degrading.

. . . .

One more scene, and this the last, and I shall have done.

When Robert Ross was arranging to bury Oscar at Bagneux he had already made up his mind as soon as he could to transfer his body to Père Lachaise and erect over his remains some worthy memorial. It became the purpose of his life to pay his friend's debts, annul his bankruptcy, and publish his books in suitable manner; in fine, to clear Oscar's memory from obloquy while leaving to his lovable spirit the shining raiment of immortality. In a few years he had accomplished all but one part of his high task. He had not only paid off all Oscar Wilde's debts; but he had managed to remit thousands of pounds yearly to his children, and had established his popularity on the widest and surest foundation.

He crossed to Paris with Oscar's son, Vyvyan, to render the last service to his friend. When preparing the body for the grave, Ross had taken medical advice as to what should be done to make his purpose possible. The doctors told him to put Wilde's body in quicklime, like the body of the man in "The Ballad of Reading Gaol". The quicklime, they said, would consume the flesh and leave the white bones—the skeleton—intact, which could then be moved easily.

To his horror, when the grave was opened, Ross found that the quicklime, instead of destroying the flesh, had preserved it. Oscar's face was recognizable, only his hair and beard had grown long. At once Ross sent the son away, and when the sextons were about to use their shovels, he ordered them to desist and, descending into the grave, moved the body with his own hands into the new coffin in loving reverence.

Those who hold our mortal vesture in respect for the sake of the spirit will know how to thank Robert Ross for the supreme devotion he showed to his friend's remains; in his case at least love was stronger than death.

One can be sure, too, that the man who won such fervid self-denying tenderness, had deserved it, called it forth by charm of companionship or magic of loving intercourse.

27

A Last Word

IT WAS THE INHUMANITY of the prison doctor and the English prison system that killed Oscar Wilde. The sore place in his ear caused by the fall when he fainted that Sunday morning in Wandsworth Prison chapel formed into an abscess and was the final cause of his death. The "operation" Ross speaks of in his letter was the excision of this tumour. The imprisonment and starvation, and above all the cruelty of his gaolers, had done their work.

The local malady was inflamed, as I have already said, by a more general and more terrible disease. The doctors attributed the red flush Oscar complained of on his chest and back, which he declared was due to eating mussels, to another and graver cause. They warned him at once to stop drinking and smoking and to live with the greatest abstemiousness, for they recognized in him the tertiary symptoms of that dreadful disease which the brainless prudery in England allows to decimate the flower of English manhood unchecked.

Oscar took no heed of their advice. He had little to live for. The pleasures of eating and drinking in good company were almost the only pleasures left to him. Why should he deny himself the immediate enjoyment for a very vague and questionable future benefit?

He never believed in any form of asceticism or self-denial, and towards the end, feeling that life had nothing more to offer him, the pagan spirit in him refused to prolong an existence that was no longer joyous. "I have lived," he would have said with profound truth.

Much has been made of the fact that Oscar was buried in an out-of-the-way cemetery at Bagneux under depressing circumstances. It rained the day of the funeral, it appears, and a cold wind blew. The way was muddy and long, and only a half-a-dozen friends accompanied the coffin to its resting-place. But after all, such accidents, depressing as they are at the moment, are unimportant. The dead clay knows nothing of our feelings, and whether it is borne to the grave in pompous procession and laid to rest in a great abbey amid the mourning of a nation or tossed as dust to the wind, is a matter of utter indifference.

Heine's verse holds the supreme consolation:

> Immerhin mich wird umgeben
> Gotteshimmel dort wie hier
> Und wie Todtenlampen schweben
> Nachts die Sterne ueber mir.

Oscar Wilde's work was over, his gift to the world completed years before. Even the friends who loved him and delighted in the charm of his talk, in his light-hearted gaiety and humour, would scarcely have kept him longer in the pillory, exposed to the loathing and contempt of this all-hating world.

The good he did lives after him, and is immortal, the evil is buried in his grave. Who would deny to-day that he was a quickening and liberating influence? If his life was given over-much to self-indulgence, it must be remembered that his writings and conversation were singularly kindly, singularly amiable, singularly pure. No harsh or coarse or bitter word ever passed those eloquent laughing lips. If he served beauty in her myriad forms, he only showed in his works the beauty that was amiable and of good report. If only half-a-dozen men mourned for him, their sorrow was unaffected and intense, and perhaps the greatest of men have not found in their lifetime even half-a-dozen devoted admirers and lovers. It is well with our friend, we say. At any rate, he was not forced to drink the bitter lees of a suffering and dishonourable old age. Death was merciful to him.

My task is finished. I don't think anyone will doubt that I have done it in a reverent spirit, telling the truth as I see it, from the beginning to the end, and hiding or omitting as little as might be of what ought to be told. Yet when I come to the parting I am painfully conscious that I have not done Oscar Wilde justice; that some fault or other in me has led me to dwell too much on his faults and failings and grudged praise to his soul-subduing charm and the incomparable sweetness and gaiety of his nature.

Let me now make amends. When to the sessions of sad memory I summon up the spirits of those whom I have met in the world and loved, men famous and men of unfulfilled renown, I miss no one so much as I miss Oscar Wilde. I would rather spend an evening with him than with Renan or Carlyle or Verlaine or Dick Burton or Davidson. I would rather have him back now than almost anyone I have ever met. I have known more heroic souls and some deeper souls; souls much more keenly alive to ideas of duty and generosity; but I have known no more charming, no more quickening, no more delightful spirit.

This may be my shortcoming; it may be that I prize humour and good-humour and eloquent or poetic speech, the artist qualities, more than goodness or loyalty or manliness, and so over-estimate things amiable. But the lovable and joyous things are to me the priceless things, and the most charming man I have ever met was assuredly Oscar Wilde. I do not believe that in all the realms of death there is a more fascinating or delightful companion.

One last word on Oscar Wilde's place in English literature. In the course of this narrative I have indicated sufficiently, I think, the value and importance of his work; he will live with Congreve and with Sheridan as the wittiest and most humorous of all our playwrights. "The Importance of Being Earnest" has its own place among the best of English comedies. But Oscar Wilde has done better work than Congreve or Sheridan. He is a master not only of the smiles, but of the tears of men. "The Ballad of Reading Gaol" is the best ballad in English; it is more, it is the noblest utterance that has yet reached us from a modern prison, the only high utterance indeed that has ever come from that underworld of man's hatred and man's inhumanity. In it, and by the spirit of Jesus which breathes through it, Oscar Wilde has done much, not only to reform English prisons, but to abolish them altogether, for they are as degrading to the intelligence as they are harmful to the soul. What gaoler and what gaol could do anything but evil to the author of such a verse as this:

> This too I know—and wise it were
> If each could know the same—
> That every prison that men build
> Is built with bricks of shame,
> And bound with bars, lest Christ should see
> How men their brothers maim.

Indeed, is it not clear that the man who, in his own wretchedness, wrote that letter to the warder which I have reproduced, and was eager to bring about the freeing of the little children at his own cost, is far above the judge who condemned him or the society which sanctions such punishments? "The Ballad of Reading Gaol", I repeat, and some pages of "De Profundis", and, above all, the tragic fate of which these were the outcome, render Oscar Wilde more interesting to men than any of his peers.

He has been indeed well served by the malice and cruelty of his enemies; in this sense his word in "De Profundis" that he stood in symbolic relation to the art and life of his time is justified.

The English drove Byron and Shelley and Keats into exile and allowed Chatterton, Davidson and Middleton to die of misery and destitution; but they treated none of their artists and seers with the malevolent cruelty they showed to Oscar Wilde. His fate in England is symbolic of the fate of all artists; in some degree they will all be punished as he was punished by a grossly materialised people who prefer to go in blinkers and accept idiotic conventions because they distrust the intellect and have no taste for mental virtues.

All English artists will be judged by their inferiors and condemned, as Dante's master was condemned, for their good deeds (*per tuo ben far*), for it must not be thought that Oscar Wilde was punished solely or even chiefly for the evil he wrought. He was punished for his popularity and his pre-eminence, for the superiority of his mind and wit; he was punished by the envy of journalists, and by the malignant pedantry of half-civilised judges. Envy in his case overleaped itself. The hate of his judges was so diabolic that they have given him to the pity of mankind forever; they it is who have made him eternally interesting to humanity, a tragic figure of imperishable renown.

EPILOGUE

Epilogue

GEORGE BERNARD SHAW ordered a special copy of this book of mine: "Oscar Wilde: His Life and Confessions," as soon as it was announced. I sent it to him and asked him to write me his opinion of the book.

In due course I received the following MSS. from him in which he tells me what he thinks of my work:—"the best life of Wilde, . . . Wilde's memory will have to stand or fall by it"; and then goes on to relate all his own meetings with Wilde, the impressions they made upon him and his judgment of Wilde as a writer and as a man.

He has given himself this labour, he says, in order that I may publish his views in the Appendix to my book if I think fit—an example, not only of Shaw's sympathy and generosity, but of his light way of treating his own kindness.

I am delighted to be able to put Shaw's considered judgment of Wilde beside my own for the benefit of my readers. For if there had been anything I had misseen or misjudged in Wilde, or any prominent trait of his character I had failed to note, the sin, whether of omission or commission, could scarcely have escaped this other pair of keen eyes. Now indeed this biography of Wilde may be regarded as definitive.

Shaw says his judgment of Wilde is severer than mine—"far

sterner", are his words; but I am not sure that this is an exact estimate.

While Shaw accentuates Wilde's snobbishness, he discounts his "Irish charm", and though he praises highly his gifts as dramatist and story-teller he lays little stress on his genuine kindness of nature and the courteous smiling ways which made him so incomparable a companion and intimate.

On the other hand he excuses Wilde's perversion as pathological, as hereditary "gigantism", and so lightens the darkest shadows just as he has toned down the lights.

I never saw anything abnormal in Oscar Wilde either in body or soul save an extravagant sensuality and an absolute adoration of beauty and comeliness; and so, with his own confessions and practices before me, I had to block him in, to use painters' jargon, with black shadows, and was delighted to find high lights to balance them—lights of courtesies, graces, and unselfish kindness of heart.

On the whole I think our two pictures are very much alike and I am sure a good many readers will be almost as grateful to Shaw for his collaboration and corroboration as I am.

Postscript

Since writing this foreword I have received the proof of his contribution which I had sent to Shaw. He has made some slight corrections in the text which, of course, have been carried out, and some comments besides on my notes as Editor. These, too, I have naturally wished to use and so, to avoid confusion, have inserted them in italics and with his initials. I hope the sequence will be clear to the reader.

F. H.

APPENDIX A

MY MEMORIES OF OSCAR WILDE

By George Bernard Shaw

My Memories of Oscar Wilde

GEORGE BERNARD SHAW

My Dear Harris:—

I have an interesting letter of yours to answer; but when you ask me to exchange biographies, you take an unfair advantage of the changes of scene and bustling movement of your own adventures. My autobiography would be like my best plays, fearfully long, and not divided into acts. Just consider this life of Wilde which you have just sent me, and which I finished ten minutes ago after putting aside everything else to read it at one stroke.

Why was Wilde so good a subject for a biography that none of the previous attempts which you have just wiped out are bad? Just because his stupendous laziness simplified his life almost as if he knew instinctively that there must be no episodes to spoil the great situation at the end of the last act but one. It was a well made life in the Scribe sense. It was as simple as the life of Des Grieux, Manon Lescaut's lover; and it beat that by omitting Manon and making Des Grieux his own lover and his own hero.

Des Grieux was a worthless rascal by all conventional standards; and we forgive him everything. We think we forgive him because he was unselfish and loved greatly. Oscar seems to have said: "I will love nobody: I will be utterly selfish; and I will be not merely a rascal but a monster; and you shall forgive me everything. In other words, I will reduce your standards to

329

absurdity, not by writing them down, though I could do that so well—in fact, *have* done it—but by actually living them down and dying them down."

However, I mustn't start writing a book to you about Wilde; I must just tumble a few things together and tell you them. To take things in the order of your book, I can remember only one occasion on which I saw Sir William Wilde, who, by the way, operated on my father to correct a squint, and overdid the corrections so much that my father squinted the other way all the rest of his life. To this day I never notice a squint; it is as normal to me as a nose or a tall hat.

I was a boy at a concert in the Antient Concert Rooms in Brunswick Street in Dublin. Everybody was in evening dress; and—unless I am mixing up this concert with another (in which case I doubt if the Wildes would have been present)—the Lord Lieutenant was there with his blue waistcoated courtiers. Wilde was dressed in snuffy brown; and he had the sort of skin that never looks clean, he produced a dramatic effect beside Lady Wilde (in full fig) of being, like Frederick the Great, Beyond Soap and Water, as his Nietzschean son was beyond Good and Evil. He was currently reported to have a family in every farmhouse; and the wonder was that Lady Wilde didn't mind—evidently a tradition from the Travers case, which I did not know about until I read your account, as I was only eight in 1864.

Lady Wilde was nice to me in London during the desperate days between my arrival in 1876 and my first earning of an income by my pen in 1885, or rather until, a few years earlier, I threw myself into Socialism and cut myself contemptuously loose from everything of which her at-homes—themselves desperate affairs enough, as you saw for yourself—were part. I was at two or three of them; and I once dined with her in company with an ex-tragedy queen named Miss Glynn, who, having no visible external ears, reared a head like a turnip. Lady Wilde talked about Schopenhauer; and Miss Glynn told me that Gladstone formed his oratorical style on Charles Kean.

I ask myself where and how I came across Lady Wilde; for we had no social relations in the Dublin days. The explanation must be that my sister, then a very attractive girl who sang beautifully, had met and made some sort of innocent conquest of both Oscar and Willie. I met Oscar once at one of the at-homes; and he came and spoke to me with an evident intention of being specially kind to me. We put each other out frightfully; and this odd difficulty persisted between us to the very last, even when we were no longer mere boyish novices and had become men of the world with plenty of skill in social intercourse. I saw him very seldom, as I avoided literary and artistic society like the plague, and refused the few invitations I received to go into society with burlesque ferocity, so as to keep out of it without offending people past their willingness to indulge me as a privileged lunatic.

The last time I saw him was at that tragic luncheon of yours at the Café Royal; and I am quite sure our total of meetings from first to last did not exceed twelve, and may not have exceeded six.

I definitely recollect six: (1) At the at-home aforesaid. (2) At Macmurdo's house in Fitzroy Street in the days of the Century Guild and its paper *The Hobby Horse*. (3) At a meeting somewhere in Westminster at which I delivered an address on Socialism, and at which Oscar turned up and spoke. Robert Ross surprised me greatly by telling me, long after Oscar's death, that it was this address of mine that moved Oscar to try his hand at a similar feat by writing "The Soul of Man Under Socialism". (4) A chance meeting near the stage door of the Haymarket Theatre, at which our queer shyness of one another made our resolutely cordial and appreciative conversation so difficult that our final laugh and shake-hands was almost a reciprocal confession. (5) A really pleasant afternoon we spent together on catching one another in a place where our presence was an absurdity. It was some exhibition in Chelsea; a naval commemoration, where there was a replica of Nelson's Victory and a set of P. & O. cabins which made one seasick by mere association of ideas. I don't know why I went or why Wilde went; but we did; and the question what the devil we were doing in that galley tickled us both. It was my sole experience of Oscar's wonderful gift as a raconteur. I remember particularly an amazingly elaborate story which you have no doubt heard from him; an example of the cumulation of a single effect, as in Mark Twain's story of the man who was persuaded to put lightning conductor after lightning conductor at every possible point on his roof until a thunderstorm came and all the lightning in the heavens went for his house and wiped it out.

Oscar's much more carefully and elegantly worked out story was of a young man who invented a theatre stall which economized space by ingenious contrivances which were all described. A friend of his invited twenty millionaires to meet him at dinner so that he might interest them in the invention. The young man convinced them competely by his demonstration of the saving in a theatre holding, in ordinary seats, six hundred people, leaving them eager and ready to make his fortune. Unfortunately, he went on to calculate the annual saving in all the theatres of the world; then in all the churches of the world; then in all the legislatures; estimating finally the incidental and moral and religious effects of the invention until at the end of an hour he had estimated a profit of several thousand millions: the climax of course being that the millionaires folded their tents and silently stole away, leaving the ruined inventor a marked man for life.

Wilde and I got on extraordinarily well on this occasion. I had not to talk myself, but to listen to a man telling me stories better than I could have told them. We did not refer to Art, about which, excluding literature from the definition, he knew only what could be picked up reading about it. He was in a tweed suit and low hat like myself, and had been detected and had detected me in the act of clandestinely spending a happy day at Rosherville Gardens instead of pontificating in his frock coat and so forth. And he had an audience on whom not one of his subtlest effects was lost. And so for once our meeting was a success; and I understood why Morris, when he was dying slowly, enjoyed a visit from Wilde more than from anybody else, as I understand why you say in your book that you would rather have Wilde back than any friend you have ever talked to, even though he was incapable of friendship, though not of the most touching kindness[1] on occasion.

Our sixth meeting, the only other one I can remember, was the one at the Café Royal. On that occasion he was not too preoccupied with his danger to be disgusted with me because I, who had praised his first plays handsomely, had turned traitor over "The Importance of Being Earnest". Clever as it was, it was his first really heartless play. In the others the chivalry of the eighteenth century Irishman and the romance of the disciple of Théophile Gautier (Oscar was really old-fashioned in the Irish way, except as a critic of morals) not only gave a certain kindness and gallantry to the serious passages and to the handling of the women, but provided that proximity of emotion without which laughter, however irresistible, is destructive and sinister. In "The Importance of Being Earnest" this had

[1] Excellent analysis. (F. H.)

332

vanished; and the play, though extremely funny, was essentially hateful. I had no idea that Oscar was going to the dogs, and that this represented a real degeneracy produced by his debaucheries. I thought he was still developing; and I hazarded the unhappy guess that "The Importance of Being Earnest" was in idea a young work written or projected long before under the influence of Gilbert and furbished up for Alexander as a potboiler. At the Café Royal that day I calmly asked him whether I was not right. He indignantly repudiated my guess, and said loftily (the only time he ever tried on me the attitude he took to John Gray and his more abject disciples) that he was disappointed in me. I suppose I said, "Then what on earth has happened to you?" but I recollect nothing more on that subject except that we did not quarrel over it.

When he was sentenced I spent a railway journey on a Socialist lecturing excursion to the North drafting a petition for his release. After that I met Willie Wilde at a theatre which I think must have been the Duke of York's because I connect it vaguely with St. Martin's Lane. I spoke to him about the petition, asking him whether anything of the sort was being done, and warning him that though I and Stewart Headlam would sign it, that would be no use, as we were two notorious cranks, and our names would by themselves reduce the petition to absurdity and do Oscar more harm than good. Willie cordially agreed, and added, with maudlin pathos and an inconceivable want of tact: "Oscar was NOT a man of bad character: you could have trusted him with a woman anywhere." He convinced me, as you discovered later, that signatures would not be obtainable; so the petition project dropped; and I don't know what became of my draft.

When Wilde was in Paris during his last phase I made a point of sending him inscribed copies of all my books as they came out; and he did the same to me.

In writing about Wilde and Whistler, in the days when they were treated as witty triflers, and called Oscar and Jimmy in print, I always made a point of taking them seriously and with scrupulous good manners. Wilde on his part also made a point of recognizing me as a man of distinction by his manner, and repudiating the current estimate of me as a mere jester. This was not the usual reciprocal-admiration trick. I believe he was sincere, and felt indignant at what he thought was a vulgar underestimate of me; and I had the same feeling about him. My impulse to rally to him in his misfortune, and my disgust at "the man Wildes" scurrilities of the newspapers, was irresistible: I don't quite know why; for my charity to his perversion, and my recognition of the fact that it does not imply any general depravity or coarseness of character, came to me through reading an observation, not through sympathy.

I have all the normal violent repugnance to homosexuality—if it is really normal, which nowadays one is sometimes provoked to doubt.

Also, I was in no way predisposed to like him. He was my fellow-townsman, and a very prime specimen of the sort of fellow-townsman I most loathed: to wit, the Dublin snob. His Irish charm, potent with Englishmen, did not exist for me; and on the whole it may be claimed for him that he got no regard from me that he did not earn.

What first established a friendly feeling in me was, unexpectedly enough, the affair of the Chicago anarchists, whose Homer you constituted yourself by *The Bomb*. I tried to get some literary men in London, all heroic rebels and skeptics on paper, to sign a memorial asking for the reprieve of these unfortunate men. The only signature I got was Oscar's. It was a completely disinterested act on his part; and it secured my distinguished consideration for him for the rest of his life.

To return for a moment to Lady Wilde. You know that there is a disease called gigantism, caused by "a certain morbid process in the sphenoid bone of the skull—viz., an excessive development of the anterior lobe of the pituitary body" (this is from the nearest encyclopedia). "When this condition does not become active until after the age of twenty-five, by which time the long bones are consolidated, the result is acromegaly, which chiefly manifests itself in an enlargment of the hands and feet." I never saw Lady Wilde's feet; but her hands were enormous, and never went straight to their aim when they grasped anything, but minced about, feeling for it. And the gigantic splaying of her palm was produced in her lumbar region.

Now Oscar was an overgrown man, with something not quite normal about his bigness—something that made Lady Colin Campbell, who hated him, describe him as "that great white caterpillar." You yourself describe the disagreeable impression he made on you physically, in spite of his fine eyes and style. Well, I have always maintained that Oscar was a giant in the pathological sense, and that this explains a good deal of his weakness.

I think you have affectionately underrated his snobbery,

mentioning only the pardonable and indeed justifiable side of it; the love of fine names and distinguished associations and luxury and good manners.[2] You say repeatedly, and *on certain planes*, truly, that he was not bitter and did not use his tongue to wound people. But this is not true on the snobbish plane. On one occasion he wrote about T. P. O'Connor with deliberate, studied, wounding insolence, with his Merrion Square Protestant pretentiousness in full cry against the Catholic. He repeatedly declaimed against the vulgarity of the British journalist, not as you or I might, but as an expression of the odious class feeling that is itself the vilest vulgarity. He made the mistake of not knowing his place. He objected to be addressed as Wilde, declaring that he was Oscar to his intimates and Mr. Wilde to others, quite unconscious of the fact that he was imposing on the men with whom, as a critic and journalist, he had to live and work, the alternative of granting him an intimacy he had no right to ask or a deference to which he had no claim. The vulgar hated him for snubbing them; and the valiant men damned his impudence and cut him. Thus he was left with a band of devoted satellites on the one hand, and a dining-out connection on the other, with here and there a man of talent and personality enough to command his respect, but utterly without that fortifying body of acquaintance among plain men in which a man must move as himself a plain man, and be Smith and Jones and Wilde and Shaw and Harris instead of Bosie and Robbie and Oscar and Mister. This is the sort of folly that does not last forever in a man of Wilde's ability; but it lasted long enough to prevent Oscar laying any solid social foundations.[3]

[2] I have touched on the evil side of his snobbery, I thought by saying that it was only famous actresses and great ladies that he ever talked about, and in telling how he loved to speak of the great houses such as Clumber to which he had been invited, and by a half a dozen other hints scattered through my book. I had attacked English snobbery so strenuously in my book "The Man Shakespeare", had resented its influence on the finest English intelligence so bitterly, that I thought if I again laid stress on it in Wilde, people would think I was crazy on the subject. But he was a snob, both by nature and training, and I understand by snob what Shaw evidently understands by it here.

[3] The reason that Oscar, snobbish as he was, and admirer of England and the English as he was, could not lay any solid social foundations in England was, in my opinion, his intellectual interests and his intellectual superiority to the men he met. No one with a fine mind devoted to things of the spirit is capable of laying solid social foundations in England. Shaw, too, has no solid social foundations in that country.

This passing shot at English society serves it right. Yet able men have found niches in London. Where was Oscar's?—G. B. S.

Another difficultly I have already hinted at. Wilde started as an apostle of Art; and in that capacity he was a humbug. The notion that a Portora boy, passed on to T.C.D. and thence to Oxford and spending his vacations in Dublin, could without special circumstances have any genuine intimacy with music and painting, is to me ridiculous.[4] When Wilde was at Portora, I was at home in a house where important musical works, including several typical masterpieces, were being rehearsed from the point of blank amateur ignorance up to fitness for public performance. I could whistle them from the first bar to the last as a butcher's boy whistles music hall songs, before I was twelve. The toleration of popular music—Strauss's waltzes, for instance—was to me positively a painful acquirement, a sort of republican duty.

I was so fascinated by painting that I haunted the National Gallery, which Doyle had made perhaps the finest collection of its size in the world; and I longed for money to buy painting materials with. This afterwards saved me from starving. It was as a critic of music and painting in the *World* that I won through my ten years of journalism before I finished up with you on the *Saturday Review*. I could make deaf stockbrokers read my two pages on music, the alleged joke being that I knew nothing about it. The real joke was that I knew all about it.

Now it was quite evident to me, as it was to Whistler and Beardsley, that Oscar knew no more about pictures[5] than anyone of his general culture and with his opportunities can pick up as he goes along. He could be witty about Art, as I could be witty about engineering; but that is no use when you have to seize and hold the attention and interest of people who really love music and painting. Therefore, Oscar was handicapped by a false start, and got a reputation[6] for shallowness and insincerity which he never retrieved until it was too late.

Comedy: the criticism of morals and manners *viva voce*,

[4] I had already marked it down to put in my book that Wilde continually pretended to a knowledge of music which he had not got. He could hardly tell one tune from another, but he loved to talk of that "scarlet thing of Dvorak," hoping in this way to be accepted as a real critic of music, when he knew nothing about it and cared even less. His eulogies of music and painting betrayed him continually though he did not know it.

[5] I touched upon Oscar's ignorance of art sufficiently I think, when I said in my book that he had learned all he knew of art and of controversy from Whistler, and that his lectures on the subject, even after sitting at the feet of the Master, were almost worthless.

[6] Perfectly true, and a notable instance of Shaw's insight.

was his real forte. When he settled down to that he was great. But, as you found when you approached Meredith about him, his initial mistake had produced that "rather low opinion of Wilde's capacities," that "deep-rooted contempt for the showman in him," which persisted as a first impression and will persist until the last man who remembers his esthetic period has perished. The world has been in some ways so unjust to him that one must be careful not to be unjust to the world.

In the preface on education, called "Parents and Children", to my volume of plays beginning with *Misalliance*, there is a section headed "Artist Idolatry", which is really about Wilde. Dealing with "the powers enjoyed by brilliant persons who are also connoisseurs in art," I say, "the influence they can exercise on young people who have been brought up in the darkness and wretchedness of a home without art, and in whom a natural bent towards art has always been baffled and snubbed, is incredible to those who have not witnessed and understood it. He (or she) who reveals the world of art to them opens heaven to them. They became satellites, disciples, worshippers of the apostle. Now the apostle may be a voluptuary without much conscience. Nature may have given him enough virtue to suffice in a reasonable environment. But this allowance may not be enough to defend him against the temptation and demoralization of finding himself a little god on the strength of what ought to be a quite ordinary culture. He may find adorers in all directions in our uncultivated society among people of stronger character than himself, not one of whom, if they had been artistically educated, would have had anything to learn from him, or regarded him as in any way extraordinary apart from his actual achievements as an artist. Tartufe is not always a priest. Indeed, he is not always a rascal; he is often a weak man absurdly credited with omniscience and perfection, and taking unfair advantages only because they are offered to him and he is too weak to refuse. Give everyone his culture, and no one will offer him more than his due."

That paragraph was the outcome of a walk and talk I had one afternoon at Chartres with Robert Ross.

You reveal Wilde as a weaker man than I thought him. I still believe that his fierce Irish pride had something to do with his refusal to run away from the trial. But in the main your evidence is conclusive. It was part of his tragedy that people asked more moral strength from him than he could bear the burden of, because they made the very common mistake—of

which actors get the benefit—of regarding style as evidence
of strength, just as in the case of women they are apt to regard
paint as evidence of beauty. Now Wilde was so in love with
style that he never realized the danger of biting off more than
he could chew. In other words, of putting up more style than
his matter would carry. Wise kings wear shabby clothes, and
leave the gold lace to the drum major.

You do not, unless my memory is betraying me as usual,
quite recollect the order of events just before the trial. That
day at the Café Royal, Wilde said he had come to ask you to
go into the witness box next day and testify that *Dorian Gray*
was a highly moral work. Your answer was something like this:
"For God's sake, man, put everything on that plane out of
your head. You don't realize what is going to happen to you.
It is not going to be a matter of clever talk about your books.
They are going to bring up a string of witnesses that will put
art and literature out of the question. Clarke will throw up his
brief. He will carry the case to a certain point; and then, when
he sees the avalanche coming, he will back out and leave you
in the dock. What you have to do is to cross to France to-night.
Leave a letter saying that you cannot face the squalor and
horror of a law case; that you are an artist and unfitted for such
things. Don't stay here clutching at straws like testimonials to
Dorian Gray. I tell you I know. I know what is going to
happen. I know Clarke's sort. I know what evidence they have
got. You must go."

It was no use. Wilde was in a curious double temper. He
made no pretence either of innocence or of questioning the
folly of his proceedings against Queensberry. But he had an
infatuate haughtiness as to the impossibility of his retreating,
and as to his right to dictate your course. Douglas sat in silence,
a haughty indignant silence, copying Wilde's attitude as all
Wilde's admirers did, but quite probably influencing Wilde as
you suggest, by the copy. Oscar finally rose with a mixture
of impatience and his grand air, and walked out with the remark
that he had now found out who were his real friends; and
Douglas followed him, absurdly smaller, and imitating his
walk, like a curate following an archbishop.[7] You remember

[7] This is an inimitable picture, but Shaw's fine sense of comedy has misled
him. The scene took place absolutely as I recorded it. Douglas went out first
saying—"Your telling him to run away shows that you are no friend of
Oscar's." Then Oscar got up to follow him. He said good-bye to Shaw,

MY MEMORIES OF OSCAR WILDE

it the other way about; but just consider this. Douglas was in the wretched position of having ruined Wilde merely to annoy his father, and of having attempted it so idiotically that he had actually prepared a triumph for him. He was, besides, much the youngest man present, and looked younger than he was. You did not make him welcome. As far as I recollect you did not greet him by a word or nod. If he had given the smallest provocation or attempted to take the lead in any way, I should not have given twopence for the chance of your keeping your temper. And Wilde, even in his ruin—which, however, he did not yet fully realize—kept his air of authority on questions of taste and conduct. It was practically impossible under such circumstances that Douglas should have taken the stage in any way. Everyone thought him a horrid little brat; but I, not having met him before to my knowledge, and having some sort of flair for his literary talent, was curious to hear what he had to say for himself. But, except to echo Wilde once or twice, he said nothing.[8] You are right in effect, because it was evident that Wilde was in his hands, and was really echoing him. But Wilde automatically kept the prompter off the stage and himself in the middle of it.

What your book needs to complete it is a portrait of yourself as good as your portrait of Wilde. Oscar was not combative, though he was supercilious in his early pose. When his snobbery was not in action, he liked to make people devoted to him and to flatter them exquisitely with that end. Mrs. Calvert, whose great final period as a stage old woman began with her appearance in my *Arms and the Man*, told me one day, when apologizing for being, as she thought, a bad rehearser, that no author had ever been so nice to her except Mr. Wilde.

Pugnacious people, if they did not actually terrify Oscar, were at least the sort of people he could not control, and whom he feared as possibly able to coerce him. You suggest that the Queensberry pugnacity was something that Oscar could not deal with successfully. But how in that case could

adding a courteous word or two. As he turned to the door I got up and said:—"I hope you do not doubt my friendship; you have no reason to."

"I do not think this is friendly of you, Frank," he said, and went on out.

[8] I am sure Douglas took the initiative and walked out first.

I have no doubt you are right, and that my vision of the exit is really a reminiscence of the entrance. In fact, now that you prompt my memory, I recall quite distinctly that Douglas, who came in as the follower, went out as the leader, and that the last word was spoken by Wilde after he had gone.—G. B. S.

Oscar have felt quite safe with you? You were more pugnacious than six Queensberrys rolled into one. When people asked, " 'What has Frank Harris been?' the usual reply was, "Obviously a pirate from the Spanish Main."

Oscar, from the moment he gained your attachment, could never have been afraid of what you might do to him, as he was sufficient of a connoisseur in *Blut Bruderschaft* to appreciate yours; but he must always have been mortally afraid of what you might do or say to his friends.[9]

You had quite an infernal scorn for nineteen out of twenty of the men and women you met in the circles he most wished to propitiate; and nothing could induce you to keep your knife in its sheath when they jarred on you. The Spanish Main itself would have blushed rosy red at your language when classical invective did not suffice to express your feelings.

It may be that if, say, Edmund Gosse had come to Oscar when he was out on bail, with a couple of first class tickets in his pocket, and gently suggested a mild trip to Folkestone, or the Channel Islands, Oscar might have let himself be coaxed away. But to be called on to gallop *ventre à terre* to Erith—it might have been Deal—and hoist the Jolly Roger on board your lugger, was like casting a light comedian and first lover for *Richard III*. Oscar could not see himself in the part.

I must not press the point too far; but it illustrates, I think, what does not come out at all in your book: that you were a very different person from the submissive and sympathetic disciples to whom he was accustomed. There are things more terrifying to a soul like Oscar's than an as yet unrealized possibility of a sentence of hard labour. A voyage with Captain Kidd may have been one of them. Wilde was a conventional man; his unconventionality was the very pedantry of convention; never was there a man less an outlaw than he. You were a born outlaw, and will never be anything else.

That is why, in his relations with you, he appears as a man always shirking action—more of a coward (all men are cowards more or less) than so proud a man can have been. Still this does not affect the truth and power of your portrait. Wilde's memory will have to stand or fall by it.

You will be blamed, I imagine, because you have not written

---

[9] This insight on Shaw's part makes me smile because it is absolutely true. Oscar commended Bosie Douglas to me again and again and again, begged me to be nice to him if we ever met by chance; but I refused to meet him for months and months.

a lying epitaph instead of a faithful chronicle and study of him; but you will not lose your sleep over that. As a matter of fact, you could not have carried kindness further without sentimental folly. I should have made a far sterner summing up. I am sure Oscar has not found the gates of heaven shut against him. He is too good company to be excluded; but he can hardly have been greeted as "Thou good and faithful servant." The first thing we ask a servant for is a testimonial to honesty, sobriety and industry; for we soon find out that these are the scarce things, and that geniuses[10] and clever people are as common as rats. Well, Oscar was not sober, not honest, not industrious. Society praised him for being idle, and persecuted him savagely for an aberration which it had better have left unadvertized, thereby making a hero of him; for it is in the nature of people to worship those who have been made to suffer horribly. Indeed I have often said that if the crucifixion could be proved a myth, and Jesus convicted of dying of old age in comfortable circumstances, Christianity would lose ninety-nine per cent of its devotees.

We must try to imagine what judgment we should have passed on Oscar if he had been a normal man, and had dug his grave with his teeth in the ordinary respectable fashion, as his brother Willie did. This brother, by the way, gives us some cue; for Willie, who had exactly the same education and the same chances, must be ruthlessly set aside by literary history as a vulgar journalist of no account. Well, suppose Oscar and Willie had both died the day before Queensberry left that card at the Club! Oscar would still have been remembered as a wit and a dandy, and would have had a niche beside Congreve in the drama. A volume of his aphorisms would have stood creditably on the library shelf with La Rochefoucauld's Maxims. We should have missed the "Ballad of Reading Gaol" and "De Profundis"; but he would still have cut a considerable figure in the Dictionary of National Biography, and been read and quoted outside the British Museum reading room.

As the "Ballad" and "De Profundis," I think it is greatly to Oscar's credit that, whilst he was sincere and deeply moved when he was protesting against the cruelty of our present system to children and to prisoners generally, he could not write

---

[10] The English paste in Shaw; genius is about the rarest thing on earth whereas the necessary quantum of "honesty, sobriety and industry," is beaten by life into nine humans out of ten.—F. H.

If so, it is the tenth who comes my way.—G. B. S.

about his own individual share in that suffering with any conviction or sympathy.[11] Except for the passage where he describes his exposure at Clapham Junction, there is hardly a line in "De Profundis" that he might not have written as a literary feat five years earlier. But in the "Ballad", even in borrowing form and melody from Coleridge, he shews that he could pity others when he could not seriously pity himself. And this, I think, may be pleaded against the reproach that he was selfish. Externally, in the ordinary action of life as distinguished from the literary action proper to his genius, he was no doubt sluggish and weak because of his gigantism. He ended as an unproductive drunkard and swindler; for the repeated sales of the Daventry plot, in so far as they imposed on the buyers and were not transparent excuses for begging, were undeniably swindles. For all that, he does not appear in his writings a selfish or baseminded man. He is at his worst and weakest in the suppressed[12] part of "De Profundis"; but in my opinion it had better be published, for several reasons. It explains some of his personal weakness by the stifling narrowness of his daily round, ruinous to a man whose proper place was in a large public life. And its concealment is mischievous because, first, it leads people to imagine all sorts of horrors in a document which contains nothing worse than any record of the squabbles of two touchy idlers; and, second, it is clearly a monstrous thing that Douglas should have a torpedo launched at him and timed to explode after his death. The torpedo is a very harmless squib; for there is nothing in it that cannot be guessed from Douglas's own book; but the public does not know that. By the way, it is rather a humorous stroke of Fate's irony that the son of the Marquis of Queensberry should be forced to expiate his sins by suffering a succession of blows beneath the belt.

Now that you have written the best life of Oscar Wilde, let us have the best life of Frank Harris. Otherwise the man behind your works will go down to posterity[13] as the hero of my very

[11] Superb criticism.

[12] I have said this in my way.

[13] A characteristic flirt of Shaw's humour. He is a great caricaturist and not a portrait-painter.

When he thinks of my Celtic face and aggressive American frankness he talks of me as pugnacious and a pirate: "a Captain Kidd". In his preface to "The Fair Lady of the Sonnets" he praises my "idiosyncratic gift of pity"; says that I am "wise through pity"; then he extols me as a prophet, not seeing that a pitying sage, prophet and pirate constitute an inhuman superman.

inadequate preface to "The Dark Lady of the Sonnets."

G. BERNARD SHAW

I shall do more for Shaw than he has been able to do for me; he is the first figure in my new volume of "Contemporary Portraits". I have portrayed him there at his best, as I love to think of him, and henceforth he'll have to try to live up to my conception and that will keep him, I'm afraid, on strain.

God help me!—G. B. S.

APPENDIX B

❧❀❧

OSCAR'S LAST DAYS

Oscar's Last Days!

LETTER FROM ROBERT ROSS TO——

Dec. 14th, 1900.

On Tuesday, October 9th, I wrote to Oscar, from whom I had not heard for some time, that I would be in Paris on Thursday, October the 18th, for a few days, when I hoped to see him. On Thursday, October 11th, I got a telegram from him as follows:—"Operated on yesterday—come over as soon as possible." I wired that I would endeavour to do so. A wire came in response, "Terribly weak—please come." I started on the evening of Tuesday, October 16th. On Wednesday morning I went to see him about 10.30. He was in very good spirits; and though he assured me his sufferings were dreadful, at the same time he shouted with laughter and told many stories against the doctors and himself. I stayed until 12.30 and returned about 4.30, when Oscar recounted his grievances about the Harris play. Oscar, of course, had deceived Harris about the whole matter—as far as I could make out the story—Harris wrote the play under the impression that only Sedger had to be bought off at £100, which Oscar had received in advance for the commission; whereas Kyrle Bellew, Louis Nethersole, Ada Rehan, and even Smithers, had all given Oscar £100 on different occasions, and all threatened Harris with proceedings—Harris, therefore, only gave Oscar £50 on account,[1] as he was obliged

---

[1] Fifty pounds was all Oscar asked me: the whole sum agreed upon. As a matter of fact I gave him fifty pounds more before leaving Paris. I didn't then know that he had ever told the scenario to anyone else, much less sold it; though I ought perhaps to have guessed it.—F. H.

347

to square these people first—hence Oscar's grievance. When I pointed out to him that he was in a much better position than formerly, because Harris, at any rate, would eventually pay off the people who had advanced money and that Oscar would eventually get something himself, he replied in the characteristic way, "Frank has deprived me of my only source of income by taking a play on which I could always have raised £100."

I continued to see Oscar every day until I left Paris. Reggie and myself sometimes dined or lunched in his bedroom, when he was always very talkative, although he looked very ill. On October 25th, my brother Aleck came to see him, when Oscar was in particularly good form. His sister-in-law, Mrs. Willie, and her husband, Texeira, were then passing through Paris on their honeymoon, and came at the same time. On this occasion he said he was "dying above his means" . . . he would never outlive the century . . . the English people would not stand him— he was responsible for the failure of the Exhibition, the English having gone away when they saw him there so well-dressed and happy . . . all the French people knew this, too, and would not stand him any more. . . . On October the 29th, Oscar got up for the first time at mid-day, and after dinner in the evening insisted on going out—he assured me that the doctor had said he might do so and would not listen to any protest.

I had urged him to get up some days before as the doctor said he might do so, but he had hitherto refused. We went to a small café in the Latin Quartier, where he insisted on drinking absinthe. He walked there and back with some difficulty, but seemed fairly well. Only I thought he had suddenly aged in face, and remarked to Reggie next day how different he looked when up and dressed. He appeared *comparatively* well in bed. (I noticed for the first time that his hair was slightly tinged with grey. I had always remarked that his hair had never altered its colour while he was in Reading;[2] it retained its soft brown tone. You must remember the jests he used to make about it, he always amused the warders by saying that his hair was perfectly white.) Next day I was not surprised to find Oscar suffering with a cold and great pain in his ear; however, Dr. Tucker said he might go out again, and the following afternoon, a very mild day, we drove in the Bois. Oscar was much

[2] I (Frank Harris) noticed at Reading that his hair was getting grey in front and at the sides; but when we met later the grey had disappeared. I thought he used some dye. I only mention this to show how two good witnesses can differ on a plain matter of fact.

better, but complained of giddiness; we returned about 4.30.
On Saturday morning, November 3rd, I met the Panseur Hennion (Reggie always called him the Libre Penseur), he came
every day to dress Oscar's wounds. He asked me if I was a great
friend or knew Oscar's relatives. He assured me that Oscar's
general condition was very serious—that he could not live
more than three or four months unless he altered his way of life
—that I ought to speak to Dr. Tucker, who did not realise
Oscar's serious state—that the ear trouble was not of much
importance in itself, but a grave symptom. On Sunday morning,
I saw Dr. Tucker—he is a silly, kind, excellent man; he said
Oscar ought to write more—that he was much better, and that
his condition would only become serious when he got up and
went about in the usual way. I begged him to be frank. He
promised to ask Oscar if he might talk to me openly on the
subject of Oscar's health. I saw him on the Tuesday following
by appointment; he was very vague; and though he endorsed
Hennion's view to some extent, said that Oscar was getting
well now, though he could not live long unless he stopped
drinking. On going to see Oscar later in the day I found him
very agitated. He said he did not want to know what the
doctor had told me. He said he did not care if he had only a
short time to live and then went off on to the subject of his
debts, which I gather amounted to something over more than
£400.[3] He asked me to see that at all events some of them were
paid if I was in a position to do so after he was dead; he suffered
remorse about some of his creditors. Reggie came in shortly
afterwards much to my relief. Oscar told us that he had had a
horrible dream the previous night—"that he had been supping
with the dead." Reggie made a very typical response, "My
dear Oscar, you were probably the life and soul of the party."
This delighted Oscar, who became high-spirited again, almost
hysterical. I left feeling rather anxious. That night I wrote to
Douglas saying that I was compelled to leave Paris—that the
doctor thought Oscar very ill—that . . . ought to pay some of
his bills as they worried him very much, and the matter was
retarding his recovery—a great point made by Dr. Tucker. On
November 2nd, All Souls' Day, I had gone to Père la Chaise
with . . . Oscar was much interested and asked me if I had
chosen a place for his tomb. He discussed epitaphs in a perfectly light-hearted way, and I never dreamt he was so near
death.

[3] Ross found afterwards that they amounted to £620.

On Monday, November 12th, I went to the Hotel d'Alsace with Reggie to say good-bye, as I was leaving for the Riviera next day. It was late in the evening after dinner. Oscar went all over his financial troubles. He had just had a letter from Harris about the Smithers claim, and was much upset; his speech seemed to me a little thick, but he had been given morphia the previous night, and he always drank too much champagne during the day. He knew I was coming to say good-bye, but paid little attention when I entered the room, which at the time I thought rather strange; he addressed all his observations to Reggie. While we were talking, the post arrived with a very nice letter from Alfred Douglas, enclosing a cheque. It was partly in response to my letter I think. Oscar wept a little but soon recovered himself. Then we all had a friendly discussion, during which Oscar walked around the room and declaimed in rather an excited way. About 10.30 I got up to go. Suddenly Oscar asked Reggie and the nurse to leave the room for a minute, as he wanted to say good-bye. He rambled at first about his debts in Paris: and then he implored me not to go away, because he felt that a great change had come over him during the last few days. I adopted a rather stern attitude, as I really thought that Oscar was simply hysterical, though I knew that he was genuinely upset at my departure. Suddenly he broke into a violent sobbing, and said he would never see me again because he felt that everything was at an end—this very painful incident lasted about three-quarters of an hour.

He talked about various things which I can scarcely repeat here. Though it was very harrowing, I really did not attach any importance to my farewell, and I did not respond to poor Oscar's emotion as I ought to have done, especially as he said, when I was going out of the room, "Look out for some little cup in the hills near Nice where I can go when I am better, and where you can come and see me often." Those were the last articulate words he ever spoke to me.

I left for Nice the following evening, November 13th.

During my absence Reggie went every day to see Oscar, and wrote me short bulletins every other day. Oscar went out several times with him driving, and seemed much better. On Tuesday, November 27th, I received the first of Reggie's letters, which I enclose (the others came after I had started), and I started back for Paris; I send them because they will give you a very good idea of how things stood. I had decided that when I had moved my mother to Mentone on the following Friday, I would go to Paris on Saturday, but on the Wednesday evening, at five-thirty, I got a telegram from Reggie saying, "Almost hopeless." I just caught the express and arrived in Paris at 10.20 in the morning. Dr. Tucker and Dr. Kleiss, a specialist called in by Reggie, were there. They informed me that Oscar could not live for more than two days. His appearance was very painful, he had become quite thin, the flesh was livid, his breathing heavy. He was trying to speak. He was conscious that people were in the room, and raised his hand when I asked him whether he understood. He pressed our hands. I then went in search of a priest, and after great difficulty found Father Cuthbert Dunn, of the Passionists, who came with me at once and administered Baptism and Extreme Unction—Oscar could not take the Eucharist. You know I had always promised to bring a priest to Oscar when he was dying, and I felt rather guilty that I had so often dissuaded him from becoming a Catholic, but you know my reasons for doing so. I then sent wires to Frank Harris, to Holman (for communicating with Adrian Hope) and to Douglas. Tucker called again later and said that Oscar might linger a few days. A *garde malade* was requisitioned as the nurse had been rather overworked.

Terrible offices had to be carried out into which I need not enter. Reggie was a perfect wreck.

He and I slept at the Hotel d'Alsace that night in a room upstairs. We were called twice by the nurse, who thought Oscar was actually dying. After 5.30 in the morning a complete change came over him, the lines of the face altered, and I believe what is called the death rattle began, but I had never heard anything like it before; it sounded like the horrible turning of a crank, and it never ceased until the end. His eyes did not respond to the light test any longer. Foam and blood came from his mouth, and had to be wiped away by someone standing by him all the time. At 12 o'clock I went out to get some food, Reggie mounting guard. He went out at 12.30. From 1 o'clock we did not leave the room; the painful noise from the throat became louder and louder. Reggie and myself destroyed letters to keep ourselves from breaking down. The two nurses were out, and the proprietor of the hotel had come up to take their place; at 1.45 the time of his breathing altered. I went to the bedside and held his hand, his pulse began to flutter. He heaved a deep sigh, the only natural one I had heard since I arrived, the limbs seemed to stretch involuntarily, the breathing came fainter; he passed at 10 minutes to 2 p.m. exactly.

After washing and binding the body, and removing the appalling *débris* which had to be burnt, Reggie and myself and the proprietor started for the Mairie to make the official declaration. There is no use recounting the tedious experiences which only make me angry to think about. The excellent Dupoirier lost his head and complicated matters by making a mystery over Oscar's name, though there was a difficulty, as Oscar was registered under the name of Melmoth at the hotel, and it is contrary to the French law to be under an assumed name in your hotel. From 3.30 till 5 p.m. we hung about the Mairie and the Commissaire de Police offices. I then got angry and insisted on going to Gesling, the undertaker to the English Embassy, to whom Father Cuthbert had recommended me. After settling matters with him I went off to find some nuns to watch the body. I thought that in Paris of all places this would be quite easy, but it was only after incredible difficulties I got two Franciscan sisters.

Gesling was most intelligent and promised to call at the Hotel d'Alsace at 8 o'clock next morning. While Reggie stayed at the hotel interviewing journalists and clamorous creditors, I started with Gesling to see officials. We did not part till 1.30, so you can imagine the formalities and oaths and exclamations and signing of papers. Dying in Paris is really a very difficult and expensive luxury for a foreigner.

It was in the afternoon the District Doctor called and asked if Oscar had committed suicide or was murdered. He would not look at the signed certificates of Kleiss and Tucker. Gesling had warned me the previous evening that owing to the assumed name and Oscar's identity, the authorities might insist on his body being taken to the Morgue. Of course I was appalled at the prospect, it really seemed the final touch of horror. After examining the body, and, indeed, everybody in the hotel, and after a series of drinks and unseasonable jests, and a liberal fee, the District Doctor consented to sign the permission for burial. Then arrived some other revolting official; he asked how many collars Oscar had, and the value of his umbrella. (This is quite true, and not a mere exaggeration of mine.) Then various poets and literary people called, Raymond de la Tailhade, Tardieu, Charles Sibleigh, Jehan Rictus, Robert d'Humieres, George Sinclair, and various English people, who gave assumed names, together with two veiled women. They were all allowed to see the body when they signed their names. . . .

I am glad to say dear Oscar looked calm and dignified, just

as he did when he came out of prison, and there was nothing at all horrible about the body after it had been washed. Around his neck was the blessed rosary which you gave me, and on the breast a Franciscan medal given me by one of the nuns, a few flowers placed there by myself and an anonymous friend who had brought some on behalf of the children, though I do not suppose the children know that their father is dead. Of course there was the usual crucifix, candles and holy water.

Gesling had advised me to have the remains placed in the coffin at once, as decomposition would begin very rapidly, and at 8.30 in the evening the men came to screw it down. An unsuccessful photograph of Oscar was taken by Maurice Gilbert at my request, the flashlight did not work properly. Henri Davray came just before they had put on the lid. He was very kind and nice. On Sunday, the next day, Alfred Douglas arrived, and various people whom I do not know called. I expect most of them were journalists. On Monday morning at 9 o'clock, the funeral started from the hotel—we all walked to the Church of St. Germain des Près behind the hearse—Alfred Douglas, Reggie Turner and myself, Dupoirier, the proprietor of the hotel, Henri, the nurse, and Jules, the servant of the hotel, Dr. Hennion and Maurice Gilbert, together with two strangers whom I did not know. After a low mass, said by one of the vicaires at the altar behind the sanctuary, part of the burial office was read by Father Cuthbert. The Suisse told me that there were fifty-six people present—there were five ladies in deep mourning—I had ordered three coaches only, as I had sent out no official notices, being anxious to keep the funeral quiet. The first coach contained Father Cuthbert and the acolyte; the second Alfred Douglas, Turner, the proprietor of the hotel, and myself; the third contained Madame Stuart Merrill, Paul Fort, Henri Davray and Sar Luis; a cab followed containing strangers unknown to me. The drive took one hour and a half; the grave is at Bagneux, in a temporary concession hired in my name—when I am able I shall purchase ground elsewhere at Père la Chaise for choice. I have not yet decided what to do, or the nature of the monument. There were altogether twenty-four wreaths of flowers; some were sent anonymously. The proprietor of the hotel supplied a pathetic bead trophy, inscribed, "A mon locataire," and there was another of the same kind from "The service de l'Hotel," the remaining twenty-two were, of course, of real flowers. Wreaths came from, or at the request of, the following: Alfred Douglas, More Adey, Reginald Turner, Miss Schuster, Arthur Clifton, the Mercure de France, Louis Wilkinson, Harold Mellor, Mr. and Mrs. Texeira de Mattos, Maurice Gilbert, and Dr. Tucker. At the head of the coffin I placed a wreath of laurels inscribed, "A tribute to his literary achievements and distinction." I tied inside the wreath the following names of those who had shown kindness to him during or after his imprisonment, "Arthur Humphreys, Max Beerbohm, Arthur Clifton, Ricketts, Shannon, Conder, Rotherstein, Dal Young, Mrs. Leverson, More Adey, Alfred Douglas, Reginald Turner, Frank Harris, Louis Wilkinson, Mellor, Miss Schuster, Rowland Strong," and by special request a friend who wished to be known as "C.B."

I can scarcely speak in moderation of the magnanimity, humanity and charity of John Dupoirier, the proprietor of the Hotel d'Alsace. Just before I left Paris Oscar told me he owed him over £190. From the day Oscar was laid up he never said anything about it. He never mentioned the subject to me until after Oscar's death, and then I started the subject. He was present at Oscar's operation, and attended to him personally every morning. He paid himself for luxuries and necessities ordered by the doctor or by Oscar out of his own pocket. I hope that——or——will at any rate pay him the money still owing. Dr. Tucker is also owed a large sum of money. He was most kind and attentive, although I think he entirely misunderstood Oscar's case.

Reggie Turner had the worst time of all in many ways—he experienced all the horrible uncertainty and the appalling responsibility of which he did not know the extent. It will always be a source of satisfaction to those who were fond of Oscar, that he had someone like Reggie near him during his last days while he was articulate and sensible of kindness and attention. . . .

Robert Ross

Index